# RESHAPING
## THE POLITICAL ARENA
## IN LATIN AMERICA

*From* Resisting Neoliberalism *to the* Second Incorporation

EDITED BY **EDUARDO SILVA** AND **FEDERICO M. ROSSI**

University of Pittsburgh Press

Published by the University of Pittsburgh Press, Pittsburgh, Pa., 15260
Copyright © 2018, University of Pittsburgh Press
All rights reserved
Manufactured in the United States of America
Printed on acid-free paper
10 9 8 7 6 5 4 3 2 1

Cataloging-in-Publication data is available from the Library of Congress

ISBN 13: 978-0-8229-6512-1
ISBN 10: 0-8229-6512-7

Cover art: *Mural* by David Hernández, licensed under CC BY-SA 2.0
Cover design by Melissa Dias-Mandoly

# RESHAPING
### THE POLITICAL ARENA
### IN LATIN AMERICA

# PITT LATIN AMERICAN SERIES

JOHN CHARLES CHASTEEN AND CATHERINE M. CONAGHAN, EDITORS

For Paul Drake

# CONTENTS

# PART III: POLITICAL PARTIES

# ACKNOWLEDGMENTS

This volume originated in Federico M. Rossi's proposal for a conference based on key ideas and concepts published in his dissertation (2011) from the European University Institute, which have subsequently appeared in *Latin American Politics and Society* (2015) and in a revised version of the dissertation published by Cambridge University Press (2017). We thank Cambridge University Press for the permission to reprint portions of Federico's book here.

The editors wish to thank Ludovico Feoli, director of the Center for Inter-American Policy and Research (CIPR) at Tulane University, for his steadfast support of this project. CIPR made available generous resources to hold the initial conference "From Resistance to Neoliberalism to the Second Wave of Incorporation: Comparative Perspectives on Reshaping the Political Arena," Tulane University, October 26–27, 2012. Those resources were augmented with funds from the Friezo Family Foundation Chair in Political Science. CIPR subsequently provided invaluable assistance in the preparation of the manuscript for publication. We owe a deep debt of gratitude to the contributors to this collection who labored through several revisions of their original papers as well as to the anonymous reviewers of the manuscript whose suggestions for revisions greatly strengthened the final product. The editors also thank Sefira Falcoff, assistant director of CIPR, and Ezra Spira-Cohen, PhD candidate in political science at Tulane University, for their assistance in preparing the manuscript for publication.

Federico would like to thank Donatella della Porta (Scuola Normale Superiore), Sid Tarrow (Cornell University), Jeff Goodwin (New York University), and Philippe Schmitter (European University Institute) for believing that it was worth mentoring and supporting his endeavors for over a decade.

Eduardo would like to give a special acknowledgment to Christopher Mitchell (New York University) for encouraging him to take up an academic career. Paul Drake (University of California, San Diego) is a mentor, colleague, and friend who taught him the basics—as well as the finer points—of just about everything in the profession.

# RESHAPING
### THE POLITICAL ARENA
### IN LATIN AMERICA

Chapter 1

# INTRODUCTION

Reshaping the Political Arena in Latin America

## FEDERICO M. ROSSI AND EDUARDO SILVA

Neoliberalism changed the face of Latin America and left average citizens struggling to cope with changes. The popular sectors, broadly defined, were especially hard-hit as wages declined and unemployment and precarious employment expanded.[1] Protracted backlash to neoliberalism in the form of popular sector protest and electoral mobilization opened space for left governments throughout Latin America (Silva 2009). Where do the popular sectors that struggled so long to create the conditions for the left turn stand today?

Neoliberal reforms unquestionably caused profound transformations in the relationship of the popular sectors to the political arena. Collier and Collier (1991) argued that the national populist period (1930s to 1970s) selectively incorporated popular sector actors (mainly unions) into the political sphere. Later, neoliberal policies sought to exclude them, especially from socio-economic policy-making arenas. Because the neoliberal period marginalized urban and rural popular sectors, the turn to left governments raised expectations for a second wave of incorporation (Rossi 2015a, 2017). And yet, although a growing literature has analyzed many aspects of left governments (Burdick, Oxhorn, and Roberts 2009; Cameron and Hershberg 2010; Weyland, Madrid, and Hunter 2010; Levitsky and Roberts 2011), we lack a systematic, comprehensive, comparative study of how the redefinition of the organized popular sectors, their political allies, and their struggles have reshaped the political arena to include their interests.

Our volume analyzes this problem in five paradigmatic cases: Argentina, Bolivia, Brazil, Ecuador, and Venezuela, following Rossi's (2015a, 2017) thesis of the second wave of incorporation in Latin America. The subject is critical for understanding the extent of change in the distribution of political power in relation to the popular sectors and their interests. This is a key issue in the study of post-neoliberalism because the emerging new developmental path in Latin America includes an expansion of the political arena.

Case selection centered on the most paradigmatic instances of incorporation in countries that include varying levels of socioeconomic and political development in high-to-medium to low-middle-income countries. These were cases that experienced significant anti-neoliberal mobilization precisely because of the economic, social, and political exclusionary nature of that project where popular sectors were concerned—a contemporary version of Polanyi's double movement against the imposition of contemporary forms of market society (Polanyi 1944; Silva 2009; Roberts 2014). Because the expressed interests of aggrieved popular sectors were plainly revealed in protests and electoral mobilization, one can measure the extent to which those interests were incorporated. We also have variation on institutional constraints and how they affected the incorporation process. These were greater in Brazil and Argentina, where incorporation was more bounded in existing institutional frameworks, and weaker in the Andean cases, where experimentation was consequently greater.

We ask three central questions. How did neoliberal adjustment and its second-generation reforms affect the transformation of key popular sector social and political actors, their interests, demands, and actions? How have reconstituted organized popular sectors been (re)incorporated into politics by center-left or left governments and what is their role in the social coalitions that support them? What are the consequences of the mode of incorporation for policy and politics?

The book addresses these questions in three sections focused on transformations affecting social movements, trade unions, and political parties. The section on social movements analyzes the emergence of new movements and the transformation of more established ones in terms of their demands, repertoire of strategies, and their relationship to political parties, the state, and the policy-making process in general. The section on unions concentrates on transformations in the structure of representation and redefinition of demands, repertoire of action, and strategies, as well as changes in their connection to the state, political parties, and the policy-making process in general. The section on political parties and party systems analyzes transformations in party systems, such as the emergence of new labor parties, populist parties, and transformation in existing ones. It also examines the social coalition they appeal to and their connections to the social groups that compose them. Each section also explores cooperation and tension among the principal actors on key policy issues, such as reforms to free-market economics and democracy.

We use a historical analytic framework to address these questions. The book analyzes how the transformations produced by neoliberal economic and political reforms affected patterns of popular sector incorporation in the political arena from the 1980s to the present. The country chapters begin with a brief overview of the previous conditions that set a benchmark by which to assess each process of relative disincorporation under free-market economic restructuring and the politics that supported it.

The chapters then trace key processes through two distinct periods. The first of these is the neoliberal period. The chapters begin with a quick review of how neoliberal economic and political reforms (1980s to early 2000s) attempted to dismantle the arrangements of the national populist period by decollectivizing popular sector organizations, especially unions. However, we do not ignore how neoliberal projects also reordered politics in ways that opened spaces for new popular sector actors at the local level and/or in other spaces disconnected from economic policy making. We then turn to an examination of the reactive phase to neoliberal reforms (1990s to 2000s). During this phase, popular sectors and their allies mobilized in the streets and electorally. How labor unions, left political parties, and social movements reconstituted themselves to challenge neoliberal economic, political, and social reforms profoundly affected the second incorporation in each case.

The second period, of course, is that of the second incorporation and reshaping of the political arena under left governments claiming to advance post-neoliberal projects (1999 to the present). This is the heart of the case studies. Here we examine the rearticulation of unions and social movements to political parties and the state. We also analyze the role of the politically significant popular organizations in the policy process and in social coalitions that support left projects. We pay careful attention to patterns of cooperation and conflict between popular organizations, parties, and the state, as well as to cooperation and conflict *among* popular organizations: who is in, who is out, and why.

The substance of the book spans a period from the late 1990s to the mid-2010s, which is when the second incorporation took shape in Latin America. To be sure, the end of the commodity boom and shifting winds to the right raise questions about the legacies of this new incorporation. However, incorporation projects began before the commodity boom during the reactive phase to neoliberalism and thus they cannot be attributed to windfall increases in the price of raw material exports.[2] Because these shifting economic and political winds are new, their impact cannot yet be fully gauged, only guessed at. We cannot yet discern what was fleeting and what sank deeper roots. Therefore, we end our study just before these very recent events. We are confident that this volume will set a benchmark for measuring what was lasting from this push for popular sector incorporation and what was more fleeting, which will most certainly be a matter of degrees in many instances rather than wholesale rollback.

Here in one collection, then, we have detailed studies of the three key actors—social movements, trade unions, and political parties—in a process of transformation that has profoundly affected politics in Latin America. Most studies only analyze one of the actors, and frequently only in single cases. Understanding the broader, cumulative effects and meanings of those discrete processes eludes us. We offer this volume as a corrective and hope that it will open a lively conversation.

## CENTRAL CONCEPTS

### Neoliberalism

This book focuses on the consequences of neoliberalism for the second incorporation of popular sectors in the political arena in the left governments that followed. Thus, it behooves us to clarify what we mean by the concept. In so doing, we also lay a narrative foundation for the country cases that reduces repetition of its core elements.

We use the concept of neoliberalism to refer to a specific form of capitalism and a series of reforms to reorganize economic relations along neoclassical economic principles beginning in Chile in 1975. The neoliberal project also had a political and social dimension once redemocratization got under way in the 1980s. This development model stressed the price system as the sole allocator of capital, labor, and land. Politics, meaning the state and representative institutions of democracy, as well as social policy, should be restructured so as to minimally interfere with the market (Silva 2009).

The timing, sequencing, and intensity of policies designed to accomplish neoliberal restructuring varied significantly across cases (Weyland 2002). However, all followed a similar pattern. So-called first stage stabilization policies addressed deep fiscal crises, balance of payments crises, and hyperinflation of the national populist period. Policy prescriptions emphasized balanced budgets, stable unitary exchange rates, and restrictive monetary and fiscal policies, primarily high interest rates and slashing government expenditures by firing state employees and cutting programs (Birdsall, de la Torre, and Valencia Caicedo 2011).

Structural adjustment reforms followed initial stabilization policies (Edwards 1995). First stage structural adjustment focused on the liberalization of trade, finance, investment, and agricultural sectors. They encouraged deregulation, privatization of public enterprise, and foreign investment. The idea was to free the price system to allocate resources more efficiently. Second stage structural adjustment restructured social institutions along market principles in health care, education, pensions, and social assistance programs. Policy encouraged privatization of services, decentralization, and means-tested coverage. These policies shifted risk onto individuals and downsized public services, narrowly targeted basic services, and social safety nets to the poor.

Neoliberal economic reforms had a political corollary: the consolidation of liberal, representative democracy and state reform (Silva 2009). Liberal democracy was understood as small government structured to support the neoliberal economic and social project. Thus, redistributive issues and a larger role for the state in economy and society were off the table. State reform meant strengthening central banks and finance ministries and circumscribing the reach of most other ministries. Having abdicated an active role of the state in economic and social development, liberal democracy emphasized procedural processes and rights for fair and free elections. Individual rights against discrimination by creed, race, religion, and gender were also advocated. Who was elected to office, however, should not affect neoliberal economic and social policy.

Electoral reforms and advances, however, could have unintended consequences. They opened spaces for popular and subaltern groups to organize against the neoliberal project. This was sometimes the case with decentralization, electoral engineering, and cultural inclusion for indigenous peoples (Falleti 2010; Lucero 2008; Willis, da C. B. Garman, and Haggard 1999; Weyland 2002; Yashar 2005). They opened the door for the development of left parties at the local level who then learned to compete on a national basis, as in the case of Brazil. They could also strengthen the organization of indigenous social movements that later pressed their territorial and material claims, as occurred in Bolivia and Ecuador.

**Popular Sector Incorporation**

The concept of popular sector incorporation is multidimensional because it refers to the recognition of the claims of politically active popular sectors, the creation or adaptation of formal and informal rules that regulate their participation in politics, and their links to the policy process (Collier and Collier 1991; Rossi 2015a, 2017). Thus, one may conceptualize the principal relationship of popular sectors to the state on three dimensions: individual rights (particularly the universal right to vote); collective rights (the right to form associations and to participate in the polity); and substantive citizenship rights (the capacity to influence public policy to ensure that governments respond to core social and economic claims).

However, popular sector incorporation is a historical process and its specific forms vary over time. Collier and Collier (1991) analyzed the processes that culminated in the initial incorporation of the mid-twentieth century. Following Rossi (2015a, 2017), the neoliberal period and the ensuing reaction to them that culminated in left governments can be understood as periods of relative *disincorporation* and *reincorporation*. This volume examines these processes in depth.

The *first incorporation* in the mid-twentieth century focused on the formal recognition, legalization, and regulation of labor unions; it codified the relationship of unions to the state, business, and policy making. Corporatism emerged as the dominant (but not only) form of popular interest intermediation, in which party-affiliated unions were the politically dominant representatives of popular sectors. The state chartered and licensed privileged union confederations to represent the interests of workers in the political arena and vis-à-vis business (Collier and Collier 1991; Collier in this volume).

The neoliberal period was one of relative *disincorporation* as a result of the application of economic and political reforms that reduced the power of the organized popular sectors vis-à-vis other segments of society (Rossi 2015a, 2017). It involved efforts by the political and economic elites to weaken and exclude collective popular actors and their organizations from the political arena. It was never absolute, as in returning to the conditions of the nineteenth and early twentieth centuries. Popular sector organizations, especially unions, were still recognized legally and regulated. However, the point was to decollectivize and depoliticize them as much as possible. This entailed measures to weaken popular organizational capacity, to tightly circumscribe their sphere of legitimate action, and to remove them from influencing socioeconomic policy making (Cook 2006). The goal was to atomize and fragment them and limit their action to the private sphere; that is, a firm-level union can only bargain with the firm's management under conditions that greatly tilt power in favor of the firm. Labor code changes that emphasized labor flexibilization, along with high unemployment and underemployment due to the shedding of formal sector jobs created by privatization, the decline of domestic industry with trade liberalization, subcontracting, and state downsizing, all took their toll. Of course the extent to which this occurred varied significantly across the cases, as we shall see. Furthermore, because state corporatism was the principal type of interest intermediation that emerged from the national populist period, neoliberal economic social reforms sought to supplant it with neopluralist forms (Oxhorn 1998).

By contrast, the period after neoliberalism is one of *partial reincorporation* for the popular sectors (Rossi 2015a, 2017). Because reincorporation takes place after redemocratization, basic individual rights (such as voting) already existed, as did the collective rights to organize. The emphasis, therefore, is on the third dimension: the expansion of substantive rights in ways that the expressed interests of major, politically significant new and old popular sector organizations find, at minimum, programmatic expression in left governments. Reincorporation also involves the concrete institutional mechanisms that link popular sector organizations to the political arena and policy making. These are the mechanisms by which popular sector organizations connect to new, transformed, or established political parties and the state in order to have their expressed interests recognized and acted upon in the policy process (Rossi 2015a, 2017).

The best way to understand the second incorporation is to contrast it to the first because it is fundamentally different (this comparison is developed by Rossi in the next chapter). Disincorporation under neoliberalism left traditional labor unions weakened. They could not lead challenges to neoliberalism from below nor subsequent reincorporation efforts. Instead, neoliberalism and the reactive phase to it gave rise to a fragmented, heterogeneous popular sector landscape. New, often territorially based popular actors rose to the fore, such as indigenous peoples' movements, unemployed workers, neighborhood organizations, shantytown dwellers, and landless peasants, among others (Rossi 2015a, 2017). In this context, the labor movement was one more participant among many in anti-neoliberal protests, and its relationship to territorially based movements varied greatly from case to case (Silva 2009).

This context was not propitious for the re-creation of state corporatism as the modal form of popular interest intermediation. Instead, as Rossi points out in the next chapter and as Silva argues in the conclusion, when governments developed reincorporation strategies they acted selectively and with differentiated mechanisms, depending on the type of popular social subject and their needs. Under these circumstances, the fate of organized labor differed greatly. In some cases, unions were not subjects of reincorporation strategies; instead, they were largely marginalized. In other cases, they fared somewhat better.

Because of the heterogeneity and fragmentation of the popular sectors in the context of democratization in highly unequal societies, the second incorporation is less structured, less institutionalized, and exhibits a greater variety of mechanisms of incorporation for a much more varied sociopolitical base than the first incorporation. The new incorporation is primarily *not* about state corporatism; it is about social citizenship (as Roberts and Rossi each stress in this volume), mechanisms of direct participatory democracy, and social inclusion. The inclusion of territorially based rather than functionally differentiated groups is part of what makes the second incorporation both potentially more democratic but also potentially fraught (as Rossi argues in this volume and elsewhere). Fragmented and territorially based groups can win collective and individual rights but can also be co-opted and managed by technocrats and clientelistic brokers.[3]

In sum, as Rossi (2015a, 2) has persuasively argued, the new incorporation amounts to " . . . the second major redefinition of the sociopolitical arena . . . caused by the broad and selective inclusion of the popular sectors in the polity after being excluded or disincorporated by military authoritarian regimes and democratic neoliberal reforms." The second incorporation is about the recognition and inclusion of popular and poor subaltern social groups' interests in the political arena, which comprises political parties, elections, executive and legislative institutions, and policy making. However, the mechanisms that articulate the popular sectors are more varied, often ad hoc, and less institutionalized with the presence of more informal arrangements (Rossi 2017).

Significantly, inclusion in reincorporation processes frequently but not necessarily concerns popular sector organizations. At the very least, however, they entail policies that attend to their expressed or revealed interests, especially those raised during the cycles of anti-neoliberal contention that preceded left turns (Roberts 2014; Silva 2009). Therefore, social policy may be considered reincorporation when programs found a new explicit or implicit social contract that extends or universalizes basic social rights to groups that had been disincorporated or marginalized by neoliberalism (Rossi 2015a). This is especially true when the implementation of social policy entails new ministries with staff and budgets. In that respect, their heading and staffing with persons representative of the popular sectors becomes a characteristic of incorporation (Rossi 2017).

The fragmentation and heterogeneity of politically significant popular sectors in the context of highly unequal democracies also shaped popular interest intermediation, another crucial dimension of incorporation. As the union hub weakened, a new form of interest representation and intermediation emerged, the associational network (Collier and Handlin 2009; Chalmers et al. 1997). As an ideal type, the A-net comprises networks of heterogeneous, small, local organizations whose actions are generally circumscribed to local-level action. National-level interest intermediation was rare and generally dependent on linkage with national unions (Collier and Handlin 2009). This interpretation, however, limits intermediation to two forms: corporatist or neocorporatist and pluralist forms.

In the concluding chapter, Silva posits the emergence of what he calls segmented popular interest intermediation regimes. This involves differential responses by governments to the diverse segments of the popular sector writ large, which includes a variety of other poor and marginalized subaltern social groups (Luna 2014; Roberts 1998). In the second incorporation, governments establish a mix of different forms of intermediation to cover the needs of specific segments of the popular sectors. This means that corporatism may persist in diminished or modified form. In some cases, it may involve labor unions. In others, reincorporation strategies may focus on socio-territorially organized segments.

In this formulation, modified corporatism may exist alongside traditional forms of interest intermediation, such as clientelism, as well as newer forms that are emerging, which Silva calls "state managerialism" and "informal contestatory types." State managerialism refers to recognition of popular sector demands and the technocratic formulation and delivery of public policies to address them, but the state does not involve the popular sector organizations that raised them in the policy process. Informal contestatory types involve routinized exchanges: governments propose policy, vigorous protest by affected popular sector organizations erupts, negotiation ensues, following which governments adhere to negotiated agreements. Because the pattern repeats, it constitutes an informal institutional mechanism of interest intermediation.

## PRINCIPAL OUTCOMES OF THE SECOND INCORPORATION

In synthesis, what makes the second incorporation period unique is that, generally speaking, it is about the extension of initial incorporation centered on unions to other popular sector groups who had never organized successfully, been important demand makers, or gotten significant social programs (Collier in this volume; Rossi 2015a, 2017). The relatively privileged position of unions of the original incorporation period has given way to indigenous and landless peasant organizations, urban popular organizations of people employed in the informal economy or the unemployed, senior citizens demanding pensions, women, and environmentalists, to mention some of the most prominent actors. As effective enfranchisement expanded, these new groups became crucial electoral support bases for left governments in our cases.

That said, we find significant diversity in the degree to which the privileged position of unions has given way to the interests of other popular actors and their organizations. The trend is stronger in Venezuela, Bolivia, and Ecuador than in Argentina and Brazil. In the first group, left governments, at one point or another, saw unions more or less as obstacles to their projects for change. This has been constant in Ecuador under Rafael Correa and the case throughout most of the Bolivarian Revolution under Hugo Chávez. Meanwhile, in Bolivia under Evo Morales, unions have established an uneasy arms-length relationship with the government. Given this more or less conflictive relationship with labor unions, the social policies and politics of these governments have generally favored other popular sector groups more.

The situation was qualitatively different in Argentina and Brazil. Unions fared better than in the other cases even as other popular sectors were incorporated. However, unions lost their privileged representation of the popular sectors, competing for the same constituency with a wide array of movements. In the governments of Néstor Kirchner and Luiz Lula da Silva, trade unions, unemployed workers' movements, landless peasants' movements, and other grassroots organizations competed for political space inside the governing coalition and for the access to resources coming from public policies.

The cases also suggest that political parties play a less central role in the second incorporation period than in the first (Roberts in this volume). Parties in general are weaker in relation to the executive branch and stand in a different relationship to the mass base. Again, there are differences across cases. Parties are weakest in Ecuador and Venezuela, where they do not effectively serve as transmission belts for societal interests, much less those of the popular sectors. The initiative rests with the state. But even in the case of Bolivia, with a new mass mobilization party, left parties are not particularly strong. In Argentina and Brazil, the Peronist Justicialist Party and the Workers' Party turned into catchall electoral machines (Levitsky 2003; Hunter 2010). Because their policy agenda–setting roles have declined, they mainly function to recruit people for executive and legislative office. By the same token, their electoral campaigns are much more media-centric, with individualized and professionally run campaigns.

As a result of this development, public policy has been an important mechanism for connecting the state to popular sectors in the second incorporation. These involve targeted education, health, and pension cash transfers. Subsidies to consumption are also used, such as for food, transportation, housing, and energy. These policies point to a new social contract with poor, subaltern, and underprivileged social groups, and many will be difficult to reverse.

In addition to these findings, the mode of incorporation—whether from above or below, and by political or technocratic means—also shows similarities and contrasts to the national populist period (Collier and Collier 1991). The mode of incorporation encompasses the relationship among the principal actors, mainly popular sector organizations, political parties, and the state. However, an important difference with first incorporation is that the cases of second incorporation in this volume take place in at least nominally democratic regimes and, thus, political parties play a role in all. But parties in general are weaker and less centrally involved; consequently, the state in many

Figure 1.1. Typology of modes of incorporation

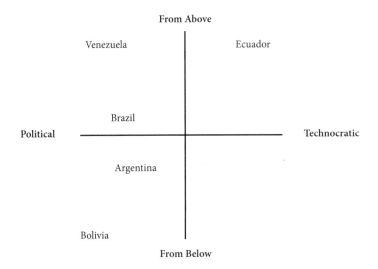

of the cases plays a deciding role. It therefore seems reasonable to distinguish between incorporations in which the state without significant party input orchestrates incorporation and where parties play a significant role.

Figure 1.1 offers a typology of reincorporation modes. Political incorporation from above occurs when state actors primarily orchestrate the process. This fits Venezuela's second incorporation, although, in a significant original contribution to the literature, we find that there has also been a substantial push from below within the United Socialist Party. By contrast, Bolivia is mainly a case of political incorporation from below, which occurs when political parties organically created by social movement organizations are the principal vehicles of incorporation. Technocratic incorporation from above happens when the party that gains power mainly mobilizes popular sectors for electoral purposes. There are no formal connections between popular sector organizations and the policy process or mobilization of popular sector organizations in the streets in support of contested policy initiatives. The link is through the implementation of social and economic policies that respond to the expressed demands of popular sector organizations. This fits Ecuador.

Argentina and Brazil suggest a mixed mode of political incorporation. Incorporation from above is probably more relevant in Brazil than in Argentina, but both cases share strong elements of incorporation from below. In the 1940s, Peronism was in charge of incorporating the popular sectors, but largely into an existing state corporatist system. However, in the 2000s reincorporation was preceded by a deep crisis of the political regime and by intense mobilizations by non-Peronist movements and unions. In Brazil, a new union movement born during the transition to democracy created the party that expanded incorporation for labor and other popular sector groups when it won the presidency with Luiz Lula da Silva in the early 2000s. But they were being incorporated into a weakened top-down corporatist interest intermediation regime dating to the authoritarian Estado Novo of the 1930s.

Overall, the second incorporation period was very complex because it involved extending incorporation to new popular actors as well as established ones. Given the number of politically relevant popular actors and their heterogeneity, we observe significant tension between new social movements that emerged in the resistance to neoliberalism and more established popular actors. In Bolivia, there was conflict between lowland indigenous peoples and highland indigenous-peasants and between the latter and labor unions. In Argentina, there was conflict between the unemployed workers' movement and new unions and the established unions. In Brazil, landless peasants' movements and peasant unions competed for resources and political power. Meanwhile, Venezuela's established labor confederation clashed with a rapidly expanding new union movement. In Ecuador, state-sponsored movements tangled with autonomous movement organizations in a ritualized game of demonstration and counterdemonstration.

## EXPLAINING SECOND INCORPORATION MODES

What explains these outcomes? The evidence from this volume suggests that the main explanation lies in a combination of popular sector struggles against the exclusionary consequences of neoliberalism and deep changes in Latin American political economy. By the 2000s, the shift away from industrialization during the neoliberal period toward reliance on comparative advantages in an open trading system partially led to a neodevelopmental "new extractive" model (Bresser-Pereira 2011; Gudynas 2012) in the context of a world commodity boom. This model emphasizes renewed state involvement in the economy and social policy along with rapid expansion of trade in mineral and agricultural commodities as the engine for economic growth and state revenue.

It has been amply documented that the neoclassical economics-inspired market-oriented reforms of the neoliberal period had the general effect of expanding the informal and service sectors of national economies to the detriment of formal employment (Egaña and Micco 2012). Privatizations, the reduction of the state bureaucracy, and the liberalization of commerce led to deindustrialization and further land concentration, with the effect of increasing informality and exclusion. Hence, the decline of urban labor unions as the key politically significant popular organizations and the increase in the relative political importance of other popular subjects was a consequence of economic and political changes (Rossi 2013, 2015a, 2017; Silva 2009, 2012).

A vigorous debate exists over what might constitute post-neoliberalism. Rather than assume a dogmatic ideological posture, we take the position that post-neoliberalism is a mixture of continuity with neoliberal policy lines and reforms to them that emphasize a sustained programmatic commitment to governing on the left (Burdick, Oxhorn, and Roberts 2009; Levitsky and Roberts 2011). That means greater state direction of the economy and social policy that, in addition to targeting to the poor, expands services and income support to broader sectors of society in an effort to approximate universality. Individual cases vary greatly in the mix. If neoliberalism was a form of capitalism, post-neoliberalism is primarily another form. It does not necessarily entail a transformation to some other economic and social formation, whether based on indigenous concepts of good living or ecological imperatives or some other formulation.

From this perspective, the left governments that ruled the cases in this collection, to a greater or lesser extent, contributed to the construction of a post-neoliberal order. Four of them remain staunchly capitalist. Venezuela thinks of itself as moving toward state socialism but still has to negotiate with its private sector. In all cases, the fiscal resources from the world commodity boom that began in the early 2000s provided left governments with the wherewithal for an increased role of the state in economic development. It also permitted governments to promote an innovative welfare model centered on targeted cash transfers that included benefits for informal sector workers (López-Calva and Lustig 2010).[4] However, governments have also steadily expanded transfers and social services to ever-broader segments of society. Poverty figures have declined markedly and inequality measures have improved (Gasparini and Lustig 2011; Huber and Stephens 2012).

The mobilized popular sectors played an important part in creating the political conditions for these left governments to come to power (Rossi in this volume; Silva 2009). However, the cases in this volume exhibit a great deal of diversity in the degree to which social movements displaced unions as the main contentious actors since second incorporation. That trend was decidedly more marked in the Andean cases than in Brazil and Argentina. A key difference marks the diverse outcomes: whether trade unions were strong and part of a corporatist system that could effectively represent a relatively significant proportion of the popular sectors.

In the Andean cases, party systems crumbled, and new left political movements and their parties appealed massively to nonunion popular voters (Roberts 2014). Constituent assemblies crafted constitutions that laid the legal foundations for a new political order. Unions were viewed with suspicion because they were, more often than not, associated with the established political system and parties that were being swept away. Brazil and Argentina, by contrast, exhibit greater institutional continuity with the past.[5] New political parties and political movements adapted to the established party system in Brazil, while in Argentina the Peronists dominant position was reinforced. In office, left governments did not think of themselves as recasting the nation. Incremental change was the order of the day. Unions were valued political allies, along with new social movements that had also become politically relevant.

Whether the extension of incorporation in the 2000s was—from above or from below, political or technocratic—depended on the relationship of the left party to the popular sectors in the context of relative institutional continuity or discontinuity. In Venezuela, a case of political incorporation from above, the leadership of the Bolivarian political movement, did not have deep organic links to organized popular sectors. Thus, it used public policy to organize nonunion popular sectors from the state. In Bolivia, political incorporation largely occurred from below because the left party in power was a mass mobilization party created by social movements. In Ecuador, the new ruling-left political movement lacked ties to popular organizations. Indeed, it competed with the major ones. Hence, it relied on public policies to technocratically incorporate from above citizens individually as voters.

The situation was different in the cases of institutional continuity, where a mixed political incorporation was the model followed. The Peronists had long dominated politics since they first incorporated labor from above in a corporatist system. Notwithstanding the collapse of the party system during the 2001–2003 crisis, part of the Peronist Justicialist Party continued that pattern in noncorporatist terms when the left faction of the party gained power in the early 2000s, extending incorporation to new unions, the unemployed workers' movement, and popular sectors in general with favorable public policies. The Brazilian case was another case of mixed political incorporation because the Workers' Party was a new mass mobilization party with strong links to a burgeoning new labor movement and urban and rural movements (Rossi 2015a, 2017).

Last but not least, there is the question of protest and sociopolitical conflict after neoliberalism. Much, but not all of it, is linked to the economic development model, which has been characterized as neodevelopmental based on intensification of natural resource extraction—hence the "new extractivism" moniker. Neodevelopmentalism refers to a return to thinking that the state has a vital role to play in directing, fomenting, and shaping economic development paths. The difference today is that the range and sophistication of policy instruments in the context of globalization has expanded from those of the mid-twentieth century (Flores-Macías 2012; Gallagher 2008). To varying degrees among our cases, economic nationalism, indicative planning, nationalization and renationalization of firms in strategic sectors of the economy (generally in the natural resources areas because they produce most state revenue), infrastructure expansion, reregulation of utilities, and industrial policy are all in vogue. Less applied are customs tariffs, discrimination against international enterprise, direct subsidies to firms, and aggressive expansion of public enterprise outside of the public utilities sector.[6]

How to finance the expansion of state economic activity and its increased social welfare effort? The international commodity boom, fueled to a large extent by the rapid economic growth of emerging market economies, especially China, offered a solution: aggressive expansion of natural resource agromineral extraction to supply increased global demand at skyrocketing prices. This of course was nothing new in Latin America; it was an old familiar pattern. What was new was the mix of commodities and the consuming nations in the context of economic globalization. The model required rapid improvements in transportation infrastructure and expansion of energy production, as well as expansion of agribusiness and large-scale mining.

This neodevelopmental extractive model was a source of tension and conflict with social movements that emerged or grew to resist its ecological impacts and—in some cases—fight for a post-neoliberal order that would embrace environmental imperatives. In the Andean region, it also included the claim for a plurinational state that fully implements indigenous rights and territorial autonomy. But the neodevelopmental extractive model ran roughshod over these concerns. Roads needed building, mega-dams constructing, water rights diverted to agribusiness and mining, land appropriated, and populations displaced regardless of environmental concerns or the newly acquired and constitutionally sanctioned indigenous rights. The chapters on Bolivia and Ecuador, especially, detail rising resistance to the model. The comparative chapter on social movements in Brazil shows that peasants and agricultural workers (landless or not) are also affected and struggle against it.

## OVERVIEW OF THE VOLUME

The book is divided into three parts: social movements, trade unions, and political parties. Each part has four chapters: a general thematic, comparative introduction, two chapters with paired comparisons, and a case study chapter.

Each chapter follows a common structure. The paired comparisons are Bolivia-Ecuador and Argentina-Brazil, with Venezuela as the country chapter. Bolivia and Ecuador both have large influential indigenous peoples' movements and sharp political-institutional breaks with the neoliberal era. Venezuela also experienced profound institutional breaks. However, oil income, differences in popular sector forces, and more radical departure from Washington Consensus policies place it in a category of its own.

Argentina and Brazil, by contrast, share a greater degree of institutional continuity and, therefore, constraints than the other cases. Thus reincorporation processes exhibited less radical departures. The five cases offer good representation of left governments on a spectrum of moderate to radical. A concluding chapter reflects on the contributions of the second incorporation for the construction of a post-neoliberal order.

Federico M. Rossi opens part 1 with a conceptualization of the two waves of incorporation, their differences, and an analysis of the role of popular movements in them. He argues that the disruption produced by social movements was important for both incorporation processes. They pushed elites to define a new "social question," innovating in both social and repressive policies to deal with the popular claims for sociopolitical inclusion. However, there are profound differences between the two waves of incorporation. In the first incorporation, labor and/or peasant movements were the main organizers of the popular sectors in their claim for well-being. The second incorporation saw the emergence of what Rossi defines as "reincorporation movements"—a type of movement that built upon, but simultaneously decentered, labor-based actors. In addition, he argues that second incorporation processes were not conducted through the old corporatist institutions but through new or reformulated institutions conceived in response to the territorialized nature of the claims that emerged with reincorporation movements.

Eduardo Silva opens the case studies with a comparison of social movements in Bolivia and Ecuador. He argues that although the heterogeneous anti-neoliberal coalition was similar in both cases, their reincorporation processes differed sharply. In Bolivia, the process occurred from below via a new mass mobilization party of indigenous, peasant, and colonist (frontier settler) social movements. In Ecuador, a state-led process of reincorporation keeps national social movements at arm's-length. The chapter also analyzes conflict between Bolivia and Ecuador's left governments and erstwhile supporting social movements.

The situation was radically different in Venezuela, where María Pilar García-Guadilla shows that the Bolivarian government actively promoted the creation of popular organizations to give material substance to the constitutionally enshrined concept of the sovereign people. She traces the history of popular urban struggles in Venezuela and argues that the government discursively legitimizes the language of these movements. However, at the same time it "criminalizes" their protests and stimulates neo-clientelistic practices that facilitate political co-optation, restrain the emergence of a genuine independent popular movement, and result in a pattern of "excluding inclusion."

The book then turns to an examination of social movements and the second incorporation in Argentina and Brazil. Federico M. Rossi analyzes the struggles for incorporation of the Argentine *piquetero* (picketer) movement and the Brazilian landless workers' movement. He traces their trajectory from their origins as anti-austerity movements to the development—partially as a result of these movements—of policies for the second incorporation in Argentina and Brazil.

Part 2 opens with an introduction by Ruth Berins Collier that frames the transformation of the trade union systems in terms of a historical comparison between the first and second incorporations. She addresses three questions to understand the distinctive features of the contemporary process. First, what key features such as union density, labor law regulations, and unification or fragmentation of the organized labor movement changed? Second, how have party-labor relations changed? Third, what is the relationship between unions and the newly incorporated groups? Notably, Collier underscores the point that unions were not necessarily the central actors of reincorporation.

Jorge León Trujillo and Susan Spronk open the chapters on trade unions with a comparison of Bolivia and Ecuador. The title "Socialism without Workers? Trade Unions and the New Left in Bolivia and Ecuador" refers to the conflicted relationship of organized labor with the governments of Evo Morales and Rafael Correa. The situation is considerably worse in Ecuador, where the government has gone to greater lengths to fragment and weaken labor unions than in Bolivia.

Steve Ellner's chapter on Venezuelan union-state relations reveals notable similarities and differences with the preceding two cases. At first the Bolivarian Revolution attacked unions because they were aligned with opposition political parties. Afterwards, however, it reorganized the union movement and, ultimately, created a sector that supports the Bolivarian Socialist process of transformation.

Argentina and Brazil offer a sharp contrast. Julián Gindin and Adalberto Cardoso show that unions have fared relatively well under left governments since 2000 and that their intervention capacity has increased. However, they also note that in both cases, politics rather than collective bargaining now play the major role in labor/capital disputes.

Part 3 on political parties begins with an overview by Kenneth M. Roberts that frames key dynamics. He notes that Latin America's second wave of incorporation, like the first, was heavily conditioned by party politics. Party organizations, however, were not always the chosen vehicle for popular sectors seeking a stronger voice and enhanced participation in the democratic process at the beginning of the twenty-first century. In some cases, reincorporation was channeled through established left political parties; in others, however, it occurred outside of established party systems, effectively displacing traditional parties from their dominant roles in the electoral arena and governing institutions.

In "From Movements to Governments: Comparing Bolivia's MAS and Ecuador's PAIS," Catherine Conaghan shows how the established party systems collapsed, giving rise to New Left political movements and parties, albeit with radically different trajectories. Bolivia's MAS retains organic linkages to social movements that originated it. In contrast, PAIS emerged primarily as an electoral vehicle and never developed strong ties to groups in civil society. Distinguished by their different modes of linking to society, both parties have achieved hegemonic status and laid the foundations for controversial, transformative presidencies.

Daniel Hellinger follows up with an analysis of the Venezuelan party system through the lens of petro-politics. He shows how the late Chávez years and early post-Chávez years have produced an electoral system composed of two electoral blocks that is held together more by the polarized nature of competition than institutionalized electoral processes.

Pierre Ostiguy and Aaron Schneider close the country studies with an analysis of changing party popular sector dynamics in Argentina and Brazil. While reincorporation has occurred within the established but evolving party system, the process has differed sharply in each case. Argentina has moved closer to a de-institutionalized party system and a personalistic, "transformative" form of political leadership, as in Venezuela. Brazilian parties have increasingly institutionalized both the party system and a coalitional mode of governance across a broad ideological spectrum.

Eduardo Silva's concluding chapter reflects on the type of interest intermediation between state and society that emerged in the consolidation of second incorporation. He argues that in the cases covered by this book, we find "segmented popular interest intermediation regimes." These are mixtures of new forms of popular interest intermediation alongside reorganized corporatist regimes and clientelism. The conclusion, thus, reflects on the contributions of the second incorporation for the construction of a post-neoliberal order and raises questions for future research.

# PART I

# SOCIAL MOVEMENTS

Chapter 2

# INTRODUCTION TO PART I

## Social Movements and the Second Wave of (Territorial) Incorporation in Latin America

### FEDERICO M. ROSSI

It was through contentious political dynamics that the poor and excluded strata of society claimed to be recognized as members of society.[1] The disruption produced by social movements and their allies was an important component in the production of the conditions for the first and second waves of incorporation. Protests, marches, pickets, strikes, and—sometimes—more violent methods have been part of the relational process of building and rebuilding institutions that modified the relationship of the popular sectors with the state. These contentious dynamics, in some occasions, pushed the elites to define a new "social question," innovating in both social and repressive policies to deal with the claim of the popular sectors for being (re)incorporated in the sociopolitical arena.

The popular movement's repertoire of strategies for social change has been associated with different types of movements in each historical period. The labor and/or peasant movements, the main organizers of the popular sectors in their claim for well-being through reform or revolution, were in the liberal period (1870s–1930s) that preceded the first incorporation (1930s–1950s). In the second incorporation (2000s–2010s), a different type of movement emerged in the neoliberal period (1970s–2000s) as the central popular actor in the quest for stopping the exclusionary consequences of authoritarianism and neoliberalism while claiming for the incorporation (again) of the popular sectors as citizens and wage earners. The emergence of what I define as "reincorporation movements"—a type of movement that has built upon but simultaneously decentered labor-based actors—is the result of important transformations that occurred in the sociopolitical arena between the two waves of Latin American incorporation of the popular sectors.

## THE TWO WAVES OF INCORPORATION

The first incorporation was a corporatist process that involved a combination of the mobilization of popular claims by labor and/or peasant movements and the policies for channeling those claims into corporatist institutions. In Brazil, this was done for demobilization purposes, while in Bolivia, Venezuela, and—mainly—in Argentina, incorporation implied the mobilization of the labor movement. In Bolivia and Venezuela, first incorporation also included peasants, and in Ecuador incorporation was done by a military reformist regime with a weak labor movement (Collier and Collier 1991; French 1992; Klein 2003; Gotkowitz 2007; Yashar 2005; Collier in this volume).

The second incorporation departed from the inherited institutions and actors of the first incorporation. In addition, the two waves of incorporation were partial and selective, redefining the relationship between the popular sectors and the state. However, in this second wave, the main actor mobilizing the claims of the popular sectors were social movements organizing the excluded or *dis*incorporated poor people at the territorial level. In addition, the second incorporation was not conducted through the old corporatist institutions but through new or reformulated institutions conceived in response to the territorialized nature of the claims that emerged with popular movements.

This second wave was "territorial" because the incorporation of the popular sectors was predominantly done through institutions created or reformulated for the articulation of actors that were *not* functionally differentiated. This was a result of the emergence of contentious claims for reincorporation outside the trade union system. Instead, urban and rural land occupations, neighborhoods and shantytowns became central spaces for claim making for the organized poor people (Merklen 2005) once neoliberal reforms and authoritarian regimes had weakened or dissolved neocorporatist arrangements for resolving sociopolitical conflicts. For this reason, the social policies to reincorporate the popular sectors were not based on function or class but on territory (i.e., defined by the physical location of the actors). This was an important shift from the functionalist logic of corporatism, which had articulated the popular sectors' claims through trade unions as their sole representative actor and through the Ministry of Labor or Peasant Affairs as their exclusive state department. To sum up, because they were not seen as serving a clear "function" for institutions with a corporatist logic, the disincorporated popular sectors were targeted by policies based on where they were located and the multiplicity of needs associated with their situation, not only as workers or peasants.

That the second incorporation was defined by territory-based logics did not mean that corporatist arrangements were abandoned altogether. The most important sources of cross-national variance on the degree of territorialization seem to be four. First is the profundity of the reformulation of the locus of politics conducted by the last authoritarian military regime in each country, whereby democratization proceeded from the local to the national level. Second is the effect wrought by neoliberalism on the mainstream parties claiming to represent popular sectors (see Roberts in this volume). Third is the ways that the trade union system was modeled by the corporatist period and remodeled by neoliberalism. Fourth is how the first incorporation of the popular sectors (urban or rural) was produced and how its achievements have been eroded by the military regimes and neoliberalism.

As part of the recursive dynamics of incorporation, both waves shared some elements in the sequencing of incorporation. Both incorporation periods were preceded by a (neo)liberal phase that created a new "social question." This "social question" in both cases evolved into a political question with a contentious actor that was gradually recognized and legitimated. In the period from the 1990s to the 2000s, the emergence of recommodification and marginalization (i.e., unemployment, impoverishment, exclusion, etc.) as a new "social question," the modification of policing techniques, and the creation of massive social programs can be seen as a process equivalent to that of the preincorporation dynamics. Between the 1870s and the 1950s, anarchists, communists, syndicalists, and socialists posing the "social question" pushed the liberal elites to create anti-immigration and security laws and increase control and repression in the countryside and indigenous communities (Isuani 1985; Suriano 1988; French 1992; Gotkowitz 2007). This gradually led to populist or leftist leaderships that emerged to recognize the claim to social rights and later the actors behind this new claim, the labor and peasant movements (Collier and Collier 1991; Welch 1999; Suriano 2000; Becker 2008). Concerning social policies, in the first wave this process led, ultimately, to the creation of the first Ministries of Labor or Peasant Affairs, the application of agrarian reforms (except for Argentina), the production of comprehensive social rights policies, and constitutional reforms. In the second wave, it also led to constitutional reforms in Bolivia, Ecuador, and Venezuela, the creation of new ministries such as the Ministry of Agrarian Development in Brazil and the Ministry of Social Development in Argentina, and the production of wide-ranging cash-transfer policies and universal citizenship income-rights policies in all these countries.

Equally significant has been the introduction of the "indigenous social question" by indigenous movements in Bolivia and Ecuador (Yashar 2005;

Lucero 2008). Even though indigenous movements in Latin America achieved
"first" incorporation during their struggles against neoliberal policies, in national terms and as part of the popular sectors (as broadly defined), indigenous peoples had already been incorporated as "peasants" during the period
of corporatist first incorporation. The emergence of a social question involving stronger ethnic and territorial identifications than those raised during the
first incorporation is a trend common to the second incorporation period.
Since the 1990s, the struggles for recognition of indigenous peoples as part
of the polity in the Andean region have evolved into reincorporation struggles. In Ecuador, the Confederación de Nacionalidades Indígenas del Ecuador
(CONAIE) even created its own party, Pachakutik, while in Bolivia some indigenous groups reached office as allies or members of the Movimiento al Socialismo (MAS) party-movement (Van Cott 2005; Lucero 2008; Becker 2011;
Pearce 2011; Fontana 2013; Conaghan in this volume).

A pattern of interaction between government and movement was thus established through new institutions or the redefinition of roles of existing institutions. The struggle against disincorporation was a contentious one, which
included a reincorporation movement: the unemployed in Argentina, the indigenous and coca growers in Bolivia, the indigenous in Ecuador, landless
peasants in Brazil, and—with less strength—urban movements in Venezuela.
Generally, these movements coordinated campaigns with trade unions and
left-wing parties (see Silva 2009). Later on, reincorporation was conducted
in territorial terms, with institutions such as the *territórios da cidadanía* in
Brazil (Delgado and Leite 2011), the *misiones* and *círculos bolivarianos* in Venezuela (Ellner 2008; García-Guadilla in this volume), and the partly formalized articulation of movement claims through the General Secretariat of the
Presidency in Argentina, Bolivia, and Brazil. Also, new institutions such as
social councils were created to deal with multiple noncorporatist claims in
Brazil (Doctor 2007; Rossi in this volume), and even constitutional reforms in
Bolivia, Ecuador, and Venezuela were promoted to deal with the new "social
question" (Lupien 2011; García-Guadilla in this volume; Silva in this volume).

These transformations did not imply that the relationship between popular movements and the elites have been harmonious. First incorporation divided movements, some supporting governments while others becoming critical or even suffering persecution and repression. In the first wave, the labor
movement kept a conflictive relationship with Perón's governments in Argentina (James 1988). In Brazil, rural incorporation was also conflictive (Welch
1999), while trade unions resisted some of the control mechanisms associated
with urban incorporation (French 1992). In Bolivia, Gotkowitz (2007) argues
that peasants and indigenous movements were very important in building the

conditions for first incorporation and, later, the main losers of incorporation policies during the revolution of 1952.

This holds also true for the second wave of incorporation. How to deal with the Néstor Kirchner and Cristina Fernández de Kirchner administrations divided the *piquetero* movement, with one sector supportive and another that was critical (Rossi 2015b). In Ecuador, the CONAIE had a very conflictive relationship with Rafael Correa's government (Becker 2008; Silva in this volume). And the Movimento dos Trabalhadores Rurais Sem Terra (MST) suffered a delusion with the modest advances of agrarian reform during Luiz Inácio Lula da Silva and Dilma Rousseff presidencies (Rossi in this volume). However, this is just half of the story. Cooperation and participation in the coalition in government have been very important, with the inclusion in office of thousands of middle- and lower-rank members of social movements, most of them in state departments related to social policies (Abers and Tatagiba 2015; Rossi in this volume). As García-Guadilla (in this volume) points out for urban movements in Venezuela, the issue faced by many social movements is that of the autonomy of grassroots popular organizations from the consequences (or intentionality) of incorporation policies. This concern seems to be common to all the other countries and movements analyzed in this section.

While these parallels allow us to talk about two waves of incorporation, they do not mean that history has repeated itself. There are elements of iteration and innovation in a process that is, as such, like a collage. It is also important to bear in mind that incorporation waves should *not* be equated with the constitution of a more equal society or the creation of a welfare state but with the reshaping of the sociopolitical arena by redefining and expanding the number of legitimate political actors. In some countries, the urban and rural poor were first incorporated into very unequal societies, as in Brazil under Getúlio Vargas (Cardoso 2010), while in other countries, a more equal society and some welfare policies emerged as a result of incorporation, as in Argentina under Juan Domingo Perón (Torre and Pastoriza 2002).

Affecting all these cross-nationally is the timing of each particular process. Reincorporation may be a relatively quick process, as it was in Argentina after 2002 and Venezuela since 1998, or long processes brought on by several regime breakdowns, as in Bolivia and Ecuador; or even the result of gradual change over the course of a protracted struggle, as in Brazil. Moreover, reincorporation processes involve the remobilization of popular sectors in more than defensive struggles, but this does not necessarily imply the ideological transformation of the popular sectors' political culture. For instance, in Argentina, Peronism has continued to supply the main political ethos of the popular sectors, while Katarism has emerged as relevant for Bolivian indigenous and coca growers' movements (Yashar 2005; Albó 2007; Lucero 2008).

## FROM RECOGNITION TO (RE)INCORPORATION STRUGGLES

It is because of the transformations produced by neoliberalism and authoritarianism that Latin America experienced a change in the focus of protest, now mainly occurring in the quest for recognition by the state (Delamata 2002; Auyero 2003). This quest for recognition is part of what I call the "struggle for (re)incorporation."[2] I use this term because although most actors in this quest present discourses of radical societal transformation, those discourses have actually unfolded as types of collective action that can be deemed "bridging with the state" (apart from the unintended transformations produced by the incorporation of the actors). By "bridging with the state," I mean types of collective action that aim to (re)connect excluded segments of society with state institutions to recover—or for the first time, gain—access to rights and benefits that the state had failed or ceased to secure or provide. Examples of this "bridging" collective action are the claims for land of the indigenous in Bolivia and Ecuador and the landless peasants in Brazil, the *piqueteros'* claim to unemployment subsidies and jobs in Argentina, and the long-standing struggle of urban movements in Venezuela for water, housing, and health services. All these claims aim to reconnect the popular sectors with the state as a provider of some benefits and rights.

Protest is thus a substantial and moral tool for popular sectors to form a bridge between the state as it actually is and the state as it should be. In other words, what the popular movements analyzed in this section struggle for is the presence of the state as more than a merely repressive institution. In this sense, reincorporation struggles are historically linked to the heritage of the incorporation of the first laborers and peasants into the sociopolitical arena. The consequences of the neoliberal reforms explain the demand for a return of the state presence as an articulator of social relationships.

Therefore, what differentiates recognition struggles from those for (re)incorporation? I argue that the two are intimately related. The pursuit of recognition might be defined as the initial quest linked to the popular sectors' disruptive emergence in protest. After some degree of recognition has been achieved (i.e., unemployment subsidies, media attention, etc.), the claim organized as a movement will usually lead to socioeconomic conflicts and the quest for incorporation. In societal terms, a struggle for recognition might lead to a struggle for incorporation—or reincorporation—as a subject and member of society who merits esteem and is entitled to some of the rights that the (neoliberal) context has (abruptly) altered. In this sense, it is both a moral economy issue and a specific process attached to the constitution of the polity through its expansion or contraction.

Another reason for defining recognition and reincorporation as intimately linked struggles is that no quest for reincorporation can emerge without a prior claim for recognition; it is that first claim that constitutes a new "social question." However, the quest for recognition does *not* necessarily evolve into one for reincorporation, as it can be a goal in itself (e.g., claims for a multilingual society). In other words, when popular sector movements are discussed, struggles for recognition should be considered as the first stage of the legitimation of both the claim and the actor. If organized into a movement, this process will generally evolve toward the dynamics of incorporation.

## REINCORPORATION MOVEMENTS

Reincorporation movements share many of the long-standing characteristics of the popular sector movements' quest for social transformation through inclusion, by revolution or reform. At the same time, they have specific attributes that mark them as particular expressions of the historical process of struggle for incorporation that emerged with neoliberalism in Latin America. As such, reincorporation movements use the repertoire of strategies and legacies accumulated in the initial incorporation period while pushing for the reestablishment of the tie between the popular sectors and the sociopolitical arena in the quest for reintegration into the polity. The reconstruction of these ties was executed through the intertwining of preexisting practices in a new scenario with somewhat different actors: a social movement (albeit heavily influenced by trade unionist strategies in Argentina and Brazil and by indigenous and peasants' practices in Bolivia and Ecuador) and a state prepared to deal only with already established neocorporatist actors. This new context for the inherited repertoire led to the recycling of strategies with new claims; for example, trade union–style negotiations for food or housing provision, the use of indigenous organizational practices, and rhetoric for water access or redistributive claims.

Therefore, "reincorporation movements" can be defined as a gestalt composed of six categories.[3] Two of these are central and universal, with four subcategories that logically depend on the first two and must be adapted to each cluster of cases studied to explain more specific national or regional patterns.

The central categories in this definition of reincorporation movements are two. First, the period of emergence: these movements are by-products of the disincorporation process that started in the 1970s and a result of the crisis of party communities[4] and mass-based labor parties set up in the 1980s and 1990s. The second is the characteristics of their demands: claims for inclusion predominate, even though these could be framed by the leaders as "revolutionary" in their long-term goals.[5]

Reincorporation movements are also defined by four noncentral categories, which can be seen to have some common attributes. The first is the method and locus of protest: radical methods of protest, such as insurrectional direct actions, tend to be used, while the movements are contemporaneously open to negotiation with government. Their locus of protest is generally the territory. The second concerns the leadership: leaders come mainly from trade unions, Christian-based communities, and former guerrilla organizations. A third subcategory is the organizational format: these movements are loose territorialized networks of highly vertical organizations. Finally, it is their perception of democracy: reincorporation movements make a positive reevaluation of the value of democracy as a political regime, insofar as it is perceived as necessary and reforms are, in some cases, achieved by electoral means.

To summarize, the basic assumption underlying the historicist definition proposed here is that the second wave of incorporation is attached to the emergence of a specific type of political actor. Therefore, many contemporary movements are not of the reincorporation type because even though they may share some of the noncentral categories, they are not explained by at least one of the central categories. Examples of this are cultural or countercultural movements, environmental movements, anti-immigration or xenophobic movements, and separatist or pro-independence movements.

## CONCLUSION

Latin America went through a cycle of continental mobilization against neoliberal disincorporation from the mid-1990s to the first decade of the 2000s (Schefner, Pasdirtz, and Blad 2006; Almeida 2007; Silva 2009). As the chapters in this section show, these mobilizations were not limited to resistance struggles, reshaping the sociopolitical arenas of Argentina, Bolivia, Brazil, Ecuador, and Venezuela following the partial and selective reincorporation of urban and/or rural popular sectors. The second incorporation of the popular sectors was the result of a dynamic of pressure from below of the popular sectors organized in social movements and trade unions and the political and economic elites attempts to co-opt, demobilize, repress, and—eventually—incorporate the popular sectors in the sociopolitical arena. This was mostly done through established relationships with political parties and unmediated—and sometimes informal—links with state departments (Rossi 2015b).

Even though the context has changed since first incorporation ended in the 1950s, the popular sector's movements that emerged since then share many of the long-standing characteristics of the demands made by popular sectors for social transformation through inclusion by way of revolution or reform. However, these reincorporation movements also have specific attributes that define them as particular expressions of the historical process of struggle for a second incorporation that emerged due to authoritarianism and neoliberal reforms. The movements analyzed by the chapters in this section can be deemed as examples of this type of struggle and actor.

Chapter 3

# SOCIAL MOVEMENTS AND THE SECOND INCORPORATION IN BOLIVIA AND ECUADOR

## EDUARDO SILVA

If labor unions were the principal subjects of the first incorporation under national populism, indigenous, indigenous-peasant, colonist, and urban poor social movements were the preferred subjects of the second incorporation in Bolivia and Ecuador in the post-neoliberal era. Yet, despite these and other similarities, the forms and substance of incorporation were radically different.

Bolivia under Evo Morales (2006–present) was a classic case of incorporation from below via a new mass mobilization party, the Movimiento al Socialismo-Instrumento Político para la Soberanía Popular (MAS-IPSP). Given the party's origins, it directly incorporated key indigenous-peasant and indigenous social movements in policy making. Labor unions and other popular sector organizations were incorporated via different mechanisms in a more arm's-length manner. These involve regularized, predictable patterns of contestation and negotiation on the one hand and assembly-style consensus building to resolve tensions on the other hand.

By contrast, Ecuador under Rafael Correa (2007–2017) was a case of state-led incorporation via a technocratic public policy–driven electoral mechanism. It resembles Collier and Collier's (1991) electoral mode of incorporation because it rejects a direct relationship between the state and organized social movements in policy making. It differs in that policy does not favor any social movement organization, as had been the case with labor during the first incorporation. In the main, it is directed at poorer, vulnerable citizen groups as individuals. It connects individual citizens to the state. Meanwhile, traditional forms of clientelism are also alive and well. I come back to what this implies for popular interest intermediation at the end of the chapter.

Why are Bolivia and Ecuador so different? This chapter argues that a series of key changes wrought by neoliberal reforms and resistance to them profoundly shaped variation in their modes of incorporation. Two of those legacies of neoliberalism were similar in both cases and set up the puzzle for explanation. First, powerful indigenous peoples' movements led broad heterogeneous social coalitions that encompassed urban popular sectors (including labor unions) and peasant social movements. Second, in their struggles against the authorities, social movements, in an alliance with left political parties and NGOs, crafted similar post-neoliberal policy programs. Thus, one might have expected similar outcomes. However, differences in three additional conditions that resulted from anti-neoliberal struggles explain the variation in outcomes for popular incorporation. These were the strength of social movements, their connections to left parties at the time left governments came to power, and the ideational frames of the political leadership that took office.

The chapter also analyzes emerging conflicts between left governments and the social movements that helped to bring them to power. Following Collier and Collier (1991), I argue those conflicts were caused by differences in the political and socioeconomic projects proposed by the heterogeneous social coalition forged during the struggle against neoliberalism (the project from below) and the governments of Evo Morales and Rafael Correa (the project from above) once they were in office.

## NATIONAL POPULISM: ORGANIZING AN INDIGENOUS PEASANT MOVEMENT, 1950S–1970S

To fully appreciate the significance for the second incorporation of transformations in relationships among social movements during the neoliberal period, let us quickly review their initial positioning in the national populist era. As the following chapters on unions and parties in Bolivia and Ecuador establish, the first incorporation followed the union-party hub model (Collier and Handlin 2009). In this model, urban labor movements allied with political parties. But that was not the whole story. Labor unions and allied political parties also organized the peasantry in a subordinate position, a development that involved rural highland indigenous peoples. Military governments pushed the process too, because they sought to break cross-class coalitions. The unintended consequence for the second incorporation was that the formation of peasant unions laid the associational foundation for the indigenous peoples' movements that later led resistance to neoliberalism.

As León Trujillo and Spronk's chapter shows, in Bolivia the Confederación de Obreros Bolivianos (COB), dominated by mining unions, articulated popular sector demands. Both the COB and the Movimiento Nacionalista Revolucionario (MNR) helped to organize a largely Aymara and Quechua peasantry along union lines. The new indigenous peasant unions quickly established their independence from the COB and took over large estates, which forced the MNR to start agrarian reform to calm the peasantry. Satisfied with land ownership, peasants became a conservative force that the MNR used against the more radical COB. Because the MNR promoted state-led development along national populist lines, peasant union leaders received important positions in state agricultural agencies and were incorporated into the policy-making boards (Klein 2003). In remote rural areas, indigenous peasant unions took on local government functions and represented their communities to national authorities. Moreover, in return for political support, the MNR allocated patronage positions, resources for peasant organizations, and policy concessions (Lazarte 1989).

Bolivian democracy collapsed in 1964, giving way to a populist military regime that influenced important changes in the organized peasantry. First, the military formed a pact with peasant unions promising to address their demands and, more importantly, unifying them into a state-controlled national confederation. Second, tax increases on land, repression, and the rise of indigenous ethno-cultural identity developed an independent indigenous peasant movement from 1968 to 1979. Katarismo blended defense of the peasant class with claims for traditional ethnic and cultural rights. They demanded tolerance for ethnic diversity and integration of indigenous and Western forms of government (Healy and Paulson 2000). Third, the intertwining of class-consciousness with ethnic rights facilitated alliances with other social movements and left political parties (Van Cott 2005, 2008). Thus, in 1978, the COB helped the Katarista unions to form a unified and politically independent *campesino* organization, the Confederación Sindical Única de Trabajadores Campesinos Bolivianos (CSUTCB). The CSUTCB mainly represented highland indigenous peasants from Cochabamba; it was affiliated to the COB (Healy 1991). Labor-peasant cooperation contributed to two waves of contention in the struggle for democracy between 1979 and 1985.

Ecuadorian national populism was mainly the work of progressive military governments in the 1960s and 1970s when Amazonian oil provided the state with sufficient resources for a measure of independence from coastal agricultural export elites (Isaacs 1993). Although more attenuated than in Bolivia, the numerous ministries and government agencies created to administer the national populist state stimulated popular sector organization to access the rights and benefits conferred by them. In Ecuador as in Bolivia, the development of indigenous social movements that resisted neoliberalism and that are among the main subjects of post-neoliberal popular sector incorporation begins during this period.

Land reform addressed peasant concerns over land security and working conditions and had a greater impact in the highland areas where Ecuador's indigenous population concentrates. Land reform also encouraged Indians to register as peasants (Zamosc 1994). Peasant communities constituted under agrarian reform strengthened indigenous peasant communities' authority structures and customary law. Peasant unions, mainly affiliated with the Federación Nacional de Organizaciones Campesinas (FENOC), helped highland communities organize along state corporatist lines to receive benefits such as land, credit, and infrastructure improvement (Yashar 2005). They also brought indigenous communities into contact with leftist political parties (Selverston-Sher 2001). These were the foundations of the highlands indigenous peoples' confederation, ECUARUNARI. Meanwhile, Amazonian oil development and an influx of colonists stimulated the organization of lowland indigenous peoples, principally the Shuar. This was the foundation for the lowland confederation, CONFENIAE.

As in Bolivia, these organizations melded class and cultural concerns. ECUARUNARI emphasized indigenous ethnic and cultural consciousness as well as land, crop prices, credit, and working conditions. CONFENIAE stressed ethnic and cultural survival along with defense of territory against oil companies, colonists, and landowners (Gerlach 2003). Later, this facilitated working with urban labor and popular sector organizations in resistance to neoliberal policies.

## CRUCIAL TRANSFORMATIONS DURING NEOLIBERALISM

Bolivia and Ecuador experienced twin transitions to free-market policies and liberal democracy roughly at the same time. Although the intensity and consistency of neoliberal reforms were greater in Bolivia (Conaghan and Malloy 1994; Andrade 2010), the reaction to the rollback in protections from the market won during the national populist period was similar (Silva 2009). Protests escalated into expanding cycles of contention that built popular sector power by forming heterogeneous coalitions led by indigenous peoples' movements as the power of labor unions waned under an onslaught of anti-union policies. As established political parties disintegrated, the leading popular organizations crafted a policy agenda for a post-neoliberal period. However, significantly for variation in second incorporation outcomes in these two cases, there were marked differences in the type of New Left parties that emerged, how social movements connected them (see Conaghan in this volume), and the ideational frames of the emerging political leadership that eventually took office.

## Bolivia, 1985–2003

The first significant consequence of the neoliberal period for the second incorporation in Bolivia involved a transformation in the sources of resistance to neoliberalism from labor unions to indigenous peoples' movements capable of articulating broad heterogeneous coalitions with other urban and rural social movements and subaltern social groups, including labor unions. In 1985, at the beginning of the neoliberal period, Víctor Paz Estenssoro's administration moved aggressively against the mining unions to break the COB's political power (León Trujillo and Spronk in this volume).

However, new movements representing a wide array of aggrieved social subjects took up the struggle. By the 2000s, the CSUTCB had replaced the COB as the main organizer of resistance. Its framing of the struggle against neoliberalism articulated a broad set of demands such as calls for state-led development, controls over the foreign sector, land reform, and a constituent assembly to establish a plurinational state. Thus, the CSUTCB became the fulcrum for coalition building among a heterogeneous collection of social movements that included highland and lowland indigenous peoples, peasants, colonists, and urban popular sector movements (Silva 2009). They mobilized escalating cycles of contention that forced the resignations of Presidents Gonzalo Sánchez de Lozada in 2003 and Carlos Mesa in 2005.

These changes were the product of more than fifteen years of struggle against governments that supported free-market policies. Following the defeat of the COB, resistance shifted to the countryside as coca-grower unions mobilized against government coca field eradication policies. The militarization of coca eradication at the behest of the United States government exacerbated the problem. In the late 1980s, 160 Cochabamba coca-grower unions organized five federations and a coordinating committee (Van Cott 2005, 58), with the largest affiliated with the CSUTCB.

In the 1990s, coca-grower federations became the nucleus of resurgent resistance to neoliberalism in Bolivia because they alone enjoyed a measure of success. They forced the government to negotiate with them. The coca federations' relative success encouraged the CSUTCB to support coca-grower mobilization. Herein lay the birth of an enduring close relationship between the *cocaleros* and the CSUTCB. By the same token, the relative success of the coca growers also gave the COB an incentive to support them, especially with negotiating expertise (Healy 1991; Healy and Paulson 2000). In short, the framing of the coca issue contributed significantly to the revitalization of peasant/

indigenous resistance and the emergence of a peasant-urban node protest and mobilization.

Second-generation Washington Consensus reforms in the 1990s, however, sought to include subaltern social groups in ways that complemented the liberal thrust of free-market reforms (Grindle 2003). This too had a positive impact on indigenous organizing. Indigenous peoples were included through bilingual education (1994) and recognition of ancestral lands as a vital component of cultural survival (1996). The primary beneficiaries were lowland indigenous nations. These peoples had organized into the Confederación Indígena del Oriente, Chaco y Amazonía de Bolivia (CIDOB) in the 1980s in tight collaboration with international and national NGOs, a collaboration that second-generation Washington Consensus reforms encouraged and reinforced. The land reform act of 1996 granted rights over common ancestral lands to indigenous peoples—the Territorios Comunitarios Originarios (TCOs). Since highland indigenous Aymara and Quechua were mostly peasants with small private landholdings, the land reform act mainly benefited lowland indigenous peoples. It was a victory for the CIDOB, which had participated in the policy process.

Privatization, political decentralization, and coca eradication policies brought the CSUTCB, CIDOB, and COB together in opposition (Farthing and Kohl 2014). CIDOB joined because it felt cultural values around coca were under threat and because it had developed more ambitious goals around demands for territorial and political autonomy. In the 1980s and 1990s, then, we see decline of the COB, rise of a *cocalero*-centered CSUTCB, emergence of the CIDOB, and the beginnings of coordination among them.

The tenuous connections between these organizations strengthened dramatically in the early 2000s. The Cochabamba Water War of 2000 and the Gas War of 2003 saw the development of new politically relevant movements and increased CSUTCB and *cocalero* leadership of opposition mobilization (Webber 2011). The new movements in the Water War were the many community groups that made up the informal water production and distribution system of Cochabamba (Olivera and Lewis 2004). These were local community-based artisanal well diggers and owners, cistern builders, truck distributors, and the cooperatives and associations that controlled the informal water supply. They formed FEDECOR and became politically relevant locally. Local labor unions (the Fabriles), the CSUTCB, and the *cocaleros* catapulted that local struggle to national political significance. The Fabriles mobilized them; *cocaleros* joined in because government coca eradication efforts were strongest in Cochabamba department; the CSUTCB saw an opportunity to advance an indigenous nationalist agenda.

The Gas War reinforced the importance of community organizing, especially along territorial (district and geographical) rather than producer lines (Assies 2004). The origins and development of the Gas War and the broad, heterogeneous coalition that fought it were complicated. For our purposes, one significant aspect was the emergence of close-knit neighborhood associations (*juntas vecinales*) that represented an urban informal sector movement born of squatter settlement struggles for land titling, basic services, and infrastructure focused on local municipalities. They formed a Federation of Neighborhood Associations (FEJUVE) and were among the most militant protesters during the Gas War.

Two more El Alto community associations played important roles in the Gas War. In the informal sector, the Women's Federation organized associations to support food security, education, public services, and production. Youth organized in student federations, especially in the newly created University of El Alto, along with many other youth associations (Lazar 2008)

Nevertheless, just as in the Water War, it fell to other movements and movement organizations to draw out their political potential and elevate their struggles to national significance. First, a regional COB federation initially realized their potential. As in the Water War, the regional COB's distinctive characteristic was that it also organized informal sector workers. Again, it was the CSUTCB that, alongside the water coordinator and the rising MAS party, framed the issue in a manner that mobilized large numbers at the national level (Assies 2004).

This long chain of events contributed to a second major consequence of the neoliberal period for the second incorporation. The social movements that led the backlash to neoliberalism set a broad left agenda for an eventual left government. This project from below was summed up as the "October Agenda," in reference to the October 2003 uprising that forced the resignation of President Sánchez de Lozada. It consisted of four fundamental planks. First, it called for the nationalization of hydrocarbons to fund state-directed economic development with social equity. Second, it demanded a constitutional assembly to set the legal foundations for recovering national sovereignty in the face of globalization, to carry out redistributive policies, and to set up a decolonized plurinational state with autonomy for indigenous nations. Third, the October agenda demanded agrarian reform to bring social and economic justice to the countryside. Fourth, it called for trials for criminal politicians, including those of the military governments of the 1960s and 1970s (Schilling-Vacaflor 2011).

As we shall see, this trajectory of struggle was similar in Ecuador. What occurred with respect to the crucial developments that explain why the two cases had such different modes of reincorporation? First, Bolivia's broad het-erogeneous social movement coalition centered on rural indigenous-peasant and indigenous peoples' movements was at the apogee of its power when the left government took power. It had led several national cycles of mobilization that had forced the resignation of two presidents: Sánchez de Lozada (2003) and his successor, Vice President Carlos Mesa (2005). Thus, it would be a cru-cial ally for an eventual left government against a relatively strong opposition.

Secondly, the coca federations, the CSUTCB, the CIDOB, and the CONA-MAQ formed the core of an organic mass mobilization party, the MAS-IPSP, to contest neoliberalism electorally. This became the primary vehicle for their incorporation in the political arena when Evo Morales became president in 2006. The COB, meanwhile, declared itself an autonomous strategic ally.

The organic connection between the MAS and its core social movement organizations influenced a third crucial development on which Ecuador dif-fered sharply (Harten 2011; Zuazo 2010). The ideational frames of the MAS leadership stressed direct inclusion of the core movements in the political arena. They also emphasized the importance of engaging with movement or-ganizations and negotiating differences with them. This frame of mind had permitted cooperation in the struggle against neoliberalism and was at the center of attitudes toward governing. The phrase "to lead by obeying" was not an empty slogan.

### Ecuador, 1984–2006

Ecuador's story is similar to Bolivia's with respect to the development of resis-tance to neoliberalism and the first two consequences of the neoliberal period for the second incorporation. The first consequence of neoliberalism was that the Indigenous Uprising (*levantamiento*) in 1990 firmly established the indig-enous peoples' movement as the principal articulator of resistance to neolib-eral reforms (Zamosc 2004).

Organizational developments in reaction to León Febres Cordero's eco-nomic stabilization policies (1984–1988) preceded the uprising. Those poli-cies threatened the base communities of ECUARUNARI and CONFENIAE because they had grown accustomed to state support for agricultural inputs, credits, infrastructure, technical assistance, and education. Thus, in 1985 the two united and formed the Confederación Nacional de Indígenas Ecuatoria-nos (CONAIE) in 1985 (Yashar 2005). CONAIE became the most powerful indigenous peoples' organization in South America. It also helped to create an indigenous peoples' political party, Pachakutik (see Conaghan in this volume).

Between 1990 and 2001, CONAIE was the undisputed leader of resistance to Washington Consensus economic, social, and political reforms. It led several uprisings in expanding cycles of contention that brought down two presidents. CONAIE also understood that openness to and coordination with non-indigenous movements was the key to successful resistance to neoliberalism in Ecuador. Thus, it became the fulcrum for the organization of a heterogeneous coalition that included organized labor (the FUT), the Frente Popular (teachers, students, and a leftist political party, the Movimiento Democrático Popular, MDP), and the Coordinadora de Movimientos Sociales (CMS), which I focus on below (Silva 2009). Indeed, after the mid-1990s, CONAIE coordinated mobilization more closely with the CMS than the FUT.

The CMS emerged in the mid-1990s due to the unreliability of the FUT during protest campaigns. It was an encompassing organization for nonindigenous social movements and some unions linked to small leftist political parties. In addition to the oil and electrical workers' unions, the CMS encompassed many different types of informal sector associations. These included vendors, retail merchants, artisans, youth centers, and rural sector retirees. Christian base communities were another important element of the CMS. The Ecuadorian chapter of Jubilee 2000-South, a transnational Christian base anti-neoliberal globalization movement, was a key component of the CMS. It brought in human rights and environmental NGOs, as well as legal and civic-oriented NGOs. It was also the point of connection into the *barrios*, mobilizing neighborhood associations and, very importantly, the myriad self-help squatter organizations created around urban land invasions for land titling, housing, and services in Quito (Collins 2004; Zamosc 2004).

In comparative perspective, what was similar to Bolivia was that indigenous peoples' social movements led the struggle against neoliberalism and that they formed a political party. But there were also significant differences. The Ecuadorian indigenous peoples' movement was more cohesive and the political party was smaller and electorally less successful.

With respect to the second consequence of neoliberalism, as indigenous movements had done in Bolivia, CONAIE articulated a broad policy agenda that addressed the major grievances, demands, and programmatic platforms of the heterogeneous social and political coalition it led. CONAIE developed a platform with deep rural indigenous roots. Effective land reform and funds for rural smallholder development was key. So were state recognition of CONAIE as the official representative of indigenous and peasant interests, abrogation of unused oil concessions in Amazonia, reorganization of the bilingual intercultural language program, and calls for a plurinational state. Broader demands that reached out to all popular sectors included appeals for a constituent assembly with representation for all sectors of society, an end to privatization programs, increased state direction of the economy, financial sector reregulation, subsidies for popular sector consumption, and greater welfare effort (Saltos 2001; CONAIE 1994). Again, this was broadly similar to the Bolivian agenda.

Temporary gains were achieved. A CONAIE-led cycle of mobilization in 1997 that culminated in President Abdalá Bucaram's ouster resulted in a constitutional convention in which CONAIE and the Pachakutik congressional bloc achieved much of the indigenous cultural rights agenda (Andolina 2003). However, they were unable to affect privatization policy and the free market–oriented thrust of economic policy in general. Thus, CONAIE's socioeconomic demands remained unchanged, as did the demand for a plurinational state.

This brings us to the three developments that explain the variation in Ecuador and Bolivia's model of incorporation. First, Ecuador differed sharply on the strength of the principal social movements when left governments came to power. Unlike in Bolivia, by 2006, when Correa was running for president, the once mighty indigenous peoples' movement had weakened significantly due to a series of political misadventures. The first episode occurred in 2000. In the midst of escalating mobilization against President Jamil Mahuad's dollarization plan and a deep banking crisis, demands for his resignation culminated in an ill-fated (and ill-considered) putsch by CONAIE in alliance with a group of mostly junior and middle-rank military officers in 2000. This antidemocratic adventure died almost as soon as it was born, but it did lasting damage to CONAIE, beginning with its democratic credentials. It also caused internal splits in CONAIE because many of its leaders did not approve of the putsch (Zamosc 2007).

The second episode began in 2002 when Lucio Gutiérrez, the colonel who had led the putsch in 2000, was elected president at the head of the newly formed Partido Sociedad Patriótica (PSP) with the support of CONAIE and urban popular sectors. During his campaign, he vowed to reverse market-oriented policies. He invited Pachakutik and CONAIE to join the government, offering them important positions in his administration. Their participation in his government accelerated CONAIE's decline. First, discord broke out among its leadership as they clashed over strategy, tactics, and government posts. Second, local indigenous communities, CONAIE's basic building blocks, wellspring of its legitimacy, and mobilization capacity, viewed their national directorate's political ambitions with suspicion. Thus, they were reluctant to support CONAIE's call to mobilize in 2003 when Gutiérrez reneged on his campaign promises with renewed commitment to foreign debt repayment, a strict economic stabilization program, and structural adjustment (Collins 2004; Wolff 2007; Zamosc 2007).

Gutiérrez' government, however, grew ever more unpopular with its cynical support for market reforms, crass political manipulation, and seemingly limitless corruption. Thus, it fell to the myriad movements and organizations that had formed the CMS, citizens in general, and, to a lesser extent, unions—who also believed that CONAIE had become just a narrow Indian interest group—to step up the struggle against him. In 2005 a heavily middle class and partially spontaneous cycle of mobilization escalated against Gutiérrez (Wolff 2007; Zamosc 2007). The *forajido* (outlaws) movement was made up of new, loosely organized citizen groups and middle-class intelligentsia demanding clean, technically competent government (Conaghan in this volume; De la Torre 2012; Larrea 2009). As the *forajido* movement grew, it attracted support from urban, rural, and indigenous peoples' organizations. In 2005, a *forajido*-led mass mobilization created an opportunity for a coalition of progressive and conservative parties abetted by the military to oust President Gutiérrez.

Although major policy changes were not forthcoming in the caretaker government that followed, the movement reinforced a national demand from middle classes, popular sectors, and indigenous peoples for economic, social, and political policies that emphasized economic nationalism, state-led development, redistributive social policies to improve social equity, ecologically sustainable development, clean government, observance of citizen rights, agrarian reform, and effective support for indigenous peoples' rights, especially over territory. There was also a call for a constituent assembly to set the legal foundation for a state and political system capable of implementing such policies (Ramírez Gallegos 2010a).

The second factor on which Ecuador differed from Bolivia—the relationship of social movements to new political parties—further debilitated the CONAIE and associated movements. As Conaghan's chapter will show, the CONAIE formed an indigenous peoples' party, Pachakutik. However, because it never overcame a narrow indigenous orientation, it did not perform well in national elections, especially after 2002. Meanwhile, as Conaghan details, the *forajido* movement gave rise to a new political party, PAIS, to contest the 2006 presidential elections. This political movement had no direct connection to CONAIE or most other social movements. Some of the leadership, however, did have links to some of the movements in the CMS, principally environmentalists (Alberto Acosta) and the urban anti-Free Trade Area of the Americas (Gustavo Larrea).

The relative disconnection of PAIS leadership from social movements, especially Correa and his inner circle, had important implications for the third major development on which the cases differed: the ideational framework of its top leadership. It tended to be technocratic; sought autonomy from social-movement organizations, especially CONAIE; and preferred inclusion of popular sector interests through public policy that addressed their demands but did not include their organizations in the policy process (De la Torre 2012). This was very different than the situation in Bolivia, and the tendency became more accentuated after passage of the new constitution in 2009. The relative weakness of the opposition to Correa's government also facilitated its autonomy-seeking preference.

## REORGANIZING THE POLITICAL ARENA: SOCIAL MOVEMENTS AND THE GOVERNMENTS OF EVO MORALES AND RAFAEL CORREA

### Bolivia

In Bolivia, the popular sectors had an opportunity for reincorporation in the political arena from below during a period of deep political crisis. Evo Morales came to power at the head of a movement-driven political party based on a broad coalition of rural and urban movement organizations following three cycles of mobilization between 2000 and 2005 during which they forced the resignation of three presidents. With ample support from his mobilized base, Evo's first government (2006–2009) pursued radical reform policies and incorporated popular sectors in the policy process. In close alignment with the popular sectors, indigenous peoples, and peasant organizations, it addressed all four planks of the policy agenda. It brought hydrocarbon production under much tighter state control and used the increased revenue to boost social spending and state involvement in the economy (Kaup 2010; Gray Molina 2010). It established a constituent assembly, reformed land laws, and issued warrants for the arrest of high-profile public figures—former president Sánchez de Lozada, who fled into exile, foremost among them. During Evo Morales's second government (2009–2014), however, the situation changed abruptly. Conflict erupted between the state and some of the social movements that had been in the core social coalition as well as others in strategic alliance as the project from above began to diverge from that of key sectors of the project from below.

*First Evo Morales Government: Constituent Assembly and Defensive Mobilization, 2006–2009*

The cross-class and multiethnic social coalition that brought Evo Morales and the MAS to power not only played a key role in shaping the policy agenda, it also sought participation in the policy process. This was clearest in the constituent assembly process (Harten 2011; Tapia 2008). During this process, the government incorporated social movements in two ways. First, it worked with them to formulate many of its key philosophical underpinnings and articles that mandated implementation of social movement demands. The core rural social movements of the MAS independently formed a Unity Pact (Pacto de Unidad) that worked closely with the MAS bench in the assembly (Garcés 2010). Second, in classic mass mobilization party style, the MAS government formed those same movement organizations into the Coordinadora Nacional de Movimientos Sociales (CONALCAM) for defensive mobilization against seditious opposition (Eaton 2007).

The opposition failed and the new 2009 constitution enshrined economic nationalism, industrialization, agrarian production reform, land reform, and labor law reform (Garcés 2010; Mendoza 2009). This outcome reflected the interests of the CSUTCB (indigenous peasants), colonists, and urban labor. Autonomy for indigenous territories was another major theme (Albró 2009; Ardaya 2009), largely supported by indigenous communities from the lowland nations represented by the CIDOB and highland communities not well integrated to the capitalist economy, represented by CONAMAQ. Both were backed by NGOs that vigorously supported the measure as well. In the end, a limited form of territorial autonomy was adopted, a somewhat disappointing outcome from the organization's perspective. A particular bone of contention was that rights to subsoil resources remained with the state, although communities would need to be consulted about their development. As we shall see, this eventually led to a rift between Morales's administration and the CIDOB and CONAMAQ.

There were also more institutional forms of incorporation into the political arena during Morales's first government. To varying degrees, the organizations of the government's broad, heterogeneous social coalition had access to key ministries in the policy-making processes. Since rural movements were at the core of the MAS coalition, this was particularly strong in the agriculture ministry. For example, early on, CIDOB and CONAMAQ were able to influence key officials with whom they shared strong ideological affinities to decree a reform of land laws that granted significant extension of territory to lowland indigenous communities.

### Second Morales Government: Tension and Conflict in the Social Coalition, 2009–2014

After a resounding victory in the 2009 constitutional referendum, Morales again won the presidency in first-round balloting, the MAS obtained a majority in the Congress, and the erstwhile secessionist conservatives retreated, limiting themselves to institutional opposition. After the solid support social movements had given the government in the struggle over the constitution, the stage seemed set for a close alignment between them as the government set about the business of formulating new laws to implement the "October Agenda" as mandated by the new constitution. But it was not to be. As other chapters note, tension escalated among the heterogeneous and contentious social movement organizations that supported the government. Any dream of co-government by the social movements vanished (Zuazo 2010).

As discussed by León Trujillo and Spronk in this volume, tensions began with massive, spontaneous demonstrations against sharp fuel-price hikes in December 2010 involving urban labor, transport sector workers, and informal urban labor sectors, among others. Following that, the ongoing conflict over indigenous rights and land, symbolized by the confrontation over the TIPNIS (Territorio Indígena Parque Isoboro Sécure), erupted with the VIII and IX Indigenous Marches for Life in August–September 2011 and June–July 2012 (Guzman 2012). Salaried and cooperative miners struck and took over mines as they appealed to the government to resolve their differences in 2011 and 2012. The COB formally declared an end to its strategic alliance with the government in early 2012. This chapter focuses on tensions with informal urban popular sectors and indigenous peoples' movements not covered in León Trujillo and Spronk's chapter.

A significant cause of these conflicts was that the project from above—from the state—began to diverge from the broad, consensual project from below in several key areas. The 2009 constitution obligated the government to enact that broad agenda into legislation. However, in the absence of institutional mechanisms for conflict resolution, several major decisions by the second Morales administration signaled clear choices in its policy priorities that contributed to the disaffection of significant sectors of the founding core coalition (Do Alto 2007).

First, its overriding commitment to a state-led economic development model focused on natural resource extraction, infrastructure expansion, and macroeconomic stability (IMF 2011; Weisbrot, Ray, and Johnston 2009). The first clear manifestation was the December 2010 decision to cut subsidies to fuel prices in the interest of preserving long-term macroeconomic stability, thus sharply increasing their cost to consumers (García Linera 2011). The government did this in an arbitrary manner reminiscent of the "neoliberal" period. It caused massive, spontaneous mobilization by urban social groups, especially by the informal sector (e.g., FEJUVEs) in addition to transport workers and labor unions. Subsidies were part of the compact Evo and the MAS government made with them to raise their income, increase purchasing power, and improve their lives. It had been broken. Faced with such massive resistance from his own social base, Morales rescinded the order in January 2011 (Rojas 2011).

A second cluster of decisions made it clear that the government believed that national development, based on natural resource extraction, required overriding regional or local interests. Choices regarding funding for hydro-electric dams, exploration for hydrocarbons, and road construction have alienated indigenous movements as represented by CIDOB and CONAM-AQ, not to mention environmentalists. Many of these communities oppose these megaprojects and feel the government has violated their constitutionally granted autonomy (Ayala et al. 2009; Lanza and Arias 2011). It has simply proceeded as if those objections—and constitutionally mandated rights to prior consultation and subsoil riches—did not exist. Environmentalists chafe at the blatant contradiction with the government's "Mother Earth" (*Pachamama*) rhetoric.

Third, and related to the previous, Morales's government signaled a preference for maintaining state control over the national territory by dragging its feet on legislation regarding territorial autonomies for indigenous peoples. This has further inflamed CIDOB and CONAMAQ against Morales's second administration, a situation compounded by his preference for placing middle-class leftist intellectuals (*invitados*) in significant government jobs rather than people of clear first peoples (*pueblos originarios*) or indigenous descent (Harten 2011). This raises doubts about the government's commitment to the decolonization of the state, hence critiques from supporters of the decolonization effort.

The TIPNIS controversy is emblematic of these tensions. The government decided to build a tranche of paved highway connecting two of Bolivia's departments (as well as Bolivia to Brazil) in a protected area that claimed status as an autonomous indigenous territory. The MAS administration did not—as it should have—consult the local indigenous communities as to whether they approved of the road passing through their territory. This rallied the CIDOB and the CONAMAQ to defend the violated autonomy rights of the TIPNIS and pitted colonists and coca growers against CIDOB in support of the road (and the government's preference). In protest, the CIDOB and the CONAM-AQ, with support from NGOs and environmentalists, organized two indigenous peoples' marches to La Paz. The first one, launched in August 2011, was successful. It received significant support and media attention and the administration backed off the plan. When the administration started backtracking, CIDOB and CONAMAQ launched a second march that was less successful (Lanza and Arias 2011; Fundación Tierra 2012; Calla Ortega 2012). While the marchers were camped in front of the government house, dissident factions of CIDOB organized an election in Santa Cruz to replace the sitting executive director who, along with most of the leadership that supported him, was in La Paz with the marchers. They duly elected a female executive director, which divided the CIDOB.

Subsequently, manipulation of a consultation process in the affected communities in 2013 severely eroded the government's public approval ratings. Because of the potentially de-legitimatizing quality of the controversy, Evo Morales put a moratorium on the project. This is further evidence that, as argued by León Trujillo and Spronk in this volume, Evo's claim to "lead by obeying" the social movements is not an empty slogan. Concerted resistance from below can cause him to reconsider a policy. This sets his government apart from those of the neoliberal era. So too did Morales's pronouncement giving a green light to the project in June 2015, after the moratorium was up.[1] In the intervening period, Morales spent considerable resources on economic and social development for the region, thus dissipating much of the original opposition and generating considerable support. Governments during the neoliberal era would not have gone to the effort. They would simply try to ramrod projects through after the hiatus. The situation, however, remains politically delicate, and by the end of 2016, Morales had still not begun construction.

Another consequence of the TIPNIS and other conflicts is the consolidation of a core social movement coalition that remains steadfastly loyal. Throughout these episodes, the CSUTCB, the Bartolinas-Sisa, and the Interculturales (ex-colonos) have publicly declared their support for the government's choices. The government has also revived the CONALCAM and used it to organize counterdemonstrations with these social movement organizations. Throughout both MAS governments, these groups and their organizations have benefited from political empowerment (appointments) and favorable public policies such as agricultural inputs, social policies to reduce poverty, and infrastructure.

*Policy Process*

Incorporation, however, is about more than who is in or out of a governing or party coalition and how governments mobilize popular sectors. It is also about the articulation of popular sector interests to the policy process itself, its inclusion in it, and the conditions of participation. In Bolivia, this occurs through three different mechanisms. The first one is more of an analytical construct. At the strategic planning level of policy making, interest intermediation is more of an abstraction, an analytic construction on the part of state policy makers. At this level, the state has sought relative autonomy from social forces. Yet, the argument goes, it is also connected to popular sector, indigenous, peasant, and first peoples because many of its agencies are staffed by invited left intellectuals of middle-class extraction who understand the needs and demands of the popular sectors, indigenous peoples, and peasants (Cunha and Santella 2010; García Linera 2011). In practice, the government has insulated the Ministry of Finance and Planning from social forces and instituted a technocratic policy-making style. The state's autonomy from social movements is most forcefully asserted in the government's choice for macroeconomic stability, which restricts spending and whereby the government respects the rules of the capitalist international political economy (García Linera 2011). The finance ministry prioritizes components of the general development plan through its power to set investment and spending ceilings for ministries and agencies charged with implementing the plan. By the same token, leftist intellectuals and technocrats transformed the electoral mandate for state intervention in the economy into a full-fledged state-led development program, with an initial emphasis on infrastructure development and conditional and universal cash transfers to promote social equity and to reduce poverty.[2]

In the second mechanism of inclusion in the policy process, social group organizations have direct connections to line ministries where they participate in the formulation of sectoral policies based on the strategic plan of the nation. This is especially true of the Ministry of Rural Development and Lands, given the MAS's rural base (Do Alto and Stefanoni 2010). This ministry probably has the greatest number of high- to midranking staff drawn from the social movements at the core of the MAS (including the minister and undersecretaries). Moreover, as the following examples show, social movement organizations have the capacity to formulate policies and to negotiate them with authorities.

There are several examples of this. In 2006, the minister of rural development was an intellectual with a strong affinity for lowland indigenous peoples as represented by the CIDOB ("true" first peoples from their perspective, not Indians-cum-peasants, as they disparagingly thought of highland indigenous). He passed a decree granting the expansion of land to Territories for the Communities of First Peoples (TCOs), a legal figure established in the 1990s that mostly applied to lowland indigenous nations. In 2010, the CSUTCB prepared draft legislation for the government entitled The Productive Decade, 2010–2020 (CSUTCB 2011). It called for the transfer of resources for peasant production concentrated in the highlands, which were to be controlled and disbursed by the five organizations that made up the Pacto de Unidad. The plan also proposed state funding for storage and marketing facilities, as well as price supports. This proposal became the basis for policy formulation within the Ministry of Rural Development and Lands, whose new minister had a greater affinity with the CSUTCB. Formal working committees were established with representation from ministry technical personnel and the CSUTCB (Colque 2011). The 2011 Ley de Revolución Productiva Agropecuaria adopted core CSUTCB proposals (Urioste 2011) with an important exception: the CSUTCB's pitch for a guaranteed funding formula to ensure ample, stable budgets. The government demurred on budgeting commitments because the institutional, organizational, and operating mechanisms to implement them were deemed too complicated and, ultimately, unworkable.

The third mechanism of incorporation involves direct contact with the president or his agents in assembly-style meetings designed to foment consensual agreements. In this mechanism, Evo Morales has structured relations with popular sectors based on traditional highland indigenous practices in which he was schooled as a "*cocalero*" leader (Harten 2011; Zuazo 2009). He discusses policy with social movement organizations in sessions that continue until a consensus is reached. This works best with organizations and communities that structure decision making based on these practices, such as the "*cocalero*" federations, the CSUTCB, and the "Bartolinas." In this style, Morales also negotiates directly with local communities, sometimes bypassing national organizations. The "Evo Cumple" program is an example of this. Municipal governments, sometimes with help from their department governments, bring local needs to the executive's attention. With public fanfare, Morales delivers the goods.

Evo's government engages in a fourth mechanism of incorporation, which I call informal contestatory. Aggrieved popular social actors protest a policy, the government negotiates, and a settlement is reached. The process repeats in a routinized pattern whose rules are understood by all involved. We see examples in Leon Trujillo and Spronk's chapter, with the cooperative mine workers' associations over ore vein allocations in renationalized mines and labor unions, especially over minimum-wage raises. In this chapter, we see the same dynamic at work in the TIPNIS episode, which spanned several years.

In sum, social movement organizations have the capacity to participate in the policy process beyond protesting and raising demands. However, I do not wish to exaggerate their influence. Their policy proposals form the basis for policy formulation by technical personnel within the respective ministries, who then periodically consult with the social organizations over the content of the emerging bill. Moreover, the resulting policies at times may be more symbolic political victories than substantive policy wins. Be that as it may, this is more active participation facilitated by the state than in the "neoliberal" past or, as we shall see, in Ecuador.

## Ecuador

Rafael Correa began his presidency in 2007 at the head of a new political movement created expressly for the 2005 presidential campaign, a movement lacking in its own cadres that attracted seasoned political leaders from a number of left political tendencies, as well as some more conservative figures. Because of the strong anti-interest group orientation of Alianza PAIS (AP), there was a built-in tension between Correa's political project and the project of the broader social coalition that had helped him to win the presidency. Correa and his team preferred a technocratic, meritocratic policy-making style and intended to keep CONAIE (which it mistrusted) and labor unions (which it disdained) at arm's length from the national policy process (see Conaghan in this volume; León Trujillo and Spronk in this volume; De la Torre 2012).

Correa's government mobilizes citizens electorally around a policy agenda that appropriates the program of the social movements that had resisted neoliberalism. For although the movements themselves had declined, Correa, his team, and AP genuinely shared many of their socioeconomic policy goals. It was a winning formula.

It is also a strategy that weakens popular associations as potential interest intermediation organizations. First, much public policy, especially social assistance, links individuals qua citizens and the state. Second, the government also establishes direct connection to the base organizations of CONAIE in indigenous communities—that is, municipalities—to deliver more public goods such as infrastructure projects, educational facilities, and other benefits. These two strategies undermine CONAIE's national leadership, whose main function historically had been to mediate between indigenous communities and the state in the pursuit of goods, services, and legislation for the community.

The general weakness of CONAIE after 2000 contributed to this outcome. It had always maintained an independent stance from political parties, even Pachakutik, which it helped to create. But by 2005, after the ill-fated adventure with Gutiérrez's government, CONAIE, as we saw, was plagued by internal strife. To recover, it retreated into a shell, emphasizing an indigenous agenda and avoiding the articulation of broader material demands and coalitions with other social groups and parties. CONAIE did not support Correa in first-round balloting for the presidency in 2005, preferring to run its own candidate, Luis Macas, under Pachakutik's wing. The result was disastrous. They received very few votes. This choice contributed to later tensions, as did CONAIE's new reputation for being just another narrow interest group—a form of organization and politics the founders of AP despised.

*First Government of Rafael Correa: The Constituent Assembly, 2006–2009*

At the beginning of Correa's first administration, tension with social movements and left political figures was muted as he sought to consolidate both his government's authority and the support of a fragmented but broad-based social and political coalition. Indeed, for a time it seemed as if there might be significant congruence between the project from Correa's administration and project from below forged during the cycles of anti-neoliberal contention. To ensure broad-based support, Correa appointed a cabinet and other high government positions that included people from a wide spectrum of leftist parties and tendencies beginning with Socialists, Pachakutik, and many smaller parties. A great many enthusiastically supported his citizen's revolution (Larrea 2009, 76; Martínez Abarca 2011). They backed alternative development policies, agrarian reform, participatory democracy, indigenous peoples' rights and autonomy, and sound environmental husbandry.

Similar to Bolivia, social movement leaders had significant access and influence in the constituent assembly process. Most of the indigenous peoples' agenda was incorporated into it, with the exception of autonomy for indigenous territories (Becker 2011). So were the environmental, peasant, small entrepreneur, and social equity agendas (Carter Center 2008). On a much smaller scale, social movements were called upon to mobilize in the streets to defend the constitutional process. The most significant event occurred early on during the conflict that ensued when Correa bent procedural rules to unseat fifty-six opposition deputies and replace them with their alternates in order to ensure that the legislature would vote to establish a constitutional convention.

However, divergences between the project from above (Correa's inner circle) and the project from below (the broader left social and political coalition) also surfaced. These tensions appeared in four different areas: the establishment of a technocratic political style that insulated policy makers from social movement organizations; the consolidation of a ruling bloc and the purging of many left leaders in the government; the deepening of an extractive development model contradictory to indigenous peoples' and environmentalists' agenda; and frontal assault against those movements when they protested.

From the very beginning, Correa's government instituted a technocratic policy-making style that insulated state planners from social forces, especially representatives of popular sectors, indigenous peoples, and labor (Ramírez Gallegos 2010a). The Planning Secretariat epitomized the trend, largely staffed with young professionals without ties to leftist parties or social movements. The same applied to state economic agencies (Nicholls 2014). Yet Correa and his technocrats addressed most of the policy demands that the social movements had raised during the cycles of anti-neoliberal mobilization. He reasserted state involvement in the national economy and greater state control over international companies. Significantly larger government takes—along with proceeds from high commodities prices—are mainly invested in development programs, improving social services, poverty reduction, and income supports.

As in Bolivia, however, the priorities assigned to different components of the broad anti-neoliberal sociopolitical-movement agenda caused problems that led to a gradual purging of leftists with ties to parties and social movements. An early sign of this was the removal of Alberto Acosta as the president of the Constituent Assembly in favor of Vice President Lenin Moreno (Larrea 2009). Acosta had close ties to left parties, environmentalists, and the indigenous peoples' movements. The official reason for his removal was that he was not efficient enough in keeping the constituent assembly process on schedule.

These tensions over policy prioritizing spilled over to relations with social movement organizations. The emphasis on government as the definer of the common good over the interests of organized social groups, concern over governability, and desire to control government expenditures led to an early confrontation with organized labor. Public sector unions, including teachers, were among the first under attack (León Trujillo and Spronk in this volume). Moreover, the government refused to recognize the CONAIE as the legitimate representative of indigenous peoples in the policy process, a core CONAIE demand since the dark days of the "long neoliberal night."

### Second and Third Correa Administrations, 2009–2017

Tensions between Correa's government and national social movement organizations deepened in his second administration following the successful plebiscite for Ecuador's new constitution. The government's technocratic policy-making style intensified with the centralization of power in Correa's administration. Many early leftist and social movement leaders in high government positions suffered a similar fate to Alberto Acosta's or resigned over growing policy differences with the Correa administration. The rest, such as loyalist Socialist party members, were, for the most part, shunted into relatively minor positions.[3]

The impact of these developments for popular sector incorporation was significant. They deprived social movement organizations of key personal linkages to the policy-making process. The absence of informal articulating mechanisms to government was a heavy blow to national social movement organizations. Moreover, as we shall see, the availability of such channels at less important government agencies suggests a government effort to fragment and control them.

In addition to technocratic rule, the government's emphasis on extractive economic development (mining), infrastructure expansion, and national state control over subnational units terminally alienated CONAIE and environmentalists. Mining projects were a fulcrum for conflict. For example, Correa's government summarily rebuffed CONAIE national leaders when they protested its refusal to consult with indigenous communities over proposed mining projects. Correa also publicly rebuked and belittled them. The major mining projects also alienated environmentalists, whom Correa did his best to publicly delegitimate (Becker 2011, 176–84; Martínez Abarca 2011, 109–12).

The purging of leftists from government, technocratic rule, and alienation of social movement organizations spurred a fragmented left to unite in opposition to Correa in order to challenge him in the 2013 presidential elections (Conaghan in this volume). A number of smaller political movements joined them along with many social movement organizations, such as CONAIE, barrio associations, and labor unions that have declared their support. Moreover, CONAIE showed signs of recovering from its internal problems and organized some successful protest events against government policies. A protest against a government-backed and Canadian-financed mammoth copper-mining project in 2012 was emblematic. CONAIE claimed to defend territorial rights, consultation rights, and to protect families from eviction.[4]

President Correa, however, maintained the upper hand. His administration reacted to growing leftist opposition in several ways leading up to the 2012 election, practices that he maintained after he won them. To begin with, it organized loyal social movement organizations as countermobilization forces against CONAIE, environmentalists, and MDP-controlled unions. In addition to restructured public sector unions, the government aggressively courted African Ecuadoreans, as well as coastal peasant unions (FENOCIN). It developed numerous programs to advance the citizen rights of African Ecuadoreans and spent considerable sums in impoverished northern coastal areas where they are demographically strongest. With respect to FENOCIN, Correa's government has had an on-and-off relationship (Herrera 2013; Becker 2014). When it is on, FENOCIN enjoys privileged access to agricultural ministry officials and is asked to provide input for policies related to peasant agriculture. Some say it also receives some material benefits. Secondly, Correa's governments attempted to break national movements, especially CONAIE. It criminalized protest, thus putting leadership and followers at risk of prosecution and jail. The government also attempted to divide CONAIE internally—for example, by supporting more government-friendly leadership and undermining strong opposition leaders (Lalander 2009).

Correa's administration's attempts to divide the labor and indigenous people's movements were successful up to a point. However, the FUT and CONAIE, while weakened, did not collapse. Indeed they rallied against Correa during the 2017 presidential election. Their mobilization, however, was not sufficient to win against the AP candidate, former vice-president Lenin Moreno.

*Policy Process*

As we just saw, the Correa administration instituted a largely technocratic policy-making process in which social movement organizations play little role at the national level. As in Bolivia, policy makers with leftist sympathies, or at least pro-poor sympathies, occupied many of the planning positions. But, with the exception of Socialists relegated to secondary posts, they had, at best, tenuous connections to left parties. However, these young technocrats saw themselves as articulating leftist policies—if by left we mean a disposition to favor state intervention in the economy and distributional policies that favor lower-income sectors (Levitsky and Roberts 2011).

Nevertheless, the Correa administration believed, correctly, it needed to legitimize its rhetoric of citizen participation in policy making. To that end, it organized new participatory mechanisms to involve citizens in policy making. Most of this activity was around the drafting of a third five-year development plan after the 2013 presidential election. However, the social organizations involved were small local ones drawn from each of the subnational territorial units. Representatives were elected by their peers in events organized by the planning secretariat SENPLADES. Established national-level organizations, for the most part, were absent. New local ad hoc groups formed to take advantage of the opportunity, as did individuals from existing small local self-help organizations unconnected to any major social movement organizations, including civic associations. Moreover, their status was strictly consultative. SENPLADES officials considered their recommendations to be potential policy inputs if deemed useful (Nicholls 2014).

Much more than in Bolivia, however, the Correa administration's strategy relied on public policies to connect citizens (individuals) and local communities to the state. This allowed it to bypass national social movement organizations (which it maintained at arm's length) and to generate electoral support. Tuaza (2011) has detailed case studies of how this worked in some highland indigenous communities. The policies that benefit individuals directly are the housing program, the Bono de Desarrollo Humano; a microcredit program for up to USD 5,000; universal subsidy for domestic-use natural gas and gasoline; the Tarifas de Dignidad (subsidized electricity, telephone, and potable water consumption); the Misión Solidaria Manuela Espejo (aid for the handicapped); school programs (nutrition, uniforms, books); and health (expansion in coverage and medical attention at reduced prices or free). Meanwhile, central (and subnational) government public works expenditures benefited municipalities. According to Tuaza, local residents were grateful to Correa for the individual benefits. No one before him seemed to care about them. Meanwhile, municipal governments with ties to CONAIE could not but accept the public works that the government offered. This drove a wedge between the base units of CONAIE and its national leadership.

Were the dynamics similar in the barrios of major cities? Here we have data from a study conducted by the Centro de Documentación e Información de los Movimientos Sociales del Ecuador (CEDIME) that suggests a positive answer in some respects.[5] The Correa administration's social policies generated electoral support at the national and local level for the president and his party among popular sectors in Quito. Although some of the programs existed before Correa, the expansion of coverage and larger individual benefits convinced people that this government cared about them. Thus, a greater variety of programs covering more needs reached localities and people who in the past had felt abandoned with greater consistency. There were indications that the programmatic, citizen rights, and means-tested approach to benefit distribution was beginning to break down established patron-client networks where a few families controlled most of the local social and political organizations of the barrio. It is also clear from the CEDIME interviews that neither militancy nor membership in AP was a prerequisite to be a local leader or to receive benefits. By the same token, there was no perceived pressure to turn out for pro-government demonstrations in return for services.

The local orientation of barrio organizations and their demands naturally led them to connect with local municipal political authorities and left them out of national policy-making processes. This suited the Correa administration well. There were no national organizations to contend with. These small, atomized territorial associations were the recipients of national welfare and urban-development planning without aspiration in participation at the national planning level. This was very different from CONAIE, the national labor federations, and professional associations that expected and demanded a place at the table in crafting agricultural (including land reform), industrial relations, health, and educational policies. What did exist was a system of top-down administrative articulation from the national executives (ministries) to newly established regional units that aggregated several departments, to the departments themselves, and on down to municipalities. At the municipal level, there was a dense network of local organizations that got the word out regarding available programs. Naturally, this was not a seamless system.

Despite these changes, clientelism, a traditional form of popular interest intermediation, was alive and well in the barrios of Ecuador's major cities such as Guayaquil (especially) and Quito. In these cities, clientelist networks involved politically powerful patrons (people with electoral machines that get them elected to prominent positions or appointed to plum government posts) who run organizations that reach all the way down to neighborhood bosses who mobilize their people to vote (Freidenberg 2003). The CEDIME study reveals that local neighborhood bosses were jumping ship to the Correa camp, mobilizing voters for him. The reasoning was straightforward. The AP government marshaled and distributed greater resources than the old parties. Data from the 2012 presidential election support such conclusions. Guayas voted heavier for AP than in the past and key barrios in the south of Quito remained loyal despite a net reduction in voting for AP (Universidad Andina Simón Bolívar 2012).

A large degree of continuity is expected from Lenin Moreno's administration. Just how much, however, is an open question. His campaign emphasized continuity and expansion of Correa's social policies. However, given the end of the commodity boom he has fewer resources at his disposal than Correa had for most of his presidency. He is also expected to differ in leadership style from Correa. So far this has translated into an anti-corruption campaign. Whether it will also result in a less conflict-prone relationship with the labor, indigenous peoples, and other critical social movements remains to be seen.

## CONCLUSION

What were the consequences of the neoliberal historical juncture for the incorporation of social movements in the post-neoliberal political arena in Bolivia and Ecuador? The first consequence was similar for both cases. Indigenous peoples' movements articulated broad, heterogeneous coalitions with class-based, territorial, and ethnic-based groups that often spearheaded cycles of contention against governments implementing free market–oriented policies. These shared characteristics also differentiate the contemporary period from the first wave of incorporation in the 1950s and 1960s in Bolivia and Ecuador. In the earlier period, urban unions allied with political parties were the main popular sector actors (Collier and Handlin 2009). If they articulated other popular sector and subaltern groups, it was from a class perspective, especially indigenous peoples based on a peasant (not indigenous) identity.

The second consequence of the neoliberal period was also similar in the two cases. The principal actors of the heterogeneous coalition generated a broad policy agenda for an eventual New Left government that included their expressed interests. The difference with the first wave of incorporation was that many interests were integral components of a potential New Left government's platforms, not just those of labor and peasants and their interpretation of the grievances of other social sectors.

Ecuador and Bolivia, however, differed sharply on three other developments. The first of these was the strength of the principal social movements that had led anti-neoliberal mobilization at the time that left governments came to power. The second one involved the connection of those social movements to the left political party that won the presidency. In Ecuador, the principal indigenous social movement and articulator of the heterogeneous social coalition was considerably debilitated and, as Conaghan shows in this volume, had not forged linkages with the main "New Left" political movement—AP. In Bolivia, the social movements that composed the heterogeneous social coalition against neoliberalism were at the apogee of their power (having forced the resignation of President Carlos Mesa), and its rural indigenous movements had founded a new, electorally successful mobilization party—the MAS.

The two cases also differed on a third major development: the ideational frames of the leaders of the New Left governments. In Bolivia, the organic connection between the MAS leadership and its core social movement organizations shaped ideational frames that stressed direct inclusion of those movement organizations in the political arena. Another key feature was their belief in the necessity of engaging and negotiating differences with social movements. By contrast, in Ecuador the disconnect between the political leadership of Correa's government and the social movements that led anti-neoliberal struggles reinforced ideational frames that emphasized technocracy and autonomy from social movements, especially CONAIE (and labor unions). Thus, Correa's government stressed inclusion of popular sector interests via public policies but excluded social movement organizations from the policy process.

The relative strength of the opposition to the governments of Evo Morales and Rafael Correa also influenced these outcomes. In Bolivia, opposition to Evo was strong, with regional claims to autonomy to topple Morales. This reinforced the tight connection between Morales's government and the social movements that defended it. However, the ideational frames of the top leadership had independent influence as well, for once the opposition had been defeated, the government still displayed a robust understanding of social movements. By contrast, the opposition was weak in Ecuador. Correa did not need to build alliances with social movements to defend his government, and the ideational frames of its leadership were relatively unfettered in shaping the second incorporation of popular sectors.

What were the consequences of these factors for the reorganization of popular interest intermediation regimes? In both Bolivia and Ecuador, and in the context of great institutional flux, the new governments had to contend with many more relatively well-organized social movements than in the first wave. Moreover, these movement organizations had their own identities and policy demands, independent (although complementary) from each other.

In this context, neither Correa nor Morales were interested in rebuilding state corporatism as the dominant interest intermediation regime, nor were they interested in pluralism. Instead, they constructed *segmented popular* interest intermediation regimes. The proliferation of popular and poor subaltern social groups that mattered politically led their left governments to establish separate forms of interest intermediation with specific social subjects and their organizations (see Rossi and Silva introduction and Silva conclusion to this volume). Thus, the primary characteristic of segmented interest intermediation regimes is that they are a mixture of old and new forms of interest intermediation. Its primary virtue is its flexibility and malleability; thus, the combination of interest intermediation forms can vary from country to country.

In Bolivia, Evo Morales introduced a state corporatist–like form of interest intermediation, primarily for the CSUTCB. Its similarity with corporatism lies in that the state recognizes the CSUTCB as the representative organization for indigenous-peasants and includes it in the policy-making process. The difference is that this arrangement is not formal, legally codified, and institutionalized. It must be stressed that this is only one of several forms of interest intermediation, nor is it dominant.

For the intermediation of popular interests and the state in other cases, the government relies on other, more novel forms of interest intermediation. I have called these contestatory when protest is used to draw the government's attention to unattended demands and consensual when protest is not a catalyst. Although they are informal, the principles, norms, procedures, and rules of engagement are understood by all parties. These processes are iterative and binding in that the state abides by the results, and so do the social organizations, at least until the next round. For example, the interest intermediation with CIDOB now tends to be contestatory, as it is with cooperative miners and, at times, the COB. It tends to be consensual with the coca federations.

Ecuador, by contrast, relies overwhelmingly on two forms of popular interest intermediation. One can be called state managerial. It refers to recognition of popular sector demands and public policy to address them, but the state does not involve the popular sector organizations that raised them in the policy process. In this type, the state manages popular sector demands directly. Traditional clientelism is the other form. Although there is protest, the informal contestatory type is not present because the government does not negotiate.

Evo Morales will remain president until 2019. Thus we can expect continuity in these arrangements. Correa gave way to his vice president in 2017, and a great deal of continuity in the broad outlines of the second wave of incorporation in Ecuador is anticipated.

Chapter 4

# THE INCORPORATION OF POPULAR SECTORS AND SOCIAL MOVEMENTS IN VENEZUELAN TWENTY-FIRST-CENTURY SOCIALISM

## MARÍA PILAR GARCÍA-GUADILLA

Hugo Chávez's ascent to power in 1999 initiated a definitive break with the Punto Fijo political system by defining a new anti-neoliberal socioeconomic project and by establishing a constitutional assembly to recast the political foundations of the nation. The resulting constitution enshrined the principles of participatory democracy and incorporated the demands for inclusion of mobilized popular sectors and social movements. In the absence of an organized grassroots social base of its own, the Bolivarian Revolutionary project stimulated the creation of new organizations, especially among the popular sectors, to implement participatory democracy and to build "people's power" (*poder popular*). These organizations also functioned as mechanisms to redistribute oil rents and, in moments of political crisis, as vehicles to mobilize people in support of President Chávez. The new organizational forms tend to exclude middle- and upper-class sectors, and the enabling law that the legislature granted Chávez in 2000 facilitated the passage of laws that negatively affected those groups, thus initiating their mobilization and precipitating the April 2002 coup d'état against Chávez (see Hellinger in this volume).

This chapter studies the diverse forms and instances of the incorporation of organized popular sectors and social movements in the Bolivarian Revolution, the evolution of their practices, the logics that guide their relationship to the state, and the processes behind the construction and transformation of those logics.[1] In short, it analyzes the role of the organized popular sectors and social movements in Venezuela's transition toward twenty-first-century socialism. Although the chapter emphasizes the Chávez period (1999-2013), it briefly describes the previous one (1958–1999) during which social organizations and movements played a significant role in pushing for constitutional transformation of the Punto Fijo political system and touches on President Maduro's presidency (2013-2017).[2]

The ways popular organization and social movements incorporated their demands during the 1999–2013 period are diverse and do not always respond to a dynamic strictly from above or below; sometimes they are mixed. Nevertheless, for analytical purposes we can group them into two main tendencies: incorporation from "below" and incorporation from "above." Incorporation from "below" involved popular and social movement mobilization for, and participation in, the process that culminated in the Bolivarian Constitution of 1999 while President Chávez promoted incorporation from "above" as part of the Bolivarian Revolutionary project. This had two modalities: the creation of Bolivarian social organizations and the implementation of ambitious social policies via the "social missions." Within this trend, we can define three models of incorporation: the constituent; the tutelary, clientelist, and exclusionary; and the assistance-welfare.

Nevertheless, many pre- and post-Chávez social movements resisted incorporation from above and opposed the government's continuation of the "neo-extractive" developmental economic and social project (see Rossi and Silva for a definition of those projects). This has generated serious conflicts, especially with the socio-environmental movement, which includes indigenous, environmental, and human rights activists. Although they generally support the government's political project, these movements mobilize to defend hard-won constitutional rights, which they feel the government's developmental socioeconomic model violates. Moreover, these movements do not inscribe themselves in government-promoted forms of social organization because they consider it sufficient that the constitution recognizes their demands. They fear that a direct, institutionalized relationship with the state would invite bureaucratization and co-optation, problems that have plagued many Bolivarian organizations.

## REFORMIST POPULAR ORGANIZATIONS: THE "DEMOCRATIZATION OF DEMOCRACY," 1958–1988

Toward the end of General Juan Vicente Gómez's dictatorship in the 1930s came the emergence of the first popular organizations in the barrios of Caracas demanding democratic rights in close association with emerging political parties. However, democracy did not flourish and these organizations languished. Popular organization in the barrios gained new momentum after the fall of the Pérez Jiménez dictatorship in December 1958. In the context of a nascent democracy, the provisional junta's populist Emergency Plan to tackle high unemployment gave birth to communal juntas (*juntas comunales*) to distribute unemployment benefits at the local level. The Emergency Plan was short-lived. Rómulo Betancourt's newly elected government eliminated it in August 1959 because it had become an economic burden due to substantial increases in rural migration to Caracas, in part because of the very availability of unemployment benefits. The Emergency Plan's short duration notwithstanding, the populist and clientelistic practices of Venezuela's political parties ensured that this pioneering form of popular organization was born co-opted.

In keeping with the Pacto de Punto Fijo (see Hellinger in this volume), the 1961 constitution inaugurated a liberal, representative democracy that sacrificed citizen participation for political stability. In this system, political parties exercised the representative function. Social interlocutors were limited to the organizations that were signatories to the pact together with the political parties: the military, business, labor unions, and the Catholic Church.

The 1970s witnessed the rise of neighborhood associations in middle-class urbanizations (Lope Bello 1979; Santana 1986, 1988; García-Guadilla 2003, 2005). Because they emerged to defend middle-class urban neighborhoods they frequently excluded popular sectors from them via campaigns to impede building the social infrastructure capable of serving massive populations. They also fought to keep out high-density public housing that could affect the exclusivity, privacy, and quality of life of their local habitat. Given the absence of legal and institutional mechanisms to defend their class interests, these neighborhood associations created the Federación de Asociaciones de Comunidades Urbanas (FACUR—Federation of Urban Neighborhood Associations). Neighborhood associations, which existed in cities across Venezuela, and especially in Caracas, were the bedrock of a self-proclaimed citizens' movement, which was active from the 1970s to the 1990s. Despite its origins, this movement transcended narrow, local class interests. It also expanded its agenda dramatically into the national political arena by calling for a "democratization of Venezuelan democracy."

By the end of the 1970s, popular sectors began organizing neighborhood associations of their own called Juntas de Desarrollo y Pro-Mejoras (Development and Improvement Councils). These suffered from clientelism and co-optation by whichever political party was in power. Nevertheless, more autonomous "committees" also existed (in the health and women's issues areas, for example), as well as other organizations that expressed the diverse concerns of the barrio's people. The demands of these organizations focused on poverty and inequality reduction along lines recommended by the United Nations Economic Commission for Latin America and the Caribbean (ECLAC). They did not question the general capitalist cast of ECLAC's development model for Latin America or its predominantly "developmental and functionalist" character.

In the 1980s and 1990s, the more autonomous popular organizations constituted a social movement that joined the citizens' movement led by FACUR in calls for democratizing reforms to the Punto Fijo system. The government responded by creating the Commission for State Reform in 1984. The commission's recommendations, however, remained stalled in the legislature until 1989 at which time, facing a grave political crisis, Carlos Andrés Pérez approved them via presidential decree (Gómez Calcaño and López Maya 1990; Combellas 1993; García-Guadilla and Roa 1996).

During the same period, emerging social movements for environmental, women's, indigenous, and human rights, among others, aligned with the citizens' movement. They believed that democratization was a fundamental condition if they were ever to be recognized as relevant actors and for the institutionalization of their demands. Paradoxically, although former members of leftist parties such as the Movimiento al Socialismo, the Communist Party of Venezuela, and the Movimiento de Izquierda Revolucionario participated in these movements, they did not demand structural transformations or revolutionary paths to change. Instead, they supported the state reform and political decentralization agenda of the Inter-American Development Bank and the World Bank.

## POPULAR ORGANIZATIONS, SOCIAL MOVEMENTS, AND ANTI-NEOLIBERALISM, 1989–1998

Because Venezuela is a petro-state, significant anti-neoliberal protests lagged behind the rest of Latin America by nearly a decade. It did not make an appearance until the second presidency of Carlos Andrés Pérez in 1989, when he applied an IMF-style structural adjustment program. That program deepened poverty, social inequality, and intensified urban popular struggles (López Maya 1999; Cariola and Lacabana 2005). The *Caracazo*—widespread rioting and protest in February 1989—became the iconic expression of popular rejection of Pérez's neoliberal macroeconomic policies.

An institutional consequence of the *Caracazo* was the implementation of social policies designed to ameliorate soaring exclusion and poverty and to secure a minimum of governability. Another consequence was the approval of long-awaited constitutional reform and political decentralization laws via decree in 1989 (see Hellinger in this volume). These reforms made the direct election of governors and mayors possible, which opened channels for the expression of discontent against economic stabilization and structural adjustment and institutionalized some of the demands of the "democratization of democracy" movement.

Decentralization laws offered space and voice, albeit limited, to emerging social organizations, which multiplied with the expansion of committees, cooperatives, and neighborhood associations in the areas of health, culture, sport, education, youth, and women, among others. Some organizations also advocated "street democracy" and sowed the seeds for the popular assembly and direct democracy movements associated with rising popular movements in the 1990s. Thus, some analysts argue that the *Caracazo* made possible the development of a popular movement that displayed greater transformative capacity than those of the 1970s and 1980s (Denis 2006).

One of these organizations was the Asamblea de Barrios de Caracas (1991–1993). Although it was short-lived, it had an important impact. Its members included MBR-200 militants and many leaders of Caracas barrios. As a result, it contributed significantly to the formulation of a plan for popular struggle in the Caracas barrios.

With the deactivation of the Asamblea de Barrios, the popular movement lost an important space for debate over alternatives for popular incorporation in a post-neoliberal setting. Nevertheless, the experience had significant consequences for the development of the Bolivarian organizations created by President Chávez. According to its founders and activists, the Asamblea de Barrios was the incubator of an autonomous popular movement struggling for the transformation of society envisioned by Chávez.

Throughout the 1990s, the citizens', environmental, indigenous, women's, and human rights movements, among others, were active nationally. Some also gained experience in co-government with novel participatory budgeting experiments implemented in the Municipality of Caroní in Ciudad Guayana under Mayor Clemente Scotto. In addition, the popular barrios witnessed the development of a relatively autonomous organizational base made up of a variety of committees (health, sport, and women), the cooperative movement, and Christian base communities. Many of these organizations advanced structural critiques of Venezuelan democracy to explain the lack of constitutional mechanisms for popular participation and expression of demands in the face of acute social conflict. In 1998, Hugo Chávez incorporated their demands for participatory democracy in his presidential campaign. Chávez's platform also called for the creation of a new post-neoliberal order based on participatory democracy and social inclusion as the vehicle for the empowerment of popular sectors more generally. This platform won him the presidency in 1998 (see Hellinger in this volume).

## POST-NEOLIBERAL INCORPORATION MODES, 1999–2013

### Incorporation from Below: The Constituent Assembly and the 1999 Bolivarian Constitution

The Venezuelan Constituent Assembly could be identified as a participatory-democratic process nourished from below. First, the nomination to be a constituent member was based on individuals, not on political parties; thus, the majority of the constituents elected came from social organizations and movements or were renowned individuals. The agenda discussed came from proposals previously made by those social organizations and movements to Hugo Chávez when he was a candidate for the presidency and later to the Constituent Assembly. Members of social organizations and movements participated and presented proposals in the agenda, not only as constituent members but also through the many participatory ways and an open system created by the constituent process that called all citizens to present such proposals. The close alliances between social organizations and movements and the constituents, as well as the continuous consulting work of social organizations and movements to the constituents, were ways to push their agendas from "below." As a result, many of those proposals were incorporated, almost verbatim, into the constitution (García-Guadilla and Hurtado 2000).

The resulting 1999 Constitution became the vehicle for legal recognition and the inclusion—or granting—of citizen rights to historically excluded popular sectors, their organizations, and social movements. These organizations and movements, which since 1992 were demanding more participation and new rights, along with the expansion of existing rights, participated directly in the constituent process on equal footing with other sociopolitical actors. Indeed, they were incorporated as essential actors of the process, and their demands were institutionalized.

The 1999 Constitution defined a new order. It not only emphasized citizen rights, it mandated new models of community organization to give them substance. Although the constitution included representative democracy, it privileged so-called participatory democracy. This involved institutionalizing participation in the implementation of public policy, granting peoples' organizations and social movements that presumably incarnated the sovereign people a primary role (*poder protagónico*). This led to the establishment of the concept of popular power as the foundation for popular sector organization. In addition to the expansion of civil and political rights already present in the 1961 Constitution, the new charter included social, economic, environmental, indigenous, and gender rights, among others. In sum, the 1999 Magna Carta constitutionally recognized *el pueblo* (the people) as the social subject of the

Bolivarian Revolution, meaning, in government discourse, the popular sectors. It granted new rights and defined participatory democracy as the primary mechanism to guide public policy and to resolve conflicts. In the process, the 1999 Constitution not only redrew the legal and social context of the old order, it opened the possibility of creating new forms of incorporation and of institutionalizing them.

### Incorporation from Above: Popular Local Organizations, the Commune, and the Social Missions

The discrediting of political parties (Roberts and Hellinger in this volume), and above all, the new government's need for an organized social base to support its political project, caused the presidency to focus on popular organizations and social movements as the preferred interlocutors and beneficiaries of the "refounding of the republic." This led to a second mode of incorporation—one from the state. It was necessary to create a strong, hegemonic popular movement as the foundation for the social transformation envisioned in the Bolivarian Revolution. A strong popular movement was also necessary to compensate for the organizational weakness of Chavismo and generalized distrust of political parties, including Chávez's own newly created Movimiento Quinta República (MVR).[3] Thus, as President Chávez emphasized, the new order required a social base for the construction of twenty-first-century socialism.

From an ideological perspective, this organized social base would incarnate the Revolutionary Bolivarian Project and be the concretion of participatory democracy's main social subject. Thus, in this second mode of incorporation, popular organizations and social movements were not only the legitimate interlocutors of participatory democracy but were also assigned the strategic task of constructing popular, or people's, power, especially in the case of popular organizations. As a result, government policy promoted social organization to give substance to the rights enshrined in the 1999 Constitution. This applied especially in the case of rights to habitat and habitation, meaning the recognition of informal urban settlements, regularization of real estate titles, proper zoning of popular barrios, and adequate social and transportation infrastructure. It is worth stressing that although this mode of incorporation supposes incorporation of popular sectors "from above" via state-promoted social organization, in some cases the organizational dynamics escaped control from above and generated a dynamic from below that is more similar to that of the social movements. (See note 1 for the distinction between popular organizations and social movements.)

A consequence of President Chávez's promotion of social organizations since 2000 has been the emergence of a "broad, heterogeneous, and diffuse popular social tissue characterized more by its capacity to mobilize and re-spond to changing situations than by its organic continuity" (Lander 2011). This extensive social tissue consists of social organizations and movements meant to incorporate popular sectors in the management of local issues. Among the latter, we can distinguish between those that originated before 1999 and those that emerged in response to President Chávez's Bolivarian project.

In addition to participating in the management of their habitat as a means to guarantee citizen rights in the area of basic services and social infrastruc-ture, Bolivarian organizations are considered an important support for the government's Social Missions. These missions constitute yet another form of "clientelist " inclusion paid for by oil revenues. They are essentially pal-liative social assistance programs aimed at improving popular consump-tion of basic needs (D'Elía 2006). One may differentiate Bolivarian popular organizations according to their degree of prior politicization, their func-tional purpose, membership characteristics (including prior organizing ex-perience), the reproduction of clientelist practices with the state, and their potential for co-optation, especially in the case of organizations financed by the government.

Government promotion of social organizations has marked clientelist-palliative social assistance characteristics. This frequently results in their co-optation by the government, the Partido Socialista Unido de Venezuela (PSUV), or other ideological organizations such as the Frente Francisco de Miranda. Moreover, to the detriment of the emergence of a genuine, autono-mous popular social movement, many of the organizations that received gov-ernment financing suffer from a lack of economic and social accountability and from high levels of corruption.

*Bolivarian Circles: Politicized Popular Organizations?*

Bolivarian Circles were the first attempt to incorporate popular sectors as the leading social subject of participatory democracy. However, this was primar-ily a politicized form of incorporation. Upon taking power, President Chávez called on the MBR-200 to create a countermovement to the political parties and social organizations that opposed his governing project. This transformed the MBR-200 into a civil-military source of support for the government's rev-olutionary process. In 2000, President Chávez launched the idea of the Boli-varian Circles, which were created by presidential decree in 2001 using Arti-cle 52 of the Bolivarian Constitution as justification. Chávez then, during his television program Aló Presidente on October 6, 2001, called on the MBR-200, women, peasants, students, and "honest and patriotic workers" to form Bolivarian Circles in order to strengthen the revolutionary process and to turn the constitutional promise that the popular sectors would be the protagonists of participatory democracy into reality. In addition to these political objectives, the Bolivarian Circles were also the first organizations that promoted social inclusion. One of their charges was the construction of spaces where people could discuss community problems and propose solutions to the government through official channels.

The Bolivarian Circles were under the jurisdiction of the Ministerio de Secretaría de la República. Many of its members had experience with the Asambleas de Barrio (barrio assemblies) of the 1990s and thus from the beginning had strong bonds to Bolivarian ideology and the MVR, which was Chávez's electoral political movement. Given this political profile, the Bolivarian Circles implicitly shared the government's political "identity and objectives," and they were the first mobilized to support the government's policies threatened by the 2002 coup d'état. According to Hawkins and Hanson (2006), the Bolivarian Circles are not based on the "type of autonomy that democracy requires" (127). Instead, they function on client-patron logics in the distribution of state resources, which makes them instruments of populism (Hawkins 2003; Arenas and Gómez Calcaño 2006; De la Torre 2013). Moreover, they exhibit a low degree of institutionalization, function as a political movement, possess a direct relationship to the charismatic leader (Chávez), and lack an identity and objectives beyond those of the supreme leader (Hawkins 2010a, 2010b).

Their apogee spanned from 2001 to 2004. During that period, Bolivarian Circles played an important political role at a time of extreme polarization, organizing numerous demonstrations in support of President Chávez and against the 2002 coup d'état (Hawkins and Hanson 2006). Although they have been surpassed by other organizations, they still exist.

### Technical Boards: Participation in Small Spaces

Building on the experience of the barrio assemblies during Aristóbulo Istúriz's mayoral tenure in metropolitan Caracas during the 1990s, in 2001 Chávez's government stimulated the creation of community organizations to collaborate in the provision of public services, such as water, housing, transportation, health, and food. The Water Technical Boards (Mesas Técnicas de Agua) were the first, created by the Organic Law for Potable Water and Waste Service. They were conceived as spaces for direct participation in the implementation of public services at the community level Thus, their reach, or territorial jurisdiction, is very limited. These boards quickly expanded into energy, transportation, telecommunications, and solid waste (Cariola et al. 2010). Although they were superseded by the communal councils in 2006, which they were supposed to fold into, they too still exist.

*Urban Land Committees: Incorporation of Socio-Territorial and Sociocultural Identities*

Comités de Tierra Urbana (CTUs, Urban Land Committees) were a form of incorporation with greater potential for inclusion and autonomy. Although they too have roots in the barrio assembly movement, they constituted a new form of popular organization with the promulgation of Presidential Decree 1666 in 2002. The CTUs' function was to regularize land use and to guarantee the right to housing established in the Bolivarian constitution.[4] They gave substance to broader citizen rights, such as the right to urban spaces and recognition of their socio-territorial and cultural identities (Antillano 2005; García-Guadilla 2011).

Although the CTUs were created by presidential decree, on occasion their organizational dynamics escaped control from above, generating their own dynamic from below, especially when they confront the state regarding conflicts that involve their identities and rights. Thus, they may at times behave like social movements when they demand freedom from state interference in their decision-making processes and reject government financing to avoid co-optation. Indeed, during moments of national political crisis, or during electoral campaigns, they may even behave like political movements.

Their sociocultural identity is tied to territory inhabited by diverse types of people and therefore plural; thus, they advance claims concerning the territorial and cultural nature of the barrio (Asamblea Metropolitana 2004, 7). Their struggles reveal a class identity built on a shared sense of exclusion from the formal city that has forced them to construct their own habitat. In addition to their struggles against social, political, and economic exclusion, CTUs demand participation in decision-making processes advocating democracy within difference or complex equality (Hopenhayn 2000, 116).

Given that their demands are political, the CTUs' claims go beyond the right to a dignified home and land titles and include the right to participate in policy formulation and in urban planning. In other words, CTUs also struggle to exercise a political right, the right to participate in the affairs of the polis. This posture springs from the tension between their resistance to the dominant discourse and their subordinate position as inhabitants of the city's poor barrios.

Despite being promoted by the government, many CTUs consider themselves autonomous, given their self-management and independence from the state in their decision making. In other words, their sense of autonomy springs from their participation and impact in state policy that affects them and from the possibility of infusing urban policy with their own project for an alternative society. Their rejection of state funding, coupled with their lack of formal legal standing to receive such, has reduced the development of clientelist practices. Moreover, their collective identity and their focus on rights have permitted a more critical stance toward the government in general.

. That said, there are tensions and contradictions concerning their autonomy. CTUs are susceptible to manipulation by pro-Chávez political parties, such as the erstwhile MVR and now the PSUV and by the executive himself. They have frequently used CTUs as a political clientele, mobilizing them electorally in support of the president and his political project.

To the degree that Venezuela's polarization and political crisis deepen, there is the risk that these temporary political "loyalties" may become permanent and, thus, displace the plural identity of CTUs. This is due to mounting pressure for their coordinators and members to officially join and militate in political parties that support the Bolivarian project. The institutionalization of the communal councils created in 2006 is another factor that threatens the survival of CTUs; according to the law, CTUs should be part of these councils. Although in dwindling numbers, autonomous CTUs still exist, have formed networks, and exhibit social movement characteristics, especially in the Metropolitan Region of Caracas.

*Communal Councils: Popular Power or New Forms of Populism?*

The communal councils are, perhaps, among the most significant popular organizations promoted by President Chávez. Formally created in 2006, they are larger in number, functions, and resource allotments than CTUs (García-Guadilla 2008)[5]. In contrast to other popular organizations, the 2006 Law of Communal Councils elevated them to the primary form of community organization for participation in the policy process. Given their registration in the Presidential Commission of Popular Power, discursively they are considered the essential grassroots base for the development of popular power. Moreover, the law obliges CTUs and other earlier forms of community organization to be placed under the direction of the communal councils.

President Chávez went even further in his address during the program *Aló Presidente* on September 4, 2006. He defined the communal councils as the "primary units for a new sociopolitical order," focused on solving community problems, and the incarnation of "popular power in action, participatory democracy." They were considered the locus of the people's sovereignty, the vehicle for the construction of a social subject capable of sustaining the Chavistas' popular sociopolitical project. By the beginning of 2007, when the process of change radicalized, communal councils were defined as the revolutionary subject par excellence—the keystone for the construction of popular power and for the necessary transformations to implement the Bolivarian Revolution and, thus, to arrive at twenty-first-century socialism.

Communal councils share attributes such as socio-territorial, political, and sociocultural incorporation with CTUs. However, in contrast to CTUs, they are legally entitled to receive public financing for the self-management and execution of community projects and empowered to administer and keep accounts of those resources. The political opposition and even some sources sympathetic to the Bolivarian Revolution (such as CTUs) have questioned the direct management of funds by the communal councils due to the lack of external accountability (Álvarez and García-Guadilla 2011). They have also questioned their autonomy and have cast doubt on their inclusiveness.

When originally proposed, the communal councils were open to all social groups irrespective of their political sympathies. However, Venezuela's extreme polarization led to changes in the wording of the new 2009 Organic Law of Communal Council that defines them as part of the "socialist project" and aligns them with the Bolivarian Socialist government. Thus, with increasing frequency, they must align ideologically with the government's project in order to receive public funds; the closer to the government, the more funding they receive, and the greater the funding, the more probable is their co-optation and the display of clientelist practices. Their close connection with government agencies that disburse funds stimulates these types of relationships and makes the communal councils more vulnerable to pressure by the government for electoral mobilization and partisan practices.[6]

Despite these pressures, some communal councils defend their decision-making autonomy from political parties and the state. In this respect, they seem closer to social movements, as in the case of the Frente Nacional Comunal Simón Bolívar and the Frente Nacional Campesino Ezequiel Zamora. They think of themselves as contributing to popular power from an independent position, but nevertheless have formed communal councils to access public funds. The first National Meeting of Communal Councils in 2007 concluded that public funding "is their *due*" even though they defend their autonomy.

Other communal councils with "double membership" include committees on health, culture, and women, among others. They must play the government's political game when acting as communal councils to obtain resources, but they also behave as social movements when they join networks and raise rights-based demands related to gender or culture from an independent stance. At times, they even manage to transcend Venezuela's political and ideological polarization. According to the First Assembly of Popular Revolutionary Movements in May 2012, a shared objective of these hybrid communal councils-cum-social movements is "planning actions against . . . the criminalization of popular struggles and protest" by the government.

### The Commune and the Communal State

The commune constitutes a second form of incorporation from "above" that should result from the aggregation of communal councils and other local organizations. Its creation has been difficult and legally uncertain since the 1999 Bolivarian Constitution did not explicitly mention them. Moreover, the 2007 constitutional referendum convoked by President Chávez, which included a new geometry of power based in the concept of the *commune*, was defeated. The need to give this new form of political-territorial organization legal standing led to the 2010 Popular Power laws, which expanded objectives beyond what had been contemplated in the 2007 referendum. According to the Organic Law of the Commune (Asamblea Nacional 2010), the commune would aggregate existing local-level popular organizations, such as the communal councils and the various committees, at a higher level of political-territorial administration: the commune. The aggregation of communes in federations, confederations, and communal cities would form the basis for the communal state. Participatory democracy, expressed in self-governing communes, would be the foundation for Socialist society in Venezuela (Asamblea Nacional 2010, Article 4). As President Chávez proclaimed, "The commune must be the space from which socialism is born" (from Hugo Aló Presidente Teórico, No. 11, June 2009, cited in Harnecker 2009). Defined as the pillar of Venezuela's "socialism," the communal state excludes community organizations that do not share this ideology becoming exclusionary.

The government has promoted the commune in its development plans as the economic, political, social, and territorial foundation for constructing the communal state. It involves people's participation in the definition, design, management, and evaluation of policies at levels that transcend the purely micro and local levels to encompass the urban, regional, and national scales. However, the process is not developing organically from "below" as a product of participatory democracy. It is a being created from the state, and the articulation of participatory democracy at higher levels has yet to materialize.

According to the Ministerio de las Comunas, there were four hundred communes in 2017, and the Second Simón Bolívar Socialist Plan for the Nation (2013–2019) set an ambitious target of three thousand communes by the year 2019. In contrast, our own census survey revealed that the number of communes that complied with all requirements did not reach 120 communes by the period 2014–2015, since most are classified as Salas de Batalla Social or "communes under Construction" (GAUS 2000–2017)—that is, "spaces for social struggle" given their lack of formal prerequisites for forming a commune. Those requirements include the territorial proximity or contiguity of the communal councils involved; additionally, those communal councils need to share the same territorial and social history, have institutions for self-government and direct democracy (the Communal Parliaments), and a common social economy, which implies solidarity and self-sustaining economic projects. Difficulties in meeting institutional requirements limit the communes' potential to fulfill the main objective of participatory democracy— that is, to achieve popular participation in the "formulation, execution, and control of public policies" (Asamblea Nacional 2010, Article 7). However, since the death of Chávez in 2013 and as the economic crisis has accentuated in Venezuela in the 2013–2017 period, the transference of economic resources not only to the communes but to the communal councils as well has become critical, and it is contributing either to demobilize or to co-opt further more of these organizations.

*The Social Missions*

The Social Missions, which are not that different from populist social assistance programs of Carlos Andrés Pérez's first Presidency, also constitute a third form of incorporation from "above." The radicalization of the opposition toward the end of 2001, its attempt to overthrow Chávez in April 2002, and its decision to force a recall referendum against president Chávez forced the Bolivarian government to develop a strategy to build legitimacy in order to win the recall referendum of 2004. One strategy was the implementation of the Social Missions. From the beginning, they were social assistance programs designed to deactivate discontent over deficient basic services (health, education) and food shortages (D'Elia and Cabezas 2008; D'Elia and Quiroz 2010). Thus, at the same time that the government promoted the development of Bolivarian social organizations, it also stimulated popular incorporation via Social Missions to reduce poverty, inequality, and persistent social exclusion. This form of incorporation has generated clientelism and, ironically, the exclusion of those who do not align with the government ideologically.

## Social Movements: Contestation to Co-opted Incorporation and Resistance to the Economic Development Model

Although some social movements demobilized after the institutionalization of their demands in the 1999 Constitution, others redoubled their efforts to raise claims in the political arena. This was the case of the socio-environmental movement, which, as in Bolivia and Ecuador, challenged the development model based on intensive extraction of hydrocarbons. The socio-environmental movement organized around constitutional rights to territory, identity, tolerance of plural citizenship, and a clean environment. Despite its shared critique of neoliberal globalization, the socio-environmental movement has seriously called the Bolivarian government to account. It has mobilized against the negative environmental effects of its "developmental-extractive" economic model, as expressed in the national development plans of 2002–2007, 2007–2013, and 2013–2019. It has also criticized the development model for not being the product of participatory democracy and from being imposed from above (García-Guadilla 2013).

An illuminating example is the long struggle of the socio-environmental movement[7] in the Sierra de Perijá against environmentally and socially harmful large-scale coal mining that violates constitutional guarantees, such as the right of indigenous peoples to the preservation of their identity and habitat. In the "alternative" workshop held in the World Social Forum in Caracas, the Venezuelan socio-environmental movement criticized the Bolivarian model. According to the Venezuelan environmental organization AMIGRANSA, the government's economic plans and policies "not only maintained the old paradigm, they deepened a capitalist, neoliberal development model based on the over-exploitation of natural resources in which the environment is totally subordinated and the leading, participatory role of communities and social movements is undervalued."[8]

Previous megadevelopment projects involving the construction of large infrastructures such as transnational pipelines, ports, and highways to carry gas and oil to the Caribbean and Latin America under the Iniciativa para la Integración de la Infraestructura Regional Suramericana (IIRSA) are virtually paralyzed due to the severe economic crisis facing Venezuela. Instead, since 2016 President Maduro's government is promoting large extractive-mining projects to be developed in ecologically fragile areas and, in some cases, in indigenous lands. One of these projects is El Arco Minero, which implies the opening (*apertura*) of mining of the Orinoco that covers almost twelve hundred thousand square kilometers in a fragile area where the main basins of the Orinoco and Caroní rivers that supply most of the energy and water to the country are located.[9] This megaproject has been rejected by all social movements and even by ex-ministers and ex-high-ranking representatives of the government because of the severe negative impacts that will result.

According to the socio-environmental movement, despite the government's strong anti-neoliberal, anticapitalist, anti-imperialist, and antiglobalization discourse, all of the national development plans constitute a continuation, indeed a strengthening, of the logics of industrial capitalism and globalization, with all of their negative impacts on vulnerable populations. Paradoxically, this economic model, which causes exclusion and strong negative social impacts, is promoted as the principal weapon in the fight against neoliberalism. For this reason, its implementation has caused sharp conflicts between the government and social movements that protest against it despite the fact that many movement members supported Chávez's government politically. Nevertheless, the reactive nature of demands and the government's rejection of their claims and criminalization of their protests bodes ill for their becoming the form of popular power envisioned in the constitution.

## CONCLUSION: FROM NEOLIBERAL EXCLUSION TO AN EXCLUSIONARY, TUTELARY, CLIENTELIST, AND PARALLEL POST-NEOLIBERAL INCORPORATION

The Punto Fijo political system excluded popular sectors from the founding pacts of representative democracy in Venezuela despite their numeric importance, their struggle for state reform, the deepening of democracy alongside the citizen's movement, and—after 1989—their rejection of neoliberal structural adjustment programs. As of 1990, resistance to neoliberalism led to the creation of organizational opportunities in popular barrios such as the barrio assemblies, whose members later formed the organizations that President Chávez promoted to incorporate popular sectors, such as the Bolivarian Circles.

Between 1999 and 2013, we can distinguish at least three models of popular incorporation. The first one can be called the "constituent model"; it was the result of a bottom-up process that focused on the recognition and legitimation of the popular sectors, along with other organized sectors of society, in the new order. The political opportunity for this process was Chávez's call for a constituent assembly. While the 1999 Constitution recognized and legitimized all sectors of society, the Bolivarian project implicitly defined the erstwhile excluded popular sectors as the main protagonist of the process and as the principal interlocutor with the state. Thus, almost from the very beginning, it excluded middle classes from the various modalities of incorporation.

The second model of incorporation was tutelary, clientelist, and exclusionary. It was tutelary because it involved the creation and promotion of popular organization by President Chávez from the state. It was exclusionary because Chávez's reason for mobilizing and controlling a social base of support for his government's project—meant the rejection of social organizations that did not align politically and ideologically with Chavismo. This form of incorporation also perpetuated time-honored clientelist practices and undermined representative democracy at the local level. Not only that, it compromised the autonomy of aligned popular sector organizations vis-à-vis the state because direct supply of resources stimulated co-optation and lax accounting abetted corruption.

In other words, these organizations suffer the contradictions of the polarization that has characterized the Bolivarian Revolution. In theory, these organizations should enrich the concept of citizenship. They should also stimulate the emergence of new social subjectivities associated with socioterritorially based identities anchored in cultural diversity and deepening democracy. Society should experience greater inclusion of material and postmaterial concerns, equality within difference and cultural pluralism, and citizen participation in political decision making. In the praxis, the result was exclusion based on ideological criteria. This applies not only to those who oppose the regime—mainly the middle and upper classes—but also to popular sectors that do not align ideologically with the Bolivarian process of transformation. Strong tensions exist between the objective of giving substance to constitutional mandates for inclusion, equality, and participation and the empirical evidence for authoritarianism and politically motivated exclusion.

Tensions also run deep between the objective of self-government and autonomy from the state of popular organizations and the need of the government to control, orchestrate support, and mobilize partisans. This leads the government to stimulate political co-optation and clientelistic practices. In the final analysis, this results in the exclusion of all of those who do not align ideologically with the Bolivarian revolutionary process leading to what we will call "inclusionary exclusion."

The third model of incorporation, the assistance-welfare model, rests on social assistance programs run by the presidency in parallel to line ministries outside of their control. This undermines formal state institutions by duplicating functions and syphoning off resources. This model also replicates populist welfare schemes that stimulate clientelist practices, political co-optation, and exclusion of all who do not share the government's ideology.

In sum, the three modes of popular sector incorporation in the Bolivarian Revolution reflect a type of inclusion that stresses the satisfaction of basic material needs but not postmaterial ones. Moreover, it excludes all social groups that do not share the government's ideology. It also contradicts an ideal of equity rooted in formal equality because popular assemblies violate the principle of minority protection, and because local-level participation cannot be scaled up to higher levels of political-territorial administration. As the economic crisis has accentuated in the post-Chávez era, so too has the exclusionary, clientelist model.

More than tutelary organization promoted from above, the creation of autonomous popular power requires social movements and vibrant networks of organizations gestated organically from below capable of making strategic decisions free from state interference. They should be able to do so whether or not they receive government financing. Moreover, they should possess the capacity to stimulate both the new forms of citizenship and the construction of a hegemony that would give substance to the type of popular power envisioned in the 1999 Constitution. Unfortunately, the very organizations capable of doing so are being demobilized, given the legal requirement that they register in clientelist and politicized organizational schemas, which is the case with most communal councils and, more recently, communes.

Last but not least, the Bolivarian processes of transformation face several paradoxes. First, the inclusion of erstwhile excluded social sectors rests on the accentuation of Venezuela's traditional extractive model of development; oil rents principally finance the Social Missions and the diverse and complex network of Bolivarian social organizations. Second, the social movements that were the central actors of the constitutional incorporation process and that from the very beginning shared the Bolivarian project's anti-neoliberal discourse were the proponents of an alternative development model capable of creating autonomous popular power envisioned in the constitution. Unfortunately, they are now in a process of demobilization because of laws that privilege formal organizations, such as the communal councils and, more recently, the communes. A third and final paradox is that a self-described left government that appropriated the social movements' agenda for change—and which constitutionally recognized social movements—marginalizes, excludes, and criminalizes them. This occurs when they take an autonomous and critical stance in defense of hard-won constitutional rights and of an alternative economic model of development that transcends global capitalism. It is particularly the case with the socio-environmental movement that defends the right to territorial expansion and demarcation, the right to make decisions concerning the environmental protection and use of said territory and, above all, the right to their identity and way of life.

Chapter 5

# SOCIAL MOVEMENTS, THE NEW "SOCIAL QUESTION," AND THE SECOND INCORPORATION OF THE POPULAR SECTORS IN ARGENTINA AND BRAZIL

## FEDERICO M. ROSSI

This chapter analyzes two paradigmatic examples of reincorporation struggles and movements in Latin America. These are the unemployed workers' movement in Argentina and the landless peasants' movement in Brazil. These movements have been struggling for the reincorporation of the popular sectors as wage earners (members of the socioeconomic society) as well as citizens (members of the political society). The aim is to understand how pressure from below built the conditions for the second incorporation of the popular sectors in Argentina and Brazil (see Rossi 2015a, 2017, and the introduction to this section).

The transformation of sociopolitical arenas in Argentina and Brazil from import-substitution industrialization (ISI) to neoliberalism and beyond was a contentious process. In Argentina, the crisis of 2001–2003 produced a larger rupture with the neoliberal past than in Brazil. In the latter, the process was incremental and mild if compared with the rest of the cases covered by this book. However, in Argentina and Brazil, a key social movement mobilized to resist the disincorporation consequences of neoliberal reforms and struggled to achieve the reincorporation of the popular sectors. In both countries, a new "social question" emerged as a result of these struggles, and social policies and policing techniques were created or modified to deal with the popular sectors' organized unrest. Finally, both movements were incorporated into the coalition in government, though with a marginal influence in the policy-making process. Using a historical and comparative method, this chapter identifies the stages of this process of second incorporation.[1]

# FROM DEMOCRATIZATION TO DISINCORPORATION

## Argentina

*The Failed Relaunch of the ISI Model (1983–1989)*

Democratization in 1983 brought with it both pluralism and an expectation of the recovery of welfare through the relaunching of the ISI model of development. However, with the failure of the Austral plan, ISI was rapidly dismissed. Argentina's economy suffered from stagnation, with a 7.2 percent contraction from 1983 to 1985, and during 1989–1991 a hyperinflation crisis, reaching 3,079.8 percent in 1989 (Saad-Filho, Iannini, and Molinari 2007). In 1989, the rate of unemployment reached 8.1 percent, and 47.3 percent of the population was in poverty, which led to a series of lootings in urban areas. As a result, Raúl Alfonsín ended his presidency six months early, handing power to the Peronist Carlos Saúl Menem (Partido Justicialista—PJ).

*Neoliberal Reforms and the Lack of Policies for the Disincorporated Popular Sectors (1989–1996)*

Despite Menem's promise of reestablishing the ISI model, continued high levels of inflation (197 percent), unemployment (7.1 percent), and poverty (33.7 percent) pushed him toward a heterodox neoliberal reform program with the purpose of urgently solving the crisis (Palermo and Novaro 1996). It began in 1989 with the restructuring and privatization of almost all the state-owned companies and public services. In 1991, the peso was pegged to the U.S. dollar at a one-to-one exchange rate with the Convertibility plan.

After the Convertibility plan, inflation fell dramatically, which gave Menem's reforms substantial public support. Menem's government had a parliamentary majority in both chambers thanks to an alliance with small conservative parties from the provinces (Llanos 2002) and a stable pro-reform coalition among some Confederación General del Trabajo (CGT) unions, domestic industrialists, and PJ governors (Levitsky and Murillo 2005).

In 1992, Menem initiated the first fiscal pact, an agreement with governors for the reduction of public sector jobs. This same year, the main losers of the neoliberal reforms organized the Congreso de Trabajadores Argentinos (CTA, later renamed as Central de Trabajadores de la Argentina) (see Gindin and Cardoso in this volume). In 1994, the second fiscal pact was introduced, expanding reforms to provincial service privatizations and increased reductions in expenditures. This led to the collapse of several regional economies. In December 1993 in Santiago del Estero, the first of a series of poor peripheral provinces collapsed, provoking a sequence of *puebladas* (town revolts). Since the first *puebladas*, a diffusion process started and *puebladas* took place in numerous provincial capitals, forcing some governors to resign. They were the result of resistance by state employees to provincial fiscal austerity policies (Farinetti 1999).

After most of the core reforms were passed during the first term of office, Menem's second mandate faced increasingly high levels of contention. This was the result of the combination of a worsening social situation, as well as the increased coordination of the CTA, the Peronist dissident union Movimiento de Trabajadores Argentinos (MTA), the Maoist Corriente Clasista y Combativa, and the emerging movement of unemployed workers.

Notwithstanding the magnitude and intensity of the struggle against neoliberal reforms and the consequences of disincorporation, in 1994 the Menem government had not yet recognized the existence of a "social question" in relation to unemployment. In 1995, the rate of unemployment reached 18.5 percent, with only 7.1 percent of the unemployed receiving any kind of economic compensation and just 1.3 percent of the economically active population covered by unemployment benefits (Etchemendy 2004). To make things worse, from 1989 to 1992 all the social policies inherited from the Alfonsín government were dismantled and replaced with very limited policies (Repetto 2000).

Why were there no unemployment policies? One reason was related to the changes in the PJ-CGT relationship. Though union influence on the PJ had been reduced since the 1980s, the Menem government still considered the CGT's participation in the pro-reform coalition as more important than disincorporated workers. Compensation was focused on protecting the organizational strength of the CGT rather than helping the individual victims of the reforms in exchange for union demobilization (Etchemendy 2004).

The second reason is related to the territorialization of politics, which favored a governability agreement, in place since 1992, between the national government and Eduardo Duhalde—the governor of the province of Buenos Aires (PJ). This led to the creation of an agreement for the regular provision of national resources at the discretion of the administration of the province at around USD 650 million annually for one decade (Prévôt-Schapira 1996; *La Nación*, January 29, 1998). This agreement was the most developed of a generic type of accord that Menem entered into with provincial governors in exchange for their support of his reform policies (Gibson and Calvo 2000). The implications of this agreement were manifold. The first was that Menem accepted not to interfere with any provincial politics in Buenos Aires since Duhalde won the 1993 internal party election (Levitsky 2001). The second was that Duhalde built a strong clientelistic territorial network in Greater Buenos

Aires based on the coordination of local brokers that administered the distribution of the Plan Vida in poor districts (Repetto 2000). The third was the absence of any national social policy on unemployment in Buenos Aires and the implementation of the provincial Plan Barrios Bonaerenses.

*The Emergence of the Reincorporation Movement: The* Piquetero *Movement*

The example of *puebladas* was crucial for the organization of a movement of unemployed people in Greater Buenos Aires. As part of state reforms, the government decided to downsize the workforce of the main state-owned company, Yacimientos Petrolíferos Fiscales (YPF) (Sánchez 1997). In 1996, a first *pueblada* was organized in Plaza Huincul and Cutral-Có to claim for some alternative industrial solutions that could recover local employment in the Patagonia.

The Convertibility plan also led to de-industrialization on a massive scale in several areas of Argentina but particularly affected Greater Buenos Aires. In historically industrial districts, from 1990 onwards most major factories began to close. In 1996, the Marcha contra el Hambre, la Desocupación y la Represión was organized by the Maoist Partido Comunista Revolucionario (PCR), the Trotskyist Movimiento al Socialismo, and the Marxist-Leninist Partido Comunista de Argentina (PCA) (Flores 2005). Also, in 1997, the first pickets were coordinated that succeeded in getting unemployment subsidies (Svampa and Pereyra 2003).

The main immediate goal of the *piqueteros*—the unemployed workers' movement—has been to recover full employment for the urban poor. This goal is related to the quest for reincorporating the popular sectors in the sociopolitical arena. In a mid- and long-term perspective, each *piquetero* organization has diverse goals based on their ideologies and repertoires of strategies (Rossi 2017). Some organizations claim revolutionary aims, while others expect gradual reforms in coalition with governments. The *piquetero* movement includes several organizations with the common identity of "unemployed workers." Although the number of organizations has gradually expanded, it began with three main groups: The Liberation Theology-oriented Federación de Trabajadores por la Tierra, Vivienda y Hábitat (FTV), the Maoist Corriente Clasista y Combativa (CCC), and the Guevarist and autonomist Movimientos de Trabajadores Desocupados (MTDs).

Part of the *piquetero* movement departed from the same groups that coordinated urban land occupations in the 1980s. Among them, the FTV is the organization with the strongest links to this previous process. Others, such as the CCC, are one of the outcomes of the process of reconfiguration of the left since democratization.

Since democratization, a group of left-wing organizations had systematically failed to organize employed workers at the factory level. This took them to work at the territorial level with those popular sectors mostly ignored by the Peronist CGT. In 1995, the MTD of La Juanita was created in La Matanza, and another MTD emerged in Florencio Varela, among others. The heterogeneity of this group led to permanent divisions and the creation of new organizations. The MTDs later created the strong Coordinadora de Trabajadores Desocupados (CTD) 'Aníbal Verón,' from which, in turn, several new organizations arose.

### The Emergence of a "Piquetero Social Question" (1996–1999)

From 1990 to 1994, the struggle in Jujuy against local disincorporation forced four governors to resign. The fiscal pacts led to a reduction of tax transfers to Jujuy while the province already controlled public education. The provincialization of politics and decentralization during the beginning of the neoliberal reforms moved the locus of protest to the provincial governments (Auyero 2002). For twelve days in 1997, nineteen simultaneous pickets were organized by a multisectoral coalition that included incorporated (CTA, Sindicato de Empleados y Obreros Municipales) and disincorporated unemployed workers. With the goal of making the wave of puebladas reach Buenos Aires, the coalition integrated by the CTA, CCC, FTV, and some MTDs organized the second Marcha Federal in 1997 (the first one was in 1994).

As social unrest grew, the national government started to enact some social policies. The Plan Trabajar was created in 1996 to relieve social unrest among unemployed people and to avoid using repression. The crucial element to note is that due to its timing, unlike what was applied to CGT unions and national industrialists, the Plan Trabajar was not a compensatory policy for the losers of neoliberal reforms to avoid mobilization or to include them in the pro-reform coalition. It came so late that its application appeared as a desperate solution to the increase in social unrest. World Bank and Ministry of Labor technocrats designed it, covering 20 percent of the unemployed workforce between 1996 and 2001 (Lodola 2005). This meant an almost 300 percent increase of coverage from the policies used before 1995.

The approach of the Menem government to the growing social unrest associated with unemployment came before the legitimation of the piqueteros as a political actor. Instead, the piquetero protests were merely considered a "social question" attributable to the novelty of their claim and the type of actor involved, which were both new for Argentina. The gradual recognition of a "social question" started in 1994 when the secretary of social development was created and put under the direct control of the presidency. However, it was not responsible for unemployment policies; it was merely an agency for the discretionary distribution of resources to control unrest (Repetto 2000).

The arrival of the "*piquetero* question" on a national level resulted from the termination of the informal territorial agreement between the presidency and the governorship of Buenos Aires. The process began when the secretary of social development position was given to Ramón Ortega in 1998. In an attempt to become the PJ presidential candidate, Ortega fought with Antonio Erman González (Ministry of Labor) for the responsibility of dealing with the unemployment issue, the administration of subsidies, and for the upgrading of the secretary into a ministry (*Clarín*, May 9, 1998). Ortega would lose his battle with González. However, as an unintended consequence, Ortega's ambition led to the virtual violation of a decade-long informal agreement for the distribution of territorial responsibilities among the national and provincial levels in Buenos Aires.

Ortega's short tenure was the starting point for permanent disputes about the responsibility of the "*piquetero* question" among the Ministry of Labor and the secretary of social development in subsequent governments. Simultaneously, since the Ortega-González dispute, the "unemployment question" became the "*piquetero* question." Even though the movement was not yet considered as a legitimate actor on a national level, its claim was recognized. In theoretical terms, this is the departure point for the construction of a *piquetero* policy domain. By "policy domain," I mean: "(1) the range of collective actors . . . who have gained sufficient legitimacy to speak about or act on a particular issue; and (2) the cultural logics, frameworks, and ideologies those actors bring to bear in constructing and narrating the 'problem' and the appropriate policy responses" (Jenness, Meyer, and Ingram 2005, 300). In brief, the accumulation of *puebladas* since 1993, the organization in Buenos Aires of the *piqueteros*, and the intragovernmental dispute for electoral purposes brought the "*piquetero* question" to the national agenda.

## Brazil

### *The Weak Relaunch of the ISI Model (1985–1990)*

José Sarney, the unexpected president, was a member of the ISI coalition that sustained the developmental model, so he did not do much to produce deep reforms. His government focused on the attempt to relaunch ISI with the 1986–1987 Cruzado plan and an important constitutional reform in 1988.

The process of disincorporation started in the 1980s, bringing unemployment and increasing impoverishment in the cities. Within this context, "Many people of rural origin sought shelter in the agricultural sector, but the impact of modernization on land access during the previous decades could not be wholly reverted" (Ondetti 2008, 92).

Concerning rural social policies, during Sarney's government the new constitution produced a legal framework for agrarian reform focused on the social utility of land. Even though Sarney chose the most prestigious person on agrarian reform issues for the Institute for Colonization and Agrarian Reform (INCRA), which developed the ambitious first Plano Nacional de Reforma Agrária, his government did not change the approach to agrarian reform. The strong ISI coalition that was built during the military regime between traditional landowners and industrialists was still powerful enough to stop any attempt of applying the first Plano (Branford and Rocha 2002).

In 1986, a new rural organization, the Movimiento dos Trabalhadores Rurais Sem Terra (MST), tried to meet President Sarney. They sought redress for the assassination of some of their members and an allied priest. Although Sarney did not meet with them, he arranged mediation by the Conferência Nacional dos Bispos do Brasil (CNBB) (Fernandes 2000). Despite this advance, the MST still had to wait a bit more to be considered a legitimate interlocutor in the political arena.

In 1990, the failure of the ISI relaunch manifested itself when inflation reached 1,000 percent. That same year, Fernando Collor de Mello, a neoliberal reformist outsider, was elected as the new president.

### The Emergence of the Reincorporation Movement: The Landless Peasants' Movement

The landless peasants' movement is composed of approximately 110 organizations (Feliciano 2011), but unlike the *piqueteros*, there is a central organization: the MST. It was founded in 1984 as a result of the coordination of peasant local struggles for land. In 1975, during the military government, the Brazilian Catholic Church created the Commissão Pastoral da Terra (CPT) for the organization of rural Christian base communities (CEBs). Inspired by liberation theology, the CPT sought to organize peasants for land reform and was much more successful than the urban CEBs in Argentina. The MST's central claim is land tenure solely for those persons who cultivate and live on it (Harnecker 2002). This communitarian perspective implied a radical noncapitalist land reform with the hope of building a new political and socioeconomic order (Hammond and Rossi 2013).

Even though the MST and the CPT emerged before the application of neoliberal reforms, most of the 110 organizations in the Brazilian countryside appeared between 1994 and 1998 (Fernandes 2000). This was the result of local divisions from the MST in a few cases and mostly a result of emulation of a successful method for popular sectors' reincorporation in a context of massive and abrupt social exclusion. In some cases, a couple of organizations emerged with some strength in certain regions of Brazil. The Movimento de Libertação dos Sem Terra (MLST) was founded in 1994 in Pernambuco by members of the Brasil Socialista tendency of the PT. The Liga dos Camponeses Pobres (LCP) was founded after the 1995 Corumbiara killings and is linked to the Maoist Liga Operária. Trade unions also created landless peasants' organizations to compete with the MST. For instance, the Movimento dos Agricultores Sem Terra (MAST), a middle-size organization in Pontal de Paranapanema, was created by the CGT do Brazil in 1997. Finally, other organizations emerged for related struggles, such as the Movimento de Atingidos por Barragens (MAB) in 1991, the Movimento dos Pequenos Agricultores (MPA) in 2000, and the Movimento de Mulheres Camponesas in 2004. This last group has been closely linked to the MST, covering issues that the MST is not working on and coordinating actions through the Vía Campesina Brazil. Overall, the MST has concentrated the majority of land occupations; for instance, in Pernambuco 34 percent, in São Paulo 27 percent, in Bahia 17 percent, in Pará 67 percent, in Paraná 29 percent, and in Minas Gerais, 52 percent of the families occupying land between 2000 and 2010 were MST members (Feliciano 2011, 41, graph 8).

Martins (1994, 156) argues that the struggle of the landless peasants' movement is not for agrarian reform but for their "recognition as not only workers, but as persons with the right of being paid for their work . . . Peasants, thus, want social changes that lead to their recognition as members of society" (quoted in Fernandes 2000, 21). In other words, they struggle for the same as the *piqueteros*: their reincorporation as wage earners and citizens. Fernandes (1998) argues that the growth of rural unrest was a result of the negative impact of neoliberalism in the urban and rural popular sectors, pursuing land occupation as an alternative quest for being socioeconomically integrated. Moreover, Pereira (2003) quotes sources that say that in the 1990s, approximately 40 percent of the landless peasants mobilized for land reform were previously part of the urban unemployed popular sectors. In Argentina, the resistance to neoliberalism and the quest for reincorporation was framed as an urban problem, while in Brazil, it was framed in rural terms because there was a legal framework inherited from first incorporation—mainly, the Estatuto da Terra of 1964—that was consolidated with the Constitution of 1988, building a tradition of institutions and actors that made this policy area more favorable for reincorporation struggles than the urban one (Rossi 2015a).

*Neoliberal Reforms and the Reemergence of a "Rural Social Question" (1990–1994)*

President Collor controlled inflation and initiated the first generation of neoliberal reforms with a series of privatizations. In 1990, the government closed the first Plano and 40 percent of INCRA officials were dismissed, disregarding the "rural social question" (Buainain 2008). In 1992 the Central Única dos Trabalhadores (CUT), the Confederação Nacional dos Trabalhadores na Agricultura (CONTAG), the Partido dos Trabalhadores (PT), and the MST organized a coordinated protest against neoliberal reforms and for a solution to the "rural social question."

Collor could not dismantle the ISI coalition, and his government became isolated as a result of policies that were affecting the middle classes (confiscation of savings), national and international banks (attempts to postpone debt moratoriums), and the traditional economic and political elites (verbally attacking them and trying to exercise autonomy from them). When in 1991 inflation returned and privatizations stalled, his power disappeared.

In 1992, Collor's political isolation and street protests led him to resign just before an impeachment process was initiated. Vice President Itamar Franco's transitional government was very important for the legalization of the "rural question." Since the Constitution of 1988, the legal framework had not been updated, and the new articles on agrarian issues were never regulated. In 1993, the legal framework for INCRA was produced, giving it a budget and legal power to expropriate land.

Franco's mandate was one of relative openness for movements. His presidency legitimized the MST as a national political actor; he met with its national leadership in February 1993 (Fernandes and Stédile 1999). With the goal of reducing poverty, Franco implemented a PT proposal calling for the first Conselho Nacional de Segurança Alimentar, giving its coordination to the CNBB (*Correio Braziliense*, June 9, 2011). In this meeting, neo-corporatist participation predominated, as several ministries, municipal governments, the CUT, CONTAG, CNBB, and other organizations were involved. Movements such as the MST were not formally members of this council.

Coordinated actions toward reintroducing the rural question in the political agenda increased, and in 1994, the Fórum pela Reforma Agrária e Justiça no Campo was created by several leftist and Catholic sectors, which included the CUT, CONTAG, CPT, MST, Cáritas, and the MAB, among others.

After this interlude, first generation neoliberal reforms resumed when Fernando Henrique Cardoso became minister of economy. With the 1994 Plano Real, inflation was controlled and a new currency established. Its success also paved the way for Cardoso's victorious presidential electoral campaign that same year.

# FROM RESISTING DISINCORPORATION TO THE CRISIS OF NEOLIBERALISM

## Argentina

*The* Piqueteros *Increased Resistance to Neoliberalism (1999–2001)*

By the end of Menem's second government—engulfed in a socioeconomic crisis—the *puebladas* continued to spread across the country. Even though inflation was no longer an issue, the economic recession, coupled with de-industrialization and mass privatization, maintained high levels of unemployment (15.6 percent) and increased the number of those living below the poverty line (27.1 percent) in 1999. Within this context, the province of Corrientes, like many others, was trying to operate with fiscal restraint. However, in 1999 a series of events kicked off a new *pueblada* that ended with the intervention of the federal authorities in the province. In October, the presidential elections were held, and the Unión Cívica Radical-Frente País Solidario (UCR-FREPASO) Alianza beat the PJ candidate (Sánchez 2000).

The Alianza consisted of the UCR, a centennial catchall party with several governorships and thousands of local governments, and the FREPASO coalition of small center-left parties that was less than a decade old with no executive posts. Due to the poor showing of FREPASO in the crucial elections for the province of Buenos Aires, the executive cabinet was almost totally formed by UCR members.

For more than ten days in May 2000, the Unión de Trabajadores Desocupados (UTD) of Mosconi organized a third *pueblada,* which was followed by strong police repression (*Clarín*, May 12–13, 2000). Parallel to this conflict, the Dissident CGT (ex-MTA) called for the first national strike against President Fernando De la Rúa to resist the approval of a new labor law that would increase flexible working conditions. Notwithstanding social unrest and union resistance, the government decided to decrease the pensions and salaries of state employees. Unions responded by organizing a new general strike coordinated by the Dissident CGT and the CTA.

From July to August, the CTA, in cooperation with the Dissident CGT and other organizations, staged a 300-km march to Buenos Aires to demand a universal unemployment subsidy and a monthly allowance for poor families with children. This march would later evolve into the Frente Nacional contra la Pobreza (FRENAPO), a popular front for the universal right to income for citizens.

In 2000, a corruption scandal affected the UCR members of the coalition. FREPASO leader and vice president Carlos "Chacho" Álvarez supported an investigation against the will of President De la Rúa. This unsustainable situation forced De la Rúa into a major reshuffle of the cabinet without consulting

Álvarez. This increased the already marginal position of FREPASO and resulted in the resignation of Álvarez and almost all the FREPASO members in government.

It was also in 2000 that the FTV and CCC initiated the Matanzazo, the first massive picket carried out in Greater Buenos Aires. It had the support of the CTA, part of FREPASO, the La Matanza mayor, and the vice-governor. This new correlation of forces was particularly unfavorable for the reluctant new minister of labor Patricia Bullrich. There was no other way out for the national government than to finally provide the FTV and CCC with legitimacy as national political actors, something the rest of the political spectrum did during the Matanzazo protest (Calvo 2006).

In June 2000, a fifth *pueblada* was organized in Mosconi. This *pueblada* introduced an innovation in the policing of protest. It was the first disruptive event in which the *gendarmería* intervened within the framework of the recently reformed Código Procesal Penal that allowed the military police to intercede in social protests (Law 24,434; *Página/12*, May 2006 and June 21, 2001). Even though the *gendarmería* was already in charge of conflicts in rural and enclave areas since the first *puebladas* in Cutral-Có and Plaza Huincul, in such occasions the intervention was done within a different legal framework. The *gendarmería's* role from redemocratization to the emergence of the *puebladas* and *piqueteros* was as guards for borders and national roads. Thus, when *piqueteros* blocked a national road, the *gendarmería* was in charge of applying the right to free transit. Since the reform, the *gendarmería* included among its duties taking part as an antiriot force.

### The Piquetero *Movement's Legitimation and the Neoliberal Crisis (2001)*

The sustained conflict in Mosconi, Tartagal, and La Matanza, plus the new cabinet changes, placed the resolution of the *piquetero* issue high on the government's agenda. Since the Matanzazo and the legitimation of the FTV, CCC, and UTD of Mosconi, the dispute centered on the definition of the political or social character of the *piqueteros'* policy domain and for the control of this policy domain. Within a new context, these conflicts implied the continuation of the struggle for the policy domain that emerged at the end of the Menem presidency. Throughout De la Rúa's mandate, the resolution of the *piqueteros'* claims would continue to be the purview of the Ministry of Labor, with a secondary role for the Ministry of Social Development. A difference in this period was that the latter was a more active contender than before in the quest of gaining some participation in the *piqueteros'* policy domain.

As contention grew, the *piquetero* movement expanded. For instance, in 1999 the Trotskyist Partido Obrero created the Polo Obrero (PO). The first public action of the PO was participating in the first Asamblea Nacional Piquetera (July 2001), after which it grew exponentially. The Asamblea was the first massive convention of the *piqueteros* coordinated by the FTV and CCC. The second Asamblea (September) represented the crystallization of the movement's diversification during this period. The FTV and CCC called for the continuation of this coordinating body, but most of the other organizations refused to follow. Unlike the MST in Brazil, for the *piqueteros* it was impossible to achieve centralized coordination through a dominant organization.

In October, economic stabilization policies caused unemployment to reach 19 percent (plus 16.2 percent underemployment), and levels of poverty were at 35.4 percent in Greater Buenos Aires. The government lost the legislative elections and its majority in both chambers. This meant the end of any possibility for De la Rúa to propose policies without PJ agreement. As a result, part of the PJ believed that the president should step down before the end of his term (*Página/12*, December 7, 2001). What the PJ semiloyal opposition could not foresee was that the legislative election had not favored the PJ as the winner (19.3 percent). In a country that never had less than 75 percent electoral turnout, this election had for the first time more nonvoters (27.2 percent) and negative voters (15.7 percent) than votes for any single party (Calvo and Escolar 2005). The effect of this election was the deterioration of the legitimacy of the entire political elite. To make things even worse, in November there was a rush into dollars that forced the government to limit the maximum weekly amount that could be taken from banks. This caused the emergence of a protest movement of bank savers.

During December, social unrest grew as the government weakened and reduced the economic survival alternatives for the population. From December 14 to December 22, 261 lootings were organized in several cities (Auyero and Moran 2007). The mobilized middle classes and the PJ semi-loyal factions (but not the *piqueteros*) were the key figures in the national *pueblada* of December. To stop the intensification of lootings, De la Rúa declared a state of emergency on December 19. The first reaction to the speech given that day by the president was a general defiance to the resolution. The urban middle classes spontaneously started a *cacerolazo* (saucepan banging) in Buenos Aires and in other big cities. Later that night, thousands went to the Plaza de Mayo to demand the resignation of the government, the Supreme Court, and all the governors, deputies, senators, and union leaders (Rossi 2005).

On December 20, the accumulated lootings and *cacerolazos* pushed the national cabinet to quit in favor of the formation of a government of national unity with the PJ. However, the continuation of protests and lootings for the rest of the day led to the resignation of the president. Finally, on the December 23, the governor of San Luis, Adolfo Rodríguez Saá (PJ), was named by the parliament as interim president.

During the inaugural ceremony, Rodríguez Saá declared that the country had defaulted on the national external debt and promised to create a new currency and one million jobs in his ninety-day mandate. Although during his government's tenure no substantial public policy decision was taken in the *piquetero* policy domain, it nevertheless represents the national legitimation moment for the whole movement. In five days, the president met with the main social actors that had resisted disincorporation: the CTA, the non-Menemista CGT, the pensioners and retired groups, the human rights movement, and the *piqueteros*.

The consequences of this first meeting of the *piqueteros* with a president were similar to those achieved by the MST, CPT, and CONTAG with Itamar Franco: an enlargement in the number of legitimate actors by including the reincorporation movement as a core actor in the policy domain. Since that moment, meeting with the president became a common practice for the *piqueteros*, beginning a process of increased incorporation.

On December 27, Rodríguez Saá declared his interest in continuing beyond the agreed mandate, but that night a third *cacerolazo* emerged, rejecting his desires. Three days later, the weakened president resigned (Rossi 2005).

## Brazil

### *The Landless Peasants' Increased Territorial Resistance to Neoliberalism (1994–1996)*

President Cardoso continued with the privatization process started by Collor. From 1994 to 1999, Brazil experienced the largest process of denationalization of its history. Some of the most important and profitable companies, such as the Companhia Vale do Rio Doce and the Companhia Siderúrgica Nacional, were sold, as well as state monopolies such as the telecommunications company Telebrás.

During this period, unemployment grew—though never as much as in Argentina—to numbers doubling those of the previous two decades. While in 1986 unemployment was at its lowest levels (3.3 percent), during Franco's mandate it reached 6 percent (1993), and during Cardoso, it hit 9.6 percent (1999) due to the serious external trade imbalances produced by the Real currency stabilization program, as well as important losses in gross domestic product (GDP). On the other hand, inequality was decreasing in a slow but stable fashion, though preserving the very high historical Gini coefficients, particularly in rural areas.

Cardoso's policies were—intentionally and unintentionally—dismantling the ISI model. Among the unintentional consequences of his policies was the lowering of land price by 45 percent (on average), economically weakening traditional landowners (Sallum 2003). In addition, pressure from the landless peasants' movement and CONTAG for reincorporation in rural terms put land distribution into question, one of the pillars of the ISI model in Brazil. In Pontal de Paranapanema (São Paulo), one of the most contentious areas of Brazil in the 1990s, the MST discovered that there were 900,000 hectares of public land illegally occupied. The success of the MST in achieving several expropriations in Pontal provoked the reactivation of the União Democrática Ruralista (UDR) in 1996.[2] During this period, in Pontal as elsewhere, several new organizations emerged emulating the MST, such as the MAST in 1997. However, in contrast to what was happening in Argentina, the MST kept its dominant position and avoided the fragmentation that the *piqueteros* suffered.

The coordination among movements, unions, and churches to resist disincorporation increased in this period. In 1995, the Fórum pela Reforma Agrária e Justiça no Campo organized its first national campaign called Grito da Terra to press the government for giving INCRA autonomy from landowners, upgrading it from a department of the Ministry of Agriculture to a presidential department. March to May also witnessed the organization of the Campanha Nacional em Defesa dos Direitos dos Trabalhadores e da Cidadania contra as Reformas Neoliberais by a coalition of leftist parties, movements, and unions, which included the MST, MAB, CPT, CUT, and the PT. In September, the CNBB started to organize the Grito dos Excluídos to protest against "the situation of growing social exclusion in Brazilian society" (Vieira 2004, 12). However, not only was the government ignoring these claims against disincorporation, it also continued with neoliberal reforms. In 1995, the Conselho Nacional de Segurança Alimentar was closed, suffering the same fate of all the other neo-corporatist councils. Instead, the family-based cash-transfer program Rede de Proteção Social was created as the main social policy.

There was also an intensification of competition between the main organization coming from first incorporation and the more expressive reincorporation movement. As the MST increased land occupations, the demobilization of CONTAG became evident. It was in Pernambuco, the state where CONTAG originated, where this competition emerged strongest. The CONTAG was created in 1963 during first incorporation, and since its origins, the Federação dos Trabalhadores na Agricultura do Estado de Pernambuco (FETAPE) has been its most powerful federation (Pereira 1997). In Pernambuco, disincorporation was as abrupt and massive as in the YPF enclaves and Greater Buenos Aires. Economically, the main industry of Pernambuco collapsed in

1994–1995, closing most sugar cane mills and tomato sauce factories (Carvalho Rosa 2010).

From 1995 to 1996, the expansion of the landless peasants' movement of disruptive power and higher degrees of subnational violence ended in two repressive situations that became turning points in the correlation of forces between the MST and the national government. In August 1995 in Corumbiara (Rondônia), at least ten peasants and two policemen were killed in a violent confrontation between the Sindicato dos Trabalhadores Rurais de Corumbaia and the police. One year later, in Eldorado dos Carajás (Pará) another violent confrontation between the MST and the police led to nineteen peasants killed and earned Brazil international condemnation of the treatment that the Cardoso government was giving to the "rural social question." The repercussions of these two events were such that for a second time a president received the MST national leadership (May 1996). In addition, they produced a reduction of state repression, which stimulated the MST's national diffusion.

### The "Rural Social Question" as a Reincorporation Policy (1996–2001)

Since 1996, the national government promoted several innovations toward institutionalizing the "rural social question" and reducing the levels of social unrest in what became the most ambitious land reform program in Brazil, settling around 375,453 families by the end of Cardoso's second mandate (fig. 5.1). The program was done within the tension of two simultaneous logics. On the one hand, it applied the expropriation model based on the 1988 legal framework, a model defended by the landless peasants' movement. On the other hand, in 1998 the government implemented the Banco da Terra, a program of negotiated or market-based land reform through which peasants could purchase land with the help of a flexible loan given by the state. This second model was designed by the World Bank and rejected by the movements (Branford and Rocha 2002; Navarro 2008).

Thus in Brazil, the "rural social question" reemerged as a compensatory policy for disincorporated workers instead of the massive program of unemployment subsidies implemented in Argentina. Land reform in Brazil was a result of the existence of a dense network of rural organizations struggling for land issues that could mobilize the mass of expelled urban workers; there were no equivalent urban reincorporation movements. The pressure of the landless peasants' movement on the government led to the elaboration of what Cardoso's minister of agrarian development, Raúl Jungmann, called a "sponge" land reform program: "Capitalism expels people [from the system], and you sponge it up, capitalism expels again, and you sponge it up" (author's personal interview, 2008). This means that agrarian reform was done to reincorporate

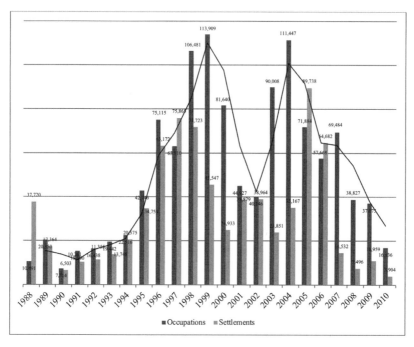

FIGURE 5.1. Number of families in land occupations versus number of families in rural settlements in Brazil, 1988–2010.

*Source*: DATALUTA (2011).

the disincorporated urban and rural popular sectors when the economic system could not absorb them by its own. Moreover, during the 1980s–2000s, the popular sectors occupying lands were mostly unemployed urban workers (Ondetti 2008, 124).

Since the 1980s, the agrarian question went through several cycles of reabsorbing excluded popular sectors. Overall, agrarian compensatory policy expanded in the 1990s–2000s due to three developments. These were the magnitude of disincorporation, the emergence of a rural reincorporation movement, and the lack of a universal unemployment subsidies program.

In 1996, INCRA recovered its autonomy and budget. It was moved from the landowner-controlled Ministry of Agriculture to the new Extraordinary Ministry of Land Policy. Simultaneously, the Cardoso administration passed two crucial laws for facilitating agrarian reform. One established the procedure for land expropriation, and the second increased taxation of unproductive land, which rose from 4.5 percent to 20 percent (Pereira 2003). In addition, the Department of Agrarian Conflicts was created for the resolution of contentious events associated with the "rural social question" (Buainain 2008).

As unemployment grew, the fragility of laborers created by disincorporation produced a reduction in the strike power of unions (see Gindin and Cardoso in this volume). At the same time, the reincorporation movement increased its capacity to mobilize the popular sectors under territorial logics (see fig. 5.1). While the MST consolidated as the main reincorporation organization, movements were weaker in the urban space, though they coordinated their efforts through the Central dos Movimentos Populares (CMP) since 1993. In 1996, the Grito da Terra was organized again and has continued annually since then. In 1997 the parties that participated in the Fórum das Oposições, the CGT do Brasil, the CUT, CONTAG, CMP, MST, and other organizations, constituted the Fórum Nacional de Lutas, a permanent coalition that planned several mobilizations against Cardoso's reforms.

For the MST, the problem with Cardoso was not land reform but the lack of concern for the "social question" produced by neoliberal reforms (Pereira 2003; Ondetti 2008). In April 1997, the MST organized the Marcha Nacional por Reforma Agrária, Emprego e Justiça. More than a thousand landless peasants walked for one thousand kilometers to Brasília on the date when the first anniversary of the Eldorado dos Carajás killings was commemorated. From 1998 on, this march would be transformed into Abril Vermelho, an annual event focusing on land occupations across Brazil for an entire month. This massive action of land occupations became the MST's most important coordinated contentious event. From April to May, the Fórum Nacional de Lutas organized the Campanha Reage Brasil to generate an equivalent mobilization to that of rural popular sectors by the urban middle classes and popular sectors. In December, the Encontro Popular Contra o Neoliberalismo por Terra, Trabalho e Cidadania brought together six thousand social movement delegates in São Paulo.

In 1999, the Department of Agrarian Conflicts was upgraded into the National Agrarian Ombudsman. The Ombudsman was created with the goal of mediating in rural conflicts to reduce the degree of violence and earn some time to find the best expropriation deal or an alternative solution for each conflict. In this sense, the new institution introduced mechanisms similar to those used by trade unions' tripartite negotiations—linking ministries for the resolution of conflicts and developing a common procedure for the state involvement in the "rural question" (Buainain 2008). However, the Ombudsman was partially different from first incorporation tripartite institutions due to its territorialized nature that took it to work across the country in association with each subnational branch of INCRA.

Most conflicts were territorially resolved on the spot after an occupation was done. However, neo-corporatist negotiations for rural organizations also emerged in this period. Once CONTAG controlled the Grito da Terra, its annual mobilization routinized in trade-unionist claims, with Minister Jungmann centralizing negotiations and linking each claim with the corresponding ministry.

The "rural question" was for Brazil the main expression of the "social question" produced by the massive disincorporation of popular sectors since the ISI model failed and neoliberal reforms were applied. The "rural social question" was not new for Brazil, but its reemergence was the result of a strong network of rural organizations that could reframe the struggle for reincorporation as a territorial struggle for land. Land occupations during the disincorporation period played an equivalent role in Brazil to the pickets and factory occupations in Argentina: they allowed disincorporated popular sectors to achieve access to resources that could allow them to struggle for their reincorporation into wage-earning society. This, however, does not mean that agrarian reform was synonymous with reincorporation, but in Brazil it substituted for social policies to assist the victims of neoliberalism.

Immediately after starting his second mandate, Cardoso sharply devaluated the real. Then, in 1999, his government began to replace agrarian reform with cash transfers as its main social compensation policy. This new approach represented an expansion of the Rede de Proteção Social, with twelve cash-transfer programs organized by territorial (municipal level) and income (family unit) logics covering urban and rural populations. This program reached 37,572,173 people by the end of 2002 (Draibe 2003).

The two sides of a new "social question" are the emergence of new social policies as well as new policing techniques. The Cardoso administration was under pressure due to increased contention organized by the landless peasants' movement. In its attempt to reduce land occupations, the government issued Interministerial Ordinance (PI) 325 of 1998 that established a procedure to limit the occupation of INCRA offices by landless peasants' organizations. In 2000, the Provisional Measure (MP) 2027 determined that each land occupied would not be subject to land expropriation for two years and, if occupied again, for four years. And in 2001, the government started to reduce INCRA's financial support for the MST's educational and health programs. In addition, the PT gradually distanced itself from the MST's radical methods because it planned to present candidate Luiz Inácio Lula da Silva as a moderate social democrat. Due to these factors, the landless peasants' movement faced difficulties in performing its two main contentious strategies, with a consequent sudden drop in the number of land occupations in 2001 (see fig. 5.1). Though it certainly diminished the MST's power "to lead the opposition to neoliberalism" (Ondetti 2008, 180), this did not mean a total demobilization. Among others, the Fórum Nacional de Lutas coalition continued organizing national campaigns against neoliberalism.

## THE SECOND INCORPORATION: BETWEEN CONTINUITY AND CHANGE

### Argentina

*Defining the Relationship between the Reincorporation Movement and the State (2002–2008)*

In Argentina, 2002 was a very contentious year. Even though lootings were mostly controlled, the *piqueteros* increased the number of protests and continued to grow. The *cacerolazos* became organized as part of the assemblies' movement, a short-term ally for the *piqueteros* (Rossi 2005). The process of factory occupations that started back in 2000 expanded and became organized with the support of left-wing parties, unions, assemblies, and *piqueteros* (Rossi 2015c). Simultaneously, levels of poverty (54.3 percent) and unemployment (21.5 percent), plus an 18.6 percent rate of underemployment, reached their worst peaks in Argentina's history.

Duhalde was chosen by the parliament as an interim president until elections were called for in 2003. After meeting with the CCC and FTV, Duhalde publicly promised to expand unemployment subsidies under a new system that implied an enlargement of the restricted *piqueteros'* policy domain to a general-policy constituency. The Programa Jefes y Jefas de Hogar Desocupados (PJJHD) became part of a redefinition of the state's approach to the legitimated *piqueteros* and its claim. From then on, it would involve an agreement between the FTV, CCC, and Duhalde. In the case of the FTV, Duhalde offered them the opportunity to direct the Programa Arraigo (in charge of legally regulating land occupations). This was the first time that a *piquetero* organization had become part of the national state structure.

Days later, Duhalde declared a 29 percent devaluation of the peso, which quickly reached 400 percent. During the next week, Duhalde called for a social-Christian approach to the resolution of social conflicts through the massive expansion of the PJJHD and the constitution of the Mesa del Diálogo Argentino—a space for negotiation and articulation inspired by the Moncloa Pact.

The government invited all *piqueteros* to the dialogue, but only the FTV, CCC, and the Movimiento Independiente de Jubilados y Desocupados (MIJD) participated. The rest of the movement not only rejected state incorporation but also the multisectoral types of strategies promoted by the FTV and the CCC. The original division of the movement that had emerged in the first and second Asambleas Piqueteras created a clear inside/outside division during this period. The PO, MTL, MTR, and other *piqueteros* organized the Bloque Piquetero Nacional (BPN) for the escalation of the national *pueblada* of December toward reaching the immediate end of the Duhalde government. The BPN also worked in alliance with the MIJD, the Coordinadora de Trabajadores Desocupados (CTD) "Aníbal Verón," the Movimiento Sin Trabajo (MST) "Teresa Vive," and Barrios de Pie (Burkart et al. 2008). This sector of the movement adopted a confrontational strategy.

The core of the government's approach toward the *piqueteros* was the promotion of governability agreements with some organizations and the demobilization of the social movement sector that promoted an insurrectional path through certain policies. To achieve this, the Duhalde cabinet adopted three simultaneous strategies.

The first strategy was the expansion of the restricted unemployment policy domain to a general constituency. The Duhalde government initially opted to expand preexistent policies: the Programa de Emergencia Laboral of the De la Rúa mandate reached 287,079 people in November 2002 and was later quickly extended without much control. The other was the PJJHD, the most far-reaching unemployment program ever applied in Latin America, which distributed almost two million unemployment subsidies (Neffa 2008).

The second strategy was the rebuilding of the state's capacity for governability. This strategy involved reconstructing the link with the PJ territorial network and avoiding confrontation with any—electoral or contentious—actor. This strategy also involved the return of the administration of unemployment subsidies to the municipalities, which included the creation of several local Consejos Consultivos. This decentralization process was done to reestablish the municipal role in controlling social unrest, which included the rebuilding of PJ clientelistic networks.

The third strategy was the state's selective distribution of resources and use of policing of protest to weaken the insurrectional component within the *piqueteros*. Duhalde's demobilization strategies were, however, not effective with the MTR and CTD "Aníbal Verón." During Duhalde's mandate, these organizations carried out the most contentious actions, and his government offered the most drastic repressive response, killing two *piqueteros* during a roadblock on the Pueyrredón bridge in Buenos Aires.

Massive media coverage of the killings and the swift international and national outcry in favor of the *piqueteros* brought forward the date for the elections, originally scheduled for October 2003, to April, with no clear favorite for president. The elections showed the effects of the 2001–2002 crisis period on the party system (see Ostiguy and Schneider in this volume). It atomized the party system, diluted the UCR's electoral power, but reinforced the hegemonic tendency of the Peronist electoral alternatives. As a result, Néstor Kirchner (Peronist Frente para la Victoria, FpV) won the election with 22.2 percent of the vote.

### Territorial Incorporation and the Establishment of a Piquetero Policy Domain

Kirchner was a Duhalde-backed candidate, but he had received fewer votes than the combined number of unemployed and underemployed people (34.4 percent in 2003). In addition to this, Kirchner had no parliamentary majority and was faced with a highly conflictive context. His government would be characterized by the territorialized incorporation of the *piqueteros* as part of the mobilization base of the Peronist FpV coalition, the decrease in protest repression, but the preservation of the judicialization of social conflicts.

The meetings of Kirchner with the *piqueteros* were organized by the social movement sector and never included all the movement simultaneously. The purpose was to provide each sector with specific resources in order to incorporate, co-opt, and/or demobilize the organizations. After these meetings, the FTV, Barrios de Pie, and the newly created Movimiento "Evita" joined the governmental coalition. In 2004, the CCC ended its alliance with the government, and the Organización Barrial (OB) "Túpac Amaru" (a former member of the FTV, located in Jujuy) and part of the MTL would participate in the coalition as external allies. In 2007, part of the MTD "Aníbal Verón" of Florencio Varela joined the sector that was supportive of the government. The *piqueteros* went on to occupy several executive posts at the national, provincial, and municipal levels, but preserved a secondary role in the decision-making process of the *piqueteros'* policy domain. Additionally, this period would be related to the initial entry of the *piqueteros* into the provincial and national parliaments, though not all as part of the governmental coalition.

The rest of the movement did not accept the government's invitation and continued with a contentious strategy. Overall, the *piqueteros* started to demobilize, while roadblocks entered into the Argentine repertoire of contention—as the 2008 peak of roadblocks by landowners shows (fig. 5.2). Those organizations that did not support the government unsuccessfully reorganized their forces to confront it. As a result, the 2003–2008 period consolidated a dynamic but clear division of the movement into two sectors based on the position of the *piqueteros* as either inside or outside the Kirchner government.

The incorporation of the *piqueteros* and their relationship with the government went through a process of formalization. This went hand in hand with the need to build a territorial base for the governmental coalition. While

Figure 5.2. Annual number of pickets in Argentina, 1997–2011

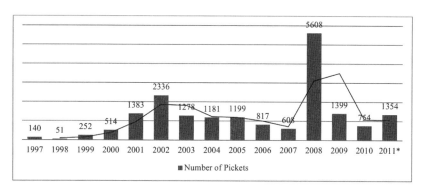

* Until September
*Source:* Centro de Estudios para la Nueva Mayoría. Reproduced from Rossi (2017, fig. 3.1).

the Secretary of Employment was still the main institution responsible for the administration of unemployment subsidies, the *piqueteros* were never allowed to participate within the structure of the Ministry of Labor. Instead, the Secretary General of the Presidency was the main governmental department that was opened up to the movement. The reincorporation process initiated by Duhalde and expanded by Kirchner implied—just like the first incorporation—the institutionalization of political conflict and the development of spaces for its resolution. Due to the territorialized nature of the second incorporation (Rossi 2015a, 2017, and the introduction to this section), the departments of the state in charge of this process were not those of the first incorporation (the Ministry of Labor). Instead, the main spaces were two newly created ministries—the Ministry of Social Development and the Ministry of Federal Planning—and the redefinition of the role of the Secretary General of the Presidency.

The FTV joined the coalition by viewing the Kirchner period as "a government under dispute" between the traditional PJ and the new forces coming from movements. The role of the FTV in government was to push the coalition—as it also attempted during the Alianza—toward a more progressive position. Within the multiclass electoral popular front strategy, the FTV followed different stages in its interaction with the government. From 2003 to 2005, personalized links with governmental officials prevailed, and the FTV could be considered as an ally that was external to the government. Once the Kirchner government was able to realign its correlation of power with Duhalde and ended the joint government agreement, the FTV also redefined its relationship. From 2005 to 2006, the FTV emulated a strategy that Barrios de

Pie had adopted since the beginning: colonizing spaces inside the state. This led to the creation of the Subsecretary of Land for Social Habitat under the new Ministry of Federal Planning. In this subsecretary—as in all the other departments of the Ministry of Federal Planning—there was no participation from any other *piquetero* organization.

Barrios de Pie entered government as an external ally in the quest to colonize spaces inside the state. Even though it had a different strategy from that of the FTV, it shared the interpretation of the Kirchner presidency as a government under dispute. Due to this, Barrios de Pie adopted the strategy of occupying as many elective or appointed state posts as possible. In a similar vein to what happened with the FTV, an area for the exclusive control of Barrios de Pie was created. The Subsecretary of Training and Popular Organization was under the responsibility of its national coordinator until 2008.

The Movimiento "Evita" was created in 2005 from above and below. This organization was the result of Kirchner's goal of building a territorial group and the coordination of non-PJ left-wing Peronists. The origins of the Movimiento "Evita" go back to when a sector of the CTD "Aníbal Verón" created the MTD "Evita" in 2002 in La Plata. This organization focused its strategy of government participation on the province of Buenos Aires from 2003 to 2007. The aim of the national government was to expand the weak Kirchnerista networks in this province, colonizing the governorship. In 2003, an agreement with Governor Felipe Solá made Vice-Chief of Cabinet Emilio Pérsico the movement leader. Since his 2003 gubernatorial reelection, for Solá, the Movimiento "Evita" meant the chance to build a territorial base to compete with Duhalde. For the Movimiento "Evita," it implied the possibility to build the network it needed and access resources to expand the organization just as Barrios de Pie was doing at the national level.

Kirchner would end the distribution of PJJHD and divide tasks related to the "*piquetero* question." Even though the responsibility for all unemployment programs and subsidies always remained under the control of the Secretary of Employment, a clear distribution of roles between the Ministry of Labor and the Ministry of Social Development was established for the first time in 2004. Since Decree 1506/04, the Ministry of Labor's responsibility over unemployment subsidies and training to reenter the labor market would be confirmed as exclusive, while the Ministry of Social Development gained responsibility for the rest of the social policies related to the *piquetero* policy domain (i.e., the territorial claims for access to water, health, education, and so forth). Only a third ministry would be directly involved in the *piquetero* policy domain, and this was the Ministry of Federal Planning, mainly for house-building and legalizing occupied land. In this way, the dispute for the responsibility of the *piquetero* policy domain initiated in 1999 was closed because it formalized the state departments' responsibilities for the "*piquetero* social question."

In 2007, Kirchner ended his mandate with an unemployment rate of 8.5 percent, just one national strike in April (which was not related to wage demands), and an increasingly demobilized *piquetero* movement. Concerning the parliament, the legislative elections were crucial for the expansion of the partial incorporation of the *piqueteros*. It led to the election of the first *piquetero* representatives to the national parliament and increased the number of provincial and local legislative posts occupied by the movement. Barrios de Pie was the organization in government that gained the most from this legislative election, getting two national deputies. The FTV did not manage to elect national legislators but did gain four Buenos Aires provincial senators and a provincial deputy.

However, the 2007 presidential elections demonstrated the limits of the process. Cristina Fernández de Kirchner won the elections with 45.29 percent of the vote, putting her government in a much better position than her husband's previous mandate. This was not expressed through more posts for the *piqueteros*; rather, their number remained roughly the same. Simultaneously, Néstor Kirchner became PJ party president and increased his reliance on the PJ mayors' territorial network. This decision led Barrios de Pie to consider that it had been defeated by the PJ in the internal struggle for power, gradually leaving the coalition between 2007 and 2008. The FTV continued to characterize the Fernández de Kirchner mandate as a government under dispute, and the Movimiento "Evita" opted for the consolidation of its strategy, joining the national council of the PJ.

For those *piqueteros* outside of government, the 2007 elections represented a new electoral opportunity. The MIJD presented Raúl Castells as its presidential candidate and Nina Pelozo for the Buenos Aires governorship. Néstor Pitrola, the national leader of the PO, was the Partido Obrero's presidential candidate, while the MST "Teresa Vive" supported a presidential ticket with no *piqueteros'* representatives of their Movimiento Socialista de Trabajadores. For all these parties, the national electoral results were below 1 percent. However, the PO achieved a relatively good result in Salta and elected some provincial legislators. The MTD of La Juanita entered the Coalición Cívica party and its leader won a seat as national deputy. Finally, the CCC rejected electoral politics and promoted electoral abstention.

Until December 2008, Fernández de Kirchner preserved the Secretary General of the Presidency as a *piqueteros'* collegiate body. Simultaneously, the FTV expanded its control over executive posts. This set of affairs would be preserved until the rural lockout would shock the government and alter the configuration of the *piquetero* movement.

### The End of the Incorporation Process (2008)

Just one year after the Fernández de Kirchner mandate started, the new minister of the economy changed taxes to agricultural exports to increase state revenues and control food inflation. For the government, this tax was crucial for the sustainability of the second incorporation process.

Rural associations contested this decision as it would mean a decrease in their profits in a period of worldwide growth in the price of commodities. A coalition of all rural associations called for a lockout of agricultural production, causing scarcity of certain products in supermarkets. The president gave a televised speech rejecting the protest and their demands, which on the same night was responded with some *cacerolazos* in small and medium cities that were dependent on agribusiness production and in the traditional upper-middle-class districts of all the main cities. During that same night, some FTV, Movimiento "Evita," Barrios de Pie, and Frente Transversal Nacional y Popular leaders went to the square with a clear purpose: "Tonight we mobilize to confront the pro-coup sector that wants to overthrow the popular government lead by President Cristina Kirchner" (FTV communiqué quoted by *La Nación*, March 26, 2008). While those sectors promoting the lockout were accused of attempting to destabilize the government, the sectors supporting the government were accused of being authoritarian.

On May 20, a second lockout ended, but negotiations failed again, and on May 25 in Rosario around 250,000 people participated in a protest in favor of the lockout (*La Nación*, May 26, 2008). The president decided in a last desperate move to send a bill to parliament legitimating the tax resolution. In an extremely polarized situation, two massive protests were organized on July 15 to separately press for the approval or rejection of the law. In an extended parliamentary debate that finished with a tied result, the vice president, in clear disagreement with the president's position, rejected the law with his deciding vote. The next day, the tax resolution was annulled and with it the possibility of making reincorporation policies economically viable in the long term.

## Brazil

### Defining the Relationship between the Reincorporation Movement and the State (2002–2005)

When the first Brazilian president of worker origins took power, the ISI model had been abandoned and replaced by a liberal-developmental model, whose "aim [was] not to rebuild the entrepreneurial national State but to reform the State so that it might push private development and social equality" (Sallum 2003, 198–99). Cardoso had built a quite technocratic state structure that controlled the policy agenda. Lula's two mandates were mostly defined by continuity in economic terms, but, in political terms, they represented a breaking point in the incorporation of social actors into the political arena. The model of reincorporation initiated in the period of government under the PT was a state multisectoral model, combining neo-corporatist and territorial dimensions.

Even though the MST, MPA, MAB, MLST, CONTAG, and other organizations expressed their support for Lula's government, they saw Lula's moderation process as a negative signal of the will to produce major transformations similar to the ones happening in Bolivia and Venezuela. First, Lula's vice president José Alencar came from the center-right Partido Liberal (PL). Moreover, during the electoral campaign, Lula published the Carta ao Povo Brasileiro to assure international creditors that he would not declare a default, avoiding the path of Argentina. In addition, the PT lacked a clear majority in parliament (though it was the main party, it had less than 20 percent of the lower chamber and senate) and won only the governorships of three peripheral states (Acre, Mato Grosso do Sul, and Piauí). As a result, the transformative possibilities of the new government were quite limited (Gonçalves Couto and Fernandes Baia 2004; Hunter 2010). Finally, the lack of a major crisis of neoliberalism—as the ones of Argentina and Bolivia—did not produce a radical break with the past. For these reasons, the MST interpreted Lula's government as "a government under dispute" between a right-wing sector that would push for the preservation of the neoliberal path initiated by Collor and a left-wing sector that would push for the introduction of a new development path.

During 2003–2004, a huge increase in land occupations happened as a result of a combination of the growing expectations for agrarian reform, the MST leadership strategic decision of pushing the government toward the left to produce a rupture with the neoliberal path, and the government decision of not applying MP2027. However, the government did not react with more expropriations or settlements to the increased number of occupations. Only in 2005 did the government start to settle more families, but soon after winning reelection the decreasing tendency returned and consolidated with the lowest numbers of settlements and expropriations until that moment (see fig. 5.1; Ondetti 2008).

As a coalitional government, Lula distributed ministries by political party and organization that provided the legislative, neo-corporatist, and territorial support for his mandate. The amplitude of the coalition was such that the groups in government had overtly contradictory aims and perspectives, confirming—according to the movements—that this was a government under dispute. The first cabinet distributed ministries between the PT, the PL, the Partido Comunista do Brasil (PC do B), the Partido Trabalhista Brasileiro (PTB), the Partido Verde (PV), and some business representatives. In the rural policy domain, this logic was also reproduced. The Ministry of Social Development was given to a CONTAG ally, the INCRA to a MST and CPT ally, and the Ministry of Agriculture to the president of the Sociedade Brasileira de Agribusiness.

The developmental-liberal coalition excluded the traditional landowners. In 2003, the government met with the MST leadership and decided to stop applying MP2027. The traditional landowners reacted informally and institutionally against this decision. First, in Paraná they founded an armed organization against land occupations. Second, between 2003 and 2005, the landowners' legislative group created a commission to investigate the main organizations of the landless peasants' movement (Ondetti 2008).

The critical moment in the dispute for influencing the direction Lula's government should take on the rural question and the role of the reincorporation movement in this coalition emerged with the struggle of the Fórum Nacional pela Reforma Agrária e Justiça no Campo for the application of the most ambitious agrarian reform program in Brazilian history. The strategy was to occupy positions inside the state while pushing for the creation of the second Plano Nacional de Reforma Agrária (the INCRA presidency was the main position occupied by an ally of the Fórum). At the end of 2003, in a context of increased rural unrest and after a year of vacillating on agrarian reform, Lula upon request of the MST asked for a second Plano with the goal of launching the much-promised agrarian reform. The resulting draft relied exclusively on the expropriation model and initially aimed to settle around one million families in the remaining three years of government. While the government accepted the condition to use only the expropriation model—closing the Banco da Terra program—the goal proposed by the second Plano was considered too ambitious, and it was reduced to around four hundred thousand families. This new goal was accepted by CONTAG but rejected by the landless peasants' movement (Navarro 2008).

In other words, Lula continued with the same approach to the "social question" started by Cardoso in 1999, replacing agrarian reform with cash-transfer policies as the main reincorporation policy. In 2003, Lula integrated three previously existing programs (Bolsa Escola, Bolsa Alimentação, and Auxilio Gás) with a new one—called Cartão Alimentação—into the Bolsa Família program. By the end of 2003, the program had reached around 11,100,000 vulnerable families. As a key element of the reincorporation process, in 2004 the government created the Ministry of Social Development as the main institution for the administration of the "social question" (Fenwick 2009).

Lula's government retained and expanded other institutions created by Cardoso. Concerning the policing dimension of the reincorporation process, in 2004 the National Agrarian Ombudsman was upgraded into a permanent department of the Ministry of Agrarian Development. Before becoming the Department of the Agrarian Ombudsman and for Conflict Resolutions, it was a group of mediators working inside INCRA and the ministry, but with no formal structure.

The direction taken by the government did not please the landless peasants' movement, which gradually distanced themselves from the coalition. By 2005, the MST and CPT had abandoned any position inside government and became openly critical of it.[3] While the MST and MLST continued supporting Lula for reelection in 2006, the CPT—among others—did not. The lack of a total rupture with the government led to the emergence of the Movimento Terra, Trabalho e Liberdade (MTL) as the result of the unification of a series of smaller landless peasants' organizations linked to some tendencies of the PT that had defected from the party to create the Partido Socialismo e Liberdade (PSOL) from 2004 onwards. Being in opposition to the government did not exclude the MTL from being received by Lula on more than one occasion.[4]

*Reformulating Neo-Corporatism: The Participatory Expansion and Routinizing of Contentious Politics*

Lula cannot be considered a president that produced a total renewal of the Brazilian political setting. In Brazil, "Modifications to corporatism are likely to be incremental, seeking to *overlie* rather than *replace* old corporatist institutions" (Doctor 2007, 135). The changes that Cardoso made were expanded or reformulated by Lula as a partial break with the neo-corporatist past.

In January–February 2003, several councils were created with the aim of integrating ministries with corporatist, territorial, and individual actors, building a participatory infrastructure for the elaboration of social policies. The main council was the Conselho de Desenvolvimento Econômico e Social (CDES): "The CDES did not erase past traditions of state-society relations but built on what was already a multipolar hybrid system of interest representation in which corporatist and pluralist associations worked together, clientelistic practices survived alongside open lobbying, and sector-oriented tripartite negotiations took place alongside the particularistic access of large firms to high-level bureaucrats and members of the government" (Doctor 2007, 135).

The goal of the CDES was to help in the production and implementation of social policy reforms. However, the CDES gradually changed its purpose into an economically focused council. The subrepresentation of social movements—getting just sixteen of the ninety-one available seats (which included ten seats for ministries and one for Lula)—led to their informal organization into a subgroup that could articulate their positions and tried to push the CDES toward the development of social policies that could produce policy recommendations in several areas (Doctor 2007).

The "rural question" was partially handled through the reopening of the Conselho Nacional de Segurança Alimentar e Nutricional. This council was originally created by Franco, later closed by Cardoso, and reopened by Lula. In 2003, this council had some participation from movements such as the MST, unions including CONTAG, CUT, Confederação Geral dos Trabalhadores (CGT of Brazil), and Força Sindical, and institutions of the CNBB such as the Pastoral da Criança, among others.

These were not the only councils; by the end of Lula's second mandate, there were thirty-four councils, eighteen of them with social movement participation. Most of these councils were part of the structure of the ministries, such as the new Conselho Nacional do Meio Ambiente or the expanded Conselho Nacional de Desenvolvimento Rural Sustentável. However, not all of these councils produced effective participatory policy-making processes. For instance, while the Conselho Nacional de Segurança Pública of the Ministry of Justice was a technocratic council, the Conselho Nacional das Cidades—during Minister for Cities Olívio Dutra's (PT) mandate—was a very participatory council, with much involvement from urban movements. In 2005, when Dutra left the ministry, the new minister Márcio Fortes (Partido Progressita) developed a quite technocratic and clientelistic relationship with movements. Participation of movements was also very important in the Ministry of the Environment until Marina Silva left the government in 2008 (Abers, Serafim, and Tatagiba 2014). In other words, it was mostly in ministries created for dealing with territorial and reincorporation movements that the development of more participatory councils was possible.

As in Argentina, the Secretary General of the Presidency played a central role in the informal relationship with the reincorporation movement. In 2003, its historical role of articulating the executive with the other branches of the state was transferred to the newly created Secretary of Institutional Relations. Meanwhile, the National Secretary for Socio-Political Articulation was created as a subsecretary of the secretary general with the aim of coordinating the relationship of the state with social organizations. In contrast with Argentina's secretary general, in Brazil no members of social movements participated in the Articulation Secretariat in Brazil. The Articulation Secretary included only public officials, all coming from the PT, and most of them from CUT or the PT tendency Campo Majoritário.

Even though the Articulation Secretariat was an institutional space for the informal relationship with movements, only CONTAG could routinize and—as a result—formalize its relationship with the secretariat. Since 2005, annual demonstrations by Grito da Terra and the Marcha das Margaridas (women's sector), both exclusively organized by CONTAG, accomplished this. As a neo-corporatist organization, after each annual demonstration CONTAG presented its claims to the Articulation Secretariat, which then arranged meetings with the ministries that were in charge of the policy areas of CONTAG's interest. The only equivalently routinized mobilization of the MST—the Abril Vermelho annual campaign of land occupations—has not reached this type of neo-corporatist relationship, being solved through informal dialogues between the MST, the articulation secretary, the agrarian ombudsman, INCRA, and the local governments that are being affected by land occupations.

*The End of the Incorporation Process (2005–2007)*

If social movements still held any hopes that the PT government might alter its approach to the "rural question," the *mensalão* corruption scandal dashed them. This break point introduced new divisions in the landless movement. In 2005 it was discovered that PT officials and members of the cabinet were buying some legislators' support. The *mensalão* showed social movements that the PT had transformed into a catchall party and that it had reduced the power of the left-wing sectors inside the coalition (Wainwright and Branford 2006; Hunter 2010). However, the dissatisfaction with the government started *before* the *mensalão*. The less ambitious second Plano was under risk of failing earlier that year: a 25 percent budget cut made impossible the fulfillment of a promise to settle 115,000 families (*Folha de São Paulo*, March 30, 2005; fig. 5.1).

Social movements had a different reaction to the corruption scandal than unions. In August 2005, the CUT and the Coordinadora dos Movimentos Populares organized a demonstration in Brasília for justice, political reform, and to defend the government of Lula from what they considered an attempt to destabilize it. In December, the MST started to publicly criticize the government (*Folha de São Paulo*, September 8, 2005). Thus, despite the *mensalão*, the MST remained ambivalent about their opposition to Lula's government.

The lack of influence of the reincorporation movement in the policy agenda led to the decision of the MLST to occupy the national parliament in 2006. The MLST still believed Lula's government could be pushed towards the left in its second term, and it partially achieved its goal: the MLST received an increase in resources for land settlements. Simultaneously, however, the PT national council decided to expel Bruno Maranhão—the MLST leader and PT national secretary for popular movements (*Folha de São Paulo*, June 7, 2006).

The MTL had not supported the Lula government since 2004. However, the *mensalão* created more PT dissidences, and the PSOL grew in number. Because of this, the MTL experienced some increase in its human and material resources. In 2006, the MTL became part of a coalition of unions and movements that opposed the government.

In parliament, there were also changes concerning social movements and CONTAG representatives. On the one hand, in 2006 CONTAG won three seats for federal deputies, increasing its representation in parliament by two seats. This change allowed CONTAG to create the Frente Parlamentar de Agricultura Familiar. On the other hand, in 2006 the MST, MBA, and MPA's discussions about how to interpret and face Lula's government caused the first coordination difficulties for the Frente Parlamentar da Terra created by the MST.

The reincorporation process played out over two social policy stages. The first took place from 1993 to 1999, when agrarian reform was the main reincorporation policy. The second occurred from 1999 to 2012, when cash-transfer programs such as Bolsa Família gradually replaced it. This process had two important consequences for the movement. First was an increase in the movement's divisions, as the MST never decided on a total rupture with the PT and continued to support PT presidential candidates. The second was a decrease in the number of land occupations due to the demobilization effects of Bolsa Família. While there was an increase in the number of settlements from 2003 to 2005, from 2006 to 2010 there was a constant decrease, until they reached the lowest historical numbers since redemocratization (see fig 5.1). In parallel, but in the opposite direction, the Bolsa Família program expanded its coverage consistently, from 3,600,000 families in 2003 to 11,100,000 in 2006 and 12,900,000 in 2010.[5]

Because the main constituencies mobilized by the landless movement were the disincorporated urban popular sectors, the application of policies that provided some partial reincorporation made it difficult for the MST leaders to convince the urban poor of the benefits of abandoning shantytowns to occupy land in the countryside. The MST leaders perceived the demobilizing effect of cash-transfer programs, considering that it was not offering real reincorporation: "We are struggling against welfarist social policies that do not create employment . . . Here you have Bolsa Família, Vale Gás, Vale Alimentação, and other stuff that kill hunger on people but they also produce complacency on people . . . the public of agrarian reform is the poor population of the city. It has always been. But now this population does not want anymore to go to the countryside, and face the difficulties of settlements. . . ." (MST coordinator in Roraima, quoted in *Jornal do Brasília*, April 28, 2008).

The application of the liberal-developmentalist first Programa de Aceleração do Crescimento (PAC) (January 2007–December 2010), which had not included agrarian reform as part of its goals, was a clear signal of the end of agrarian reform as a reincorporation policy. However, movements still resisted this strategic decision taken by the government. In 2008, the Fórum Nacional pela Reforma Agrária e Justiça no Campo created the Campanha pelo Limite da Propriedade da Terra, and the same year the left-wing tendencies of the PT could reopen the Núcleo Setorial Agrário of the PT (closed in 2002).

## THE AFTERMATH OF SECOND INCORPORATION

### Argentina

*The Neo-Developmental Model (2008–2012)*

The rural lockout had important effects on the process of reincorporation in Argentina. Due to the enormous political costs of the defeat for the government, there was an increase in institutionalization, but the process reached a stalemate that signaled the end of the second incorporation stage. Even though a neo-developmental model was introduced, this model lacked institutional sedimentation to reach the degrees of strength necessary to become sustainable in a period of low commodity prices. Among the main reasons were the impossibility of reducing agribusiness' and traditional landowners' centrality in the balance of trade. This led to an eternal trap for Argentine growth: much of the reincorporation resources came from commodity exports.[6]

For the *piqueteros*, there were some important changes in their alliances as a result of the lockout and the decision of Néstor Kirchner to become PJ president. In December 2008, Barrios de Pie made its departure from the Fernández de Kirchner coalition official. This meant in many cases that the Movimiento "Evita" occupied most of the national and provincial positions in Buenos Aires that had been vacated by the former.

In 2009, the activities of the collegiate body of *piqueteros* in the Secretary General of the Presidency ended due to marginal results and the increased space conferred to the traditional Peronist leaders to the detriment of the *piqueteros*. As part of a process of augmented institutionalization, this informal space was replaced in March 2009 with the Subsecretary of Relationships with Civil Society. However, there was no access to the Ministry of Labor for disincorporated workers' organizations, as unions preserved the control of this department (the struggle to officially participate in this ministry by several *piqueteros* notwithstanding). In 2008, the Movimiento "Evita" had particularly struggled for a position in the Ministry of Labor, but was instead appointed to the Subsecretary of Social Economy Commercialization in the Ministry of Social Development. In other words, the *piqueteros* could never transcend the secondary role that was given to them; neither could they overcome the informal, territorialized, individualized, and horizontally and vertically uncoordinated interactive logic of politics that traditional Peronist leaders dominate.

Since 2010, unions recuperated their mobilization power as inflation grew and employment was recovered. However, issues over the definition of the relationship with the government kept them divided (see Gindin and Cardoso in this volume). The *piqueteros* were less mobilized than before, but still organized and divided. The sector that continued supporting the government attempted several times to create a group that could give them more power inside the coalition.

Regarding the evolution of the *piquetero* policy domain, a new employment program was created that weakened the *piqueteros'* position vis-à-vis PJ mayors even more. The Programa de Ingreso Social con Trabajo "Argentina Trabaja" meant that the *piquetero* policy domain partially returned to the control of the PJ mayors' network for the first time since 2003. As a sign of the coalition's reconfiguration, the "Argentina Trabaja" meant a reversal from previous policies that were developed alongside the *piqueteros*. In any case, the relationship between movement and government was less formalized in institutions, preserving the movement's secondary role as well as a higher degree of autonomy in comparison to the one achieved by unions during the first incorporation.[7]

## Brazil

### *The Liberal-Developmentalist Model (2007–2012)*

With the beginning of the first PAC, the reincorporation process finished due to the building of specific midterm policies that established a liberal-developmental model.[8] The period 2007–2012 should be considered as the aftermath of the reincorporation period because no substantial change was produced on the institutions and state-social movements' relations since that year. Finally, the presidential election of Dilma Rousseff (the main brain behind the first PAC) consolidated the path initiated by Lula.

Lula's last three years in government and Rousseff's mandate exhibited continuity in economic and social policies. During the first two years, Rous-

seff's government was paralyzed by several corruption scandals that led to numerous cabinet reshuffles, and it was very much limited in its transformative
possibilities by the coalitional nature of Brazilian politics. The government
was mostly focused on solving these scandals, controlling inflation, reducing
public expenditures, and expanding cash-transfer policies (von Bülow and
Lassance 2012).

The MST gave its customary critical support to Rousseff, but the relationship was more distant than with Lula. Social policy continued to expand Bolsa
Família, reaching 13,400,000 families in 2011.[9] The expansion of cash-transfer
policies was done in a similar fashion to that of her predecessor. In June 2011,
Rousseff launched the Brasil Sem Miséria program, which combined Bolsa
Família with Bolsa Verde and Plano Viver Sem Limite. In October 2012, this
expansion continued with the creation of Brasil Carinhoso. During Rousseff's
tenure, the logic of incremental changes continued by combining preexistent
programs toward building a bigger one that covered more vulnerable people.

Meanwhile, agrarian reform was dismissed as a reincorporation policy.
The lack of interest for agrarian reform was such that the INCRA presidency was vacant for the first three months of Rousseff's government until an
MST-ally director occupied it. In addition, due to the lack of budget for land
expropriations, Rousseff's first year offered the lowest number of settlements
(22,000 families) since redemocratization. During 2012, the situation deteriorated so much that INCRA and Ministry of Agrarian Development officials
initiated a strike for more budget, more employees, and the improvement of
the infrastructure for agrarian reform (*Brasil de Fato*, April 4 and June 18,
2012).

Finally, Rousseff did not redefine the roles of the main institutions responsible for the "social question" inherited from Lula's administration. Almost
all councils were kept open and working as before. The informal relationship
between social movements and the Secretary General of the Presidency continued to be structured as during the Lula mandate after an attempt to expand
and institutionalize social participation inside each ministry failed when the
Congress annulled Decree 8,243 in October 2014.

Since then, Rousseff's weakness increased by means of the government's
difficulties to produce a clear rupture with the neoliberal past in a coalition
that gradually gave more power to its conservative allies. Rousseff debilitated
even more due to more corruption scandals, economic recession, and massive
protests in 2013 and again in 2015–2016. Showing the recursive logic of incorporation waves, a civic coup d'état against Rousseff by the conservative sector
of the coalition consolidated the aftermath of second incorporation in 2016.

## CONCLUSION

Brazil can be defined by its gradual metamorphosis, while Argentina by its quick rupture and change. This makes Brazil a case more difficult to define as post-neoliberal than Argentina, though in both cases there was a second wave of incorporation that combined elements from below and above. While in Brazil the process had a mixture of neo-corporatist and territorial features, in Argentina it was mostly territorial. In both countries, however, first and second incorporation actors started to share institutional spaces. In Brazil, these spaces were increasingly formalized and corporatized, leading to the gradual exclusion of the territorially based actors. In Argentina, competition produced a dispute over weak reformed corporatist institutions and the creation of less-formal territorially based spaces inside the state. However, this also led to the gradual reduction of *piqueteros'* power vis-à-vis unions. In both countries, nevertheless, the social policies implemented since the emergence of territorial contention led to a process of collapse or gradual change of the neoliberal political setting. Argentina and Brazil incorporated popular movements into the state as (almost) equals to first incorporation actors. In both countries, though, this new relationship with a government open to receiving and (at least) listening to their claims resulted in divisions among reincorporation movements in their disputes over the determination of degrees of change and continuity produced between the 1990s and the 2010s.

More recently, in both countries, the return to power of conservative neoliberals signaled the possible consolidation of the aftermath phase. However, there was an important difference between Argentina and Brazil. While the latter went through a novel democratic electoral transition, in the former the logic of first incorporation was reproduced, ending the reincorporation process with a coup d'état.

# PART II

# TRADE UNIONS

Chapter 6

# INTRODUCTION TO PART II

Labor Unions in Latin America

Incorporation and Reincorporation under the New Left

## RUTH BERINS COLLIER

The strikingly novel aspect of the "second incorporation" is the inclusion of previously excluded, marginalized segments of the population, particularly the informal urban and rural popular sectors. However, key questions arise concerning the second incorporation also from the point of view of formal sector workers and their organizations, labor unions, which were the main subject of the initial incorporation in the first half of the twentieth century (Collier and Collier 1991). To what extent does the second incorporation represent a reincorporation in the sense that basic features have changed both from the now distant first incorporation and also from the more proximate and recent changes of what may have been an intervening period of "disincorporation?" And given the new incorporation of previously excluded groups, what is the overall relationship between unions during the second incorporation and newly incorporated popular groups and associations?

Unions in the second incorporation are usefully seen in terms of a changing political economy that occurred since the initial incorporating period. The first incorporation occurred during a specific world historic moment of early industrialization and expanding production of primary goods as inputs. The terms of incorporation were sustained during a period when industrialization advanced and was largely oriented to the domestic market. Demand-side economic models (ISI in Latin America and Fordism/Keynesianism in advanced economies) provided the leeway for policies that introduced union-friendly "rigidities" into the labor market. The economic setting has since changed fundamentally. In the last decades of the twentieth century, a more open, globalized economy has brought more challenging supply-side models as a structural context for unions. These models of marketization included labor market flexibilization. As emphasized in the introduction to this volume, a harsh economic transition of market reform imposed widespread hardships on the popular sectors, including unionized workers. Subsequently, in the opening decades of the twenty-first century, and partly in reaction to the hardships imposed by the marketizing reforms, left governments took power in several countries in Latin America, and previously excluded lower-class or popular sector constituencies became key political actors. The chapters in this section focus on the position of unions under these left governments.

In this introduction to the section on unions, I will thus raise three questions. First, to what extent have *key features* of the organized labor movement changed? These traits include the labor law that regulates and structures unions and their activities, the density of unionization, and the unification or fragmentation of the labor movement. Second, how have *party-labor relations* changed? Third, what is the relationship between unions and newly incorporated groups? These relations are a component of what has been conceptualized as the *"popular interest regime"* (Collier and Handlin 2009). These three questions will be discussed, *grosso modo*, during three analytical periods: the initial incorporation; the period of military rule and neoliberal reform, when unions were challenged with "disincorporation," or rolling back of earlier gains, relationships, and patterns; and the subsequent period of left government and potential "reincorporation" of unions.

## THE INITIAL INCORPORATION

In Latin America as in Europe, popular politics in the twentieth century was characterized by the primacy of labor unions. Having emerged in the last decades of the nineteenth century as a new social technology for organizing and representing a subset of the lower classes, unions were legalized and "incorporated" as economic and political actors in what proved to be a historic and consequential shift in each country. Workers came to constitute the core constituency for mass parties, and forms of labor-based or union-affiliated parties became one of the most important—often the most important—political party. These labor-based parties took various forms, generally classist or the more cross-class populist form quite common in Latin America.

The initial incorporation in the first part of the twentieth century brought about three notable transformations. New labor laws legalized unions, institutionalizing a system of industrial relations to resolve labor-capital conflict and to structure the labor movement. In addition, the politics of incorporation established the partisan affiliation of the labor movement. Finally, the initial incorporation established the first popular interest regime, one which privileged unions as the most important organizations for popular sector representation.

## The Labor Movement

The new labor laws established what has been understood as a system of state corporatism. The common goal of the presidents who carried out labor incorporation in Latin America was to control the labor movement, specifically to address the "social question"—what was seen as the problem of the radical and militant working class. Existing labor movements contained important currents that were anarchist, syndicalist, socialist, and/or communist, which were perceived as threatening the capitalist order; strikes and protests were economically disruptive. Institutionalization through acceptable channels of rule-based industrial relations, rather than repression, came to be seen as a more appropriate response that would institutionalize class conflict.

Within this commonality, two subpatterns have been distinguished according to whether or not the incorporating president had a second, additional goal of mobilizing the political support of the working class (Collier and Collier 1991). Of the countries covered in the present volume, Brazil followed the nonmobilizational pattern, and accordingly its labor law defined a more constrained and less favorable structure for unions. In Ecuador as well, the incorporating government did not attempt to mobilize labor support. However, confronting a much less developed working class, it was less demobilizational and introduced fewer structures of control.

In the other three countries, where the goal was not only to control the labor movement through institutionalization but also to actively mobilize its political support, labor law was, to different degrees, more favorable to workers and unions. Indeed, given the desire to attract the support of extant unions, the incorporation period itself could be quite pro-labor. In these cases, the process of incorporation took place in coalition with the labor movement and in a way that empowered unions as political actors. This labor power threatened conservative interests, typically leading to a conservative reaction that brought the more pro-labor, incorporating period to an end. Nevertheless, in these latter cases labor law remained more favorable to unions.

Of the countries in the present volume, Brazil ended up with the most controlling, state corporatist labor law in Latin America. Its corporatist model placed many constraints on unions and organized them in an elaborate hierarchical structure from the local level to a small number of peak sectoral confederations at the national level. These eventually came together in the CGT.

In Ecuador, a reformist military government oversaw the incorporation project and brought in Socialist intellectuals when shaping the labor code.

However, the government did not seek popular support or the political mobilization of the labor movement. The country lacked both industrialization and export enclaves, so that unionization rates were very low. Furthermore, the labor movement remained more fragmented than in the other cases: the more conservative Confederación Ecuatoriana de Obreros Católicos (CEDOC) was soon joined by the more leftist Confederación de Trabajadores del Ecuador (CTE) and later, in 1962, by the anti-Communist Confederación Ecuatoriana de Organizaciones Sindicales Libres (CEOSL).

Argentina's pattern of incorporation, combined with its historically early industrialization, led to a highly mobilized and powerful union movement with high density, greater centralization under a single national confederation, the CGT, and a pattern of national sectoral collective bargaining. Although Venezuela and especially Bolivia embarked on industrialization later, strong unions were formed in the important petroleum and mining sectors, respectively. Furthermore, the incorporation also included peasant unions. These came together in the Confederación de Trabajadores de Venezuela (CTV) in Venezuela and the COB in Bolivia.

## Union-Party Relations

The pattern of party affiliation was affected by the nature of the initial incorporation period. In cases where incorporation was instituted by a president with the goal of mobilizing labor support, new cross-class "populist" parties were founded to channel that support. These new populist parties were electoral vehicles for attracting workers' votes and recruiting unionist candidates. Just as corporatist labor laws legalized unions but channeled their activities into acceptable institutions, so too were populist parties established to both activate and channel labor's political activities and participation into an acceptable, non-Marxist political party—the populist party was meant to be a tool to balance the twin goals of labor control and electoral mobilization. In various forms, the unions and the populist party were often organically connected, with unions having formal or informal representation in the party organization. The Venezuelan political party, Acción Democrática (AD), is a classic example of this model.

In the other two mobilizing cases that are analyzed in this volume, however, the incorporating party did not sustain these simultaneous goals over an extended period. In Argentina, the populist PJ was banned by the military after the incorporation period of the Perón presidency, and, as a result, unions, rather than electoral machinery, became the organizational backbone of the party. Hence, unlike most other cases of populist party formation, the PJ did

TABLE 6.1. Unions after initial incorporation

|  | Argentina | Bolivia | Brazil | Ecuador | Venezuela |
|---|---|---|---|---|---|
| Main confederations | CGT | COB | CGT | CEDOC, CTE, CEOSL | CTV |
| Union-party ties | CGT with PJ | None (after 1956) | CGT with PTB (loose) | CEDOC with MSC/PSC; CTE with PSE; CEOSL: none | CTV with AD |
| Union density (1980)[1] | 45% | 25% | 14% | 10% | 25% |

*Key*: PSE: Partido Socialista Ecuatoriano; MSC/PSC: Movimiento Social Cristiano/Partido Social Cristiano.

*Note*: 1. *Source*: Roberts, n.d.

not discipline unions in the post-incorporation period. In Bolivia, the populist MNR drew on the support of miners and peasants along with the urban lower and middle class. During the first four years following the 1952 revolution, party-union ties took the form of an experiment with co-government between the MNR and the COB. After this collaborative effort failed, however, the COB maintained autonomy from the MNR.

No cross-class populist party was founded in countries where authoritarian governments undertook the initial incorporation and did not seek to mobilize labor support. In the absence of a government project of labor mobilization in Ecuador, the divided labor movement had diverse partisan attachments. The conservative and Catholic CEDOC was affiliated to the Christian Democrats, and the CTE to the Socialists. The anti-Communist CEOSL had no partisan affiliation and entered into ad hoc cooperation with various parties. Similarly, in Brazil, where the initial incorporation took place under the authoritarian Estado Novo and had the sole goal of controlling unions, no such cross-class populist, or labor-based, party was founded. In its absence, the labor movement continued to be affiliated to more classist parties. However, when Marxist parties were banned shortly after the reintroduction of elections, the labor movement became increasingly oriented toward the Partido Trabalhista Brasileiro (PTB), which Vargas had founded at the end of the Estado Novo as a labor vehicle for the subsequent period of democratic politics. As it came under growing union influence, the party developed an increasingly classist program; but organic party-union organizational linkages seen in Argentina and Venezuela never developed.

### Popular Interest Regime

The result of the first incorporation was a particular type of popular interest regime. With the exception of Argentina, where most workers came to be covered by collective bargaining agreements, formal workers were and remained a minority (and often a small minority) of the popular classes. Nevertheless, even in these cases unions were the predominant organizations that represented lower-class interests. They were not the only popular-sector organizations, but they were politically privileged. Their own resources and organization gave them a unique capacity to scale up and to undertake collective action. Through legal recognition, the government further supported unions as organizations, their collective rights, and their capacity to represent and defend worker interests vis-à-vis employers and the state. Unions became important actors in the party-electoral arena, as well as in industrial relations. Indeed, the initial incorporation, by legally recognizing and privileging unions, defined a divide between labor market insiders and outsiders, and it politically privileged the unionized vs. the nonunionized popular classes, which were not well organized, attached to recognized representative structures, or so closely or organizationally affiliated with major political parties.

## CHANGE AND CHALLENGES

The last decades of the twentieth century brought two challenges to the patterns established by the initial incorporation. The first was military rule. Military rule became pervasive in Latin America, instituted by a wave of coups that began in the 1960s. Of the countries covered in this volume, only Venezuela did not succumb to military rule. One of the major factors prompting military intervention was the desire to politically demobilize unions and curtail the power they had accumulated since the initial incorporation.

Despite the often extraordinarily coercive resources the military applied to the task of repressing the labor movement, it is notable how temporary any success was. Indeed, in Bolivia and Argentina, unions recovered from the repression directed at them and became important actors in the struggle to unseat the military and institute democratic regimes (Collier 1999). In Brazil, the labor movement was reorganized during military rule. The Brazilian CUT was founded as an oppositionist confederation, and the more traditional unions underwent a number of reorganizations, eventually uniting in Força Sindical (FS). In Ecuador, although the military regime was in some ways rather progressive and employed a rhetoric of social justice, it was nevertheless quite anti-labor. In reaction, the three national labor confederations formed a united front, Frente Unitario de Trabajadores (FUT), and carried out a series of general strikes.

The second challenge was economic. More enduring than political repression in terms of its impact on unions was the profound change in the economic model. The change was prompted by three factors. The first was a sense that the ISI model was stalling. The second was a change in the international economy, which saw the end of important Bretton Woods institutions and a major increase in global trade, investment, and capital flows. The third was the international debt crisis, which hit Latin America particularly hard because the region had been a recipient of much bank lending. The debt crisis meant that in Latin America the change to a more open economic model based on greater integration into the global economy took a harsh form. It led to a particular form of an open, export-oriented model, one that was shaped by IMF conditionality with high priority on monetary balances and free market mechanisms, including the labor market. The result was "the lost decade" of the 1980s with virtually no economic growth, heightened unemployment, and immiseration. Unions, which opposed the policies, were dealt notable political defeats.

The change in economic model had profound consequences for unions, union-party relations, and the strength of unions as popular sector organizations.

**The Labor Movement**

As explained in the introduction to this volume, the economic reform agenda included flexibilization of the labor market, in terms of both individual labor rights (especially regarding severance pay) and collective labor rights (such as mandating decentralized collective bargaining). Other changes also adversely affected workers and put pressure on unionized jobs and wages: firm downsizing, the privatization of state-owned enterprises, and the dramatic reduction of trade protection in sectors that had been union strongholds. Other negative effects resulted from pension reform and the removal of subsidies that had previously benefited workers.

Many initiatives were taken to modify the labor law in order to remove what reformers viewed as anti-market rigidities. Those that were actually adopted varied across cases, but in general deregulatory provisions that flexibilized the labor market with respect to individual provisions went further than deregulatory reforms concerning union structure and collective rights. Murillo and Shrank (2005, 975) and Murillo (2005, 443) report that during the period of reform in the 1980s and 1990s, the Menem government in Argentina passed deregulatory measures, though some backtracking subsequently

TABLE 6.2. Unions under challenge

|  | Argentina | Bolivia | Brazil | Ecuador | Venezuela |
|---|---|---|---|---|---|
| Changes in labor law— individual flexibility | Mostly deregulatory | Deregulatory | Mixed | Deregulatory | Deregulatory |
| Changes in labor law— collective benefits | Mixed | Deregulatory | Mixed | Deregulatory | Regulatory |
| Main confederations | CGT, CTA | COB | CUT, FS | FUT[1] | CTV |
| Union-party ties | CGT with PJ (loose); CTA: none | None | CUT with PT; FS: shifting | Varied, loose | CTV with AD and LCR |
| Union density (1995)[2] | 22% | 9% | 24% | 9% | 14% |

*Notes*: 1. FUT is a coalition of CEDOC, CTE, and CEOSL.
2. Roberts, n.d.

occurred. More dramatic than these legal changes, however, was the suspension of collective bargaining during much of the Menem period. In Venezuela, both types of deregulatory measures adopted under Pérez were followed by further measures of individual flexibilization under Caldera. Some deregulation of individual provisions occurred in Brazil under Cardoso and of both types in Ecuador under Borja.

While the direction of reform is important, it must of course be interpreted against the level of deregulation. For a comparison, one may consider the 2006 de jure indices (scored from 0 to 100) presented by Burgess (2010, 204). Brazil (49) had the greatest individual flexibility, followed by Argentina (39), Ecuador (34), Venezuela (30), and finally Bolivia (25). In terms of collective rights, or what is referred to as de jure labor standards, the measures and even the rank ordering among the five countries are quite different: deregulation is highest in Bolivia (69) and Ecuador (70), followed by Brazil (81), and lowest in Venezuela (89) and Argentina (93).[1]

Perhaps more important than changes in labor law were other reforms, such as privatization, which led to layoffs and hence had a substantial impact on union density and sectoral strength. Roberts's data (see fig. 6.2) indicate that by the mid-1990s union density was halved in Argentina and Venezuela, compared to its 1980 level, and fell to about a third in in Bolivia. Density in

Brazil, on the other hand, nearly doubled from 1980 to the mid-1990s and was unchanged in Ecuador.

## Union Relations to Parties and Popular Associations

In reaction to these challenges, new currents and struggles emerged within the union movement. Some unionists considered party affiliation potentially advantageous for providing access to politicians and policymakers. Others favored partisan independence, since partisan affiliation had not enabled unions to block the new economic policies they had opposed, although some had been able to extract concessions (Etchemendy 2011). The result was a struggle within the labor movement, adding weight to currents that were autonomous from parties and more accountable to the rank and file. In many places, new confederations with such an orientation were founded.

An important question in the present context is the extent to which these unions were willing to form alliances and make common cause with other societal organizations, associations, and causes of the nonunionized lower classes. These popular sector associations had proliferated and become more active, often in reaction to the lost decade of the 1980s. The CTA in Argentina is a prominent example of a new rival confederation that eschewed partisan affiliation, adopted more militant tactics, and emphasized shop-floor organization. It forged some linkages with popular associations, primarily in the unemployed, or *piquetero*, movement. In Bolivia, the older COB was tremendously weakened by the dramatic reduction in the number of miners, who had formed the backbone of the labor movement. Having earlier become autonomous and militant, it maintained that stance. It presented itself as leading popular struggles and built coalitions with new popular organizations that had gained prominence, such as those representing urban informal workers. In Ecuador, the FUT entered into temporary, instrumental alliances with the indigenous CONAIE at various times. In Brazil, the CUT was closely affiliated to the PT, which it played a major role in founding in coordination with new social movement organizations.

Even for the historic confederations, the change in economic model often led to an alteration of the party-union relations that had been in place since the initial incorporation period. Policy under the new economic model—and specifically the harsh form it took in Latin America—seemed inconsistent with former types of union gains and positions of bargaining strength. Therefore, political parties, particularly those that were serious competitors for national power, often wanted to distance themselves from the organic relations they had previously maintained with unions.

Party-union ties were particularly strained where it fell to a union-affiliated, populist party to enact the economic reforms, as in Argentina and Venezuela. In Argentina, the PJ shifted from a labor-based party to a clientelist party that made popular appeals outside the union structure and downgraded the position of unions within the party. The PJ's new political strategy provoked the opposition of the CGT, which reacted against its demotion within the party as well as against the party's pursuit of wide-ranging neoliberal economic reforms. Between 2000–2003, the CGT split in two over the issue. In Venezuela, the struggle between the party and the CTV had a different outcome. Although AD similarly demoted the CTV within the party, the confederation opposed the economic reforms and had the political clout to turn the party against its own market-oriented presidents. This "success," however, may have contributed to the decline of AD and may have limited the CTV's reorientation toward labor market outsiders (Levitsky 2003, 235; Ellner 1993, 79 and 89). At the same time, a leftist political party, La Causa Radical (LCR), gained influence in the union movement. Finally, in Ecuador, the confederations of the fragmented labor movement maintained their earlier partisan affiliations. However, the Ecuadoran labor movement, already weakened and with a very low percentage of the economically active population covered by collective bargaining agreements, had little political influence.

By the end of the twentieth century, then, much had changed in the position of unions since the initial incorporation decades earlier. Unions were put on the defensive politically and economically, relations with parties were more distant and more fluid, and new popular sector organizations presented at once both the challenge of a competing source of electoral mobilization and the opportunity of constituting potential allies.

## THE REINCORPORATION OF UNIONS UNDER LEFT GOVERNMENTS

In the five countries that are the subject of this book, the left came to win the presidency, appearing as the champion of the lower classes in general and of those groups that had not participated in or benefited from the initial incorporation. These nonunion constituencies did not inherently pose the same challenge to the new economic model that had been adopted in these countries. To the contrary, that model was consistent with social policies oriented toward these groups in a way that would compensate for market failure rather than challenge the market model. Indeed, such social policies were widely adopted in Latin America even in countries without leftist victories. Similarly, they were advanced by international financial institutions, which were strong proponents of marketizing models. These policies have consisted of various forms of income support, health programs, and even pensions oriented toward these groups—policies that had previously been adopted for unionized insiders and had generally excluded those who had not been part of the initial incorporation. As discussed in this volume, leftist governments varied considerably in the form these policies took and the degree to which they were adopted as part of a larger program of supporting or challenging the neoliberal economic model they inherited. Pro-union policies were in greater conflict with the inherited neoliberal model, but these new left governments, to varying degrees, rejected that model. Policies toward unions reflected a combination of economic and political priorities.

### The Labor Movement

Under left governments, some pro-union changes in labor law have occurred but have generally been rather incremental. By contrast, many labor movements have been reshaped in terms of the configuration of national labor confederations. Only Bolivia shows no change. Brazil has experienced some fragmentation under left government. Fractionalization of the labor movement in Argentina was more evident: currents within both the CGT and CTA split, largely over the question of how to position the confederation vis-à-vis the Kirchner government.

The biggest ruptures occurred in Venezuela and Ecuador, where leftist presidents opposed the existing unions and undertook actions to form parallel unions supportive of the government. In both cases, new confederations were formed through a combination of top-down and union-based initiatives. In Venezuela, the traditional and dominant CTV was substantially supplanted by the Chavez-promoted labor movement. Ecuador saw the greatest fragmentation, into nine or ten confederations, most of which became grouped into and coordinated by three fronts. The FUT coordinated the historic confederations, while the Central Unitaria de Trabajadores (CUT) and Parlamento Laboral Ecuatoriano (PLE) generally grouped newer confederations. While most revisions to labor codes under left government have reversed some of the previous deregulatory changes, Ecuador's revision has significantly weakened the labor movement by restricting the collective bargaining rights of its largest component: public sector workers.

### Union-Party Relations

The advent of left governments brought a new set of dynamics to union-party relations, very different from the period of economic reform when some distancing took place on both sides. The discussions in the following chapters indicate that relations between the governing parties and unions have taken various forms, with new types of cooperation being forged. In part, the out-

TABLE 6.3. Unions under left government

| | Argentina | Bolivia | Brazil | Ecuador | Venezuela |
|---|---|---|---|---|---|
| Changes in labor law | Regulatory | Regulatory | Regulatory | Mixed | Regulatory |
| Main con- federations | CGT, CTA | COB | CUT, FS, NCST, UGT, CTB | FUT[1], PLE,[2] CUT | UNETE, CBST, CTV |
| Union-party ties | CGT[3]: Instru- mental with PJ; CTA(T) with FpV[4]; CTA(A): none | COB: In- strumental with MAS | CUT with PT; others: shifting | Varied: loose | UENTE with PSUV; CTV with AD |

*Key*: CBST: Central Bolivariana Socialista de Trabajadores y Trabajadoras de la Ciudad, el Campo y la Pesca; CEDOC-CLAT: Central Ecuatoriana de Organizaciones Clasistas; CSE: Central Sindical de Ecuador; CTB: Central dos Trabalhadores do Brasil; CTSPEC: Confederación de Trabajadores del Sector Público de Ecuador; CTSS: Confederación de Trabajadores del Seguro Social; NCST: Nova Central de Trabalhadores; PSUV: Partido Socialista Unificado de Venezuela; UGT: União Geral dos Trabalhadores; UNETE: Unión Nacional de Trabajadores de Venezuela.

Notes: 1. FUT is a coalition of CEDOC, CTE, and CEOSL.
2. PLE is a coalition of CSE, CEDOC-CLAT, CTSS, and CTSPEC.
3. Factions of CGT had instrumental relations with factions of the PJ.
4. FpV is the Kirchner faction of Peronism.

come corresponded to the nature of the popular base of the victorious left par-ty. The key distinction is whether or not the governing party had a core base of support in the labor movement. Argentina and Brazil represent cases in which the governing parties were rooted in the labor movement. In these cases, state policy showed accommodation toward unions, which, in turn, were willing to cooperate with the party. This accommodation was perhaps strongest in Argentina, where unions were particularly powerful, had become more au-tonomous in the preceding period, and extracted more generous policies from the government. Factions of both the CGT and the CTA developed strong pat-terns of cooperation with the FpV—the Kirchner faction of Peronism—which itself had become deeply divided. Some factions of the CGT subsequently co-operated with other factions of Peronism.

In those cases where the party came to power without a major base of sup-port in the labor movement, the party had more options in terms of policies toward unions. In Bolivia, where the MAS substantially grew out of a social movement, relations between the government and the COB were instrumen-tal. Evo Morales was initially supportive of the COB, and relations were coop-erative. However, in his second term, the COB adopted a more critical stance, including some protest against the government, mainly over wages and pensions. Subsequently, the COB established a more stable instrumental alliance with the MAS government.

In Venezuela and Ecuador, the leftist presidents were initially elected without a party that was socially rooted and adopted a strategy that opposed the existing unions and sponsored the creation of new confederations. In Venezuela, Chávez initially turned to mobilizing labor movement outsiders and entered a substantial conflict with the existing labor movement, which he identified with the establishment, which he opposed. His strategy was to reorganize the labor movement, substituting a new Chavista labor movement for the preexisting CTV. Ellner, in his chapter, details some dispute within the Chavista labor movement over the issue of autonomy.

In Ecuador, the Correa government initially followed a technocratic approach that did not attempt to win labor support. Its proposed revision of the labor code resulted in an uncooperative and contentious relationship between the government and the FUT, as seen in the late 2014 protests. Rather than accommodate the FUT, the government sponsored the CUT. Taking a position between the FUT and the CUT, the newer PLE has demonstrated a willingness to negotiate with the government. Despite the formation of the CUT, the opposition of the FUT and the negotiations with the PLE wrested some concessions in the labor code revision, including provisions that attempt to limit inequality by regulating salary discrepancies between employers and employees and also between formal and informal workers. Beyond advocating this policy, most labor confederations reformed their organizational statutes to allow informal workers to join, although they generally followed through with little organization or inclusion.

The result of the second incorporation, then, shows interesting variation among the cases of left government. The variation is evident along several axes. Fragmentation seems to be increasing and is greatest in Ecuador and least evident in Bolivia. Although in Argentina factionalism within the CGT is not new, it seems to be more severe than in the past and is accompanied by a parallel factionalism within the PJ. Autonomy is an issue debated in all cases: not only do different confederations within a country adopt varying stances on this issue, but it is also a matter of debate within confederations, several of which continue to reevaluate their strategies vis-à-vis parties— whether to maintain distance and the desirability of cooperation. What seems clear is that the traditional organic relationship characteristic of the classic labor-based party, with organizational integration between party and unions, is mostly a thing of the past, apparently even in Venezuela and Ecuador, where the left governments have sponsored new unionism. The exception among the current cases is in Brazil, where the PT has links to both the CUT and popular organizations. Thus, compared to the earlier period during much of the twentieth century when labor-based parties were in power, there is no single pattern of relations among unions, parties, and left governments.

This diversity raises some central questions about the reincorporation of unions and their new role and capacity to represent workers in each country. What access do unions have to policy making and how do they fare in collective bargaining? What is the effect of a shift in the popular interest regime? That is, how has the politicization of a new set of popular organizations—particularly ones that form a new support base for left parties—affected the political influence of unions? Has it diluted their clout, now that they are no longer such a dominant organized presence among popular sector groups? Or does the presence of an expanded and more diverse organized popular sector afford the possibility of making common cause with allies and thereby augmenting popular sector influence? These are central questions, which this volume begins to address.

Chapter 7

# SOCIALISM WITHOUT WORKERS? TRADE UNIONS AND THE NEW LEFT IN BOLIVIA AND ECUADOR

## JORGE LEÓN TRUJILLO AND SUSAN SPRONK

Bolivia and Ecuador share much more than amazing biodiversity and stunning geography. In the twentieth century, both countries have been home to powerful indigenous and labor movements that have been characterized as among the most powerful on the continent (Rivera Cusicanqui 1987; Yashar 2005; Hylton and Thomson 2007; Becker 2008). After long periods of political instability, they both elected left-of-center presidents who promised to end the long night of neoliberalism with impressive popular mandates. Evo Morales, Bolivia's sixth president within eight years, was elected in December 2005; Rafael Correa, Ecuador's eighth president within ten years, was elected in November 2007. Both were reelected for subsequent terms with majority shares of the popular vote.

While many scholars have highlighted the considerable accomplishments of these administrations in reducing poverty, improving social equity, and expanding citizenship rights, the fraught relationship of these administrations with labor movements has escaped critical review. In Ecuador, Correa has attempted to undercut the independent labor movement by creating parallel state-controlled workers' organizations, among other measures. In Bolivia, the MAS has collaborated with some elements of the labor movement and repressed others. For these reasons, with respect to relations between trade unions and the state, we qualify the second incorporation in Bolivia as following the pattern of contestatory interest intermediation, in which involvement of labor leaders in policy making has been selective and informal. In Ecuador, labor-state relations are best divided into two periods. In the first period, unions were included in government decision making, but in the second period the government created unions that toed the government's line, forcing independent unions to return to the streets to push their demands.

## FIRST INCORPORATION

Compared to more industrialized countries such as Brazil or Argentina, neither Ecuador nor Bolivia can be described as "corporatist" in the narrow sense. Given the structure of economies, the formal working class has always been a minority of the economically active population. In both cases, trade unions have relied on their mobilization capacity to influence government policy rather than formal relationships with parties and governments. Although labor movements in both countries have tended to be fiercely independent for most of the twentieth century, they benefited from corporatist arrangements at different points during the first period of incorporation. The organized labor movement in Bolivia has been much stronger historically than in Ecuador since it has been united under one workers' central, the Central Obrera Boliviana (COB), which was dominated by the militant miners' union, as opposed to Ecuador, where the labor movement has been more fragmented.

### Bolivia: Trade Unions and the National-Popular Revolution of 1952

Up until the 1980s, Bolivia was home to one of Latin America's most militant labor movements of the twentieth century. The industrial proletariat has always been but a small fraction of the economically active population in Bolivia. Nonetheless, industrial workers—Trotskyist miners' unions—have dominated the Bolivian labor movement for most of the twentieth century (Alexander 2005; John 2009).

The national-popular movement of 1952 was a formative moment for the organized labor movement. The revolution was led by a populist coalition of middle-class sectors, miners, urban workers, and peasants who rallied behind the Movimiento Nacional Revolucionario (MNR), which had won the 1951 elections but was prevented from taking office by a military junta. The MNR was an "alliance of various forces broadly committed to change but ideologically vague" (Dandler 1976). Workers founded the main workers' central, the COB, in the heat of the revolution. This organization, dominated by miners of Trotskyist orientation, played the leading role in the popular class struggle throughout the post-revolutionary period (1952–1964) and up to the mid-1980s (Lora 1977; Dunkerley 1984; John 2009). Facing militant miners' unions organized under the COB, the MNR government nationalized most tin mines in 1952 and created the Corporación Minera de Bolivia (COMIBOL) to administer them.

In the first four years following the revolution (1952–1956), there was a brief experiment with co-government between the COB and the state. Under this arrangement, the government included three pro-COB ministers in the cabinet and accepted the demand for *fuero sindical*, the legally autonomous status that granted the COB semi-sovereign control over the workers of Bolivia. The MNR regime gave worker representatives veto power in all COMIBOL decisions and allowed for a co-government in mine administration. The government also established special stores for the miners, increased their salaries, and rehired the workers who were fired in the conflicts leading up to the revolution (Alexander 2005; John 2009).

Despite the strong relationships between the MNR government and union leaders forged in the early years following the revolution, for most of the twentieth century the COB has resisted incorporation. The experiment with co-government ended abruptly in 1956 when the COB withdrew from the arrangement in protest of the government's acceptance of the terms of an IMF austerity package. Despite the severing of the co-government arrangement, the COB's power continued to grow. The ruling party, the MNR, increasingly relied on the military to keep COB militias under control.

The internal structure of the COB, which reflected workers' belief that the industrial proletariat was the leader of the class struggle, was at once its strength and a weakness in terms of its mobilizational capacity. To this day, the COB is dominated by militant miners' unions that are not shy to use collective action to achieve their goals, but its inflexible structure has not been able to accommodate shifts in the changing rhythm of class struggle, as indigenous and peasant organizations have become important political players. Upon its founding, on an executive committee of thirty-four members, the peasant faction of the COB only received a token representation of two seats. Furthermore, according to its internal statutes, 51 percent of the voting members of the COB came from the proletariat (blue-collar workers), while 26 percent of the voting delegates came from the peasant sector, leaving 23 percent for the middle-class sectors (white-collar professionals such as teachers, nurses, and public servants) (Chávez 2000). By statute, the leader of the COB always came from the miners' unions, the Federación Sindical de Trabajadores Mineros de Bolivia (FSTMB). This structure remains virtually unchanged to this day. As anthropologist Doug Hertzler (2005) notes, this organizational structure eventually served to further alienate the peasant participants, who eventually established their own federation in 1979, which is still part of the COB but acts independently, the Confederación Sindical Única de Trabajadores Campesinos de Bolivia (CSUTCB) (see Silva in this volume).

When the country succumbed to military rule in 1964, the COB faced intense repression, and the gulf between indigenous and proletarian organizations grew wider under the divide-and-rule strategies of military governments. The government of Hugo Banzer between 1971 and 1978 outlawed the COB altogether. Relations between the co-opted peasant unions and the miners also became increasingly tense, as the government would use the peasant militias to repress the miners under the "peasant-military pact" in force from 1964 to 1974. Despite being a clandestine organization, the COB proved its lasting influence and resilience when it resurfaced during the "dual transition" to democracy and neoliberalism. The majority of the Bolivian population considered the COB to be the only institution capable of representing the interests of the working class after the military called for elections in 1978, and it played a leading role in the popular struggles to return Bolivia to constitutional rule in 1979 and 1982.

## Ecuador: Firm-Based Unionism during the Import Substitution Era

For most of the twentieth century, the organized labor movement in Ecuador has been divided into several union centrals with different ideological tendencies. By the time of late industrialization in the 1960s and 1970s, Ecuador had developed three main, ideologically distinct union centrals: the Confederación de Trabajadores del Ecuador (CTE), which followed the line of the Third International and aligned with Communist and Socialist parties in the World Federation of Trade Unions; the Confederación Ecuatoriana de Obreros Católicos (CEDOC), aligned with Christian Democracy; and the Confederación Ecuatoriana de Organizaciones Sindicales Libres (CEOSL), primarily connected to U.S.-based unionism but following a different political tendency inspired by European social democracy (Darlic 1997).

Ecuadorian unionism involves a mixture of small organizations of few members from diverse economic sectors. As a result, unions in Ecuador have little social weight of their own. Due to this heterogeneity, the power of Ecuadorian unions depends on their ability to federate and their capacity to exert political pressure. Pronounced regional rivalries between Guayaquil and the highlands have complicated the role of the union centrals, which must engage with formal political actors from the rival regions first and then, having achieved recognition in the political arena, propose socioeconomic and political projects and reforms.

The legacy of ideological pluralism has been an enduring feature of the Ecuadorian labor movement, but in the context of military rule (1972–1979), the need for political action against measures that limited union activities and collective bargaining created incentives to unify the labor movement. Thus, the three main labor federations formed the Frente Unitario de Trabajadores

(FUT) in 1971, which was only solidified as a formal organization in the 1980s. Even so, the average rate of union membership over this period remained low, at around 16 percent of the economically active population (León 1998).

In addition to ideological pluralism, import substitution industrialization policies increased the fragmentation of labor by adding industrial workers to the mix. Fragmentation obligated the FUT to construct demands directed at the state that emphasized the general interests of labor and the popular sector as a whole: workers from the formal and informal sectors, public and private, industrial, agro-export, service, artisanal, the modern sector, and obsolete firms. The FUT's platform focused on minimum wage increases, collective bargaining rights, working conditions and benefits, price levels, economic nationalism, and the state's obligation to invest in economic development and welfare. In the mid-1970s, the FUT also channeled broader opposition to military rule, as it was widely seen as the only organization that had political presence (Pérez 1985).

This strategy elevated the FUT to the leadership of popular struggles in the late 1970s and early 1980s. The FUT intensified political pressure for either the adoption or expansion of policies and programs it championed. For example, when laws generalizing labor contracts in the public sector were passed, the labor movement had to exert pressure in the political arena to ensure recognition and full implementation of those rights, including in the resolution of labor conflicts. This meant that labor centrals had to support each other as they struggled to achieve recognition and implementation of their rights. Thus, despite their ideological differences, labor centrals began a process of concertation, albeit in the context of competitive relationships with each other (Dávila 1995; Darlic 1997; León Trujillo 2003a).

Under these circumstances, the dynamics of external conflict and internal competition both unified and divided the actions of the labor centrals. It also permitted their insertion in a political system that recognized the legitimacy of, or at least accepted, demonstrations and protest. By the same token, public pressure was the best tactic to resolve labor conflicts at the firm level. Thus, demonstrations and protest were also a means to maintain or increase union membership. This fed competition among union centrals to build up their presence in the public eye.

Redemocratization in 1979 gave unions opportunities for greater political expression, both within political institutions as well as by exerting pressure outside of them. The freedom to express grievances and demands and to influence public opinion and policy contributed to a significant increase in labor conflicts. They also led to an increase in the number of legally recognized unions.

## THE IMPACT OF NEOLIBERAL RESTRUCTURING ON TRADE UNIONS

The neoliberal historical juncture in Ecuador and Bolivia, as with many other countries of the region, is best referred to as a "double transition" from authoritarian rule and toward market-led (neoliberal) models of development. Beginning in the 1980s, governments implemented harsh measures to curtail working-class power. Austerity policies, anti-labor legislation, and privatization of state-owned enterprises were among a host of other measures that were intended to "free" the economy from the fetters of the discretionary powers of the state. As a result of these measures, labor's influence in both Ecuador and Bolivia declined substantially, although the timing of neoliberal reforms varied significantly due to workers' collective action in the public arena. While in Ecuador the efforts of labor to stymie privatization were more successful than in Bolivia, in both countries the power of traditional forms of labor organizations was severely eroded by the changing nature of the world of work: informalization and precarization of the labor force.

### Bolivia: Privatization, Decentralization, and Re-proletarianization

Like many other countries in the region, Bolivia's transition from authoritarian rule took place in the context of an unprecedented economic crisis. Bolivia emerged from the 1970s with an unmanageable debt load, which was largely accrued by unaccountable elites who transferred most of their earnings to banks in the United States and Europe. The first democratic government elected in 1982 came to office in "exceptionally difficult circumstances" (Dunkerley 1993, 125).

The coalition government under the Unión Democrática y Popular (UDP) attempted to address the pent-up demands of the working class for redistribution by pursuing a highly expansive wage policy. The power held by the trade unions, represented by the COB, reached its maximum during 1982–1985. This period was marked by an unprecedented number of strikes, stoppages, and diminished productivity. At the same time, Bolivia experienced one of the worst economic crises in its history caused by record-setting hyperinflation. Although this period of political and economic instability demonstrated the power unions had to influence governments, it also made unions and left governments targets of neoliberal ideologues, who blamed them for creating the inflationary crisis, a disciplining mechanism that the MAS administration is not shy to use (Webber 2011).

The response to the hyperinflation crisis was an orthodox shock-therapy program designed by the International Monetary Fund (IMF) and implemented with gusto by the former "revolutionary" party, the MNR (Sachs

2005). Indeed, President Víctor Paz Estenssoro, who ironically was the architect of nationalization following the revolution of 1952, also introduced the neoliberal revolution. Paz appointed U.S.-educated mining magnate Gonzalo Sánchez de Lozada head of the economic change team, who introduced the New Economic Policy via Supreme Decree 21060 that sought to overturn the "State of '52."

One of the primary goals of the Supreme Decree 21060 was to destroy the organized labor movement, particularly the militant miners' unions. Between 1985 and 1987, the government closed down the majority of the state-owned mines, reducing the workforce from 30,000 to around 7,000, demolishing the base of the organized labor movement. The government also dismissed 31,000 public service workers by the end of the decade, and 35,000 manufacturing jobs were lost due to the opening to international competition and economic contraction as over 110 factories were closed (Farthing 1991; Kruse 2001; Grindle 2003). Labor reforms established the freedom of employers to hire and fire with no restriction bypassing the job stability provisions in the General Labor Law (Cook 2006, 174).

The COB tried to stop this first stage of neoliberal reforms, but three years of confrontation with UDP government had weakened its ability to mobilize massive displays of public support. The layoff of the miners had nearly demolished the FSTMB, the backbone of the COB. As a result, by the late 1980s the CSUTCB (see Silva in this volume), representing peasants, began to challenge the FSTMB's traditional dominance of the COB. Internally divided, the COB found it increasingly difficult to effectively challenge government policy. For example, a teachers' strike in 1995 was defeated because the COB could not marshal the support of many of its members. The state also used selective martial law to keep the disruptions caused by the teachers to a minimum. The defeat of the teachers—considered to be the most militant union in the COB after the FSTMB—was another major blow to the COB, which became mired in internal corruption and infighting in the mid-1990s, making it difficult to resist the second stage of neoliberal reforms.

The second stage of neoliberal reforms under Gonzalo Sánchez de Lozada (1993–1997) further weakened organized labor. The Plan de Todos was an ambitious program that combined administrative decentralization and privatization (Kohl 2002). Under the privatization program, majority shares of the publicly owned companies at the heart of the Bolivian economy—in the energy, telecommunications, and transportation sectors—were transferred to multinational corporations. The results of the privatization program were as disappointing as they were predictable (Kohl 2004). Rather than revitalizing the economy, privatization led to increasing unemployment, escalating public budget deficits, deepening dependence on international aid, and the overall deterioration of working and living conditions.

The decentralization program—the 1994 Law of Popular Participation (LPP)—responded to long-standing demands by indigenous movements for decision-making powers but was also an attempt to displace trade unions from the role they had in public affairs. Under the law, each of the newly minted municipal governments became responsible for infrastructure and development. Importantly, the law also provided for the legal recognition of urban neighborhood councils and rural and indigenous communities as Organizaciones Territoriales de Base (OTBs), charged with identifying, prioritizing, and supervising the construction and delivery of public works and services in a participatory process. The law states explicitly, however, that "functional" (class-based) organizations such as trade unions cannot be recognized as OTBs (Kohl and Farthing 2006, 132), thus excluding trade unions from an important arena of decision making.

The political and economic decline of the formal proletariat was accompanied by an inverse process of what Bolivian sociologist (and now vice president) Álvaro García Linera (1999) dubbed "re-proletarianization"—the growth of smaller, decentralized workplaces that employ between one and four employees who confront precarious conditions of employment. In many cases, employees are family members who do not earn a fixed wage. In 1983, the number of manufacturing workers within microenterprises in La Paz and El Alto (employing one to four workers) was 20,002 and within large enterprises (employing thirty or more workers), 25,978. In 1987, the number of workers in microenterprises climbed to 25,223 but in large enterprises dropped to less than half, 12,390 (García Linera 1999). This poses a serious problem for trade unions, since the General Labor Law dictates that unions must have more than twenty members, meaning that a majority of workers are ineligible to join a trade union. The informal sector has been entrenched as a permanent part of the Bolivian economy. One study estimated that in the 1990s, the informal sector created nine out of ten new jobs (cited by Arze and Kruse 2004).

The fact that the COB retained at least some political clout over the neoliberal period was essentially due to the residual public sector, consisting mostly of public school teachers and health care workers and what remained of the state-employed miners (Dunkerley 1990; Malloy and Gamarra 1988). By the late 1990s, however, the COB invested more energy in creating coalitions with other organizations (such as indigenous organizations), which has become a strategic necessity in the neoliberal era as it found itself increasingly isolated (Kohl and Farthing 2006; Silva 2012). The COB took a new interest in the mobilized and radicalizing peasantry of the coca-growing farmers of the Tropic of Cochabamba, supporting its struggles against U.S.-sponsored eradication efforts. As Crabtree (2005, 6) argues, despite the fact that the COB was no longer able "to defend or coordinate the activities of other social organizations as in the past," it played an important role as a participant in coalitions that emerged to contest the privatization of natural resources and to prevent the deterioration of living and working conditions, such as the "Gas War" and the "Water War" between 2000 to 2005, which ushered in the election of the MAS.

### Ecuador: De-collectivization

Neoliberal reforms were not as radical in Ecuador as Bolivia. Political tensions between Ecuador's principal regions on the one hand and social mobilization on the other hand impeded the implementation of deep, sustained neoliberal reforms. The polarization between the coast and the highlands was decisive in the stalemate. Coastal elites in finance and agriculture preferred opening domestic markets and export promotion. Highland elites, however, with an economic base in large, medium, and small firms that benefited from ISI preferred protection from international competition. The prolonged political instability that followed witnessed the passing of six presidents in ten years (1996–2006), three of them deposed before the end of their terms by popular mobilization. This period of political crisis only ended when Rafael Correa came to power in 2007, which coincided with the boom in petroleum prices (Acosta 2015; Andrade 2008; Mejía Acosta 2010; Lucio-Paredes 2009; Verdesoto 2014; Varela 2010).

Under these circumstances, it was easier for governments to implement stop-go fiscal stabilization policies rather than full-out structural adjustment measures. These measures, mainly introduced by presidential decrees, included currency devaluations, the lifting of price controls, cuts to subsidies on basic consumption, and the suppression of wage demands. Attempts to liberalize imports also occurred but resistance by highland industrialists generally watered down the effort. Privatization was also an uphill battle, as every time the government tried to push through the reform large general strikes would force it to back down. Governments implementing neoliberal reforms had more permanent success in two areas. One was deregulation of the financial sector that ended in a deep financial market crash in the late 1990s. The other, given the failure to legislate central bank autonomy, was the imposition of the U.S. dollar as Ecuador's currency to control inflation, reserve balances, and foreign exchange rates in 2000 (Conaghan and Malloy 1994; Sánchez-Parga 1993).

Compared to other cases such as Bolivia, neoliberal reforms to labor policy in Ecuador were not as comprehensive or as radical, yet in the context of a fragmented, heterogeneous, weak and politically dependent labor movement it nevertheless had significant decollectivizing consequences. For example, frequent demands for the deregulation of labor yielded partial measures, such as increases in the minimum number of members required to establish a union (from fifteen to thirty). This reform had serious impacts on union organization, limiting the number of new unions that could be formed and favoring the establishment of maquiladoras and subcontracting.

The biggest change, however, occurred during the government of Sixto Durán Ballén (1992–1996), which reformed the tripartite bargaining system. Trade union formation plummeted as unions lost negotiating capacity and could not resolve conflicts in their favor, even in cases where the law was clearly on their side. The Ministry of Labor, bound by statute to find in favor of unions in unclear cases, consistently ruled against workers. In light of their declining public presence, unions lost legitimacy in the eyes of workers. One need only to compare the low number of worker actions and their unfavorable resolution in the governments of León Febres Cordero (1984–1988) and Durán Ballén to the higher numbers in the more receptive and open government of Rodrigo Borja Cevallos (1988–1992) to understand the utter dependence of unions on the relative political openness or closure of a government.

The absolute reduction in the number of collective bargaining agreements between 1990 and 1997 was a significant indicator of decollectivization. Overall, fewer than 4 percent of the economically active population were covered by them. Of greater significance was a reduction in the number of collective bargaining contracts in economic sectors with the highest number of firms and unions. In the food, beverage, and tobacco sector, they fell from 43 percent to 24 percent, and in metalworking, from 23 percent to 10 percent. Overall, then, the core industrial manufacturing sectors were the most affected (Conaghan and Malloy 1994; Dávila 1995; León Trujillo 1998; Pachano 2010).

Established trade unions and their federations also suffered during the neoliberal period from improved functioning of a parallel union system—the comité de empresa—that the military governments had created to delegitimate established unions. The comités de empresa became the sole organization legally empowered to engage in collective bargaining; only half of the workers of a firm had to belong to it in order for it to be legally recognized. In a context of growing union delegitimation and economic insecurity, the comités de empresa gave employers a mechanism to attract workers disinterested in traditional unionism. Workers, afraid of losing their jobs, would end up accepting the firm's conditions; their unions would disappear as they came under control of management (León Trujillo 1997; Montúfar 2000; Sánchez-Parga 1993).

Additional factors accelerated the decline of the Ecuadorian labor movement during the neoliberal era. These included the opening of the economy to international competition, which hit the manufacturing sector hard, followed by the financial crisis of 1999–2000, which bankrupted many firms. Dollarization of the economy in 2000 contributed to a fall in demand, and firms reorganized their business in ways that were detrimental to unions.

Two more indicators of decollectivization are worth mentioning. First, although the absolute numbers of unions did not decline dramatically, the drop in the number of new unions being legalized was notable. In the period immediately after redemocratization, 19.4 new unions were legally recognized per month. In the first presidency of the neoliberal period (Febres Cordero), the average dropped to 16.1. In Durán Ballén's government, which was the most orthodox, it plummeted to 5.17 (León Trujillo 2003a).

A second additional indicator for the decollectivization of labor was a change in the social composition of unions. Before the neoliberal period, members of unions affiliated with the major federations tended to be salaried workers in the formal sector with contracts. By 1998, the tendency was to affiliate nonsalaried workers from the informal sector. Similar to the situation in Bolivia, many of these informal workers, mainly from the commercial and peasant sectors, are subcontracted and work two or more jobs. A significant consequence of this shift has been a strong weakening of laborite platforms and the dwindling of a vanguardist vision for the traditional labor movement focused on the firm. Last but not least, the drop in unionized workers resulted in a loss of resources for unions, with the consequent limitation in union activity.

What was the cumulative effect of decollectivization on labor's resistance to neoliberalism? At first, faced with the economic stabilization program of Febres Cordero, the FUT played its traditional role as articulator, spokesman, and leader for popular resistance. In other words, the conflict with the government reinforced coordinated action by the union centrals. To underscore its leading role in the public sphere, the FUT organized thirteen national strikes from 1979 to 1989 (Dávila Loor 1995). These reactive protests not only forced government to backpedal on its policy initiatives, they also kept more drastic measures, such as privatization of public enterprises and social benefits such as social security, health, and education, off the policy agenda.

However, by the 1990s the cumulative effects of the decollectivizing effects of neoliberal reforms caused unions to lose their mobilizing and representative capacity. Their calls for mass demonstrations only received partial support from their own ranks and did not win other social sectors that opposed neoliberal reforms to their side. Nor did public officials listen to them as they had in the past. Years later indigenous organizations, which did not necessarily support the demands of labor, would play the key role in channeling this discontent (Altmann 2013; Barrera 2001; Baud 2007; Becker 2008; Lalander and Ospina Peralta 2012; Yashar 2005; Zamosc 2007; Silva in this volume).

Lastly, union leadership suffered from internal fractioning and competition with each other depending on its party political alignments. A former union leader of the CEDOC-CUT put it this way: "The weakening of the labor movement was due less to repression than to a lack of strong leadership in a context of changes" (Dávila Loor 1995, 49).

## SECOND INCORPORATION: CONTESTATORY INTEREST INTERMEDIATION

In both Ecuador and Bolivia, the harsh effects of neoliberal structural adjustment were met with massive popular resistance. In both countries, social movements took their demands to the streets, staging protests that frequently paralyzed the economy by blocking roads and airports. Unlike the previous era, however, these protests were not led by the organized labor movement but rather, eventually, by indigenous movements and "territorial organizations" that protested the looting of the countries' natural resources by multinational corporations as part of a broader anti-neoliberal agenda (Silva 2012; Spronk 2012). These contentious tactics were met with fear and disdain by the traditional political parties, which failed to effectively respond to their demands. In both countries, the political movements that rearticulated parts of the left, the Movimiento al Socialismo (Bolivia) and the Alianza País (Ecuador), were considered "political outsiders" that managed to capture the wave of social movement energy (see Conaghan and Silva in this volume).

Compared to times past when trade unions were central players in articulating popular agendas, they are now minor players in the administrations of the "New Left." From a comparative perspective, however, Bolivian trade unions remain more powerful actors in the political arena compared to their Ecuadorian counterparts, which relates to their continued willingness to take job action and the orientation of the political parties in office. Since the MAS is conceived by many to be a "political instrument" rather than a traditional political party, the Morales government derives its legitimacy from its connections to social movements, including the organized labor movement. The COB leadership has been consulted on key pieces of legislation in official dialogues in policy spaces created by government. The relationship between the organized labor movement and the government, however, has been fraught with tension. The COB has oscillated back and forth as ally and adversary of the government, following the pattern of contestatory interest intermediation, under which the government's efforts to incorporate social movements have focused on "territorially based" organizations rather than "functional organizations" such as trade unions (see Rossi in this volume).

By contrast, the Correa government's technocratic vision of governance does not necessarily include public participation and has little regard for popular movements, focusing instead on creating an individualist polity described as the "citizen's revolution." The Correa government has declared an outright war on the independent labor movement, launching a brutal attack on public sector workers and, in a second period, stimulating parallel organizations to undermine the traditional labor centrals.

## Bolivia: COB as Ally and Adversary

The election of Evo Morales raised popular hopes for a "social movement" government that would respond to the demands of the working classes. In the first years of his administration (2006–2009), Morales made a show of a pro-labor discourse and sought to actively involve the COB in the elaboration of policy, particularly in the pension reform. While these first three years were punctuated by important labor struggles in the transportation, health, and mining sectors, it was a period of relative calm, as organized labor rallied to the government's defense in the context of the constitutional reform that threatened to tear the country apart. Once the dust settled, however, the MAS took a more aggressive stance against organized workers. In its second term in office (2010–2014), the MAS tabled a new labor code that would restrict the right to strike, attempted to force public health sector workers to work longer hours, and imposed policies that were seen to be an attack on the working classes, such as the removal of fuel subsidies. In 2010, organized workers returned to the streets in an annual protest cycle to pressure the government to follow through on promises to improve living and working conditions.

Unlike Correa's government in Ecuador, however, the MAS has backed down from controversial policy reforms when they have been met with wide-scale popular protests. The most serious challenge from the organized labor movement to the MAS's hegemony has been from public school teachers, salaried miners, and manufacturing unions. These groups of workers have not been shy about using collective action to force policy change, even without the approval of their leadership. Policy reforms that affect labor—such as wage increases and the much-heralded pension reform—have therefore been the result of a complicated set of shifting alliances between the MAS government, the COB leadership, and the rank-and-file unions typical of contestatory interest intermediation regimes.

The new Constitution of Bolivia approved in 2009 institutionalizes popular participation in decision making by parts of society, establishing that Bolivia is a "participatory, representative and communitarian" democracy (Article 11). Articles 240 and 241 further stipulate that the Bolivian population, represented by the "organized civil society," is to participate in the design of public politics and to execute social control at every level of state: municipal, departmental, and national. The participatory rights and the codetermination of "organized civil society" are also mentioned with regard to sectors of the economy with strong social organizations: the health system, the educational system, the (plural) economic system, and in the realm of environmental protection (Articles 40, 78–93, 309, 343).

The precise definition of who constitutes this amorphous "organized civil society" and the institutionalization of this public participation are as yet undefined. As Moira Zuazo (2010, 132) describes, the juridical framework that shapes participation is therefore "arbitrary." Thus it is difficult to describe the current relations between the Bolivian government and the COB as "corporatist": the government recognizes the COB's jurisdiction over select pieces of legislation, but the COB is not given special place in the government's agenda. Instead, it must compete with many other social movement organizations for space at the table.

Public consultation on key areas of policy depends on a series of shifting alliances that make social movements vulnerable to the government's divide-and-conquer strategies. As Fernando Molina (2013) describes, the government "manages unity" by giving different treatment to the social movements that confront it. Social movement organizations may be considered allies or adversaries at any given moment. If a certain social movement and its organizations are deemed allies, the conflict is framed by the government as "creative tensions within the revolution" (García Linera 2012), and it seeks to avoid an escalation of protest by relying on the government's relationship with the leaders and the popularity of government officials among the potential mobilizing forces (Kohl and Farthing 2014, 16). Various concessions are made, provided that the government considers them acceptable. When the conflict cannot be prevented in this way, the mobilized sector becomes an adversary that is publicly ridiculed and accused of being "counterrevolutionary." The government also uses its selective alliances to encourage the countermobilization of other social groups that remain loyal to the government who rally to the government's cause. As we shall see further, organized labor has been deemed as both ally and adversary, depending on the issue.

### Labor Conflicts under the MAS government

The rising number of social mobilizations in Morales's second term (2009–2014) demonstrates that as a form of governance, ad hoc incorporation is highly conflictual. In a recent study, Fundación UNIR reports that the number of protests increased significantly in the period of economic instability following the 2008 crisis. While there were 288 conflicts in 2009, there were approximately 1,300 in 2011 (Quiroga et al. 2012, 50). Although Bolivia registered among the highest economic growth rate in the region, poor families were negatively affected by spiraling prices of basic foodstuffs such as cooking oil, pasta, and rice. Conflicts related to demands for better living and working conditions top the list. About 20 percent of the conflicts relate to the "economic situation," 15 percent were explicitly related to "work and salary," 4 percent related to "land," and 3.5 percent related to "natural resources" (Quiroga et al. 2012, 72). During this period, the COB and its affiliates were responsible for around 45 of 2,426 conflicts recorded. While this number may seem small, the COB has organized some of the largest protests with respect to their geographic scope.

As longtime observer of Bolivian social movements Maria Teresa Zegada (2011) argues, the uptick in conflict from 2009 to 2011 is the result of deteriorating standards of living and pressure from below rather than a rising militancy of the COB leadership. Indeed, the COB leadership has frequently been pushed from rank-and-file members to take direct action. In several instances, the COB has called national, indefinite strikes, but only after the initiative was taken by its affiliates.

### The 2010 "Gasolinazo"

While the government was able to contain protest in the first years of the administration with promises of pro-labor pension reform and significant wage increases, the first major labor protests since Morales took office erupted in May 2010, primarily over wages but also due to a host of frustrations related to unmet expectations that the "process of change" would transform the economy to benefit workers.

The relationship between workers and the government soured after the "gasolinazo" of late December 2010. On the day after Christmas, the government announced that the move to remove subsidies from gasoline intended to promote "energy sovereignty" and prevent trafficking to neighboring countries. Fuel prices were projected to rise over 73 percent for gasoline and 82 percent for diesel, whose inflationary effects on transportation and food hit the poor the hardest. Similar price increases were the triggers behind other anti-neoliberal protests, such as the Caracazo in Venezuela in 1989. As the progressive electronic newspaper BolPress editorialized, "The MAS government has succeeded in doing what no neoliberal government was able to do for 25 years" (cited in Fuentes 2010). The government hoped—wrongly—that the announcement would catch social movements off-guard by making the announcement on December 26. The COB organized massive mobilizations that paralyzed nearly every city in the country, with thousands of workers taking to the streets. The government was forced to back down, canceling the measure five days after its announcement.

The government has responded to pressure from below coming from organized labor even if it has not sought to incorporate its leaders directly into the state. The government has been increasingly called upon to arbitrate in conflicts among different sections of workers. The conflicts in the mining sector offer a window into the challenges faced by the government as it seeks to balance the contradictory expectations of different groups of workers in its response to demands to reassert popular control over Bolivia's natural resource wealth.

### Mining Policy: Dancing with Dynamite[1]

The bloodiest conflict in the first year of the MAS administration broke out in Huanuni, Bolivia's largest tin mine. In early October 2006, violent confrontations broke out between salaried workers employed by the state mining company, COMIBOL, and independent workers organized in cooperatives as the salaried miners attempted to prevent the cooperative miners from taking over one of the richest veins in the main mine. Two days of fighting left sixteen dead and scores of others injured.

The roots of such mining conflicts go back to the neoliberal period. Since many of the state-owned mines were closed in the mid-1980s and subsequently privatized throughout the 1990s, cooperative miners have come to outnumber salaried miners. The cooperative sector grew exponentially as mineral prices skyrocketed with the commodities boom from 2002 and 2012. To many progressives, it may appear at first glance that the proliferation of cooperatives in the mining sector is a good thing. Unfortunately, the opposite is true. Although mining cooperatives are technically "cooperatives" under the law, they are highly hierarchical organizations that pay workers on temporary contracts by piece rate, often at depressed prices. Most workers, as contractors, do not enjoy health and safety protections.

Cooperative and salaried miners often work in close proximity to each other, setting the stage for conflict. The salaried miners, who have access to modern equipment, have been granted concessions to work the deepest veins. The cooperative miners with their rudimentary tools have been granted concessions to work the shallower veins. Conflicts break out over veins in the middle where the two concessions meet and between two groups of workers represented respectively by the FSTMB and the National Federation of Mining Cooperatives of Bolivia (FENCOMIN).

The selective and informal nature of the contestatory interest intermediation regime established by the MAS has been exemplified in the mining sector, as the government has made concessions to one side and then another. To end the 2006 Huanuni conflict, the government absorbed the cooperative miners into COMIBOL, raising the number of salaried workers from 1,100 to 4,700 at that mine and granting COMIBOL full jurisdiction over the mine, thus "nationalizing" it. The government flip-flopped its position in the Colquiri conflict a few years later when a similar conflict between private miners, state miners, and cooperative miners broke out in Bolivia's second-largest tin mine in October 2012. This time, Morales revoked the mining license of Swiss commodities giant Glencore and turned its operations (and workforce) over to COMIBOL. In turn, COMIBOL granted a thirty-year lease to cooperative miners at the site's Rosario vein, worth an estimated $5 billion. Unlike the Huanuni conflict when all cooperative miners were hired by COMIBOL, however, only eight hundred workers were added to its payroll.

*Labor Law and Pensions*

Constitutional amendments have been part of the strategy to bury Supreme Decree 21060 of 1985 that implemented neoliberalism. Articles 14, 49, and 51 of the new constitution recognize the universal rights of all workers to organize and collectively bargain, including agricultural workers (who are excluded from the 1942 General Labor Code), and provide trade union protection for all trade union leaders. The constitution also establishes access to a worthy job without exclusion, specifies that unjustified firing from jobs is forbidden, and that the state will resolve conflicts between employers and employees (Articles 49.3 and 50). However, such rights consecrated in the constitution require a legal framework in order to enact them.

Labor law in Bolivia remains a complex web of regulations that are difficult to enforce. The 1942 General Labor Law, which has been modified over two thousand times by sixty different presidential decrees, remains the basis for employment rights in Bolivia. The Morales administration circulated a draft proposal in 2010 to reform the General Labor Law that was highly criticized by labor groups, particularly the factory workers of Cochabamba, who have a long history of militancy (see Silva in this volume). The initial draft contained several proposals that were viewed as excessive restrictions on the rights of workers. First, it would make it necessary for a union to have a two-thirds majority to go on strike instead of the current regulation of 50 plus 1 percent. In addition, the proposed legislation stipulated that workers who did not agree to strike would be allowed to work. Second, the proposal stripped all public sector workers of their right to strike, excluded agricultural workers, and would not permit employees of microenterprises to join unions (raising the minimum number of workers from ten to fifteen). Third, concerns were raised about proposals to give the state the ability to finance unions, which would compromise trade union independence. Fourth, the proposal would have penalized protest measures of civil disobedience (Webber 2011, 213–14).

The national leadership of the COB was originally prepared to accept this proposal until factory workers', teachers', and health workers' unions resisted in May 2010, which forced the national leaders to present a show of struggle, calling an indefinite general strike but then doing little to guarantee its success. As of November 2014, the labor law reform has been put on hold.

Reforms to the pension system have been among the most important benefits to labor, both informal and formal. In October 2007, President Morales announced that the privatized pension scheme established by neoliberal president Sánchez de Lozada would be replaced with a noncontributory pension scheme, Renta Dignidad, that expanded coverage to seven hundred thousand Bolivians. The benefit is funded by a tax on hydrocarbons and dividends from companies that have been re-nationalized.

In an even more ambitious reform, Morales nationalized the pension system in December 2010, which lowered the retirement age from 65 to 58 and allows mothers of three or more children to receive pensions at 55 years of age. Miners can retire at 56 years of age, or between 51 and 55 if they worked in unhealthy conditions. The government also introduced a new semicontributory pension scheme for those in the informal sector, estimated to account for about 60 percent of the workforce.

Despite the fact that forty-four of forty-seven trade unions in the COB initially voted in favor of the 2010 pension reform, with escalating popular demands in the wake of "*gasolinazo*" and the TIPNIS conflict, which was viewed by the COB leadership to be an attack on indigenous rights to consultation (see Silva in this volume), the COB's relationship with the government broke down, and Bolivia's largest workers' federation moved from ally to adversary. In May 2013, the COB launched a series of strikes, marches, and road blockades in the capital city to push for a modification of the 2010 Pensions Act, demanding that the retirement pension be raised to 100 percent of average salaries rather than the 70 percent established under the act, and for more special concessions for miners. For the first time, protests spread to all departments of Bolivia in support of the pension reform and in reaction against the government repression of the protesters. The conflict saw miners, teachers, and health workers take to the streets of La Paz, while roadblocks and strikes took place across the country.

The government strongly condemned the strike, with Minister of the Presidency Juan Ramón Quintana accusing some union leaders of trying to overthrow the state. In response to the pension increase demands, the government deployed police to break up blockades in Cochabamba and La Paz, leading to several arrests and injuries. After sixteen days of protest, COB leaders agreed to lift the strike to allow time to analyze a government offer to reform the current pensions system, increasing payments to miners. In early September 2014, the government agreed to further lower the pension age for workers who work in unhealthy conditions up to another five years.

While relations between the COB leadership and Morales soured between 2010 and 2013, the push-pull dynamic between the government and the peak labor central continues to oscillate. Disappointed with the MAS, the COB explored creating its own political instrument. At its national general assembly in November 2013, however, the COB leadership decided to drop the initiative, endorsing the MAS in the upcoming elections in October 2014 and returning to its role in supporting the government by helping to suppress popular demands. It is highly symbolic that Morales participated in the May Day events of 2008 and 2014—the only times that a president has participated in such events since 1971 (Rivas and Vásquez 2014).

In sum, since Morales came to office, despite the fact that the COB has been involved in consultations on some key pieces of legislation, there has been little semblance of formal "corporatist" arrangements with trade unions compared to the more formalized incorporation of leaders from other social movement organizations. Pushed by its base, the COB leadership has pulled out of negotiations and returned to the streets in order to protest public policies that are perceived as an attack on labor and popular sectors. Yet the push-pull dynamic between the government and the COB leadership moves with the rhythms of the electoral cycle. The COB leadership was part of the Unity Pact that helped bring Morales to office in 2006, and after a brief period of contest between 2010 and 2013, endorsed the MAS in the national elections in October 2014. Morales's resounding victory in the presidential elections in October 2014—with 61 percent of the popular vote—demonstrates that from an electoral standpoint, contestatory intermediation works.

The government's popularity is best explained by robust economic growth and the redistribution policies that have improved the lives of the majority even while reforms have fallen short of expectations. According to data compiled by the Centre for Economic Policy Research (Johnstone and Lefebvre 2014), between 2006 and 2014, the Bolivian economy has grown about 3.0 percent, compared to negative growth from 1980 to 1993, and 0.9 percent from 1994 to 2005. Public investment as a percentage of GDP also doubled from

2005 to 2014, from 6.3 percent to 14.4 percent. This combined effect of growth and redistribution has had an important impact on poverty. Between 2005 and 2010, the proportion of those in moderate poverty went down from 60 percent to 49.6 percent, while extreme poverty fell from 38 percent to 25 percent. In addition, the World Bank estimates the Gini coefficient in 2012 was about 0.47, falling from 0.58 in 2005.

## Ecuador: Labor Reincorporation, an Illusion Shattered

The history of the Ecuadorian labor movement, and social movements in general, reveals four important consequences for understanding its trajectory after neoliberalism under Rafael Correa. First, it highlights the role of protest in Ecuadorian politics in general. Second, it underscores that regional protest dynamics (coast, highlands, and lowlands) check the concentration of power in any one sector, such as unions, indigenous movements, or middle classes. Third, we see that "leading" actors may vary over time and contexts, but in the end they invariably function as social counterweights to governments. This is a lesson Correa's government has learned the hard way, with the reawakening of trade union protest capable of catalyzing broader social unrest, validated by favorable public opinion, especially as of 2013. In short, we underscore that the Ecuadorian political system is one that offers a favorable opportunity structure for social movement organization.

This brings us to our fourth point. As of the 1990s, the Ecuadorian political system has included traditionally excluded subaltern social groups such as indigenous peoples, women, African descendants, sexual minorities, and evangelicals, among others. Their political incorporation goes beyond the promotion of effective voting rights and rights to association and protest. They were active participants in various stages of the policy process. They generated counterproposals to government-sponsored reforms, crafted an agenda for a post-neoliberal Ecuador, lobbied legislators, and negotiated over those reforms at the height of mobilizations. Moreover, some of these new social movements created their own political parties, most famously Pachakutik (the indigenous peoples' political arm), which elected national legislators, mayors, and city councilors. Given these developments, further "political incorporation" was not a priority for Correa, although early on he scored points by appointing women and some indigenous people to his administration. Most noteworthy, instead, was his choice to use social policy to promote a new social contract based on greater equity as the main instrument of incorporation (Freindenberg 2012; León Trujillo 2003b, 2011; Ramírez Gallegos 2010a, 2010b; Ramírez and Guijarro 2011).

It is impossible to understand Rafael Correa's ascension to power without

the active participation of organized popular sectors. Over the various crises that wracked Ecuador during the neoliberal period, the popular sectors
led anti-neoliberal struggles and slowed down the pace of neoliberal reforms.
They also generated alternative policy proposals that Correa later incorporated in his governing platform. By the same token, anti-neoliberal resistance
struggles also generated expectations regarding state-society relationships.
Policy proposals put forward by social movements were forged in broad par-
ticipative processes that involved a myriad of networks and leaders of different
political tendencies. That process was simultaneously an affirmation of the
right of participation and a search for mechanisms of participation. In the
context of a deep economic and political crisis, this process gave birth to the
idea that civil society constitutes an alternative to tired politics as usual.

Correa channeled these social forces and their aspirations into a broad
base of support that won him the presidency and inspired him to call his
government the "citizens' revolution" (Ramírez Gallegos 2010a; Ramírez and
Guijarro 2011). Thus, as further discussed by Conaghan (this volume), initially Correa's legitimacy was intimately tied to those organizations, their policy
proposals, and their votes. Very quickly, however, he used public policy, mass
media campaigns, and the very polarization that his government created to
augment his own personal power. Erstwhile close allies were converted into
mere sources of support for his government, losing their decision-making capacity and independence. In other words, the government's actions do not
match the rhetoric of participation (see Silva in this volume; Freindenberg
2012).

*Disincorporating Labor Organizations of the "Old Order"*

In this context, the hopes for reincorporation of the trade unions and centrals
that formed the FUT were dashed from the outset. They have had to swallow
the bitter pill of disappointment as Correa's government deepened the process of disincorporation begun during the neoliberal period. Correa's efforts
took two tracks. The first one was a marked "anticorporatist" tendency. The
second one rested on a conception of state modernization that included state
enterprises, especially with respect to the rationalization of administrative
personnel and workers over the injection of financial resources (Correa 2010;
Lucio-Paredes 2009; SENPLADES 2000).

The anticorporatist stance originates in the idea that social organizations
had too much influence in the policy process in the past, which allowed them
to impose their narrow corporative interests to the detriment of the general good. This framing applied to unions, indigenous peoples' organizations,
and women, among other groups. Trade unions were guilty of seeking special

advantages for a small, privileged sector of workers, or worse, personal advantages for corrupt leaders. Their politically motivated national strikes were blamed for exacerbating instability. Similar views held for highly contentious indigenous organizations that, while financed by the state, enjoyed a great deal of autonomy.

In light of these convictions, Correa first sought to eliminate professional organizations (such as doctors, lawyers, and engineers), and he further weakened unions by eliminating the political negotiating role of union centrals. By cutting labor out of the political process, Correa deprived it of its principal strength, the capacity to articulate the demands of generally unorganized popular masses and to negotiate tangible and symbolic benefits. It was this political role that had provided trade unions legitimacy in the eyes of other popular sectors and that gave a small number of organized workers the capacity to mobilize much larger numbers. Thus, unions also lost legitimacy in the eyes of unorganized workers and the rest of the popular masses.

To underscore organized labor's exclusion from the political arena, the labor ministry further curbed union formation and in mediation generally favored employers. A long, drawn-out strike in Ecuador's largest tire manufacturing firm—ERCO—in 2009 was a paradigmatic case. The firm's *comité de empresa*, which had demanded 20 percent wage increases, rejected management's 3 percent raise proposal. Workers deemed the offer an insult since it was less than half of the collective bargaining contract obtained the year before. Despite the fact that the law was on the *comité*'s side, the labor relation's board sided with management and declared the strike illegal. One hundred and twenty workers were summarily fired, all of them union leaders or among the more militant rank and file (El Comercio 2010; Diario Hoy 2010, 2011; El Tiempo 2010; Ciudadania Informada 2009).

The economic and human resource development model of Correa's administration demands rationalization and flexibilization of the labor force in firms, including public enterprises. Correa's government set the legal basis for this policy direction as early as 2008, when the constitutional assembly issued "mandates" that relaxed rules for firing workers, especially in the public sector. These were followed up with decrees that permitted "voluntary firing" and "mandatory early retirement" in the public sector.[2] Twenty percent of the public sector workforce was affected. Additional decrees and internal ministerial rules fixed public sector salaries unilaterally without reference to collective bargaining, which had been the norm.

The rationalization of the public sector workforce has tamed public sector unions. Troublemakers and deadwood are gone, and a more compliant workforce remains. This is important because, given the state's strong role in the economy and in social policy, the overall number of public sector workers has increased. According to the National Institute of Statistics, two out of ten new jobs created between 2008 and 2013 were public sector jobs, in tandem with the growth of public sector spending, which, thanks to high oil prices in world markets, stood at 30.25 percent of the GDP in 2011 (INEC 2016; INEC-UNFPA 2015–2016; Lucio-Paredes 2009).

Correa's government has also used a heavy hand to unilaterally redefine working conditions, further weakening established unions. Here, the administration has applied a strategy based on coercion and intimidation to create a "social pact" based on union acquiescence to government policy. This, of course, is in contrast to the constant protests and demonstrations of the previous era. If necessary, Correa personally interprets labor law, which generally involves a devaluation of unions and pressure on judges to find in favor of the government in legal challenges. For example, in 2012 the journal *Vanguardia* published the minutes of a meeting at Petroecuador (the state petroleum company) that President Correa attended. An angry Correa put the navy in charge of the company, intervened, and replaced the troublemaking union with one more supportive of the government's policy.

Another indicator of Correa's onslaught against labor associations is that complaints to the International Labor Organization have multiplied. They cluster around violations of labor law, collective bargaining rights, restriction of the right to strike, arbitrary firings, and incompatibility between new labor laws, rules, and procedures on the one hand and international labor protocols to which Ecuador is a signatory. Equally troubling, many complaints refer to police repression with excessive force resulting in physical injuries, arrests at or before demonstrations organized by the labor movement, and threats and intimidation of labor leaders (see, for example, FUT 2015).

It is highly symptomatic of labor's diminished status that the Ministry of Labor no longer has data on collective bargaining contracts and other important labor statistics. Thus, we cannot empirically ascertain the current state of trade unions or labor conflicts. Nevertheless, from conversations with leaders of the labor centrals we may conclude that the number of unions at the firm level in the private sector has declined drastically.[3] Today, most unions are in the public services sector, both at the national level (education, health, and public works) and at the subnational level (provinces and municipalities). As far as union density is concerned, we estimate it has declined from approximately 10 to 2 percent of the economically active population.

As further evidence of the organized labor movement's precipitous decline, in 2016 the Ministry of Education issued Decree 16 that dissolved the National Union of Educators (teachers) and confiscated its assets. The decree was based on a law that applied to NGOs, not unions. It contradicts the right to associate.

*(Re)Incorporation of Working People, Correa Style*

To compensate for the continued disincorporation of established unions—and social movement organizations in general—Correa's government has reincorporated workers, popular sectors, and subaltern social groups in several ways. Noteworthy is the fact that two novel forms of popular inclusion affect groups that had been previously incorporated and then partially disincorporated under neoliberalism and individuals in social categories that had never been incorporated, or only weakly so at best.

One of the forms of reincorporation, perhaps the most traditional, involves the creation of new social organizations. The low level of citizen and social movement turnout to defend Correa during the bloody September 2010 police revolt in which he was taken prisoner caused him to pull back from his anticorporatist stance and to concentrate on the creation of social organizations to support him. For this, he capitalized on internal divisions and factions in existing social organizations, such as unions, indigenous peoples, medical personnel, students, women, African descendants, informal sector workers, and public sector employees.

In the labor sector, more than five new union centrals were created. Generally speaking, the new union centrals were either promoted by the government in order to weaken and devalue traditional union centrals or were formed by unions that accepted the government's proposals. The new centrals include the Confederación Sindical del Ecuador (CSE), which formed from a split in the CEOSL and took most of its unions with it. Several new sectoral confederations have also emerged. These include the Confederación de Trabajadores del Seguro Social (CTSS), the Confederación de Trabajadores del Sector Público (CTSP), the Confederación de Trabajadores Autónomos del Ecuador (CTAE, which draws its members from the informal sector of the economy), and the Confederación Unitaria de Trabajadores Azucareros (CUTAE). In 2013, the CSE, along with the CEDOC-CLAT and the CTSP, formed the Parlamento Laboral Ecuatoriano (PLE), which, although it supports the government, resists its efforts to further deregulate labor relations. Last but not least, in 2015 the government formed the Central Unitaria de los Trabajadores (CUT), led by the CTSP and a faction of the Confederación Unitaria de Trabajadores y Trabajadoras Autónomos del Ecuador (CUTTAE).

Government-sponsored fragmentation of the labor movement spurred the FUT to strengthen ties with other organizations. Of special note was the FUT's association with the Unión General de Trabajadores del Ecuador

(UGTE), which has now joined the FUT. Also notable are the FUT's joint actions with the CONAIE.

Correa's unionism follows a well-established pattern of "political marketing" in which contradictory reforms aim to selectively incorporate sectors of traditionally excluded workers as he disincorporates others, particularly the traditional labor movement of the "old order." For example, on November 15, 2014, when Labor Minister Carlos Marx Carrasco announced the formation of the CUT, he stressed that it "brings self-employed, farmers, housewives, public and private employees" into a "modern trade unionism" that promotes "the supremacy of human labor over capital, without denying the need for the latter" and works with the idea of finding solutions to the "tensions between capital and labor."[4]

The government also presented the Law for Labor Justice and Recognition of Work from Home, a minipackage of reforms that seeks to incorporate 1.5 million housewives into the social security system. It also gives greater protection to other marginalized groups, such as LGBT, women, and African Ecuadorean workers by prohibiting fixed-term contracts and punishing employers who attempt to dismiss pregnant women and labor leaders.[5] Here the right to unionize is specifically noted. Yet in a contradictory move a month later, the government introduced a constitutional amendment before the legislature that clearly states that public sector workers cannot be governed by the Labor Code, which would strip them of their right to unionize. Since the majority of formal workers are employed by the public sector, in practice this reform would imply that the number of unions would be reduced significantly. Moreover, the state would reduce its share of financing for social security pension funds to 40 percent of its previous commitment. This would result in predictable underfinancing problems (Lucio-Paredes 2015).

Aiming to promote greater income equality, the government has also attempted to modify a law that forces companies to share 15 percent of their pretax profits with all employees. This is typically paid out as a lump sum "bonus." Correa, however, has argued that this practice of profit sharing privileges some workers over others and that the money should go to the government for equitable redistribution. Earlier in 2014, the government proposed a law that aimed to reduce this amount to 3 percent for highly profitable mobile-phone companies, directing the remaining 12 percent toward the state. Due to fierce opposition, the government was forced to back down on this initial proposal.

Correa's "citizen revolution" thus represents a novel and much broader form of incorporation that promotes individual citizenship rights. These rights accrue to individuals, and the state is the guarantor of those rights without intermediaries, such as unions and collective bargaining. For example, the state promotes observance of labor laws in order to safeguard the rights of individual working people. This promotes contracts between individuals and employers, not collective bargaining. By the same token, the state has promoted observance of labor laws in the informal sector. This is the case for domestic workers or people employed in microenterprises, where labor regulations now require that these workers be enrolled in the social security system or by protecting against child labor. In other words, the state strives to formalize employment.

Finally, Correa's government appropriated the platform championed by the organizations that struggled against neoliberalism and incorporated many of their proposals into public policy. Such was the case of the war on poverty, social policy, and the very recovery of the state. New and expanded social services in health, pensions, education, pre- and neonatal care, housing, and for disabled persons compensate for greater job precariousness and most directly favor the informal sector labor (see Silva in this volume for more details). The same holds true for the citizens' revolution's aggressive policy to increase minimum wages. However, wage policy does not necessarily extend to salaried formal sector employees who already earned more than the minimum. Such employees frequently report on the absence of pay raises or, worse, since it is so easy for employers to hire and fire, there is a tendency to pay no more than the minimum wage.

Socioeconomic indicators have definitely improved. With dollarization, inflation dropped significantly, from 91 percent in 2000 to 5.4 percent in 2011 and 3.7 percent in 2014. Government statistics indicate that poverty has also dropped, from 35 percent in 2008 to 25.6 percent in 2013. Access to health and education has improved significantly. Social inequality is also dropping. In 2011, 20 percent of the poorest population had access to 3.9 percent of the wealth, compared to 2.8 percent in 2000, and while the richest 20 percent had 62 percent of the wealth in 2000, it is now 53.6 percent. The Gini coefficient has dropped to 0.46 (INEC 2015).

Given the grim fate of the labor movement in Correa's government and that of other previously organized popular sector and poor subaltern social groups, these positive figures of socioeconomic inclusion tell an interesting tale. They attest to the relative success of the citizens' revolution's emphasis on incorporation of popular sector social subjects mainly as individuals rather than their organizations, as it was in the liberal tradition. The electoral victories of Rafael Correa—with his third administration recently finished—strongly support the argument. However, capital-labor relations have also been modified to the detriment of workers who now have fewer legal defenses to prevent flexible working conditions and face stricter rules on collective bargaining and various punitive measures that make organizing independent unions much more difficult.

## CONCLUSION

Under the "New Left," the influx of royalties and taxes on natural resource exports has permitted a substantial increase in welfare spending in Ecuador and Bolivia. Due to improving economic conditions, the working classes in both countries have made gains in their living standards compared to the previous neoliberal era as measured by improvements in income, access to basic services, and benefits. An upswing in economic growth has been accompanied with an increase in social equity. Following international policy trends, the "New Left" has oriented its major policy innovations toward workers in the informal sector rather than formal sector workers employed by the state and private capital, which provided the backbone of welfare state models in the twentieth century (Esping-Anderson 1990). The improvements to social security, such as increases to pensions, health, and education benefits, have not been won through collective bargaining but through policies designed by state managers, such as conditional cash transfers that aim to reach workers in the informal sector and target women.

Compared to Ecuador, the push-and-pull relationship between organized labor and the MAS government in Bolivia has resulted in more public policy reforms that favor salaried workers. The trade unions in Bolivia have been more willing and capable of demonstrating their political strength by organizing massive mobilizations that have forced the government to back down on some of the most controversial elements of economic policy. The MAS government has had informal ties with the COB, although it no longer has pride of place. Nonetheless, there have been some important concessions to organized labor with respect to legal reform (at least at the constitutional level if not the laws and regulations to enforce it) and pension reform, often after strike action by workers thwarted the government's original plans and proposals. Under Correa, on the other hand, the establishment of parallel union centrals has further fragmented the already divided labor movement. Correa's heavy-handed anti-union stance resembles the divide-and-conquer politics that characterize authoritarian governments such as the PRI in Mexico that seek to destroy the independent labor movement.

Despite these recent trends, we also recognize that organized labor's weakness is historical due to a structural tendency that reduces formal sector salaried employees and wage earners in businesses that add value to raw materials.

Thus, nothing less than organized labor's place in society is at stake. Economic globalization has sharpened international competition in a manner generally disadvantageous to Latin America, which has intensified primary product exports to the detriment of enterprises that add value to them.

That said, how organized popular sectors are incorporated in the political arena depends in no small measure on the characteristics of the political system. As a result, in Bolivia we see more cooperative arrangements alongside protest. By contrast, Ecuador offers few opportunities for cooperation, despite the weakness and fragmentation of popular sector organizations—such as trade unions—it nonetheless offers space for protest. This is why, despite a similarity in ideology between the two cases, they exhibit strong differences with respect to popular sector incorporation.

This review of the government's relationship with the labor movements in Bolivia and Ecuador invites a broader reflection on the meaning of "twenty-first-century socialism," particularly the role of organized labor within the project. While both Morales and Correa have proclaimed themselves to be promoters of "socialism," theirs bears little resemblance to its earlier nineteenth- and twentieth-century versions, when organized industrial workers—as the most powerful section of the working classes—were considered to be the privileged subject of revolutionary change. For Morales, organized labor appears to be just another interest group to be negotiated with at some moments and sidelined at others when its demands push the boundaries of the government's agenda. Correa, on the other hand, has been outright hostile to organized labor, seeking to incorporate individuals into the state as part of his "citizens' revolution." In this sense, it appears that these two experiments with "twenty-first-century socialism" are a novel interpretation of socialism appropriate to an era of neoliberal globalization that does not aim to shift the power balance between capital and labor in favor of workers, at least not independently organized ones.

Chapter 8

# CONFLICTING CURRENTS WITHIN THE PRO-CHAVEZ LABOR MOVEMENT AND THE DYNAMICS OF DECISION MAKING

## STEVE ELLNER

Throughout the fourteen years of the presidency of Hugo Chávez between 1998 and the presidential elections of 2012, the Chavista leadership often re-sponded positively to pressure from distinct groups within the movement, even while its relations with the opposition became increasingly stormy. In-deed, President Chávez's discourse and actions convinced his heterogeneous base of support that he identified with each one of its constituent groups and defended their interests. At the same time, however, Chávez's movement was subject to ongoing strains due to the clash of internal political currents and the distinct concerns of non-elite social groups.

The Chavista social base of support included members of the working class, the nonincorporated sectors that lacked both union representation and job security, and members of the middle sectors. In addition, moderate and more radical currents coexisted within the Chavista movement and even among pro-government trade unionists. The leading Chavista trade union-ist, Nicolás Maduro, who became foreign minister in 2006, vice president in 2012, and president in 2013, represented worker interests at the national level at the same time that he promoted his own bloc within the labor movement and the PSUV that grouped a large number of labor activists. The national executive interacted with these internal currents and groups by encouraging their mobilization and that of rank-and-file Chavistas, at the same time that it articulated and helped shape popular demands as well as their transformation into policies and legislation.

The following chapter will examine how this interactive relationship played out in the labor movement in order to determine whether the Chavista government moved significantly beyond a mere statist and centralist strategy by creating the conditions for institutionalization based on participation from below. Specifically, it will address the question of whether the government's encouragement of mobilization and the organizational opportunities that were provided opened spaces conducive to institutionalization and organizational consolidation, along with the deepening of democracy and the incorporation of previously excluded sectors of the population. The chapter will explore the interaction between the state and the two major factions of the Chavista labor movement that emerged following the creation of the pro-Chavista labor confederation, the Unión Nacional de Trabajadores (UNETE) in 2003. One camp led by Marcela Máspero was more focused on exclusive working-class demands than the second camp led by Oswaldo Vera (a close ally of Maduro), which defended the multiclass and statist approach of the Chávez government. The chapter will show how the national executive granted important concessions to the Máspero camp as well as workers in general, but at the same time showed an unmistakable preference for the Vera current. After defining the differences between the two currents, the chapter will discuss several major decisions taken by the national executive that were applauded by rank-and-file workers: the nationalization of the steel industry in 2008, the elaboration of the "Plan Guayana Socialista" in 2009, and the promulgation of the Organic Law of Labor and Workers (LOTTT) in 2012.

The concluding section of the chapter will discuss the institutional and theoretical implications of these developments. A number of scholarly works draw on pejorative notions of populism to point to an empty space that allegedly existed between an assertive President Chávez and his allegedly passive followers, who are seen as lacking organizational capacity and ideological criteria. This chapter argues for a more fluid and two-way relationship and a dynamic that could lead in the direction of viable and enduring institutionalization. On the one hand, Chávez and more recently Maduro occasionally encouraged their movement's rank and file to check the state and party bureaucracies by demanding honesty and efficiency. On the other hand, the Chavista movement from the outset envisioned a statist strategy of assigning the state a central role in promoting social organizing, which in the course of time came to include the formation of labor federations, community councils, and organizations of land settlers. Furthermore, the organizational instability and deficiency of grassroots Chavista groups in spite of the opportunities provided convinced the Chavista leadership that subjective conditions were lagging and consequently initiatives needed to come from above. As the editors point out in the introductory chapter, Venezuela's relative input from below places the nation in between the more fluid popular participation that characterizes Evo Morales' Bolivia and the technocratic features of Rafael Correa's government in Ecuador.

## THE EMERGENCE OF THE CHAVISTA MOVEMENT IN THE AGE OF NEOLIBERALISM

Throughout the extended stage of import substitution industrialization beginning in the 1940s, the labor movement asserted considerable political influence within political parties and in other arenas (Ellner 2012b, 141). Thus, for instance, at the national congress of the governing Acción Democrática (AD) in 1963, the party's labor bureau nominated Raúl Leoni as presidential candidate, even though the selection was not the choice of AD's maximum leader Rómulo Betancourt, who was then president of the nation. Furthermore, AD's labor bureau and the nation's main labor confederation, the Confederación de Trabajadores de Venezuela (CTV), envisioned the party's eventual transformation into a labor party, a goal that enhanced labor's sense of efficacy. During this period, a significant number of labor leaders were elected to various legislative branches of government (Ellner 1993, 98–99).

The neoliberal-inspired policies initiated by the second administration of Carlos Andrés Pérez in Venezuela in 1989 did more than transform the nation's economic structure through the privatization of key industries almost exclusively bought out by foreign capital. The neoliberal strategy also put an end to a political model associated with import substitution industrialization. A key expression of that model had been AD's labor bureau and its equivalent in the social Christian COPEI party, which served to incorporate the organized working class in the nation's ruling bloc. In the 1990s, AD's labor bureau was stripped of prerogatives including uncontested representation on party slates for public office and as a result was forced to vie with newly created party bureaus representing youth, women, and professionals, among others. The labor bureau lost influence not only internally but also among workers in general due to its support for neoliberalism and particularly the ratification of the neoliberal-inspired labor law reform in 1997.

The passage of the labor law reform contributed to the erosion of influence of the labor leadership of all the establishment parties and the rise to power of "outsiders" led by Hugo Chávez. The reform eliminated the "retroactive" provision of the system of severance payment in which the amount paid to a worker upon leaving a company was calculated on the basis of his/her last monthly salary multiplied by length of service with the firm. Retroactivity acted as a hedge against inflation (which in the year prior to the passage of the reform exceeded 100 percent). Its elimination, which the peak business organization Fedecámaras had been calling for since its founding in 1944, served to convert the system into a veritable annual bonus (as opposed to payment upon layoff), thus depriving workers of a major safety net at the time when they most needed it (Ellner 1999a, 18–19).

As late as 1995 at its eleventh national congress, the CTV went on record as refusing to negotiate any modification of severance payment retroactivity, which it considered a sacred worker conquest. Nevertheless, a few months later the government of President Rafael Caldera established the Tripartite Commission, consisting of CTV, Fedecámaras, and government representatives, which drafted the 1997 reform as well as a proposal that virtually privatized the social security system. AD and COPEI trade unionists on the CTV's executive committee supported the reform, with only one of them, José Beltrán Vallejo, expressing reservations. Caldera had coauthored the Labor Law of 1936, which first established the principle of retroactivity, while one of the main architects of the reform, Planning Minister Teodoro Petkoff, was a top leader of the formerly leftist Movimiento al Socialismo (MAS). These reversals of positions put in evidence the profound impact of neoliberalism on actors of different political leanings who were closely tied to the political system and accepted the established rules of the political game.

In contrast, Chávez's Movimiento Bolivariano Revolucionario-200 (MBR-200) joined hard-line leftist organizations such as the Partido Comunista de Venezuela (PCV), the Causa R party, and the Patria Para Todos (PPT) party, as well as militant labor groups that stressed trade union autonomy, in protesting the 1997 reform. On July 15, 1997, a group of leftist congresspeople presented a petition to the Supreme Court requesting the annulment of the reform on grounds that by reducing the compensation paid to workers for unjustified layoffs (to a maximum of five months' salary), it undermined the constitutionally recognized goal of job security. The following day, representatives of two hundred unions allegedly representing one million workers gathered in front of the Supreme Court in support of the annulment petition. According to *El Nacional*, the peaceful protesters, who were met with a squad of National Guardsmen, raised signs that read No to the Theft of Severance Payments! (July 17, 1997, p. D-4). The labor reporter for the politically moderate Jesuit magazine *SIC* called the protest "extreme populism that will undermine the credibility" of the reform's opponents (Arrieta 1997, 261). The statement illustrated the increasing divide in the age of neoliberalism between reformists who worked within the system and those who mobilized popular sectors in favor of more far-reaching change. One result of these developments was that the impetus for opposition to the market economy came from outside of the system, in accordance with a hemispheric-wide pattern (see Roberts 2016, 117-118).

In April 1997, Hugo Chávez and his followers reversed their policy of electoral abstention by participating in the presidential elections slated for the following year. In subsequent years, the Chavistas debated and vacillated on the issue of whether to work within existing institutions and promote alliances with organizations associated with traditional political practices as opposed to creating parallel structures and following a go-it-alone approach. Two examples of organizations rooted in traditional politics that provided Chávez's Movimiento Quinta República (MVR—the MBR-200's successor) political space to its right in which to participate and form alliances were MAS and the CTV. During their moderate period, which took place during the presidential campaign and first three years of government, the Chavistas followed a broad-based strategy of working with MAS and within the CTV.

Subsequently, the MVR—and then its successor party, the Partido Socialista Unido de Venezuela (PSUV)—opted for radical transformational policies that were conducive to an aloof approach to relations with non-leftist organizations. The party's hard-line stance included the rejection of "consensus politics," which had brought political and business elites into the decision-making process prior to 1998; the breakaway of Chavista trade unionists from the CTV and the formation of a rival labor confederation in 2003; and the questioning of the legitimacy of the opposition that in turn intensified the nation's political polarization.

The Chavista movement's rejection of the old way of doing politics and hostility to traditional actors drew on a tradition that was well represented in the labor movement. Beginning in the 1980s, insurgent groups that bypassed the CTV had made important inroads, especially in the textile and steel workers' unions, and raised the banner of autonomy vis-à-vis political parties (including those on the left) and the state (Ellner 1993, 150–71). Autonomy became a major issue of concern for Chavista worker leaders and would eventually divide their movement.

Nevertheless, the MBR-200 was in many ways unique among organizations on the left in the 1990s. By that period, a host of political organizations originating from the guerrilla movement of the 1960s had opted for electoral participation. In contrast, after the failed coup of 1992, the MBR-200 advocated electoral abstention (until April 1997, when it launched the presidential candidacy of Chávez and changed its name to the MVR). During these years, Chávez expressed contempt for those reformers such as MAS and Convergencia (the party of Rafael Caldera) "that go around attached to the formal ship"—that is, the establishment—and warned against strategies for change within the existing political structure since they would "end up being utilized by the system to supply it with oxygen" (Blanco Muñoz 1998, 310). As an alternative, he called for political work with "popular organizations" in order to promote the proposal for a new constitution that would bring about "fundamental change in the economic and political system" (Blanco Muñoz 1998, 428, 630).

The MBR-200's antiparty discourse resembled that of rank-and-file dissident groups within the labor movement (which at one point included the Causa R) that dismissed the CTV as being an appendage of AD and COPEI. The MBR-200 characterized establishment institutions as dysfunctional and, in some cases, thoroughly corrupt. After its moderate stage between 1998 and 2001, the Chávez government and movement established new parallel institutions on diverse fronts including health, education, and even the armed forces. Along similar lines, the Chavista labor leaders backed by the government questioned the legitimacy of the CTV and ended up creating a rival confederation.

The MBR-200's support for autonomy vis-a-vis political parties did not extend to its vision of relations between society and the state, which diverged from the views of leftist political and social movements that distrusted central authority of any type.[1] The Chavistas envisioned the state as playing a fundamental role in the formation of new democratic institutions open to rank-and-file participation. Indeed, after 1998, the state would promote the creation of tens of thousands of worker cooperatives and community councils among other bodies that stimulated rank-and-file participation. This statist strategy was spelled out in one MVR-200 document written in the mid-1990s: "The new state should place technical, financial and legal mechanisms at the disposal [of social organizations] to further their consolidation. It is fundamental for the state to listen to their suggestions and attend to their grievances. The state also needs to put in place mechanisms of participation in the decision-making process. In this way, democracy will be a process that goes from below upward" (MBR-200 2002, 196).

The MBR-200's statist vision ruled out the effective utilization of power at the local level prior to gaining power at the national level (Blanco Muñoz 1998, 309). At the same time, however, the MBR-200 embraced the model of participatory democracy, which represented a corrective to unrestrained top-down statism as well as military hegemony. Participatory democracy and statism were two essential components of the strategy of the Chavistas after coming to power in 1998. In practice, various factors shaped the dynamic of Chavista rule: the lack of a tradition of autonomous social movements compared to nations such as Bolivia, Ecuador, and Peru; the statist vision first formulated by the MBR-200 during its early years in the 1980s and 1990s; and the all-encompassing power of the national executive buttressed by the charismatic qualities of Chávez. A fourth factor served to counterbalance the first three, namely, the government's bold actions and policies that took into consideration the demands and proposals originating from the grassroots of the Chavista movement. Thus, in spite of the slowness of the organizational consolidation of the Chavista movement and Venezuelan social movements in general, the Chavista rank and file was convinced that Chávez defended their interests.

Developments during the historical juncture of the 1990s, which was characterized by political crisis, shaped the backlash against neoliberalism that led into the extreme polarization of the Chávez years. During the 1990s, those located slightly on the left of the political spectrum, including organizations such as MAS and the CTV and leaders such as AD's Carlos Andrés Pérez, Luis Raúl Matos Azócar, and COPEI's Rafael Caldera, ended up defending neoliberal formulas, in the process pitting the more radical and intransigent left against the entire political establishment. Furthermore, Chávez's 1992 coup was directed against Pérez and other historical leaders, thus encouraging the rebels to condemn the political system per se dating back in time and not just specific policies and leaders in the present. The official Chavista discourse after 1998 was that the nation's democracy from the outset of the modern democratic period in 1958 was thoroughly corrupt and required a complete break with the past, a position conducive to polarization and the repudiation of "consensus politics."

Another lasting effect of the neoliberal period of the 1990s was the antiparty sentiment originating from both sides of the political spectrum. On the one hand, the Chavista movement viewed political parties as the bedrock of a corrupt political system. On the other hand, neoliberal stalwarts (such as the think tank Centro de Divulgación del Conocimiento Económico—Cedice) and other critics of traditional politics in the 1990s blamed clientelistic parties for holding back much-needed pro-market reforms due to their vested interest in maintaining a strong public sector. Newspapers such as *El Nacional*, for instance, opened their pages to civil society spokespeople highly critical of political parties. After 1998, some members of the opposition (such as AD's Carlos Raúl Hernández) attributed Chávez's rise to power to this aggressive campaign against political parties. On the other side of the political spectrum, the antiparty language of the 1990s had an impact on many rank-and-file Chavistas, who after 1998 distrusted party bosses, even Chavista ones, and made clear that their only loyalty was to Chávez himself (Ellner 1999b, 117).

## THE CLASH OVER DIFFERENT CONCEPTS OF STATE-UNION RELATIONS, 1999–2014

The Venezuelan political system under Chávez was more state-based (similar to other incorporation regimes, as the editors discuss in the introductory chapter) than the party-based system that prevailed during the decades after 1958. While AD's labor bureau and equivalent bodies of other parties had served as a major institutional link between trade unionists and decision-making structures in the state sphere, after 1998 the national congress's Committee of Social Development, which was led by trade unionists, played a similar function. The shift from party bureau to congressional committee was significant because the former had a greater potential to assert relative autonomy vis-à-vis the governing party and the state than did the latter.

Nevertheless, the committee provided space for trade unionists and thus helped dispel the notion that no viable intermediate structures existed in Venezuela under Chávez. Indeed, several Chavista trade unionists on the committee went on to assume important positions in the government. During Chávez's early presidential years, Nicolás Maduro presided over the committee, which included future ministers José Khan (a former metro worker) and Angel Rodríguez (formerly of the oil workers' movement). Subsequently, PCV secretary general and former trade unionist Oscar Figuera assumed the presidency of the committee and prioritized the drafting of a new labor law. After succeeding Figuera as committee president, Oswaldo Vera participated in the drawing up of the law, known as the Organic Law of Labor and Workers (LOTTT) enacted in 2012. Subsequently, both Vera and opposition trade unionist Alfredo Ramos (future mayor of Barquisimeto), who also served on the committee, submitted proposals for a new pension law to provide coverage to workers in the informal economy.[2]

Throughout the Chávez presidency, the relations between the government and organized labor were heavily debated in the Chavista workers' movement. These issues, which defined differences among internal currents, changed in response to political developments in the nation.

From 1999 until 2002, with the attempted coup and the general strike against Chávez (in effect, a company lockout), the proposed creation of parallel structures divided the Chavista workers' movement in two currents. A moderate current headed by Chávez's right-hand man Luis Miquilena (who had been a prominent dissident Communist labor leader in the 1940s) argued that the strategy of parallel unionism had historically isolated the left and that consequently the Chavistas should work within the CTV, which had been the nation's main labor confederation since its founding in 1947. Maduro, a former metro workers' leader and member of the far-leftist Liga Socialista party who became an early Chávez supporter, headed a hard-line current. The hard-liners argued for a two-pronged strategy of taking advantage of the Chavista control of executive and legislative branches as well as its rank-and-file labor influence to deliver a heavy blow to the CTV to facilitate the creation of a new authentic workers' confederation. The decision to participate in CTV elections in October 2001 represented a victory for Miquilena and was subsequently considered an error by many of the hard-liners. The Chavistas and other labor leaders

TABLE 8.1. Information on Venezuelan labor confederations

| Confederation | Date of founding | Political orientation | Degree of autonomy vis-à-vis party or state | Major leader at present |
|---|---|---|---|---|
| Confederación de Trabajadores de Venezuela (CTV) | 1947 | Pro-AD throughout its history | Little | Manuel Cova |
| Unión Nacional de Trabajadores (UN-ETE) | 2003 | Pro-Chavista | Critical of government and party | Marcela Máspero |
| Central Bolivariana Socialista de Trabajadores (CBST) | 2011 | Chavista | Little | Oswaldo Vera and Wills Rangel |

attributed the triumph of AD's Carlos Ortega as CTV president to widespread electoral fraud.

Following the attempted coup of April 2002 (when Miquilena defected to the opposition) and the general strike in 2002–2003, both of which were supported by opposition labor leaders, the Chavistas reached a consensus on the need to break with the CTV and form a new confederation. Between the founding of UNETE in 2003 and its second congress held in 2006, the issue of relations with the state divided the confederation. Trotskyist labor leader Orlando Chirino raised the banner of "absolute trade union autonomy" and insisted that worker gains be the result of collective bargaining and other union initiatives rather than presidential decrees and that worker co-management be applied to strategic state-run sectors of the economy such as oil and electricity, contrary to the position assumed by the Chavista government (Chirino 2006). A second group associated with Máspero at the time defended the importance of political criteria. The differences between the two groups came to a head in 2006 when Máspero called for the postponement of UNETE elections in order not to detract from Chávez's campaign efforts for the presidential elections in December. Chirino rejected the proposal as a violation of the principal of union autonomy and, after a scuffle at the congress, left UNETE and then the Chavista camp.

Other factions within UNETE challenged Máspero's current "Colectivo de Trabajadores en Revolución" (CTR) from the right. One current was labeled "rightist" because several of its leading members came from COPEI; its most prominent leader, steel workers' president Ramón Machuca, had allegedly failed to follow a militant course in his dealings with the multinational Ama-

zonia, owner of the nation's steel company SIDOR. Oswaldo Vera led another
current referred to as "bureaucratic" due to his close ties with the MVR (and
the PSUV) and various ministries including the labor ministry.

UNETE under Máspero's leadership increasingly clashed with the government as a result of disruptive and prolonged labor disputes that the confederation backed, as well as its outspoken positions on labor policy. Two Trotskyist
currents in UNETE (known as the Marea Socialista and the Corriente Marxista Revolucionaria–the CMR), which supported the Chávez government after Chirino's withdrawal and worked within the PSUV, played a direct role in
some of these conflicts. In 2009, for instance, state police killed two workers
in an attempt to expel members of a CMR-led union that had occupied a Mitsubishi plant in Barcelona with the intent of promoting workers' participation. The union leaders reacted by organizing protests calling for the removal
of the state's secretary general and police force head, both appointed by the
Chavista governor, as well as various labor ministry officials and judges who
were held responsible for the repression. Subsequently, the PSUV refrained
from criticizing the firing of eleven members of the union's executive committee, thus intensifying tension between UNETE and the Chavista political
leadership.

UNETE's support for workers' participation in decision making in state
companies produced clashes with managers in some cases backed by labor
ministry inspectors. At the same time, however, trade union radicals and
much of the rank and file applauded the national executive's decision to expropriate firms taken over by the workers. The issue of workers' control and
workers' participation emerged following the two-month general strike of
2002–2003, when hundreds of companies faced bankruptcy as a result of the
prolonged conflict. The government initially accepted UNETE's proposal for
government financial aid to rescue the companies in return for management's
acceptance of workers' input in decision making. In 2005, the government
expropriated the paper company INVEPAL, the valve company INVEVAL,
and several other firms that had recently closed down and refused to pay employees their accumulated benefits and were consequently taken over by the
workers. The government's nationalization of strategic companies such as
electricity, telecommunications, steel, and cement at the outset of Chavez's
third presidential period of 2007 to 2013 and then his expropriation of scores
of companies in food processing and other sectors stimulated debate and led
to worker actions in favor of participatory demands. Intense and in some
cases prolonged labor disputes broke out over UNETE-backed struggles to
achieve worker input in decision making that included companies of different
types: some facing bankruptcy that were taken over by the government due

to their failure to meet employee obligations, such as the sardine company La Gaviota in Cumana, the glass company Vivex in Barcelona, Sanitarios Maracay (production of bathroom pieces), and Cerámicas Carabobo (refractory components); companies that the government accused of creating artificial shortages and expropriated (such as the coffee firm Fama de America in Caracas); and strategic industries such as the steel complex in the state of Bolívar in the Guayana region.

In addition, UNETE put forward proposals for the new labor law under consideration in the National Assembly that some PSUV national deputies viewed as excessive. Máspero called for wage hikes that privileged lower-paid and manual workers over white-collar ones, and in doing so sharply criticized Labor Minister José Ramón Rivero (an ally of Maduro) for recommending increases that were below levels of inflation. During these years, Máspero became increasingly critical of the PSUV leadership. By the 2012 presidential elections, her CTR current called on followers to vote for Chávez on one of the tickets of the Chavista coalition (the Gran Polo Patriótico) but not that of the PUSV. The following year, the CTR refrained from openly endorsing the presidential candidacy of Maduro. Máspero's leadership, however, was undermined as a result of the failure of UNETE to achieve organizational consolidation by holding elections for its national authorities.

In response to these developments, the PSUV distanced itself from Máspero and threw its support behind the current headed by Vera. As a sign of the realignment, the PSUV bypassed Máspero in the 2008 national elections by nominating Vera, who became the party's only national deputy representing labor (with ex-Metro workers' president Francisco Torrealba, formerly identified with the moderate current headed by Machuca, as his substitute). In November 2011, Vera's current, after several years of proposing the formation of a new confederation, created the Central Bolivariana Socialista de Trabajadores (CBST) and selected Wills Rangel, head of the Federación Unitaria de Trabajadores Petroleros de Venezuela (FUTPV), as its first president. The CBST, with the participation of Vice President Elías Jaua, organized its own May Day march in 2012, separate from that of UNETE.

Concrete differences separated UNETE and the CBST. Vera of the CBST explicitly stated that the political defense of the Chávez government took preference over worker demands, even while most of the confederation's attention was devoted to the latter, and that the labor movement needed to address multiclass concerns rather than confine itself exclusively to the immediate interests of the organized working class.[3] UNETE under Máspero's leadership claimed that, in spite of its critical positions, it acted responsibly in defense of the Chávez government. According to Máspero, the issue of autonomy versus submission to the state, as framed by Chirino, and the issue of the political obligations of the labor movement versus workerism, as framed by Vera, were deceptive since they were not either-or propositions. Furthermore, the CBST's failure to assume a militant stand played into the hands of the CTV, which was able to outflank the Chavistas by pretending to champion worker interests. UNETE spokespeople attributed the triumphs of opposition trade unionists in union elections in the heavy industrial zone of the Guayana region in 2011–2012 (including the aluminum company ALCASA, the iron company Ferrominera, and the aluminum processing company Carbonorca) to the Vera camp's failure to effectively articulate worker demands. The UNETE trade unionists noted that the defeat of the pro-CBST candidates occurred in spite of the support they received from their respective companies as well as the governor's office.[4]

The polemic that produced the sharpest conflict between the two camps was the proposal of workers' participation in company decision making. Vera argued that the labor movement had to act responsibly by extending preferential treatment to state companies and avoid the formulation of co-management demands as a cover for economism. In addition, the labor movement needed to distinguish between three types of state companies. In the first place, highly strategic industries, oil in particular, needed to be off limits to workers' participation schemes, a position that the Chávez government adopted following initial attempts at worker input during and after the general strike in 2002–2003. A second category consisted of ailing companies that the government had taken over to avoid their closing and resultant mass layoffs. In these cases, government action was of a defensive nature and thus demands to inject large sums of money and promote workers' participation were unrealistic. Proposals for worker input in decision making, according to Vera, should be largely reserved for a third type of firm—namely, financially sound, nonstrategic ones.

In contrast, UNETE viewed workers' participation as a priority demand regardless of circumstances in that it served as an alternative to "state capitalism," which was nothing short of a perversion of socialism. Actually, UNETE may have overstated its argument. Even without worker input in decision making, state companies in Venezuela were hardly managed according to market criteria along the lines of state capitalism. In some cases, prices were kept artificially low and in others employees received benefits untypical of capitalism (such as the elimination of outsourcing).

The differences and confrontations between the CBST and UNETE were sufficiently sharp as to have endangered unity among the Chavistas. The explanation for the ongoing worker support for Chávez in spite of the cleavages is to be found in the dynamic whereby important government decisions were sometimes taken in response to proposals from below in favor of the working class and even the radical currents grouped in UNETE. These measures included the nationalization of SIDOR, the Plan Guayana Socialista of worker participation, and the promulgation of a new labor law (to be discussed).

The CTV, for its part, remained considerably weakened after the debacles of the early years of the Chávez presidency. The confederation lost credibility among workers as a result of its close cooperation with Fedecámaras in the drafting of the labor reform of 1997 and the general strikes leading to the 2002 coup and then the two-month shutdown in 2002–2003. Following the latter conflict, CTV president Carlos Ortega fled Venezuela, after which the organization's leadership devolved upon its secretary general, Manuel Cova of the construction workers—the one sector where the confederation retained a degree of influence. The CTV received a further setback in 2006 when the ILO recognized UNETE as the sole representative of the Venezuelan working class. In 2012, the Causa R's secretary general Daniel Santolo criticized Cova for having failed to hold CTV internal elections since 2005, when the current leadership's term had expired. At the same time, Santolo held Cova responsible for the decline in the membership of CTV-affiliated unions from one million to fifty thousand and the number of its federations from seventy to ten (Lugo 2012; Ojeda Díaz 2012).

Beginning in 2011, the inroads of opposition labor leaders in the state-run industries of Guayana opened the possibility of a CTV comeback. Nevertheless, the state's takeover of strategic sectors undermined the CTV's worker following (as was, according to the opposition, the government's intention when it decreed the expropriations). Thus, for instance, the CTV lost virtually all its backing in the oil industry (whose main federation had previously been headed by Carlos Ortega), in part as a result of the executive order that transferred workers from the payroll of oil companies with mixed capital to PDVSA. In the elections of the FUTPV held in October 2009, none of the four leading slates that together received 96 percent of the vote had ties with the CTV: many of the elected labor leaders supported Chávez while (in some cases) harshly criticizing PDVSA president Rafael Ramírez, while others defined themselves as equally antigovernment and anti-opposition.

The FUTPV election was undoubtedly the most blatant example of state favoritism—to the detriment of the CTV. During the campaign, PDVSA president Rafael Ramírez made clear that under no circumstances would his company accept union control by those who had spearheaded the general strike of 2002–2003 (Buitrago 2009). The CTV leaders' distrust of the state led them to criticize the LOTTT for assigning the National Electoral Council (CNE) responsibility for overseeing union elections. They also disagreed with the law's exclusion of minority unions from the collective bargaining process.

## GOVERNMENT RESPONSES TO PRESSURE FROM BELOW

Beginning in the 1970s, the steelworkers' Sindicato Unico de Trabajadores de la Industria Siderúrgica (SUTISS) became undoubtedly the most combative union in Venezuela, a militancy that continued under the Chávez government. SUTISS played a key role in the defeat of the 2002–2003 general strike by keeping SIDOR running and sending a contingent of workers to the neighboring state of Anzoátegui to ensure the supply of natural gas for the industrial plants in the region. A one-year conflict over the signing of a new collective bargaining agreement included a series of strikes that culminated on March 14, 2008, with protests resulting in over fifty arrests and a dozen wounded. A group of workers traveled to Caracas to help publicize the struggle, and on a television program in which they presented their case, President Chávez telephoned and announced his support for their opposition to the practice of outsourcing, one of the main issues in the dispute. As occurred on other occasions, Chávez surprised the nation by nationalizing SIDOR in an act commemorating May Day on April 30 (the same day and month chosen to promulgate the LOTTT in 2012).

Shortly thereafter, Chávez traveled to Puerto Ordaz, where he declared that the nationalization was a "victory for the workers and the popular sectors in general." He added that "now that SIDOR is recuperated, the workers will unite with us and the people to steer SIDOR, as a great motor, on the path to socialism." At the same time, Chávez replaced Labor Minister José Ramón Rivero, who SUTISS leaders had attacked for favoring SIDOR's foreign owner, with National Deputy and former Communist Roberto Hernández, who had been receptive to worker demands. The government committed itself to the incorporation of the approximately ten thousand contracted steelworkers and began the process by accepting 1,248 of them on the payroll of SIDOR. The elimination of outsourcing became a Chavista rallying cry and was incorporated in the LOTTT in 2012. In short, the sequence of events involving the nationalization of SIDOR became a well-established pattern: rank-and-file mobilization, initial government indecision, followed by its unanticipated intervention contributing to the radicalization of the process of change, empowerment of nonprivileged sectors, and the formulation of new demands.

The proposal of workers' participation in decision making, which became a central trade-union demand in the Guayana region following the nationalization of SIDOR, gained momentum as a result of a combination of autonomous worker initiatives and state actions. For two weeks in May–June 2009, six hundred worker activists met with the ministers of planning and labor to draw up the "Plan Guayana Socialista" (PGS), consisting of mechanisms of worker input at the managerial level. President Chávez hailed the plan and called it a new stage in which "the workers will be more of a protagonist." The statement signaled a change in official discourse, which began to emphasize the special role of the working class in the revolutionary process in contrast to Chávez's previous thinking (Blanco Muñoz 1998, 392–93).

The PGS formulated specific proposals including the unification of upstream, downstream, and productive operations of the iron-steel and aluminum industries. With the aim of facilitating the proposed transformation, the national executive expropriated five companies, including the seamless-tube company Tavsa located within the installations of SIDOR, as well as Cerámicas Carabobo, which had recently closed down as a result of a prolonged worker conflict. Several large Venezuelan economic groups including Boulton, Cisneros, and Banco Mercantil had investments in the firms. The PGS also called for checks on the state company bureaucracy. Along these lines, Chávez expressed concern over management's failure to accept worker input and added that some company functionaries were "enemies" of the revolutionary process and that "it is necessary to defeat resistance to change," while recognizing that the issue had to be handled "with care and responsibility" (Chávez 2009, 20; Robertson 2012). In May 2010, Chávez accepted the nominations put forward by worker committees for the positions of president of the major state companies of the region. These "worker presidents" included engineer Carlos de Oliveira (a steel industry employee for thirty years who had participated in the PGS discussion group) to head SIDOR and longtime trade union activist Elio Sayago as president of ALCASA. In addition, worker committees (*mesas de trabajo*) were created for operational and administrative areas in each company.

Following the May 2010 appointments, the issue of workers' control led to sharp confrontations within the Chavista movement in the Guayana industrial region. The "worker presidents" of ALCASA, SIDOR, and other firms faced resistance from company managers, executives of the ministerial Corporación Venezolana de Guayana (CVG), and the Chavista governor of the state of Bolívar, all of whom paid lip service to the slogan of workers' control. Several issues were at stake and played out in ways in which the real motivations of key actors were difficult to determine. UNETE labor leaders, for instance, recognized that the banner of workers' control sometimes served as a pretext for opportunistic union leaders to insist on promotions for their clients and family members within the company.[5] Moderate Chavistas, on the other hand, viewed the demand for workers' control as a rhetorical ploy designed to shift attention away from the real objective of achieving inordinate economic benefits as well as the immediate elimination of outsourcing.

Other union militants argued that by opening company books for the purpose of scrutinizing managerial operations, workers' participation served as a corrective to ethically questionable practices of company bureaucrats. In SIDOR, for instance, UNETE trade unionists supported by de Oliveira accused the company's commercialization manager Luis Velásquez of purchasing metal rods at regulated prices and then selling them in neighboring Colombia at market value. Velásquez, whose alleged contraband activity undermined the government's program of mass housing construction initiated in 2011, was eventually jailed. Some claimed that politically influential individuals close to the state's Chavista governor were also involved in what became known as the "metal rod mafia."

Along similar lines, ALCASA president Elio Sayago accused the governor and various ministers of blocking workers' participation in his company and maintaining ties with company bureaucrats who negotiated contracts with multinational firms against the interests of the nation. Sayago attempted to carry out the PGS recommendation, which had been seconded by Chávez at the time, of reducing the export of non-elaborated raw materials in order to promote national economic development. With this goal in mind, he severed the futures contracts with multinational firms that were considered contrary to national interests. Sayago not only openly clashed with important Chavista figures at the state and national level but with members of Vera's faction within the labor movement, who in early 2011 called a thirty-four-day strike and on one occasion physically attacked him on company premises. During the conflict, Sayago was forced to reroute a protest march of pro-UNETE trade unionists and community members in order to avoid a violent confrontation with another concentration led by the union's secretary general, an ally of Vera who accused ALCASA of anti-union behavior.

CBST leaders in the Guayana region criticized UNETE and other dissident trade unionists for pressing for workers' participation without considering the critical conditions faced by state companies. Not only were international prices for certain exports depressed but the lack of a unified trade union command convinced company managers in some cases to refrain from collective bargaining following the expiration of worker contracts. In February 2012, in an attempt to overcome the discord in the Guayana industrial region, the national executive replaced Sayago with a close ally of the governor of Bolívar. Several months later, in the midst of militant protests of contracted workers demanding incorporation in SIDOR's payroll (even though some of them did not engage in permanent company functions), de Oliveira was also replaced. Sayago's removal was the second time that an ALCASA president committed to workers' participation was forced out of his position, the first being ex-guerrilla leftist theoretician Carlos Lanz, who Chávez had appointed in 2005 with the expressed purpose of promoting company democratization.

In spite of the intense internal conflict in the Guayana region, several basic objectives and concerns held the Chavista labor movement together. Most important, the Chavista trade unionists as a whole were receptive to Chávez's insistence that disruptions and paralysis of production in strategic sectors had to be avoided at all costs. In addition, both UNETE and CBST worker leaders in the region rejected the thesis of absolute union autonomy, originally put forward by Orlando Chirino, by recognizing the validity of political criteria. Both sides were also wary of the inroads made by the CTV and other opposition trade unionists. Furthermore, both Chavista groups converged in their support of certain worker demands, including the negotiation of collective bargaining agreements that had expired.

In August 2012, when Chávez met with workers of the Guayana region in an encounter that was broadcast live on all television channels, trade union spokespeople associated with the CBST insisted on immediate negotiations of worker contracts along with other demands. At the encounter, they were cheered on by rank-and-file Chavistas of the various internal currents, who at times disrupted the president. Chávez ended up accepting their demands at the meeting while insisting on responsible trade union leadership. One basic concern of the workers pertained to PDVSA management of the tube company Tavsa, even though it operated out of SIDOR. Tavsa trade unionists perceived that PDVSA (through its affiliate PDVSA Industrial) maintained a hard line toward collective bargaining and that SIDOR managers would be more accessible and receptive to worker demands.[6]

The promulgation of the LOTTT also put in evidence the convergence of CBST and UNETE leaders on major worker demands, even while the latter insisted on more radical provisions. The "retroactive" character of severance payments and other labor benefits incorporated in the LOTTT united Chavista labor leaders but had met resistance from moderate Chavista political leaders over a period of time (such as Luis Miquilena at the time of the 1999 Constitution's ratification). The initiatives for breaking the deadlock in the National Assembly over the proposed labor law came from the recently created CBST, which called on the president to pass it by executive decree. In December 2011, Chávez accepted the suggestion and created a sixteen-person presidential commission to draft the law, headed by Nicolás Maduro and taking in five other trade unionists (including Vera, Torrealba, and Rangel) all associated with the CBST. UNETE trade unionists appeared before the commission with specific proposals. Among the major worker gains were the restoration of the retroactive provision of the severance pay system, the elimination of outsourcing for ongoing activity to take effect within three years, reduction of the workweek from forty-four to forty hours, and an increase of postnatal paid leaves of absence from twelve to twenty weeks.

In spite of areas of similarity in the positions of the two confederations, the more radical measures favored by UNETE put in evidence differences that were generally more quantitative than qualitative. Thus, some UNETE leaders argued that the three-year period for the elimination of the practice of outsourcing was excessive. In contrast, CBST leaders insisted that the provision was only applicable to permanent work and thus criticized protests led by radical trade unionists that demanded the incorporation of workers in the company payroll even though their jobs were temporary in nature. UNETE also advocated a thirty-six-hour workweek, as Chávez had originally favored, on grounds that it would provide workers free time in order to prepare for assuming management responsibilities (Rodríguez 2012, 5; see also Lebowitz 2010, 133–36 and 155–57). In contrast, CBST trade unionists pointed out that not only did the LOTTT reduce the workweek by four hours but its Article 174 reaffirmed the goal spelled out in the constitution of "the progressive reduction of the work day."

The intensification of worker tension in SIDOR in 2013 and 2014 among trade unionists who at one point were identified with Chavismo demonstrated clearly that Maduro was less successful than his predecessor in reining in discontent members of his movement. Thus, for instance, trade unionists aligned with Chavismo controlled SUTISS at the outset of Maduro's presidency, but then some distanced themselves from the movement as a result of work stoppages over the signing of a new collective bargaining agreement to replace the one that had expired in 2010. Sharply different positions emerged during the conflicts. Maduro loyalists, including the CBST, equated the work stoppages with economic sabotage. During a trip to the region, National Assembly president Diosdado Cabello claimed that a "union mafia" in SIDOR was carrying out disruptive tactics to obtain excessive demands, a statement that the leftist PSUV faction Marea Socialista objected to as unfounded. Marea Socialista's worker group in SIDOR, Alianza Sindical, also divided over the issue. Two members belonging to the executive committee of SUTISS signed a collective bargaining agreement in August 2014, while others sided with the union's president and secretary general in refusing to recognize the contract's validity. Marea Socialista itself maintained a middle position that criticized union intransigence but also the failure of the signers of the new contract to consult the rank and file. The sharp divisions within SUTISS were rooted in the issue of whether to prioritize the interests of the workers or the well functioning of state companies. A related thorny issue was the union demand that the government inject sufficient capital to keep SIDOR afloat in light of the system of regulated prices that undermined the company's sustainability.

## CONCLUSION

Following the guerrilla period of the 1960s, various leftist groups assumed an intransigent position toward the government and political party leaderships. The intransigents put forward a critique of the consensus politics that privileged party elites at the expense of emerging social movements and brought Fedecámaras into the decision-making process, particularly on economic matters. The intransigent currents, which took in the Liga Socialista and Bandera Roja (both the results of a schism in AD in 1960) and "Ruptura" and the Causa R (both of which emerged from the PCV), maintained a presence on various fronts. In the labor movement, they achieved leadership positions in the steel and textile industries, where they raised the banner of trade union autonomy and lashed out at the AD-controlled CTV. For many years, some of the intransigents advocated electoral abstention. At the same time, the intransigent groups harshly criticized moderate leftists such as MAS on grounds that they benefited from forming part of the system and helping to legitimize it. Intransigents at national and local levels maintained contact with military rebels and, in some cases, participated in the coup attempts in 1992. Both before and after 1998, intransigents left their respective political organizations to join the Chavista party. After 1998, a significant number of them—proportionally much higher than those coming from other parties—played leadership roles in the Chavista movement and government.

The intransigent position of the pre-1998 years found expression during the Chávez presidency. In the first place, the government rejected consensus politics and for the most part refused to negotiate with or consult non-leftist political parties as well as Fedecámaras, even though it occasionally made concessions to business and the middle class. In the second place, after 1998, the Chavista labor leaders headed by Nicolás Maduro continued to raise the banner of labor autonomy, which they interpreted as signifying the need to completely break with the CTV. Following the creation of UNETE in 2003, the issue of trade union autonomy re-emerged but in different terms. The autonomists led by Marcela Máspero, while recognizing the validity of political criteria, argued that the failure to firmly defend workers' interests in both private and state-owned companies would open opportunities to opposition trade unionists. In contrast, the Chavistas who founded the CBST advocated the prioritization of political imperatives and pointed to the 2002–2003 general strike as evidence that the workers played an essential role in guaranteeing the survival of the government.

At first glance, certain features of the Chavista government and movement appeared to resemble populist experiences of the past and lend credibility to Chávez's critics, who characterize Chavismo as tantamount to crass populism (Castañeda 2006; Corrales 2011, 36–38). Most important, major decisions that challenged established interests came from above often in the form of an executive decree, as was the case with the LOTTT in 2012. Furthermore, its announcements often surprised the nation, thus reinforcing the notion that Chavismo was a "one-man show." In these situations, intermediate structures such as government bureaucracies or (in the case of the LOTTT) the National Assembly were left on the sidelines, and sometimes (as with the nationalization of SIDOR) various prominent government figures were discredited by the executive action.

This volume has been particularly concerned with institutional comparisons between the twenty-first-century left in power and its twentieth-century predecessors. In spite of similarities between Chavismo in office and AD in the period of radical populism in the 1940s (Ellner 2012b), the latter party was characterized by a greater degree of collective leadership. Political scientists who lauded Venezuelan democracy during the modern democratic period after 1958 pointed to AD's joint leadership (in contrast to the alleged *caudillismo* of populist parties such as the Peronists in Argentina and APRA in Peru) and the political system's institutionalization that established effective mechanisms to resolve conflicts (Alexander 1973, 20; Levine 1973; Collier and Collier 1991). AD's labor bureau contributed to this institutional strength by serving as a bridge between the party leadership and rank-and-file workers. Nevertheless, AD labor leaders hardly acted in an autonomous capacity, as they were tightly bound by party discipline and nearly always complied with decisions from above (Fagen 1977, 189–92).

The discussion in this chapter suggests that the Chavista-labor influence in decision making was no less pronounced than in the case of AD's labor bureau, as discussed previously. In doing so, the chapter questions the notion that in Venezuela the Chavista rank and file blindly followed a populist-type leader. The chapter shows that in spite of its fragmentation, the Chavista labor movement achieved a degree of organization at the national level, that it was highly mobilized over a lengthy period of time, and that important sectors (grouped in UNETE) maintained positions of critical support for the Chávez government. Furthermore, government actions did not occur in a vacuum, nor were they undertaken for purely electoral reasons, but were carried out in response to extended worker mobilization that in some cases led to violence. At the same time, however, the Chavista labor leaders privileged by the government and eventually grouped in the CBST lacked an autonomous stance in that they followed the party line, much as AD's labor bureau did over a period of decades.

The heterogeneity of the Chavista labor movement and the complexity of its relations with the Chávez government cast doubt on the applicability not only of simplistic notions of populism but also the simplistic dichotomy between "constituted power" and "constituent power" derived from the works of Antonio Negri and Michael Hardt. The latter concept has been employed by leftist critics (including the Trotskyist CMR) who characterize virtually the entire government (the "constituted power"), with the exception of Chávez himself, as counterrevolutionary and pitted against the popular sectors ("constituent power") (Woods 2008, 391–95). This framework would suggest that Chávez's inner circle, along with the CBST's national leadership, formed part of a monolithic bureaucratic bloc. Nevertheless, the CBST's leading role in the drafting of the LOTT, which the more radical UNETE applauded even while formulating specific criticisms, points to a more complex relationship. Indeed, the LOTT's reestablishment of the "retroactive" provision of severance payments had been resisted by more moderate sectors of the Chavista movement as far back as 1999, when the constitution of that year guaranteed its implementation. Thus, important differences existed within the Chavista national leadership. Furthermore, the decision in mid-2012 of the "Marea Socialista," a radical group within UNETE, to join the CBST in order to further Chavista unity runs counter to the notion that the two confederations corresponded to irreconcilable visions and interests. The Marea Socialista justified its decision on grounds that the new confederation took in important labor activists.

Charismatic leadership over time often leads to institutionalization, as Max Weber pointed out a century ago. Chávez's bout with cancer beginning in 2011 brought to the fore the issue of delegation of authority, the importance of which Chávez openly began to recognize (Ellner 2012a, 18). Under the Maduro government, the main question became not whether charismatic leadership will persist at the expense of institutionalization but the form that the latter will take, and specifically whether it will lead to greater internal democracy, pluralism, and open debate.

Institutionalization involves greater precision in the definition of the decision-making role of different branches and levels of the state sphere. The decisions themselves, however, can be reached either behind closed doors or on the basis of debate and input from below. Organizational solidity and linkages are requisites for the latter. A promising development in the Chavista movement dating back to 2003 was the holding of party primaries for the selection of candidates and party authorities. Chávez prohibited media campaign propaganda for primaries in order to ensure a level playing field. In the opposite vein, about 40 percent of the delegates to the PSUV's congress in July 2014 were superdelegates, thus reducing the effectiveness of the system of primaries. In general, Maduro as president was less inclined to side with the rank and file in opposition to higher spheres of decision making.

On the trade union front, the achievement of unity would have facilitated rank-and-file input in the Chavista movement and at the level of the state. Nevertheless, the acute conflict between UNETE and other dissidents, on the one hand, and the CBST, on the other, strengthens the case of those Chavista politicians who argue that subjective conditions for far-reaching change are not ripe and that top-down leadership is required, at least for the time being. The intense political polarization that characterized Venezuela during these years reinforced this position.

Chávez's governing style of relying heavily on the "constituted power" of state bureaucrats and party bosses, but also encouraging the movement's rank and file by accepting certain demands and promoting ongoing radicalization, suggested the coexistence of statist and bottom-up approaches. Under Maduro, the rank-and-file dissidents and radicals have occupied a more limited space within the Chavista movement. The state media has eliminated programs conducted by critical Chavistas, while a much weaker UNETE has drifted from the Chavista camp. Then again, the Maduro government has responded positively to some rank-and-file demands. Thus, for instance, in August 2013 the national executive replaced the president of the food company Industrias Diana, who the workers had accused of unethical conduct, and in so doing overrode the minister for alimentation. The government also expropriated a subsidiary of the U.S.-owned Clorox, which had been taken over by the workers after it left the country and announced its decision to sell off Venezuelan assets in September 2014.

Nevertheless, these actions by Maduro, like those of Chávez before him, were no substitute for the establishment of democratic mechanisms for ongoing participation as part of the institutionalization process. Within the Chavista movement, mechanisms such as the holding of party primaries and union elections in which Chavista candidates compete on a level playing field would not only contribute to the deepening of democracy but would ensure that greater institutionalization will largely be of a bottom-up as opposed to bureaucratic nature.

Chapter 9

# THE LABOR MOVEMENT AND THE EROSION OF NEOLIBERAL HEGEMONY

Brazil and Argentina

## JULIÁN GINDIN AND ADALBERTO CARDOSO

An attentive observer, from the beginning or middle of the twentieth century, would effortlessly realize that Brazil and Argentina have become more similar countries than ever. They resemble each other in terms of GDP per capita, urban population, and the share of wage-earning population (Fausto and Devoto 2004). Though significant differences remain, both countries have also become more alike in terms of social inequality, which over the course of the last forty years rose in Argentina and dropped in Brazil. Furthermore, of particular interest for this study, they have also grown more similar in terms of the capacity for union and working-class action (which is now stronger in Brazil than it used to be).

Both countries have also undergone analogous political processes, associated with first the hegemony, and later the erosion, of neoliberalism, as well as the consolidation of governments with strong linkages to social movements. The convergence between Argentina and Brazil can be recognized despite the fact that their labor markets, party systems, and labor union structures and traditions are still considerably different. This chapter describes the role of the labor movement in these processes. The main focus is on the political activity of the organized labor movement—unionism—and, in this context, its linkages with the party system.

The political activity of unionism is singularly important in Argentina and Brazil. These are countries where labor relations are legally regulated based on the idea of "social protection," in which the state figures as a mediator between capital and labor. How labor is employed (i.e., working hours, hiring and dismissal rules, protection to women and minors, etc.) as well as labor relations (representation and union organization) are strictly regulated by federal laws.

This means that the disputes and negotiations between capital and labor unfold according to the rules on work relations laid out by the state.

If we consider neoliberalism as an historical juncture, the study of organized labor must consider its legacies in terms of the following conditions: (1) the situation of the working class; (2) labor institutions and organizations often, but not exclusively, coded in the union structure and legislation; and (3) politics, that is, the relations between organized labor and political parties and the state. These legacies influenced the contexts in which the labor movement acted, pressured, and struggled, which in turn motivated the governments elected in 2002 and 2003 to promote policies aimed at improving the situation of workers and strengthening unionism.

This chapter reconstructs these legacies over a period spanning from 2002 to 2012. During that period, the labor movement has become stronger as an institutional actor and as a representative of the interests of workers in the bargaining process with the state and the employers. Moreover, fomenting linkages with the labor movement has been important both for the Partido dos Trabalhadores (PT) in Brazil and for Kirchnerismo in Argentina, albeit for different reasons. In Brazil, the origins of the PT are in the labor movement, and many cadres of the PT government also began as labor movement militants. In Argentina, the labor movement's support was crucial in the institutional reconstruction process that followed in the wake of the 2001–2002 crisis. Be that as it may, neither governments in Brazil nor Argentina invested in the creation of a unionism "of their own" as a mobilized support base.

Significant changes in the political alignment of unions also occurred. In Brazil, almost all of the left-wing ranks of the Central Única dos Trabalhadores (CUT) abandoned the organization, while the union that traditionally vied with the CUT to represent workers (Força Sindical, FS) became closer to it and became a relatively autonomous and pragmatic unionist actor, feebly linked to the party system (a new phenomenon in Brazil). In Argentina, unions affiliated with the Movimiento de los Trabajadores Argentinos (MTA), traditional opponents of neoliberalism, were able to block a more pragmatic unionism that collaborated with neoliberals and for some time headed the powerful Confederación General del Trabajo (CGT). Moreover, between 2002 and 2008, the two main labor centrals (the CGT and the Central de los Trabajadores Argentinos, CTA), which in the recent past had been rivals, were allies of Kirchnerismo. However, between 2009 and 2012, the MTA disintegrated and important CTA and CGT unions broke with Kirchnerism. In what follows we will discuss these in detail.

## LABOR AND THE FIRST INCORPORATION

### Argentina

Juan Domingo Perón became secretary of labor in 1943 and president of Argentina from 1946 to 1955. He encountered a largely urbanized working class and a highly consolidated organized labor movement, especially in comparison to other Latin American countries (Roxborough 1994). Perón mobilized workers and leaned on them for political support, in what Collier and Collier (1991) have called "a party incorporation model," in which the labor movement is politically mobilized.

Perón's labor relations and union-organization laws recognized rights demanded by union cadres and leaders, among them the protection of union representatives in the workplace. At the same time, they established mechanisms of control, such as the requirement of union recognition by the administrative authority (via the *personería gremial*). National level unions organized by the economic sector that possessed organizational and economic resources guaranteed by the state, or union federations capable of controlling their member unions, became the major actors in the organized labor movement.

Perón was overthrown in 1955, and government after government tried, to no avail, to dismantle the labor movement. In fact, it regrouped during Perón's exile, consolidating itself as a strong and disciplined organization capable of centralizing its negotiations, in which the creation of a nationwide union-owned health system (the Obras Sociales[1]) played an important role. The movement became relatively autonomous both from Perón and the Partido Justicialista (PJ), created by Perón. Although generically identified with Peronism, different traditions consolidated within the organized labor movement: one confrontational, one pro-negotiation, and one participationist (which is, ultimately, even more willing to negotiate with other parties).

The military dictatorship (1976–1983) controlled unionism strictly and violently repressed more radical leaders. As a result, in the transition to democracy, the union movement was "purified" from a large faction of its more active members. Even so, both emerging and traditional leaders concentrated efforts to reorganize the labor movement. Despite the labor movement's protagonist role in democratization, it was politically defeated in the 1983 presidential elections because, for the first time, the Unión Cívica Radical (UCR) defeated Peronism in presidential elections. As a result, unionism positioned itself as opposition to the government, consolidating its presence in the PJ and confronting the Raúl Alfonsín government (1983–1989) with strikes and mobilizations. One of the main (positive) outcomes of the period was the ratification of the union legislation in 1988, one of Perón's legacies.

## Brazil

Unlike Argentina, in Brazil worker organizations were in dire condition on the eve of the 1930 revolution, which brought Vargas to power (Gomes 1988) and did not offer resistance to Vargas's project of controlling the labor movement. The authoritarian legislation instituted by Vargas, especially the syndical act of 1939 (which would remain in force without modification until 1988), converted unions into agents of the state among urban workers, characterized by Collier and Collier (1991) as "state incorporation, without working class mobilization" with a clear authoritarian bent. The government provided organizational and financial resources to centralized unions according to category of activity but built a geographically fragmented structure that favored municipal or intermunicipal organizations.

After this phase of authoritarian incorporation, Vargas and his main political heir, João Goulart (nicknamed Jango), politicized ties to the urban labor movement, which became the supporting base of the Partido Trabalhista Brasileiro (PTB) during the presidential terms of Vargas (1950–1954) and Jango (1961–1964). In this democratic interregnum, from 1945 to 1964, unionism strengthened despite many constraints. After 1950, it became the main social force in Brazil, capable of pressuring the political system to address social issues and demanding further democratization via redistributive reforms (Lobo 2010; Leal 2011). Meanwhile, peasants started organizing and mobilizing, thereby becoming important political actors just before the military coup.[2] Their linkages to the clandestine Partido Comunista do Brasil (PCB) and to the PTB, a coalition that became virtually hegemonic in the workers' movement (Santana 2001), greatly strengthened the political left. This process was interrupted by the military regime (1964–1985).

A number of factors during the military regime set the stage for a profound process of union renovation. These included a renewed (by mass rural-urban migration) working class that lacked strong political identities, highly selective repression during the dictatorship, a long cycle of industrial growth, and a relatively weak labor organizational structure. Ironically, when social agitation rekindled toward the end of the 1970s, workers were able to use Vargas-era labor laws for organizational purposes. This helps explain why the labor movement grew so rapidly in the 1980s, founding its own political party in 1980 (the PT) and two federations of union centrals in 1983. The new unionism formed the CUT and the old unionism created the Coordenação Nacional da Classe Trabalhadora (CONCLAT), later renamed Confederação Geral dos Trabalhadores (CGT), in 1986 (Seidman 1994; Sluyter Beltrão 2010).

Unionism was a more relevant protagonist in the democratization of Brazil than in Argentina. The new federal constitution (1988) recognized some of the grievances of the "new unionism," such as allowing the creation of union centers, freeing unions from the control of the state, and authorizing union organization in the public sector. Moreover, the most important union leader, Lula da Silva, a PT leadership, entered the 1989 presidential elections as a viable candidate.

## NEOLIBERAL HISTORICAL JUNCTURE

### Argentina

In 1989, the PJ returned to power with Carlos Menem and, contrary to his campaign promises, Menem immediately launched a program of privatization of public enterprises, passed a new employment law, and implemented an economic stabilization plan that significantly curbed inflation. These policies, notwithstanding the high levels of unemployment and de-industrialization they caused, bolstered popular support for Menem during the entire decade (see Rossi and Ostiguy and Schneider in this volume; also Cardoso and Gindín 2009).

In this context, for the first time during a Justicialista/Peronist government, the CGT divided into two factions, the CGT Azopardo and the CGT San Martín, which aligned with the government. Menem took advantage of this split. He appointed union leaders who supported him, such as Jorge Triaca, to head the Ministry of Labor. More importantly, he negotiated concessions with unions of economic sectors targeted by reform, opening up space for unions to participate in new businesses, creating the Aseguradoras de Riesgos de Trabajo and Administradoras de Fondos de Jubilaciones y Pensiones (Murillo 2001; Etchemendy 2001).

Confrontational Peronist unionism, which had its moment in the 1980s, was the major loser in the first years of the Menem government. Saúl Ubaldini, an important leader of the CGT in the 1980s, failed in his attempt to become governor of the province of Buenos Aires in 1991. In 1992, confrontationists and collaborationists realized that reunification was crucial for the CGT and called for a general strike in order to negotiate (from a strong position) the anti-unionist aspects of Menem's political project. In 1994, confrontationist Peronist unionism created the MTA, an internal strand of the CGT, with the goal of heading the union central. It had significant clout in the powerful transport sector.

Significantly, not all of Ubaldini's followers rejoined the CGT in 1992. One segment, with a significant role in public sector unionism (the teachers of the

Confederación de Trabajadores de la Educación de Argentina, CTERA, and
the Asociación de Trabajadores del Estado, ATE public servants), launched
an unprecedented project: they created a union central parallel to the CGT,
the CTA. This project lured leading cadres from other political traditions not
aligned to the various strands of the CGT.

As the regressive effects of neoliberal policies became clearer and Menemismo lost hegemony, Menemista unionism shrunk within the CGT. This
sparked competition for leadership of the CGT between pragmatists and confrontationists. Despite tensions, the two factions collaborated to limit Menem's neoliberal program, and in 1996 they organized three general strikes.

The political alignment of organized labor also changed. The confrontationist MTA, strongly identified with Peronism and possessing a solid
union project, strengthened politically as Menemista hegemony deteriorated.
During this process, it distanced itself from the PJ, and the vacuum created
was not filled. In this process, the participation of unionists in the PJ lists for
legislative elections has declined continuously since 1980, a trend that accelerated in the 1990s (Levitsky 2003). In this context, the labor movement became
more autonomous in relation to the PJ, although its structural links to the
state remained intact.

The CTA burned its bridges with the PJ when it founded a new political
movement: the Frente Grande. As detailed in Ostiguy and Schneider's chapter in this volume, in 1995 it joined forces with other anti-neoliberal political
groups to create the Frente País Solidario (FREPASO), which became the main
opposition to Menem. In 1997, the FREPASO struck an alliance with the UCR,
forming the Alianza. In 1999, the Alianza's UCR candidate, Fernando De la
Rúa, won the presidential elections. Thus, it was the CTA, a minority force
within unionism, that most capitalized on the political opportunities opened
by the opposition to Menemismo (see Gindin 2008, for the case of CTERA).

De la Rúa, however, upheld Menem's programs. Once again, the CGT divided into an "official" CGT, headed by pragmatic union leaders, and a "rebellious" CGT, led by Hugo Moyano of the MTA. The "rebellious" CGT organized five general strikes against De la Rúa's government, which was reeling
from a rapidly deteriorating economy. The government collapsed in December 2001 when, as detailed by Rossi in this volume, a multiclass opposition,
with the participation of the worker centrals, rose up against it. The end result
of this process was paradoxical. When social mobilization liquidated the political opposition to Menemismo, it partially revived the PJ, particularly its
anti-Menemista factions (Maneiro 2012).

The economic debacle that led to De la Rúa's downfall was, in large measure, caused by die-hard defense of the Argentine peso to the U.S. dollar

parity, a pillar of the neoliberal economic program. When Eduardo Duhalde (PJ) became president in the midst of a profound recession, the situation
in Argentina was critical. Duhalde took two measures that restored stability
in government-labor relations. For one, at the beginning of 2002 he ended
currency parity. This caused an uptick in employment over the following
semesters. It also caused inflation and, thus, constant bargaining to maintain wage levels. Concomitantly, Duhalde, appointed Alfredo Atanasof
(from the Confederación de Obreros y Empleados de la República Argentina, COERA, a public sector union) as minister of labor, followed by Graciela
Camaño, the wife of Luis Barrionuevo (the Unión de Trabajadores del Turis-
mo, Hoteleros y Gastronómicos de la República Argentina, UTGHRA, food-
service-workers' union). The COERA and the UTGHRA were unions of
the official CGT. Meanwhile, Moyano called for a general strike against the
Duhalde government in May 2002. It was unsuccessful because the union
movement as a whole was more concerned with the country's political and
economic stability and was aligned with the government, profiting from the
government's inability to enforce its positions in wage bargaining. Thus, the
political force of the CGT in this phase did not derive from economic growth
or the strengthening of syndical actions within enterprises at first but rather
from its key role in the stabilization of the political and economic situation
during the peak of the crisis.

An evaluation of the neoliberal period of 1989–2002 suggests that, in part
due to the labor movement's ability to pressure, modifications of the labor
legislation were moderated, and the framework for collective negotiation and
the structure of unionism did not change until 2000 (Cook 2006). However, changes in labor relations were not necessarily "moderated." Enterprises
enacted so-called "cold" labor norm flexibilization, which frequently meant
simply not complying with the law, something unionism was not capable of
limiting significantly.

## Brazil

After the 1989 presidential elections, Fernando Collor de Mello initiated neoliberal reforms in Brazil with privatizations, labor law flexibilization, anti-
labor discourse and practices, criticism of public services, inflexibility in
bargaining major worker conflicts, and subordination to U.S. foreign policy.
During Collor de Mello's administration, the most significant, pragmatically
oriented anti-CUT sectors were incorporated in the Ministry of Labor (1989)
and the FS was founded, which became the second most important union
organization in Brazil (Cardoso 1999; Trópia 2004). Collor de Mello offered
union leaders channels of participation in neoliberal programs and also of-

fered them concessions during the privatization process, such as stock partnership in privatized companies previously controlled by CUT unions, many of which were conquered by FS in subsequent elections.

Collor de Mello's presidency ended in impeachment. It was followed by the transitional government of Itamar Franco and new elections, from which Fernando Henrique Cardoso emerged as the winner. Thus, as seen in greater detail in Ostiguy and Schneider's chapter, two political coalitions consolidated in the 1990s: one led by the Partido da Social Democracia Brasileira (PSDB) identified with Cardoso, and the other led by the PT, which, after defeats in 1994 and 1998, elected Lula president in 2002.

As in the Argentinean case, one of the keys of the consensus reached by Cardoso was economic stabilization (the "Real Plan" of 1994), the implementation of which he coordinated as minister of finance in Franco's government. This won Cardoso the prestige that elected him president. As in Argentina, the plan was well received by the working class due to economic stabilization and the end of hyperinflation. However, a mood of rejection followed when commercial liberalization led to deindustrialization and unemployment (Cardoso 2003, 2004).

Cardoso began his government by imposing a political defeat in 1995 on striking oil workers, a category that was one of the supporting pillars of the CUT. He then attracted FS to the neoliberal project, even without formally incorporating it into the government. Partially for this reason, but also because economic policies were undermining the FS's worker base, this union central eventually adopted a more critical attitude. It participated in a general strike in 1996 and, starting in 1999 (when the "Real Plan" collapsed), it organized some joint campaigns with the CUT, including in the automobile industry (Trópia 2004). Although the government retained the political initiative, openly campaigning against the established union structure and the Consolidation of Labor Laws (CLT)—the main legacies of Vargas—it could not prevail. The legal basis of the labor relations' system was not modified, and the government limited itself to implementing a few reforms aimed at flexibilization (Vogel 2010).

The CUT organized broad political campaigns against neoliberal policies. However, it suffered important setbacks in collective bargaining. In fact, concession bargaining prevailed in shop-floor and work-organization reforms (Cardoso 2004; Sluyter-Beltrão 2010), which deepened divisions within the CUT, where there was an important and active leftist opposition.

It should be underscored that Brazilian union leaders are more willing than their Argentinean counterparts to abandon unionism to strengthen the political projects in which they participate by becoming federal deputies. In part, this was due to the union structure (which does not favor the consolida-tion of powerful national unions) and to the very political project elaborated by "new unionism" in the 1980s. The PT offered increasing opportunities to union cadres who devoted themselves exclusively to political activities. This was because over the course of the decade their legislative presence had in-creased and the party won municipal elections in several important cities (such as São Paulo from 1989 to 1993, Porto Alegre from 1989 to 2005, and Belo Horizonte from 1993 to 1997). They had also done well in state guberna-torial elections (as in the Federal District from 1995 to 1999, and Rio Grande do Sul from 1999 to 2003). Meanwhile, the leaders of FS also pursued political careers of their own, as in the case of Luiz Antonio de Medeiros and Paulo Pereira da Silva

It is worth noting that Cardoso abandoned currency-exchange parity in 1999, well before the PT won the presidency in 2002. This fact, in addition to weak opposition to the Lula government and the relatively minor damages (compared to Argentina) caused by neoliberalism, explains the image of con-tinuity, from the standpoint of economic policy, between the Cardoso and Lula administrations. Indeed, the labor movement, by the end of Cardoso's government, benefited from a more favorable economic, social, and political context than Argentinean unionism in 2001–2002. The opposition spearhead-ed by Lula, himself a product of "new unionism," was clearly a viable political alternative.

## LEGACIES OF THE NEOLIBERAL HISTORICAL JUNCTURE

### Argentina

A first legacy of neoliberalism concerns its labor market effects—that is, in the very structure of the working class. In Argentina, unemployment was partic-ularly high. Moreover, when employment expanded, it was in traditionally nonunionized sectors or in conditions in which class organization faced more obstacles. The privatization of important public enterprises whose employees had formed powerful unions (telecommunications, oil, steel, transportation, and electricity) entailed significant layoffs. These conditions caused a diminu-tion of workers, the fragmentation of collective demands, and less bargaining leverage for unions. In the 1940s and 1950s, in a country with a relatively high rate of urbanization and of a salaried workforce, the labor movement was practically the exclusive representative of the popular classes. The only successful attempt to unify unionism struggles with those of the movement of unemployed people, the *piqueteros*, was led by the CTA, a minor yet highly politically active central federation (see Rossi's chapter in this volume). For its part, the CGT kept its distance from the *piqueteros* in which the left, a declared enemy of traditional unionism, dominated.

A second legacy of neoliberalism refers to trade union organizations per se. As stressed previously, there were no major changes in the trade union legislation, and the rate of unionization of salaried workers dropped slightly. However, there were relevant internal changes. Some of the main traditional organizations—steel and railway workers—shrank, whereas others boomed, such as those in commerce, food services (*gastronómicos*), truck drivers, and teachers. The power injected into these organizations had a direct impact on the internal disputes around the centralization of the union structure. The outcome was that the commerce workers', truck drivers', teachers', and *gastronómicos'* federations gained substantial power within the labor movement.

In general, then, although the presence and leverage of firm-based unionism diminished (Novick 2003), it still remained stronger than in Brazil. Unionism by the end of the 1990s had become more bureaucratized, more dependent upon services, and (in general terms) more distanced from its rank and file. These factors led some union leaders to downplay their roles as channels for workers' grievances and in some cases to evolve into "entrepreneurial unionism."

A third legacy is political. It concerns the linkages of unionism with the party system. Unions that founded the "rebellious" CGT (and particularly the MTA), hewing to their Peronist identity, strained their ties to the PJ. Concomitantly, the failure of the Alianza reduced the political weight of the CTA and increased internal tensions. In global terms, there is no doubt neoliberalism strained the relationship of unionism with the party system, furthering its autonomist proclivities (see Ostiguy and Schneider in this volume).

## Brazil

With respect to the legacies of neoliberalism in Brazil, unemployment more than doubled in the period, and eight in every ten new jobs created between 1996 to 2002 were informal jobs. There was also a significant "migration" of manufacturing jobs to the country's hinterland and, as in Argentina where employment increased, it was in sectors with no union tradition or in those with significant obstacles to the organization of class action. These developments were particularly dramatic for some central actors in the labor movement (Trópia 2004).

Unlike Argentina, in Brazil the ties between unions and social movements were far more resistant. This was basically due to the existence of the CUT (heir to the struggles of the 1980s) and its links with the PT, the MST, and almost all the opposition to neoliberalism. As Rossi's chapter in this volume analyzes in greater depth, more radical groups, both within and beyond unionism, acted in Brazil as the leftist flank of this anti-neoliberal front, particularly the MST.

The share of the unionized wage-earning population remained stable, at roughly 20 percent, but, as in the Argentinean case, there were major changes in the internal composition of affiliates. Civil servant unions grew as well as those in some services sectors—such as food and catering. It is interesting to point out that the commerce workers' union in São Paulo, after leading a split from the FS, currently heads the third largest central federation in the country. Fragmentation increased due to economic and organizational incentives in a system the state lost control over after 1988. The number of unions grew, while the number of those unionized remained stable as a proportion of the economically active population. The more important unions diversified their activities and services rendered to their members as a response to this adverse situation. They focused on the consolidation of union leaders and on the process of institutionalization of the "new unionism." Both the FS and the CUT were legally recognized, consolidated their bureaucratic structures, and became participants of several state agencies or tripartite bodies, such as the Conselho Curador do Fundo de Amparo ao Trabalhador (FAT).

The main legacy of neoliberalism was bolstering the PT as an arena of militancy and as the political project of the CUT unionism. Indeed, the CUT faced widespread competition within the realm of unionism, which hindered its advancement. First, CUT unionism was never successful in replicating the experience of the metalworkers' union from the São Paulo industrial belt in terms of shop-floor presence, union participation, and so forth. The attempt to convert the metalworkers' federation into the main centralized entity for the representation of the interests of this industrial segment at the national level failed, partially due to internal fissures and partially due to the advances of the FS. Second, the ABC metalworkers, the source of the CUT, faced a particularly difficult juncture in the 1990s. Automobile manufacturers managed to place workers under the menacing threat of productive reconversion, fiscal competition, and loss of productivity—a true sword of Damocles. Third, the CUT's major project of tripartite social dialogue—the sectoral chambers— were only successful in the case of the ABC automobile industry, eventually dismantled during the Cardoso administration (Cardoso and Comin 1995; Rodriguez 2002). Lastly, despite the CUT's success in attracting most union filiations between 1992 and 2001, and although it remained either the prevalent or the only central in several sectors, the FS consolidated. In reality, the FS expanded, in relative terms, more than the CUT, shedding its almost strictly anti-CUT stance and presenting itself as a serious competitor in manufacturing, commerce, and services.[3] It is important to mention that while the main

Brazilian central federations tended toward political convergence, given the CUT's moderation and the FS's abandonment of its strict neoliberal positions, the CUT left-wing strands became gradually more isolated.

So, in Argentina and Brazil, neoliberalism meant only partial disincorporation, mostly due to two labor market effects of neoliberal policies: unemployment and informality. Since most workers' rights are employment related, to be out of a formal job is to face social and economic oblivion. Politically, disincorporation was also partial for portions of the labor movement, with other sectors allied with neoliberal incumbents that benefited from some of its policies.

## AFTER NEOLIBERALISM: A NEW POLITICAL CONTEXT FOR UNION ACTION

### Argentina

The Kirchner government came to power in 2003 facing two clear challenges: to consolidate economic recovery and to reconstitute the country's institutions. Straying from his own political history (as a former ally of Menemismo) and his political allegiance to Duhalde (who enabled his election), Kirchner stepped in with a sharp anti-neoliberal discourse, calling for a break with the 1990s. Kirchnerismo strengthened in 2005 by defeating Duhalde in legislative elections and by electing Néstor Kirchner's wife, Cristina Fernández, president in 2007 and in 2011. As discussed further in Ostiguy and Schneider's chapter, Kirchnerismo constitutes, along with Menemismo, the most successful political project of Peronism after the death of Perón. It partially revived the tradition of the Peronist left, defeated in the 1970s, by constructing an epic narrative of ruptures with neoliberalism. It incorporated—with relative success according to context—leading figures from other political parties and limited the field of action for the non-Peronist center-left that had consolidated in opposition to Menemismo.

The social movements that challenged neoliberalism never made it to the center of the political arena, as in Brazil, although they were partially incorporated by the government. As Rossi (in this volume) elaborates, the "social question" they brought to the fore was minimized because its social base was undermined, in part due to universal social assistance policies administrated by the state, but more fundamentally because of the expansion of salaried employment. Unemployment indeed dropped significantly, although the proportion of unregistered jobs remained high. Besides the promotion of registered, formal jobs, the government also promoted real minimum wage increases. The real value of the minimum wage–which declined in the 1980s[4]–recovered tangibly (doubling in 2006–2007 if compared to 1990). This growth served as

TABLE 9.1. Evolution of minimum wage, average overall wages, and average wages in manufacturing, Argentina, 2000–2010

| Year | Minimum wage | Real average wages | Wages in manufacturing |
|------|-------------|--------------------|------------------------|
| 2000 | 100.0 | | 100.0 |
| 2001 | 101.1 | | 98.4 |
| 2002 | 81.3 | 100.0 | 79.4 |
| 2003 | 84.0 | 105.0 | 85.9 |
| 2004 | 129.8 | 114.7 | 104.3 |
| 2005 | 171.1 | 123.2 | 114.8 |
| 2006 | 193.2 | 134.2 | 129.9 |
| 2007 | 219.6 | 146.4 | 145.5 |
| 2008 | 253.3 | 159.2 | 167.9 |
| 2009 | 292,0 | 177.9 | |
| 2010 | 321.2 | 200.8 | |

*Note*: Average wages: Registered workers in the private sector (2002 = 100). The official inflation index in Argentina released by the INDEC has been discredited since 2007. The chart overestimates the growth in real salaries after this year.

*Source*: Panorama Laboral 2009 and 2011 (International Labor Organization).

a baseline, enabling segments with better abilities to apply pressure and obtain gains that are even more significant. Table 9.1 shows the evolution of salary-related indicators during Kirchnerista governments.

Growth in terms of employment and minimum wage was highly welcomed by society, particularly the labor movement, contrasting with the rampant unemployment of the 1990s as well as the 2001–2002 crises. The recuperation of living standards for workers must, however, be seen in historical perspective. A significant portion of the working class had once lived in times of better wages, public services, and living standards (or at least could draw a comparison to the generation of their parents). This was not the case in Brazil.

Both in Brazil and Argentina, the growth of employment, and particularly registered employment, entails automatic effects on other labor institutions (as coverage defined by collective conventions and the social security system) and activates a series of labor and social rights that render the worker more visible to the state and affords him or her some socioeconomic security. This is what Palomino (2008) called a "labor mechanism," which also favors union action as it increases institutional revenues and the number of workers represented. So the labor market is still a very powerful incorporation institution in these countries.

TABLE 9.2. Evolution of formal employment in the private sector, Argentina, 1997, 2002, and 2012

|  | Primary activities | Industry | Electricity, gas, and water | Construction | Commerce | Services | Total | Evolution (1997=100) |
|---|---|---|---|---|---|---|---|---|
| 1997 | 310,536 | 965,777 | 45,110 | 249,501 | 587,388 | 1,607,362 | 3,714,254 | 100 |
| 2002 | 284,125 | 753,293 | 46,882 | 125,378 | 581,063 | 1,707,825 | 3.498,566 | 94 |
| 2012 | 431,436 | 1,280,345 | 60,762 | 452,504 | 1,128,261 | 2,961,207 | 6,314,515 | 170 |

Source: Boletín Trimestral de Empleo Registrado. Tercer trimestre 2012. Observatorio de Empleo y Dinámica Empresarial, Ministerio de Trabajo y Seguridad Social.

Table 9.2 shows the evolution of formal employment in the private sector. It compares the last year of the 1990s with economic growth (1997), the year with the worst economic performance (2002), and the situation in 2012 ten years after the currency devaluation and after nine years of Kirchnerismo. Further calculations from the figures in the table show that manufacturing employment, despite significant growth between 1997 and 2012 in absolute terms, fell as a proportion of the total number of registered workers, from 26 percent (1997) to 21.5 percent (2002) and 20.2 percent (2012). The decline occurred in a context of impressive expansion of salaried formal jobs. The sectors with the highest relative growth were construction (highly sensitive to economic fluctuation) and commerce (which almost doubled between 2002 and 2012).

Full recovery of the "labor mechanism" strengthened unionism amid a context of new internal shifts aimed at boosting industrial employment. Some emblematic organizations of Argentinean unionism—which had lost strength—such as the Unión Obrera Metalúrgica (UOM), were back on the scene (Collier and Etchemendy 2007). Union membership seems to have increased, although there is no available information for long-term comparisons. Different studies on enterprises employing more than ten workers, in 2000 and 2006, provide estimates of membership rates in this segment that range between 37 and 40 percent (Aspiazu and Waisgrais 2007).

The reactivation of collective bargaining has been considered one of the most relevant phenomena in recent labor relations, in view of the number of signed agreements and the return of bargaining by economic sectors. This bargaining focuses on levels of wage recovery but also involves other aspects—such as ensuring contributions toward unions or issues relating to work organization (CTA 2005; Cardoso and Gindin 2009, 57). Collective bargaining by sector of activity is stimulated, coordinated, and ultimately approved by government (which can eventually reject an agreement and render it null).

The combination of a centralized union structure and collective bargaining by sector historically conducted by the Ministry of Labor, a centralist and president-centered political tradition, and Kirchnerismo's hegemony in the provinces and in Congress, all contributed to augmenting the federal government's power in the realm of union action and in the dynamics of collective bargaining. They also strengthened the direct relationship between the executive branch and the labor movement.

However, there were also new tensions and strains. Economic growth, the existence of a solid union structure, the return of inflation, and higher formal employment rates created a context favorable to rank-and-file mobilization. Politically motivated union action expanded, resulting in nationwide conflicts within some economic sectors, in the increase of union organization in firms, and in a generational transition in unionism (still quite invisible among leading figures but evident at the base of the movement).

### Kirchnerismo and the Union Movement

Kirchnerismo followed an orthodox policy toward unions, in the sense that it strove to guarantee the economic and organizational resources that empower unions. Carlos Tomada, a lawyer with a negotiator profile who had previously worked for some large unions, was appointed minister of labor. The controversial labor reform of 2000 was repealed with the approval of the 2004 Ley de Ordenamiento Laboral (25877/04). Kirchnerismo also exploited disputes among unions by favoring factions that would support the status quo, a necessary condition to avoid a clash with the labor movement at large.

The renovation of the union cadres was by and large channeled and controlled within traditional structures, although the majority did not become full-blown Kirchnerista militants. At the same time, most union leaders did not identify with the political discourse of the Peronist left (promoted by segments of the government) and seemed to be more at ease in ideological terms with traditional Peronism. As a result, more decidedly pro-Kirchnerismo social organizations were formed beyond the scope of unionism, such as social and students' organizations.

The class-based left grew, configuring the more legitimate processes of union renovation thus far. However, it has only become a consolidated opposition in some sectors.[5] In this process, class-based unionism seems to have reassumed the role it played in the 1980s—however, this time in a different context, because contemporary unionism is, in general, more bureaucratic and dependent on internal control mechanisms than it was in the period of union normalization in the 1980s. The most eloquent case of this renovation—and of the conservatism of Kirchnerismo unionism—is that of subway workers in

Buenos Aires. Usually represented by the UTA, workers clashed with union leaders and decided to create a union of their own. The UTA, the government, and the subway company tried to no avail to thwart the workers, and the government ultimately was forced to partially recognize the new union. Still, the workers were not granted *personería gremial* (legal recognition), and the UTA remains the legal representative of this category (Montes Cató and Ventrici 2011).

From the standpoint of the relationship between unionism and the political system, the main issue is the political alignment of the large union organizations. Some comments built upon table 9.3, which lists the fifteen main unions in Argentina: First, considering leadership, ten organizations replaced their main leaders in the period from 2002 to 2012. In five of these cases, the change was prompted by either the death or illness of leaders (Sindicato de Mecánicos y Afines del Transporte Automotor, SMATA, Unión Obrera Metalúrgica, UOM, Asociación Obrera Textil, AOT) or by the imprisonment of others, convicted of crimes (UF, Asociación Bancaria). With the partial exceptions of the UTA, COERA, and the Asociación Bancaria, political continuity was not interrupted by leadership changes. The second observation refers to union structure. Although some federations fragmented in the last two decades and operate in the same manner as the Brazilian federations (federations of unions, with different political perspectives), this is not the case of the most important ones (truck drivers, FTIA, Federación de Empleados de Comercio y Servicios, FAECYS), which remain cohesive and unitarian. A third relevant feature refers to the so-called sector shifts. The traditional Unión Ferroviaria lost thousands of affiliates as a result of privatization. Manufacturing unions such as the UOM and the AOT recovered some of the importance they had lost during the 1990s. The Sindicato Argentino de Docentes Particulares (SADOPD), COERA, CTERA, and FAECYS grew. The truck drivers' federation, the Unión Argentina de Trabajadores Rurales y Estibadores (UATRE), and the UTGHRA became more important than they had ever been. In general terms, the same organizations have been dominating unionism for more than thirty years.

Among the leading figures belonging to these unions who displayed more incisive political intervention were Peronists Hugo Moyano (truck drivers), Luis Barrionuevo (UTGHRA), and Gerónimo Venegas (UATRE). These unions offer political leaders the economic resources and a disciplined contingent of midlevel cadres—in some cases covering a large territory. These figures (particularly Moyano) are also capable of mobilizing the rank and file. However, their power is coextensive and limited to the power of the organizations they lead; union leaders are not leaders "of the people" or of social movements.

TABLE 9.3. Unionist organizations in Argentina (March 2013)

| Organization | Structure and leadership | Union central |
|---|---|---|
| Federación de Camioneros (truck drivers and logistic workers) | Federation. Supported by a large union active in the city and province of Buenos Aires. Directed by Hugo Moyano since 1992. | CGT Azopardo |
| COERA (municipal public servants) | A confederation of local unions, it is the second-largest union organization in terms of membership. Amadeo Genta (city of Buenos Aires) has headed the union since 2007. Previously headed by Alfredo Atanasof (province of Buenos Aires). | CGT Azopardo |
| Asociación Bancaria (bank workers) | Nationwide union. José Zanola (president of bank workers since 1983) was arrested in 2009. The second in the chain of command, Sergio Palazzo, replaced him. | CGT Azopardo |
| UATRE (rural and ports' workers) | Nationwide union since 1988 (previously a federation). It has been led since 1991 by Gerónimo Venegas. | CGT Azopardo |
| FAECYS (trades and services) | Federation of local unions It is the largest union. Headed since the 1990s by Armando Cavallieri, member of the city of Buenos Aires union. | CGT Alsina |
| UOM (metalworkers) | Nationwide union. Antonio Caló has headed the union since 2004, following the death of Lorenzo Miguel (2002), who had headed the union since 1970. | CGT Alsina |
| SMATA (auto workers) | Nationwide union. Ricardo Pignarelli has headed the union since 2011, following the death of José Rodriguez (2009), who had headed the union since 1973. | CGT Alsina |
| UOCRA (construction workers) | Nationwide union. Headed by Gerardo Martínez since 1990. | CGT Alsina |

| Organization | Structure and leadership | Union central |
|---|---|---|
| UF (railway workers) | Nationwide union. Sergio Sasia has headed the union ever since the arrest of José Pedraza (the leader since 1983), in 2011. | CGT Alsina |
| UTA (bus and subway drivers) | Nationwide union. Juan Manuel Palacios sat as the union's director from 1984 to 2006. Since then the UTA is led by Roberto Fernández. | CGT Alsina |
| SADOP (private sector teachers) | Nationwide union. Headed by Horacio Ghilini (1995–2011) and then by Mario Almirón since 2011. | CGT Alsina |
| AOT (textile workers) | Nationwide union. Headed by Pedro Goyeneche (1984–2004) and then by Jorge Lobais. | CGT Alsina |
| FTIA (food workers) | Federation. Headed by Luis Bernabé Morán (Buenos Aires Province), but Rodolfo Daer (union leader in the city of Buenos Aires since 1984) is independently influential in unionism. | CGT Alsina |
| CTERA (public sector teachers) | Federation. Led by Marta Maffei 1994–2003 and since 2004 by Stella Maldonado, province of Buenos Aires union. | CTA Yasky |
| ATE (civil servants) | Nationwide union. Led by Víctor de Gennaro (1984–2004), Pablo Micheli (2004-2011), and by Julio Fuentes since then. | CTA Micheli |

Note: The Asociación Bancaria renounced direction of the CGT Alsina in May 2013.

Source: Fieldwork.

Besides truck drivers, UTGHRA, and UATRE, there is the anti-Menemista group that accompanied Moyano until his break with Kirchner that today can be considered Peronist-Kirchnerista unionism (SADOP). There is also a group of Peronist unions that are close to the government (UOCRA, SMATA, UOM, Unión del Personal Civil de la Nación, UPCN) and pragmatic leaderships that compete with Moyano (FAECYS). Outside the CGT, the paths of the CTERA and the ATE have diverged, which has been the case for the Argentinian center-left as a whole. The former migrated from the Alianza to Kirchnerismo, while the ATE shifted toward the non-Kirchnerista center-left (which in 2011 convened as the Frente Amplio Progresista). Smaller unions follow each one of the segments.

It is good to recall that in 2003 there was not a single unionist strand that could be considered Kirchnerista. Since 2000 there was a rift within the CGT between the official CGT, headed by pragmatic unionists, and a rebel CGT, headed by Moyano. Kirchner sought the support of the rebel CGT since Moyano's profile matched the government's project of breaking with neoliberalism. He also had autonomous mobilization capacity and the political ability to lead a unified CGT. Perhaps Moyano was the only leading figure featuring these three key conditions. And, as typical in Argentinean political dynamics, the Kirchner government built its hegemony within unionism upon internal divisions.

Already before the Kirchner government, Moyano had settled upon a course of political "expansionism" that was further stimulated by Kirchnerismo by providing the movement with more resources and members (Pontoni 2012). This expansionist policy also attracted animosity from other unionists.[6] In the wage bargaining processes of 2006, 2007, and 2008, the salary increases Moyano negotiated for the workers he represented served as a parameter used by the government for other unions in general (Etchemendy 2011). Moyano, in a new context, reiterates a practice typical of Peronist unionism in the 1960s— mystique, discipline, mobilization capacity, articulation with Peronism, and economic might.

The strengthening of Kirchner in the government occurred in tandem with the strengthening of Moyano, who became the general secretary of a re-unified CGT in 2005 and was reelected in 2009. In the meantime, some unions abandoned the CGT (one sector constituted the CGT Azul y Blanca, in 2008, and others simply resigned). In parallel, Moyano occupied one of the five vice presidencies of the Partido Justicialista in 2008 and was appointed vice president of the party in the province of Buenos Aires in 2009.

Increasingly, in part due to the consolidation of Kirchnerismo, the government attempted to control union conflicts and wage increase demands. Moyano, for his part, pressured the government with labor-related demands—against income taxes (which had greater effect on categories with more bargaining power), union-related demands (claiming a debt owed by the Obras Sociales system), and political demands (more unionists on PJ lists for the 2011 elections). His demands, however, were rejected, leading him to quit the PJ and confront the government.[7]

The CGT split after Moyano's departure, when traditionally anti-Moyano unionists, as well as others close to Kirchnerismo and even longtime MTA sectors, went their separate ways. The CGT once again was divided into an opposition CGT (led by Moyano, the CGT Azopardo) and a CGT aligned with the government (led by Antonio Caló, a metalworker, the CGT Alsina). This split followed on the heels of a similar division of the CTA in 2010. The opposing CGT, the CGT Azul y Blanca, and the opposing CTA organized the first general strike against Kirchnerismo in November 2012 and were successful. The period starting with the Kirchner presidency until 2012 was the longest without general strikes since Perón's governments (1946–1955).

## Unions and Politics in Brazil

Lula came to power facing a difficult challenge. He had to prove that a party rooted in unionism could govern the largest country in Latin America. He was reelected in 2006, and in 2010 he promoted the election of Dilma Rousseff, who, although new to the PT, had a long history as a militant in the Partido Democrático Trabalhista (PDT). Thus, a new and still unfolding political era was inaugurated in 2002–2003.

CUT and PT militants in Lula's first term, as well as a good portion of the social movements discussed in Rossi's chapter, considered—not unreasonably—that the government was also "theirs." Those who had opposed neoliberalism made it to the government. This feeling did not last long. In the wake of a corruption scandal in 2005 (the "*mensalão*"), many PT cadres left the government, which was left no choice but to seek the support of the PMDB (a pragmatic, center party) in the PT's second and third terms. It is important to stress, however, that the PT never had a majority in Congress, meaning that the party always had to fill cabinet positions with appointments from other parties in addition to relying on frequently unstable coalitions in Congress in order to pass policies.

A coalition federal government, the decentralization of collective bargaining, and the political traditions shaped by the political party system and the labor movements are key in understanding some of the differences between the Brazilian and Argentinean cases. The relative fragility of the PT in the federal government is coupled with a union structure and political negotiation framework that is less centralized than that of Argentina. During the last years of the military regime in Brazil (1978–1985), state control of unions and the collective bargaining agreements submitted to the labor justice system (usually pro-patrons) contributed toward the politicization of collective bargaining as unionism. Unionism, which usually acted from a municipal or intermunicipal perspective, saw in the federal government an actor who operated to the detriment of the labor movement in collective bargaining (Renner 2002). This situation changed with democratization. Collective bargaining is still regulated by law; however, it plays out in a decentralized and relative-

TABLE 9.4. Evolution of minimum wage, average remuneration in the private sector, and average remuneration in industry, Brazil, 2000–2010

| Year | Minimum wage | Average real wages* | Wages in manufacturing |
|---|---|---|---|
| 2000 | 100.0 | | 100.0 |
| 2001 | 109.8 | | 101.4 |
| 2002 | 114.3 | | 99.5 |
| 2003 | 117.4 | 100.0 | 95.9 |
| 2004 | 121.4 | 99.7 | 103.3 |
| 2005 | 128.5 | 98.8 | 105.7 |
| 2006 | 145.3 | 102.2 | 107.1 |
| 2007 | 154.7 | 103.2 | 110.9 |
| 2008 | 160.8 | 105.3 | 115.3 |
| 2009 | 172.7 | 107.7 | |
| 2010 | 182.0 | 109.7 | |

*Note*: Workers protected by social and labor legislation in the private sector (2003 = 100).

*Source*: Panorama Laboral 2009 and 2011 (International Labor Organization).

ly "depoliticized" environment in which unions and enterprises settle upon agreements.

As in Argentina, the Brazilian government suspended its anti-unionist policies, incorporated some union demands, promoted formal employment, increased the minimum wage, and stimulated the creation of tripartite negotiation chambers for the definition of labor policies. Informality still hovers around 40 percent of the economically active population, but contrary to the neoliberal juncture, eight in every ten new jobs created between 2003 and 2012 were formal jobs. As shown in table 9.4, recovery of the minimum wage was more moderate than in Argentina, although gains were concentrated in the period of the PT-led coalition.

Observing recovery of the minimum wage, progress seems to be less significant than in Argentina. However, this picture changes when viewed from a broader historical perspective. In Brazil, the number of registered salaried workers has never been higher, so universally protected, and with as much access to consumption (as a result of salary gains and credit expansion).

As in Argentina, the "labor mechanism" means that every new formal job, more or less automatically, is a powerful incorporation mechanism that also reinforces unionism. Collective bargaining, for example, which is systematically carried out, grants unions the possibility of collecting extra money from unionized workers.[8] Moreover, this is done in addition to the "union tax" (renamed union contribution), which is still in force and which economically benefits unions regardless of its base's membership. None of these mechanisms—unlike the registration of agreements in the Argentinean case—require government approval.

Beyond this automatic mechanism of bolstering union finances, union density increased between 2002 and 2006 among wage-earning workers in the private sector (1.1 percent) and in the public sector (2.4 percent). It is true that the sharp increase in formal employment in 2006 and the massive entry of youth in the labor market reduced union density from then on, but in absolute numbers, the private sector unions received 1.3 million additional members and the public sector, more than 300,000 between 2006 and 2011[9]. This was crucial in guaranteeing that the virtuous cycle linking economic growth, union empowerment, and progressive social policy translated into salary gains. Between 1996 and 2004, salary gains above inflation only happened twice (in 1996 and 2004, with 51.9 percent and 51.5 percent of collective negotiations resulting in real salary increases). Since 2004, the majority of unions have obtained above-inflation salary increases—sometimes well above average—every year (DIEESE 2011). The economic and political context favored union action in enterprises. This became transparent as persistent, albeit atomized, labor conflicts unfolded, as tumultuous strikes occurred in the interior (as in the enormous works in the Amazonian region for the construction of dams), and as unionism flourished in the periphery (Siqueira 2008). Union activity was further bolstered by a relatively flexible union structure. Yet, unionism still struggles to become nationally articulated by sector of professional category (with the exception of bank workers and, naturally, federal public servants).

The annual average number of strikes during the first Lula term was the lowest in recent Brazilian history. After 842 strikes in the 1993–1994 period, the number of strikes peaked at 865 in the years of resistance to Cardoso (1995–1998), then dropped to 440 during the downfall of neoliberalism (1999–2002), and then to 322 in the first Lula government (2003–2007). Although the number of strikes has dropped, the average number of nonworked days grew due to long strikes in the public sector and the higher probability of being able to negotiate gains in a favorable economic and political climate (Noronha 2009). In fact, with or without strikes, the majority of unions negotiated salary increases above the inflation rate. Be that as it may, in the four subsequent years (2008–2011), there was a slight increase of mobilizations for strikes, with an average of 482 per year, reaching almost 870 in 2012 (Boito and Marcelino 2011; Cardoso 2013).

These strikes were caused by salary disputes, dismissal negotiation, and resistance to the process of industrial reconversion, since neither the improvements of global indicators related to the labor market nor the change of government altered previous practices of dealing with labor. As in the 1990s, important unions had to negotiate concessions in order to reduce the impact of employment policies of enterprises such as General Motors or Volkswagen (Arruda 2010; Marx and Mello 2012; Soul and Gindin 2013). The increase of conflicts after 2007 in private firms and government is a reflection of the international financial crisis.

**The PT and Unionism**

Unionism in Brazil, for reasons analogous to Argentina, allowed the labor movement to accept (however more critically) macroeconomic policy and obtain salary gains. Yet in a context in which unionism had low mobilization capacity while it was strongly linked to the government, CUT-led unionism intensified its linkages to the state, while in the second Lula term, the majority of unions (including the FS) became aligned with the government.

The rise of Lula to the presidency in 2003 represented the rise of CUT unionism to government as well.[10] In general terms, Lula's government regarded the CUT as a site for training and recruitment of cadres for state administration.[11] The government attracted other unions by changing the union structure to strengthen them. The result of government's economic policy choices ultimately prompted the left-leaning segments of the CUT to leave it. These dissidents created the CONLUTAS (2004), the Intersindical (2006), and the Unidos para Lutar (2010), three groups that have not been able to unite and that have not achieved a significant presence. The departure of these militants from the CUT coincided with the departure from the PT of analogous left-leaning segments, rendering quite clear the symbiosis between the union and the party, now "purified" from groups that are more radical.

Concerning union structure, the only significant change was Law 11,648/08, which regulates the framework for labor federations, reserving for them part of the funds collected via the union tax. However, even before this incentive, union leaders had already realigned in dissidences from the CUT and the FS, and smaller federations fused in new central organizations. Outside what once was the CUT camp, sectors of the traditional union structure created the Nova Central Sindical de Trabalhadores (NCST, 2005), and three unions (one of which was part of the FS) joined as the União Geral de Trabalhadores (UGT, 2007). This contemporary strengthening of unions made it possible to aggregate, from top to bottom, this decentralized structure that had always been resilient to unification from the base.

TABLE 9.5. Representativeness of selected union central federations (2008–2013)

| | CUT | FS | UGT | NTSC | CTB | CGTB |
|---|---|---|---|---|---|---|
| 2008 | 35.84% | 12.33% | 6.29% | 6.27% | 5.09% | 5.02% |
| 2013 | 35.60% | 13.80% | 11.20% | 8.10% | 9.20% | --- |

*Note*: Public sector unionism is underrepresented; percentages relative to total unions affiliated to central federations.

*Source*: Ministério do Trabalho e Desemprego.

As in Argentina, the renewal of unionism took place almost entirely under the control of leaders of traditional unions and federations. The main cases of renewal were a result of the previously mentioned industrialization of peripheral regions (automatically creating the potential for independent unions) and of scattered union elections won by the opposition. At any rate, new and old leaders faced a new context, as the traditional dispute pitting CUT militants against CUT opponents, which had shaped the disputes within unionism since 1983, became diluted as a result of the rearrangement of power among six union centers with relative representativeness (see table 9.5). A more competitive political-unionist scenario, buttressed by the newly established union system, also favored fragmentation, with new unions being created as a by-product of interunion disputes.[12] This trend of increasing fragmentation of Brazilian unionism (at the base as well as at the top) should not, however, obscure the growing political galvanization of the labor movement (save for the former CUT left) in support of the political project led by the PT and of the union model.

The crisis spurred by the "*mensalão*" corruption scandal dealt a blow to the PT-dominated composition of the first Lula term. In the 2006 elections, Lula was reelected with an impressive majority of votes in poor neighborhoods in metropolitan areas and in the northeast region, areas traditionally averse to the PT. This result was a consequence of economic stability and income redistribution policies and was not viewed as emanating from organized unionism or social movements. The president personally claimed the laurels. Lula's trajectory—from union leader to ever-more popular political leader—gradually became detached from the PT and especially the CUT, since the parties in the coalition capitalized on his ascension. In this scenario, direct participation in a highly popular government paradoxically entailed the weakening of the CUT, which for the first time in its history put into practice the typical social-democratic tenet of restricting demands and containing the immediate demands of its constituents for the sake of a long-term political project.

Starting in 2007, fissures between the government and the CUT appeared. As mentioned, lower levels of economic growth also took a toll and led to—although not as the sole determinant—an expansion of strikes. At the same time, the CUT lost some of its connections to the government. First, in March 2007, Lula appointed Carlos Lupi (PDT) minister of labor, thus removing the CUT's control over this strategic post. Paulo Pereira da Silva (Paulinho), the president of the FS affiliated to the PDT, influenced this appointment. In other words, in order to guarantee the consolidation of a more solid coalition in Congress, Lula transferred control of the Ministry of Labor to the union in direct competition with the CUT. Second, the election of Rousseff in 2010 removed Lula— the main CUT interlocutor—from the center of power. This situation, along with more restrictive policies toward the administration of the public sector, prompted significant conflicts involving the CUT, leading to confrontation with the government concerning air transportation and public services. However, the CUT remains the most important social base of support to the PT government.

## ARGENTINA AND BRAZIL IN COMPARATIVE PERSPECTIVE

The union structure legislation passed in the Perón and Vargas governments remains to this date largely unchanged. This was one of the keys, if not the only one, to preserving the backbone of the union structure, with few major changes since the 1940s. In this respect, Argentina and Brazil are contrast cases when compared to the other countries analyzed in this book. Building on Rossi's metaphor of the "bridging collective actions" by which popular sectors reconnect with state institutions (see chapter 2 in this book), we could say that the bridges that united the labor movement and the state built in the mid-twentieth century in both countries were sufficiently strong in the 1990s to arbitrate neoliberal political, economic, and social transformations and to survive the transition. Disincorporation affected mainly the unions' rank and files because of unemployment and informality.

Nonetheless, this does not signify the absence of discontinuities in government policies—quite the contrary. Neoliberalism inverted the principle that had justified state intervention in labor relations: instead of protecting or patronizing labor, government discourse and practice were ultimately undermining regulated labor-capital relations. Although the economic and ideological context of the first half of the 1990s did not favor union action in either country, unionism was relatively strong compared to other cases in Latin America, after a decade of political and institutional victories (Cook 2006). Another commonality was how models of economic development and their effects on the labor market impacted unions.

The Kirchner and Lula governments were politically built upon neoliberalism as an instance of historical rupture, but their political projects were not as daring as those of contemporaries Evo Morales or Hugo Chávez. However, they governed a capitalistic nation incorporating the demands of unions and social movements, refusing to be subordinated to credit entities and U.S. foreign policy. At any rate, both represent renovation. In both countries, unionism was a protagonist of renovation by presenting itself as a viable alternative to power (as in the Brazilian case) and by supporting projects aimed at reforming or overturning neoliberalism (as in the Argentinean case).

Until 2007, the Lula and Kirchner governments benefited from a favorable economic climate. Redistributive policies, increase of wage-paying registered employment, higher work incomes, and all the other factors that assisted in laying the material foundation for the political projects of both groups were only possible in the face of the reduction of the foreign constraints that traditionally stunted the growth of both economies. These are frail balance sheets, the need of external financing to service public sector debt, and declining terms of trade due to a poor export portfolio. Brazil and Argentina accumulated large international reserves, reduced foreign dependency, minimized the impact and perception of internal and external debt, and broadened the possibilities for productive investment. However, in 2007, external difficulties (as a result of an economic downturn) coupled with domestic limitations and mounting tension between the government and unionism became discernible.

In Argentina, the end of neoliberal hegemony also led to the collapse of the opposition that had coalesced against the Menem government, as opposed to Brazil, where the opposition to Cardoso came to power. How the crisis of neoliberalism was processed in both countries explains why Lula, a union leader of the opposition, traditionally rejected by the Brazilian bourgeoisie, took over government as a moderate leadership and why Kirchner, a traditional Peronist politician, presented himself as a challenger willing to cast aside the neoliberal legacy and found Argentina anew.

Neoliberalism advanced without excluding workers from electoral competition, since the democracies of both countries consolidated without excluding unions from political dynamics, despite their subordination, and without modifying substantially the long-standing framework regulating labor relations, even though some significant changes were implemented. What is more, the neoliberal governments vied for the adhesion of workers and tried to neutralize union opposition with "selective incentives" and political force. The more or less heteronomous relationship between the labor movement and the state ultimately guaranteed the survival of unions, albeit with a cost. This also enabled unions to capitalize on favorable economic and political conditions for union action after 2003.

The period after neoliberalism witnessed the strengthening, in new contexts, of the "classical" mechanisms that political and economic conditions had undermined (but not destroyed) in the 1990s. On the one hand, these mechanisms create the regulated environment that wage earners, the unemployed, and the majority of the self-employed hoped for, expected to be strengthened, and acknowledged as the ideal for work and the quest for subsistence. On the other hand, these mechanisms reinvigorated traditional unionism (hit hard in the 1990s) and spurred the growth of converted sectors (with little or no union experience).

In Brazil, the most organized and influential union sector, the CUT, underwent profound transformation in the 1990s and distanced itself from the program it championed in the first half of the 1980s. In 2003, the labor movement in both countries basically demanded the return and activation of the mechanisms of state intervention in the market and the economy. It called for protection for national industries, the promotion of registered employment, minimum wage increases, and the strengthening of collective bargaining. It also demanded (with more political leverage in the Argentinean case, and based on its organic participation in government in the Brazilian case) the inclusion of the labor movement in the policy decision-making process.

The historical analysis of the labor movement in Argentina and Brazil sheds light on its contemporary evolution. When Perón sought labor union support, he was partially motivated by the fact that the working class had significant presence and unionism was already a sufficiently relevant social force to support his political project. Perón, thus, further empowered unionism. This was not the case in Brazil, where state incorporation of the working class did not guarantee the same amount of organizational resources for unions, although the union tax assured their institutional maintenance. Regardless, unionism never took root as broadly in private sector firms as it did in Argentina, nor was it capable of becoming as vertically structured.

In the 1980s and 1990s, the sectors with unquestionable capacity to mobilize the Brazilian working class concluded that union action alone (whether traditional or renewed) would not be enough to advance their political goals. Thus, they strengthened their articulation with other sectors (an articulation with roots in the struggle for democracy), as well as their political and electoral political projection with the PT.

Argentine unionism took a conservative route and sought the protection of the union structure (ratified in the 1980s) and, in time, powerlessly witnessed its own demise within the PJ. This was dramatically experienced by a segment of unionism identified with Peronism during the first half of the 1990s, which split and then reunited as it aligned with Kirchnerismo. It is noteworthy that, in contrast to the Brazilian case, union leaders did not "migrate" to the state apparatus. Instead they maintained and tried to reinforce their positions within unions.

The PT governments and Kirchnerismo were favorably evaluated by the union's rank and file, by midlevel cadres, and eventually by the majority of the working class, especially as a result of the effects of their political and economic choices in the labor market. Certainly, a few elements of nationalism (in the case of Argentina) and Lula's trajectory as a poor migrant "worker" from the northeast who made it to the presidency contributed as well. However, neither government invested in the formation of a "new" unionism of their own as a support base. Why? Because given their political projects and their circumstances, this was not necessary. In Brazil, the PT had to exorcise the specter of radicalization and show it could govern. In Argentina, Kirchnerismo had to demobilize the streets and return the country to "normalcy." In both cases, these political projects could count on hegemonic unionism as a reliable ally.

In this context, for the PT government, CUT unionism was fertile ground for the recruitment of cadres for state administration. This priority took so much precedence that in hindsight it is clear that the CUT's historical project of union reform made greater progress when it was in the opposition in 1988 than in the government. What is more, the CUT leadership practically did not lament the departure of its leftist factions.

Kirchnerismo faced a politically heterogeneous unionism, which became stronger as the government consolidated its power. In this context, the labor movement was, at the same time, a natural ally (given the government's labor and wage policies) and a sector of the government was forced to negotiate with unions due to unionism's strength. This explains why Kirchnerismo, despite its unorthodox actions in some areas, was so conservative in terms of its union policies.

We can say, then, that reincorporation was partial in both countries. Labor markets improved importantly, thus promoting millions of workers out of unemployment and informality. This activated the "labor mechanism" that fostered union strength and social protection. But neither in Brazil nor in Argentina was the heteronomy of the union structures inherited from the mid-nineteenth century an object of reform.

Although the future of the Brazilian and Argentine labor movements will ultimately be determined by the political and economic developments, some trends and scenarios can be suggested.

In Brazil, traditional unionism, dependent as it is on the structure guaranteed by the state, and absent as it is from its rank and file, has taken steps back and will continue trending in that direction. This is not so much because of the CUT and its changes but rather due to the transformation of traditional unionism itself. This is the case of many manufacturing and services sectors presently affiliated with the FS, a union central that has shed its strictly anti-CUT bearings. However, this sort of unionism is very unlikely to replicate the kind of relationship the CUT had with the PT. Thus, a relatively new development in Brazil is possible—a stronger reformist and pragmatic labor movement, more autonomous from the state, yet weakly or only pragmatically articulated with the party system.

It is harder to fathom what will happen to the CUT. On the one hand, a new generation of leadership bred in the unions will become increasingly responsible for the direction the central takes. On the other hand, a new generation of cadres shaped from within the state will assume more importance within the PT. So far, there are no signs that the CUT new generations are leaning to the left of current leaders nor of a faltering or different relationship between the CUT and the PT. For the time being, the allure of power seems strong enough to keep their relationship cohesive and supportive of the same political project. The risk of a split seems to lie in the possible effects of the state's management of the economy and if the PT coalition loses presidential elections to the opposition. The demise of the PT would also be the demise of the CUT. In this case dealing with the rubble will befall both indistinctly. Other political forces with good electoral performance can assume the role of renovators from the left (as the PSB and the PDT), both in the realm of unions and of parties.[13] In this sense, the competition for social bases, the spoils of the CUT and PT, could bring the CUT back to the left.

In Argentina, some union leaders have chosen routes that ensure stricter mechanisms of control over their base, in detriment of consensus. Generational renovation and the strengthening of the working class could lead to the repetition of the sharp conflicts involving the metro, railways, and food workers in other categories. Such a scenario would probably reinvigorate class-based unionism. The lack of legitimacy exhibited by some union organizations could also be capitalized on by the CTA, although this union's project has not proven attractive for unionism at large.

The next steps of Moyanismo are difficult to predict. Although Moyano defends more union participation in politics, there is no possibility for a labor party, and the PJ will not take him on his terms. However, he will probably retain, in any context, his ability to call upon governments. It is hard to imagine that the front integrated by the class-based unions, the CTA, and the former MTA, which consistently opposed neoliberalism, will converge in organizational or political terms as a force capable of acting in conjunction.

# PART III

# POLITICAL PARTIES

Chapter 10

# INTRODUCTION TO PART III

## Political Parties in Latin America's Second Wave of Incorporation

### KENNETH M. ROBERTS

Latin America's second wave of mass political incorporation, like the first, was heavily conditioned by party politics. Party organizations, however, were not always the chosen vehicle for popular sectors seeking a stronger voice and enhanced participation in the democratic process at the beginning of the twenty-first century. In some countries, reincorporation was channeled through established political parties—especially those located to the left of center—that were committed to redistributive policies, popular participation, and expanded social citizenship rights. In other countries, reincorporation occurred outside and even against established party systems, effectively displacing traditional parties from their dominant roles in the electoral arena and governing institutions. In these countries, traditional parties were often challenged by mass social protest and ultimately eclipsed by the electoral mobilization of a diverse array of populist "outsiders" and new political movements.

Reincorporation, therefore, did not follow a singular political model or institutional logic, as the chapters in this section make clear. It was associated with complex patterns of both change and continuity in national party systems, and it produced substantial cross-national political variation among those party systems. The most basic distinction—between systemic forms of reincorporation through established parties and extra-systemic forms of reincorporation through outsider movements—carried with it a number of major political correlates. It was related, for example, to the levels of social mobilization and protest, the organizational foundations of electoral shifts to the left, and the extent to which reincorporation produced a basic rupture in the constitutional order and/or a sharp turn away from neoliberal orthodoxy. These outcomes were central features of Latin America's political landscape in the aftermath to neoliberal reform—that is, in the "post-adjustment" political era that followed the period of market-based structural adjustment between the mid-1970s and mid-1990s.

The comparative perspective developed in the chapters by Catherine Conaghan, Daniel Hellinger, and Pierre Ostiguy and Aaron Schneider suggests that the process of market liberalization left behind very different types of party systems with distinct capacities to channel and respond to societal pressures in the post-adjustment period. Market reforms in Brazil helped to align and stabilize a previously inchoate party system along a left-right axis of programmatic contestation, encouraging a reincorporation process led by an institutionalized and increasingly moderate party of the left. Reforms in Venezuela, Bolivia, Ecuador, and Argentina, on the other hand, de-aligned party systems in ways that left them vulnerable to widespread social protest, institutional decay, and (partially excepting Argentina) the rise of more radical populist and leftist alternatives during the reincorporation process. These institutional legacies of the reform process—which I have elsewhere characterized as a new "critical juncture" in Latin America's political development (Roberts 2014)—thus conditioned the character and content of popular reincorporation as diverse societal actors articulated claims for more effective political representation and expanded social citizenship rights.

## PARTY SYSTEMS IN CYCLES OF POLITICAL INCORPORATION AND EXCLUSION

As explained in the seminal study by Ruth Berins Collier and David Collier (1991), party systems in much of Latin America were reconfigured by the political incorporation of labor and popular movements during the early stages of industrialization in the first half of the twentieth century. In Argentina, Bolivia, Brazil, and Venezuela, for example, new mass parties forged close ties to labor unions and supported redistributive social reforms and state-led policies of import substitution industrialization (ISI). This incorporation process, however, was ultimately reversed during a wrenching period of economic crisis and political exclusion. Political exclusion was enforced by military regimes in the 1960s and 1970s, leading to severe repression of labor unions and their affiliated populist or leftist parties in much of the region (O'Donnell 1973). Although democratic transitions in the 1980s restored basic citizenship rights—a vital first step in the process of reincorporation—*de facto* exclusion of popular sectors continued in the public policy sphere, as the debt crisis and inflationary pressures forced governments to adopt harsh austerity and structural adjustment measures. Economic crises and market restructuring led to a sharp reduction in trade unionization throughout the region, and levels of social mobilization in general declined during the period of market liberalization (Kurtz 2004).

Paradoxically, some of the most ambitious neoliberal "shock treatments" were imposed not by conservative pro-business and pro-market parties but rather by center-left or populist parties with strong labor bases and historic commitments to statist ISI policies. This dynamic of "bait-and-switch" liberalization—what Stokes (2001a) called "neoliberalism by surprise"—contributed to the perception of a technocratic "Washington Consensus" around the neoliberal model (Williamson 1990). The technocratic consensus, however, never fully extended to mass publics, and once stabilization had been achieved by the mid-1990s—when Brazil was the last country in the region to defeat hyperinflation—societal resistance to the neoliberal model intensified and sought political expression. This societal resistance was a driving force behind the political reincorporation of popular sectors in public policy-making arenas in Latin America's post-adjustment era. As explained in the following, however, the political expression of this societal resistance, and the institutional forms of reincorporation, were heavily conditioned by the competitive alignment of party systems around the process of market liberalization.

## ALIGNING AND DE-ALIGNING PATTERNS OF MARKET REFORM

As Karl Polanyi (1944; see also Silva 2009) famously asserted, "market society" tends to spawn social and political resistance among those who feel threatened by market insecurities. Consequently, the expansion of markets into new spheres of social relations can trigger a "double movement" of resistance to a heightened dependence on market forces for access to land, employment, consumption, and services. As the recent Latin American experience shows, however, such "double movements" can take a variety of different political forms. In some contexts, they may find expression in collective forms of social protest, from strikes, riots, and demonstrations to the occupation of public sites or highway blockades. In other contexts, they may give rise to electoral protests—that is, electoral support for "outsider," antisystem parties, movements, or leaders. Alternatively, the double movement can assume more institutional forms through support for established parties or governments that promise social protection policies. These alternatives are shaped, in part, by the capacity of party systems to articulate and channel societal claims—that is, to construct forms of social citizenship that lie beyond purely market-based allocations of income, goods, and services.

Market liberalization in Latin America left behind party systems that varied dramatically in their ability to channel such societal claims. This variation

was not simply a function of whether or not party systems were institutionalized at the start of the reform process. The recent Latin American experience
provides examples of very strong, institutionalized party systems that failed
to channel societal claims and broke down as a consequence; Venezuela is the
most prominent example. Conversely, it also provides examples of traditionally fluid and inchoate party systems that more effectively channeled societal
claims and progressively institutionalized, as in Brazil (see the chapters by
Hellinger and Ostiguy and Schneider). Such divergent outcomes would have
been very difficult to predict on the basis of their preexisting or antecedent
party system characteristics.

Indeed, the decisive factor in these outcomes was not the antecedent prop-
erties of the party systems that entered the period of structural adjustment,
but rather what happened to them *during* the process of reform itself. More
specifically, party systems were differentiated by their competitive alignments
around the process of market reform. Party systems could be programmatically aligned or de-aligned by market liberalization, depending on the political leadership of the reform process and the presence or absence of a major leftist party in opposition. Left-right programmatic alignment occurred
where conservative or centrist political actors—whether parties or military
rulers—took the lead in the reform process and a major party of the left was
present to offer consistent opposition. Such alignments produced a competitive dynamic of *contested liberalism*, with a central cleavage between supporters and opponents of neoliberal orthodoxy. Of the countries included in this
study,[1] only Brazil experienced such a programmatically aligning process of
reform; as seen in the chapter by Ostiguy and Schneider, structural adjustment was imposed by conservative president Fernando Collor de Mello and
the center-right coalition governments of Fernando Henrique Cardoso, over
the staunch opposition of the leftist Partido dos Trabalhadores (PT) and its
affiliated labor and popular organizations.

Conversely, programmatic de-alignment occurred where traditional populist or center-left parties played a leading role in the process of market reform, leaving party systems without a well-defined opponent of neoliberal
orthodoxy. Such bait-and-switch patterns of reform produced a competitive dynamic of neoliberal convergence, whereby all the major partisan alternatives adhered to the market liberalization process, effectively reifying
the Washington Consensus in the partisan sphere. In this study, Argentina, Bolivia, Venezuela, and Ecuador experienced such de-aligning patterns
of market liberalization. Historic populist parties led the reform process in
the first three countries—the Peronist Partido Justicialista (PJ) in Argentina,
the Movimiento Nacionalista Revolucionario (MNR) in Bolivia, and Acción

Democrática (AD) in Venezuela—while a succession of conservative, center-left, and populist parties all took turns in the Ecuadorean case (see the chapter by Conaghan).

During the period of structural adjustment when debt and inflationary pressures limited the range of viable policy alternatives, neoliberal convergence was not necessarily unstable. In the post-adjustment period, however, when the "double movement" of societal resistance tended to gather strength, neoliberal convergence proved to be a highly unstable competitive equilibrium. Given the absence of institutionalized channels for dissent from neoliberal orthodoxy, it was prone to disruptive "reactive sequences" in the aftermath period (Mahoney 2001). Such dissent was often expressed outside and in opposition to established party systems, including mass protest movements and/or electoral support for anti-establishment populist figures or new "movement parties" that outflanked traditional parties on the left.

Reactive sequences were far less dramatic and turbulent, however, in countries that experienced programmatically aligning patterns of reform and entered the post-adjustment period with institutional legacies of contested liberalism. Under contested liberalism, major parties of the left provided institutionalized outlets for societal dissent, muting social protest and channeling opposition to the neoliberal model into relatively stable forms of electoral contestation. The legacies of party system alignment and de-alignment during the critical juncture of market liberalization thus conditioned the character and intensity of reactive sequences, along with the patterns of popular reincorporation as Latin America turned to the left politically in the post-adjustment period.

## REACTIVE SEQUENCES AND REINCORPORATION IN THE POST-ADJUSTMENT ERA

All five countries included in this study turned to the left politically in the post-adjustment period, part of an unprecedented regional political shift that included over thirty presidential victories by leftist candidates in twelve different countries between 1998 and 2014 (Madrid 2009; Weyland, Madrid, and Hunter 2010; Levitsky and Roberts 2011). Even where the left did not capture national executive office, leftist alternatives emerged or strengthened, as seen in countries such as Mexico, Costa Rica, Honduras, and Colombia. This "left turn" was not synonymous with the reincorporation process, as the latter entailed multiple forms of recognizing rights and representing or responding to the needs of popular sectors that were not the exclusive preserve of leftist parties or governments. In some Latin American countries, popular demands and/or electoral challenges from the left induced more conservative governments to expand social programs for the poor, reducing some of the more extreme forms of social marginalization. Nevertheless, the post-1998 left turn became an integral part of the reincorporation process in much of the region, as it created opportunities to build new participatory channels and representative vehicles for popular sectors, initiate or expand redistributive measures, and recognize forms of social citizenship that broke with the market orthodoxy of the Washington Consensus.

The character and content of reincorporation, however, varied widely, depending on the institutional legacies of market reform, the reactive sequences they spawned, and the nature of the left turn in different national settings. Reincorporation could take place by systemic means, through institutionalized parties of the left, or extra-systemic means through the rise of populist outsiders or new "movement parties" that frontally challenged the political establishment. The reactive sequences that shaped these divergent paths varied along four principal dimensions: (1) the levels of social mobilization and protest; (2) levels of antisystem or "protest" voting and its corollary, the stabilization or breakdown of party systems; (3) the resort to plebiscitary forms of popular sovereignty to re-found the constitutional order of democratic regimes; and (4) the degree of departure from neoliberal orthodoxy in the post-adjustment period. Along each dimension, stark differences existed between countries that experienced programmatically aligning or de-aligning patterns of reform.

Although fragmented and localized social protests against structural adjustment policies emerged throughout the region, the most widespread and explosive forms of social protest—namely, those that led, directly or indirectly, to the removal of pro-market presidents—occurred in the four countries included in this study that experienced de-aligning, bait-and-switch patterns of reform: Venezuela, Argentina, Ecuador, and Bolivia. Venezuela had the most explosive social backlash against neoliberal reforms in the entire region during the period of structural adjustment itself—the five-day cycle of mass urban riots known as the *Caracazo* that greeted Carlos Andrés Pérez's initial "shock treatment" in February 1989. As explained in the chapter by Hellinger, Pérez never recovered politically; over three thousand smaller protest events occurred over the next four years (López Maya 2005, 90 and 94), and the president's eventual impeachment was preceded by two military coup attempts in 1992, the first led by a then-unknown army lieutenant colonel, Hugo Chávez. In Ecuador, the region's first major indigenous movement gathered strength in the early 1990s and joined with labor and other popular sectors in a series of mass uprisings that toppled three consecutive elected presidents in 1997, 2000, and 2005 (Yashar 2005). In Argentina and Bolivia, the most widespread and intense forms of social protest were concentrated in the post-adjustment period, as seen in the chapters by Ostiguy and Schneider and Conaghan. The *piquetero* (picketers) movement of unemployed workers helped trigger a popular uprising, and urban riots that brought down the UCR government of Fernando De la Rúa during Argentina's financial crisis in December 2001. Likewise, post-2000 cycles of mass protest in Bolivia known as the "Water War" and the "Gas War" ultimately toppled presidents in 2003 and 2005 (see Silva 2009 for an overview of these diverse protest movements).

Neither Brazil nor any of the other countries with a programmatically aligning process of reform experienced protest cycles of comparable breadth and intensity in the early post-adjustment period.[2] Instead, societal opposition to the neoliberal model was channeled primarily into partisan and electoral politics by the PT, which progressively strengthened and ascended to national executive office in the post-adjustment period (Hunter 2010). The PT won four consecutive presidential elections in 2002, 2006, 2010, and 2014, while Brazil's notoriously inchoate party system stabilized around a central cleavage between a center-right bloc anchored by Cardoso's PSDB and a left-leaning bloc led by the PT (see the chapter by Ostiguy and Schneider).

The party system effects of reactive sequences were dramatically different in the four countries that experienced programmatically de-aligning reforms and widespread social protest. Pro-market centrist and conservative parties declined or collapsed in all four countries, while traditional populist or leftist parties were outflanked and eclipsed on the left by new populist figures or "movement parties" with staunch anti-neoliberal platforms. In Venezuela and Ecuador, these alternatives were constructed by populist figures—Hugo Chávez and Rafael Correa—who tapped into the anti-establishment sentiments of their countries' protest movements but were not rooted in those movements themselves (see the chapters by Hellinger and Conaghan). In Bolivia, on the other hand, the *cocalero,* indigenous, peasant, and labor movements that toppled two presidents spawned a new partisan vehicle, the MAS, which elected Evo Morales of the coca growers' union to the presidency in 2005.

As seen in the chapter by Ostiguy and Schneider, Argentina was distinctive among the bait-and-switch cases because a traditional populist party, the Peronist PJ, partially channeled the social backlash against neoliberal orthodoxy in the post-adjustment period. After leading the process of market reform under Carlos Menem in the 1990s, the internally heterogeneous PJ veered leftward under the leadership of Néstor Kirchner and Cristina Fernández de Kirchner following the financial meltdown and popular uprising that toppled the UCR-led government in 2001. Drawing upon the PJ's historical linkages to labor and popular sectors, Kirchner reached out to *piquetero* organizations and labor unions while creating massive new public employment and social welfare programs to provide relief from the economic crisis (see the chapter by Ostiguy and Schneider; also Wolff 2007). In the process, he essentially created a new left "movement party"—the Frente Para la Victoria—that was located partially within Peronism but also partially outside it and very much in tension with the PJ's old-guard, non-Kirchnerista (and more conservative) leadership factions. Argentina's reactive sequences, then, produced a virtual collapse of the anti-Peronist side of the party system while reconfiguring Peronism around rival strands of a dominant, personalistic movement left and the remnants of a conservative party machine.

In contrast to Brazil, then—where the party system stabilized in the post-adjustment era—party systems in the four cases of programmatic de-alignment partially or thoroughly decomposed. Traditional party systems in Venezuela and Bolivia essentially collapsed, while in Ecuador parties withered as new populist contenders emerged on both the left and right sides of the political spectrum. Similarly, the anti-Peronist side of the party system fragmented and declined in Argentina, though the PJ provided a partial measure of institutional continuity in the electoral arena.

These party system effects had major implications for popular reincorporation in the post-adjustment period. In Brazil, reincorporation was sponsored by established parties—in particular the leftist PT, a party founded by labor and social movement activists during the early stages of democratic transition at the beginning of the 1980s, prior to the onset of market reforms. In Venezuela, Ecuador, and Bolivia, however, reincorporation was sponsored by new, anti-establishment parties of the left that emerged out of the social backlash against neoliberal orthodoxy. As the chapters by Conaghan and Hellinger explain, these parties were electoral vehicles for dominant populist figures in Venezuela and Ecuador, whereas in Bolivia the MAS emerged organically from the confluence of social movements that rocked the political establishment after 2000. The Argentine case offered a hybrid mix of these different patterns, with new personalistic leadership and movement currents pulling a traditional populist party back to the left as societal resistance to the neoliberal model intensified (see Ostiguy and Schneider).

In Venezuela, Ecuador, and Bolivia, new populist and leftist alternatives made explicit commitments to break with established regime institutions, as Chávez, Correa, and Morales all ran for office on platforms that called for the election of constituent assemblies to refound democratic institutions. In contexts of party system crises where conservative opponents were in disarray, these leaders employed their mobilization capacity to bypass judicial and legislative bodies and exercise more direct forms of popular sovereignty. In particular, they organized popular referendums to convoke constituent assemblies, ratify the constitutions they wrote, and hold new elections that strengthened their control over governing institutions. These "constituent moments" (Frank 2010), while sometimes violating existing constitutional procedures, provided unparalleled opportunities for civic groups to participate in the redesign of democratic institutions. Such plebiscitary expressions of popular sovereignty did not exist in Brazil and Argentina, where established parties that were more firmly embedded in existing regime institutions played a major role in the process of reincorporation.

The different partisan trajectories also shaped the extent to which reincorporation was associated with major departures from the neoliberal model. Although the PT held the presidency in Brazil after 2002, it did not have a legislative majority, so PT presidents Luiz Inácio Lula da Silva and Dilma Rousseff had to rely on centrist and conservative members of their multiparty coalitions to pass legislation and make public policy. This clearly constrained the PT's policy options, inducing the party to maintain relatively orthodox macroeconomic policies while it increased wages and social programs to address the needs of core popular constituencies. In the other four cases, however—where mass protests had occurred, conservative parties had been gravely weakened, and new leftist governments possessed legislative majorities—ambitious redistributive measures were coupled with sharp departures from neoliberal orthodoxy and experimentation with more heterodox and statist development policies.

By shattering the Washington Consensus of the 1990s, these policy shifts have revived political contestation over programmatic alternatives, and they have at least partially reconstructed a left-right axis of competition around which sociopolitical cleavages and party systems could be realigned and reconstituted. As the chapters by Conaghan, Hellinger, and Ostiguy and Schneider all demonstrate, however, party systems that decompose do not automatically or easily reconstitute themselves. In Bolivia, Ecuador, and Venezuela, conservative and elite actors were especially ineffectual at rebuilding partisan vehicles to represent their interests and policy preferences in the electoral arena. Instead, they relied heavily on independent personalities and fluid electoral fronts behind which fragmented and disparate actors can coalesce. In Argentina, the anti-Peronist bloc was also organizationally fluid following the 2001 collapse of the UCR–led government, although it showed some signs of consolidation around the conservative leadership of Mauricio Macri during the elections of 2015.

Where new leftist alternatives emerged in the aftermath period, party rebuilding advanced most rapidly in Bolivia, where the MAS incorporated many—though not all—of the organized popular constituencies that mobilized against the political establishment in the post-2000 protest cycles. As Conaghan stresses, however, party-society relations are strikingly different in Ecuador. The indigenous movement that played an instrumental role in Ecuador's protest cycles launched a partisan vehicle, Pachakutik (Van Cott 2005), but unlike the MAS, it failed to become electorally competitive at the national level. Pachakutik thus gave its support to a series of independent populist figures, but the indigenous movement was ultimately divided and demobilized by the controversies that surrounded these political alliances (Wolff 2007). Remnants of the movement have clashed with Correa's autocratic leadership and his support for extractive development policies that threaten community control over land, water, and resources—issues that have also driven a wedge between the MAS and lowland indigenous groups in Bolivia. Since Correa tapped into antiparty sentiments by running for office in 2006 without an organized partisan base or even an accompanying list of congressional candidates, his efforts to stitch together a party vehicle after taking office were conducted from the top down and heavily reliant on state resources to mobilize support. On both the left and the right, then, Ecuador's party "system," to the extent that one existed, was fluid and highly personalistic.

Tensions between top-down and bottom-up dynamics are also a centerpiece of Hellinger's chapter on Venezuela. Chávez was elected into office in 1998 at the head of a highly personalistic movement that had substantial mobilization capacity but very limited forms of partisan organization. After taking office, Chavismo sponsored extensive grassroots organization around government social "missions" and participatory forms of community self-governance (Hawkins 2010b). Many of the local networks that emerged, however, were only loosely connected to Chávez's party organization, and party building clearly lagged behind popular mobilization. After 2006, Chávez made a new effort to incorporate these social networks and small leftist party factions into a more cohesive and institutionalized party organization, the Partido Socialista Unificado de Venezuela (PSUV). Following Chavez's death in 2013, the PSUV provided an organizational foundation for at least one side of the left/right—or populist/antipopulist—cleavage that structures Venezuelan politics. This cleavage, however, relied heavily on charismatic leadership as a pole of attraction and repulsion to align and aggregate its rival sociopolitical blocs, and the partisan institutionalization of these blocs remains a work in progress.

Indeed, the chapters by Conaghan, Hellinger, and Ostiguy and Schneider all demonstrate the challenges of translating popular reincorporation into responsive and institutionalized partisan competition. To be sure, new leftist governments in the five countries all adopted redistributive and social welfare measures that responded to the needs of low income groups, and they were rewarded by voters at the ballot box; as of the end of 2015, leftist alternatives had won five consecutive presidential elections in Venezuela, four in Brazil, and three apiece in Bolivia, Ecuador, and Argentina—in the latter case, prior to the late 2015 defeat of the Peronists. In each case, a basic left-right structuring of political space and electoral competition emerged in the post-adjustment era, even if the partisan institutionalization of this programmatic alignment lagged behind. Very high levels of popular mobilization undergirded and reproduced those cleavages in Bolivia and Venezuela, but Ecuador's weakened popular movements were largely detached from the country's left-populist leadership, and Venezuela's grassroots Chavismo was not fully incorporated within the movement's partisan vehicle. The conservative side of the cleavage everywhere struggled to rebuild parties once they had collapsed, although conservative blocs began to show signs of political consolidation in Argentina and Venezuela by the second decade of the twenty-first century.

Although the Bolivian MAS and the Brazilian PT began as classic "movement parties" with very high levels of grassroots social activism, their ascent to state power inevitably created tensions between their movement networks· and party organizations, with the latter becoming more professionalized and bureaucratized as they competed in the electoral arena and exercised public office (Hunter 2010). As Anria (2013) demonstrates, the movement character of the MAS and the ability of its organized popular constituencies to hold the party leadership accountable vary across urban and rural areas, depending on different formative experiences in the articulation of movement and party networks. Even the Bolivian case suggests, however, that although social movements can occasionally topple governments and win national elections, they do not easily *govern* as movements; the partisan intermediaries that they form to win elections and administer public office are imperfect vehicles for the participation and representation of mobilized popular constituencies. To date, societal organizations are more fragmented and pluralistic in Latin America's second wave of mass political incorporation—and their ties to party organizations are more tenuous—than those which characterized the region's initial process of labor-based political incorporation in the twentieth century. Popular sectors in the region have long struggled to find incorporation patterns that allow for meaningful participation and responsiveness in public affairs while avoiding the autocratic personalism of populist leaders and the bureaucratic detachment of professionalized party organizations. That struggle is sure to continue.

Chapter 11

# FROM MOVEMENTS TO GOVERNMENTS

## Comparing Bolivia's MAS and Ecuador's PAIS

### CATHERINE CONAGHAN

Evo Morales captured the world's attention when he became Bolivia's first indigenous president in January 2006. A year later, Morales applauded as Rafael Correa, a young economist, was sworn in as president of the northern Andean nation Ecuador. The two men had much in common. In their inaugural speeches, both presidents renewed their sweeping campaign pledge: that they would use their political power to transform the nation. As newly minted leaders at the forefront of Latin America's left turn, Morales and Correa made clear their ideological commitment and programmatic goals. They firmly staked out their plans to jettison neoliberal economics, restore national sovereignty, and actively deploy state power to eradicate poverty and social exclusion. Both men promised to deliver an entirely new constitution, envisioned as the foundational framework for reinvigorating the role of the state in the economy and expanding citizens' rights.

For the most part, Morales and Correa made good on their promises. In doing so, they ushered in a new era of popular class incorporation that extended collective and substantive citizenship rights like never before (Rossi and Silva in this volume). Expansive social assistance programs and increased public spending were coupled with a constitutionally enshrined "rights revolution" that recognized the claims of groups across society. Indigenous communities, the disabled, women, children, adolescents, the elderly, consumers, and prisoners were accorded new status. Both constitutions established the principle that creating the conditions for "good living" (*buen vivir*) was the central task of state. Yet, as both presidents discovered, expanding consumption and rights simultaneously would not be easy to pull off in states that rely so heavily on profits from hydrocarbons and other mining industries. Reconciling the state's heavy reliance on extractive industries with popular claims challenging natural resource exploitation would prove to be one of the most contentious issues at play in the Andean second wave incorporation projects.

Under the charismatic leadership of Morales and Correa, the two countries took largely similar policy paths. Voters rewarded their governments with successive reelections and legislative majorities. Indeed, both presidents succeeded in putting an end to the political instability that had dogged each system prior to their election. Yet, as much as Bolivia and Ecuador have in common, it would be mistaken to conclude that political development in the two has been entirely equivalent. In both countries, economic stress in the 1990s and 2000s triggered popular resistance to neoliberalism (Silva 2009). Bolivians and Ecuadorians pulled away from the right, left, center, and populist parties that implemented neoliberal policies. Discontent set party system de-alignment in motion and paved the way for new partisan challengers (see Roberts in this volume). Yet, while rooted in a backlash against neoliberalism, the reconfiguration of the party systems in Bolivia and Ecuador developed in different ways. Prevailing political culture, preexisting organizational capabilities, and the political opportunity structures that crystallized during the neoliberal critical juncture gave birth to distinctive governing parties.

In Bolivia, Evo Morales came to power as the standard bearer of the Movimiento al Socialismo (MAS). As one of MAS's founders, Morales understood the movement as the "political instrument" of Bolivia's combative civil society—the product of decades of struggle by peasants, workers, and popular class organizations. Beginning his public career as a leader in the coca farmers' union, Morales recognized and embodied the organic nexus of MAS and social movements. MAS manifested a hybrid "linkage repertoire": it mobilized voters through their connections to peasant unions along with the more recent associational networks that emerged in the struggle against neoliberalism (Handlin and Collier 2011).

Morales's bottom-up understanding of how he became president starkly contrasts with Correa's top-down rendering. At his first inauguration, Correa made no mention of social movements, noting only that PAIS was formed by an inspired "handful of citizens" that turned his campaign into "crusade" (Presidencia de la República del Ecuador 2007). Trained as an economist and with no previous experience in partisan or movement politics, Correa came to power as the quintessential "outsider" who joined with other activists to rapidly mount his 2006 campaign. While giving voice to demands from lower-income groups and repackaging policy ideas long advocated by Ecuador's left, Correa and PAIS were not directly beholden to social movements or closely tied to other leftist parties. In contrast to Morales and MAS, Correa and his inner circle forged PAIS primarily as an electoral vehicle, one that relied more on using the media to connect with individual voters rather than cultivating linkages to organized society.

In order to understand exactly why and how these distinctive political movements and leaders paved the way to second wave incorporation, we begin by considering how political parties engaged with popular classes during first wave incorporation and the historical juncture of neoliberal reform. Parties of the first wave, through their failures and the fallout from their projects, set the stage for a new generation of partisan challengers.

## FIRST WAVE INCORPORATION: 1950S–1970S

In the last half of the twentieth century, Bolivia and Ecuador dealt final blows to oligarchic party politics. Bolivia took a dramatic, radical route to this end through its national populist revolution of 1952. In Ecuador, the demise of oligarchic politics came in a slower, more piecemeal fashion in the 1960s and 1970s. In both countries, military rule interrupted and complicated the development of party systems. Despite the differences in the timing and pacing of the processes that ended elite domination of the political system and secured universal voting rights, the first wave of incorporation in both countries left popular classes in a roughly similar position with respect to the party system. No single political party monopolized the votes of low-income voters in a sustained way. Instead, populist parties of various stripes competed alongside an array of left and center parties for the support of low-income voters, making for the development of a highly fragmented and volatile party system by the 1980s (Mainwaring and Scully 1995a, 8)

### Bolivia's Revolutionary Breakthrough

The populist Movimiento Nacionalista Revolucionario (MNR) served as a big "tent" uniting peasants, organized labor, and the urban middle class in bringing about the Bolivian revolution of 1952. Universal suffrage, agrarian reform, and the nationalization of tin mines were the signature policy achievements of the revolution (Gotkowitz 2007; Malloy 1970; Molina 2013). The initial phase of the MNR-led revolution also featured a unique experiment in procedural incorporation: *cogobierno.* Leaders of labor and peasant organizations became cabinet ministers while simultaneously serving as members of the MNR's executive board (Mitchell 1977, 51). But this radical fusion of popular organizations, party, and government was short-lived. By 1957, U.S. pressures on the Bolivian government and the MNR's middle-class constituents supported a conservative turn (Useem 1980). Juan Lechín, leader of Bolivia's mine workers and head of the powerful trade union confederation Central Obrera Boliviana (COB), finally bolted from the MNR in 1964 after being denied its presidential nomination. Subsequently, COB never fell under the sway of a single party; instead it became an arena in which a variety of leftist parties competed for support.

In contrast to its divorce from trade unions, the MNR maintained close ties with peasants and even mobilized rural militias during labor conflicts in the late 1950s and early 1960s. By supporting agrarian reform and organizing local peasant unions (*sindicatos*), the MNR cultivated rural support but did so in a way that kept the peasantry divided and the unions dependent on their links to party officials. After the overthrow of the MNR government in 1964, military dictators also sought peasant support; the strategy was formalized in the "Military-Peasant Pact" of President René Barrientos in 1966. In a subsequent military government, General Hugo Banzer put an end to the peasant alliance with his violent response to peasant protest in 1974 (Malloy and Gamarra 1988).

Bolivia's messy return to democracy (interrupted by General García Meza's 1980 coup) triggered intense partisan competition. The MNR, divided between left and conservative factions, faced a wide array of rivals on the left—socialists, social democrats, communists, and Trotskyites along with new indigenous parties inspired by the Aymara-based ideology Katarismo. Hope that a new era of incorporation was in the offing was stoked by the 1982 election of President Hernán Siles Zuazo. Backed by an alliance of leftist parties and his left faction of the MNR, Siles was buffeted by demands from his diverse coalition, especially the COB (Ibáñez Rojo 2000). By 1985, the Siles administration was in a full-fledged policy meltdown as it grappled with widespread labor conflicts and a staggering hyperinflation approaching 11,000 percent.

Siles's disastrous failure discredited the left and opened the door to the 1985 presidential victory of the MNR's historic founder, Víctor Paz Estenssorro. From 1985–2002, the MNR took turns in the presidency with two other parties: the social democratic Movimiento de Izquierda Revolucionaria (MIR), led by Jaime Paz Zamora, and the conservative Acción Democrática Nacionalista (ADN), founded by former dictator Hugo Banzer. Starting with Paz's famous economic shock-treatment measures in 1985, all three parties continued down a path of neoliberal reforms.

### Ecuador's Incremental Incorporation

Ecuador's popular classes never experienced a radical interlude of incorporation like that of the Bolivian revolution. Nor was there a party equivalent to the early MNR. Oligarchic politics had a long shelf life in Ecuador. Socialist, communist, and other leftist parties were on the scene in the twentieth century, but traditional liberal and conservative forces continued to dominate politics through the 1960s. Even the country's first variant of populism, practiced by five-time president José María Velasco Ibarra, was decidedly conservative and personality-centric (De la Torre 2010). Velasco never championed incorporating policies akin to those generated by classic populism found elsewhere in the region, nor did any Velasquista organization survive after his death.

With relatively weak and factionalized labor and peasant movements, progressive reforms were slow to materialize and limited in scope. The military regime's 1964 agrarian reform law abolished traditional haciendas and gave peasants ownership of their subsistence plots but did not execute significant land redistribution. It took until the 1970s for labor to entrench collective bargaining (see León Trujillo and Spronk in this volume). Universal suffrage was achieved finally in 1979 when the literacy requirement for voting was lifted.

While rhetorically committed to a "national revolution," Ecuador's military government in the 1970s fell far short of the pro-labor and pro-peasant reforms undertaken by the armed forces in neighboring Peru during the same time period (Conaghan 1988). The military's decision to hand back power to civilians in 1979 set the stage for a reconfigured party system with modernized organizations that emerged in splits from the old oligarchic parties. These included the rightist Partido Social Cristiano (PSC), the social democratic Izquierda Democrática (ID), and the Christian democratic Democracia Popular (DP). Guayaquil's populist forces, grouped in the Concentración de Fuerzas Populares, fell apart and reassembled in the Partido Roldosista Ecuatoriano (PRE) in 1981 after the untimely death of President Jaime Roldós. From 1981 to 2002, these four organizations dominated national politics, taking their turns at the presidency and fielding the largest caucuses in Congress. As in Bolivia, each of these governing parties played a role in managing Ecuador's application of neoliberalism.

## THE NEOLIBERAL JUNCTURE: 1980S–2000S

Bolivia and Ecuador did not undergo neoliberal economic reform at the same pace or to the same degree (Lora 2001; Inter-American Development Bank 1997). In the implementation of key policies (inflation reduction, trade opening, financial liberalization, deficit reduction, privatization of state-owned enterprises, market deregulation), Bolivia was judged among the most "aggressive" countries in carrying out neoliberal reform. Ecuador ranked among the most "shallow" reformers (Corrales 2003, 90–91).

The experiences of neoliberalism differed, but neither country managed to resolve its problems with achieving sustained economic growth and eradicating poverty in this period. Dependent on extractive industries and agriculture, both economies remained vulnerable to external shocks in commodities prices and natural disasters that produced intermittent "growth crises" (Solimano and Soto 2004). At the same time, no sustained improvements in overall poverty levels or reductions in economic inequality occurred (World Bank 2004, 2005a, 2005b).

By the first decade of the twenty-first century, the purported economic benefits of neoliberal reform were not in evidence to a great many Bolivians and Ecuadorians, especially those in the lower classes. On the contrary, economic stress and displacements in the labor force became synonymous with neoliberalism. Public opinion polls showed "reform fatigue" and dramatic declines in mass support for neoliberal policies such as privatization (Lora, Panizza, and Quispe-Agnoli 2004, 2–3). The public's disillusion with neoliberalism went hand in hand with declining support for the political parties that administered it. Additional concerns about crime, corruption, and fallout from the U.S.-backed counternarcotics policies fueled the breakdown in support for traditional parties in charge. A host of "state deficiencies" converged with neoliberalism (Mainwaring 2006). Meanwhile, opponents of neoliberalism were taking advantage of the new openings for activism made possible by political reforms designed to respond to popular claims for relief and inclusion: multiculturalism and decentralization.

### Bolivia's Neoliberal Revolution

As Grindle (2003, 19) observed, Bolivia in the 1980s and 1990s underwent nothing short of a "neoliberal revolution." The process began in 1985 when President Víctor Paz Estenssorro enacted the sweeping "New Economic Policy" (NEP) in a single executive decree. The law included a wide range of fiscal correctives to reduce government spending, ranging from cuts to consumer subsidies to plans to fire public sector employees. It also contained provisions aimed at deregulating and opening the economy to trade and foreign investment.

Although the NEP was successful in stopping hyperinflation, its harsh impact on lower-class groups set in motion successive waves of anti-neoliberal mobilizations (Silva 2009). Despite the rise of anti-neoliberal resistance, subsequent governments adhered to the free-market tenets established in the NEP, albeit with occasional backsliding in controlling government spending. President Gonzalo Sánchez de Lozada, the MNR's leading mind behind the original NEP, ushered in second generation neoliberal reform in his first administration (1993–1997), with a push to accelerate privatization. Along with privatization came the sweeping Plan de Todos: a set of reforms aimed at enhancing participation, transparency, and distributing profits accrued from privatization (Van Cott 2000, 149–79). The plan reached out to indigenous groups with its 1994 education law establishing bilingual, intercultural education with oversight councils run by Aymara, Quechua, and Guaraní participants.

For the party system, the most impactful reform was the 1994 Ley de Participación Popular (LPP). The law mandated the direct election of public officials in three hundred new municipalities along with the creation of a set of oversight committees under the control of grassroots organizations to monitor municipal governments. Given the continued existence of local peasant unions, the reform increased the political clout of these organizations (Thede 2011, 216). Municipal elections opened up a completely new arena for political expression, offering a foothold for new political organizations to emerge. In the words of Van Cott (2005, 220), "the face of politics changed overnight as Bolivia institutionalized direct municipal elections in 1995." The 1995 constitutional reform added to the incentives for political competition by ditching national-level proportional representation in favor of a mixed system allotting half of the seats in the Chamber of Deputies to winning candidates in single-member districts. These reforms enabled the fledgling MAS to develop first in its regional stronghold, the Chapare. A national breakthrough came when MAS captured its first legislative seats in 1997.

### Ecuador's Neoliberal Gradualism

In contrast to Bolivia's continuous implementation of neoliberal policies, Ecuador's approach was gradual and applied in "fits and starts" (Hey and Klak 1999, 67–68). Starting in 1982 and continuing through the 2000s, governments of varying partisan persuasions fell into a pattern of enacting economic stabilization measures to reduce public spending, then rescinding them wholly or partially in the face of public protests. The first fully elaborated plan of neoliberal reform came with the 1984 election of President León Febres Cordero, a PSC leader in Guayaquil's business community. But after two years of monetary, exchange rate, and fiscal policy reforms to stabilize the economy, Febres Cordero retreated from reforms after political crisis weakened his government (Conaghan and Malloy 1994).

The most concerted effort at deep structural reforms came under the conservative government of President Sixto Durán Ballén (1992–1996). For the first time, the privatization of state-owned enterprises was prioritized, and a new agrarian reform law restricted land invasions and squatting. But no single neoliberal policy had a greater long-term effect than the decision to deregulate the banking system. With no effective oversight over lending policies, Ecuador's banks became the economy's ticking time bomb (Martínez 2006).

The financial deregulation generated the catastrophic economic crisis that forced DP leader President Jamil Mahaud from office (1998–2000). As banks collapsed, Mahuad enacted a series of unpopular measures; these included a temporary freeze on bank deposits, devaluation, and finally the adoption of the U.S. dollar as the national currency (North 2004). The 1999–2000 economic crisis was among the worst in Ecuador's history as it ravaged incomes and spurred massive emigration (Jokisch and Pribilsky 2002; Hall 2005). The crisis was a turning point; it eroded public confidence in traditional parties and set the stage for "outsider" challenges.

As in Bolivia, political reforms enacted to placate the popular backlash against neoliberalism ended up facilitating changes in the party system. New election rules made for a "permissive institutional environment" that encouraged political competition (Van Cott 2005, 214–15). While elected municipal governments had been in place in Ecuador since 1980, burdensome national-level party registration rules made getting on the ballot difficult. Under pressure from the Confederación de Nacionalidades Indígenas del Ecuador (CONAIE), Durán Ballén's administration dropped the requirement for nationwide registration and opened the door for candidates to run as "independents," along with allowing groups to run as "movements" instead of parties. Thus, CONAIE was able to launch its own political vehicle, Movimiento Unidad Plurinacional Pachakutik (MUPP), in 1996. While Pachakutik never approximated MAS's electoral success, its anti-neoliberal, anti-imperialist campaign set the left's agenda. Many of Pachakutik's demands, including the proposal for an entirely new constitution, would be championed by Correa and incorporated in PAIS's platform.

## PARTIES UNDER NEOLIBERALISM: STABILITY TO DECLINE

Joseph Schumpeter's classic observation on capitalism's capacity for "creative destruction" aptly describes neoliberalism's effects in Bolivia and Ecuador. In ways that policy makers never fully anticipated, neoliberalism churned society and politics. Public dissatisfaction with the concrete results of neoliberalism was part of the problem. Chronic troubles with corruption and crime further fueled the sense that public policies were failing across the board. The leaders and parties identified with the failures of the neoliberal era fell by the wayside as the backlash against them grew and alternatives emerged.

## Bolivia's Tripartite System

Bolivia's continual implementation of neoliberal reform from 1985 to 2002 owed its existence to a remarkable "silent revolution" that transformed the party system and governance (Mayorga 1997). Between 1985 and 2002, each of the three major parties—the MNR, MIR, and ADN—became governing parties. All engaged in pact making that kept the neoliberal model in place. The desire for stability after the disastrous Siles presidency and ideological affinities explain some of this extraordinary cooperation. But pragmatic considerations also figured into the process. Under Bolivia's electoral law at the time, presidential elections were decided by Congress when no candidate received 50 percent of the vote. This forced parties into intensive bargaining and coalition formation.

By the 1990s, other parties became players in Bolivia's "pacted democracy." These included new populist parties such as Unión Cívica Solidaridad (UCS), founded by the wealthy beer baron Max Fernández, and Conciencia de Patria (CONDEPA), led by popular media personality Carlos Palenque. In exchange for their periodic cooperation in pacts with the government, these parties were rewarded with cabinet ministries or other public sector posts. In addition, the parties were given some leeway to legislate on behalf of their respective constituencies (Muñoz-Pogossian 2008, 105–8). Thus, Bolivia's neoliberal project evolved under an umbrella of "shared ownership." Consequently, voters aimed their ire at all established parties.

The MNR, MIR, and ADN drew support from a mix of voters that included urban popular classes and peasants. All three parties garnered support using clientelism and populist-sounding appeals. None of the parties made significant efforts at democratizing their internal operations, cultivating new leaders, or tapping into the new social movements developing on the ground (Calderón and Gamarra 2003). Few indigenous people were recruited to be candidates or to hold top-level positions (Madrid 2012, 47). Confidence in parties, already low, further dissipated as dissatisfaction with neoliberalism grew and conflicts intensified over the government's unpopular, military-style campaign to eradicate coca cultivation in the countryside. Weakened by the untimely deaths of their founders, CONDEPA and UCS lost their luster as anti-establishment forces.

The 2002 presidential and congressional elections revealed a shifting electoral landscape and previewed what lay ahead for the dominant parties. For the first time since 1985, combined votes for the MNR-MIR-ADN "tripod" fell below 50 percent in a national election, with the ADN taking the worst of the beating (Mayorga 2003, 97–98). In a surprising surge, the upstart MAS was suddenly Bolivia's number-two party, trailing behind the MNR by just two percentage points in the presidential and congressional vote.

## Ecuador's Four-Party System

As in Bolivia, the debt crisis and external pressures generated by the Washington Consensus pushed the governments led by Ecuador's four dominant parties (DP, PSC, ID, PRE) toward neoliberalism from 1981 through 2002. While never featuring the formal political pacts of Bolivia, Ecuador's uneven neoliberalism also relied on interparty cooperation in its implementation. Despite the power of the "big four" parties, the party system remained highly fragmented so that none of the governing parties enjoyed a sustained majority in the congress. Informal deal making was essential for governing. Legislators entered into "ghost coalitions"—behind-the-scenes deals in which they agreed to support government policies in exchange for budgetary transfers to their districts, job appointments, and even cash payments (Mejía 2009). The deal making facilitated neoliberal reform, but it also stoked the impression that Congress was a site of influence peddling and corruption.

As Simón Pachano (2012a) argues, all of the principal parties eventually became identified with the suboptimal performance of the government: "It was very difficult for the average voter to identify which [of the parties] bore responsibility in the administration of public affairs and the legislature" (Pachano 2012a, 3). Moreover, every party, including Bucaram's populist PRE, had some exposure when it came to implementing, or attempting to implement, policies that were identified as neoliberal by the public.

None of the major parties had strong historic ties to labor unions or peasant organizations. To varying degrees, all of the parties relied on clientele networks to win elections. Moreover, every party was limited by its territorially restricted base of support (Pachano 2006). For ID and DP, the region was interior highlands. For the PRE and PSC, votes came from the coastal provinces. When voters started to desert their traditional regional parties and look for alternatives, the dominant parties had no way to compensate for the decline in their geographic strongholds.

Voters demonstrated their willingness to opt for a nontraditional alternative in the 2002 presidential election. Neither of the two leading candidates hailed directly from the "big four" parties. Former army colonel Lucio Gutiérrez, the man who had led the 2000 coup that unseated President Mahuad, launched his candidacy with a rapidly assembled populist vehicle, Partido Sociedad Patriótica (PSP). Gutiérrez's rival was Álvaro Noboa, a billionaire businessman with a populist style who mounted Partido Renovador Institucional Acción Nacional (PRIAN). Garnering support from Pachakutik and other leftist parties by attacking neoliberal policies, Gutiérrez won the presidency. On the congressional side, however, the traditional parties managed to maintain sizeable caucuses. While not eradicating the "big four" parties, the 2002 presidential election showed that they were vulnerable to challenges.

## PARTY SYSTEMS TRANSFORMED: LEFT CHALLENGERS

Bolivia's MAS and Ecuador's PAIS succeeded in channeling the public's disaffection with the political establishment and eventually turned their respective party systems upside down. By the end of the first decade of the twenty-first century, both movements had won successive elections and became hegemonic governing parties. Meanwhile, the parties that championed neoliberalism either were gone altogether or greatly debilitated. The stunning electoral breakthroughs of MAS and PAIS were built on the same foundation: a charismatic leader and inclusive programmatic appeals that encapsulated the aspirations of a broad range of social groups. Still, as Silva (in this volume) and León Trujillo and Spronk (in this volume) corroborate, the two organizations diverged significantly with respect to how they engaged with society and managed relationships with their supporters.

### Bolivia's Rising MAS

Coca farmers (*cocaleros*) of the tropical zone of Cochabamba were the driving force behind the movement that eventually became MAS. These farmers organized to defend their land and livelihood from the Bolivian government's U.S.-led effort to eradicate the crop (Harten 2011, 54). By the late 1980s, the *cocaleros* were a leading force inside the national level peasant organization Confederación Sindical Única de Trabajadores Campesinos de Bolivia (CSUTCB) (Silva in this volume).

Evo Morales forged his leadership skills in the ranks of *cocalero* unionism. By 1988, he was executive secretary of the national *cocalero* federation. In 1996, he became president of the organization representing all the coca federations inside the CSUTCB. Morales became an early advocate of forming a political organization based in popular organizations. The idea had been under discussion in CSUTCB since at least the early 1990s (Harten 2011; Van Cott 2005, 68). Created as Asamblea por la Soberanía de los Pueblos (ASP) in 1994, MAS underwent a number of name changes as it maneuvered to meet the requirements for getting on the ballot in the municipal elections of 1995 and national elections of 1997.

MAS began its ascent as a national political force in 1997 by winning four congressional seats, including one for Morales. In a steady advance, MAS grew its congressional caucus to thirty-five seats in the 2002 elections. Even more astonishing was Morales's second-place finish in the presidential contest with 20.94 percent of the vote. MAS's definitive breakthrough came in the 2005 elections. Departing from the previous pattern that led Congress to select the president because no candidate had garnered more than 50 percent of the vote, Morales won the presidency outright with 50 percent of the vote. MAS's success extended to the legislature, where its eighty-four-member caucus accounted for more than half of the lower-house seats. Still, the breakthrough was not a complete one: conservative opponents clung to a majority in the senate.

As MAS surged, the old guard crumbled and then struggled to regroup. The 2005 presidential candidates of the MNR and Unidad Nacional (UN, a party formed from a split in MIR) polled in the single digits; their congressional lists picked up less than ten seats each. Rightist forces from Banzer's ADN, along with former MNR and MIR politicians, regrouped around a new organization, Poder Democrático y Social (PODEMOS), led by former president Jorge Quiroga (Singer 2007). While it placed second to MAS in the presidential and congressional races, the organization rapidly fell apart. By 2009, nothing was left of the original MNR-MIR-ADN tripod (Alpert, Centellas, and Singer 2010).

MAS's march to national political power reflected an inclusive strategy aimed at appealing to indigenous and mestizo voters across the country. MAS's synthetic political ideology welded long-standing popular demands for inclusion with an embrace of Bolivia's diverse indigenous identities (Albró 2006; Canessa 2006; Dunkerley 2007; Harten 2011; Madrid 2012; Postero 2010). In contrast to political parties organized around a single indigenous identity such as Felipe Quispe's Aymara-based Movimiento Indígena Pachakuti (MIP), MAS did not overtly exclude any ethnic group in its concept of what constituted the "nation." It wrapped indigenous rights, class demands, and nationalism in an appealing package. For MAS, defending coca production meant defending the indigenous people who use it as part of their cultural tradition as well as the peasants who depended on it for their livelihood. The coca leaf became the symbol of the fight for national sovereignty: a cause around which all Bolivians of every background could rally. MAS constructed a convincing "chain of equivalence" across issues that broadened, rather than narrowed, its appeal (Harten 2011, 74–77).

MAS's inclusive message was made all the more attractive by the leader who delivered it. Aymara by descent, Evo Morales migrated to the Quechua-speaking countryside, did his obligatory military service, and returned to earn a living as a *cocalero*. As Crabtree observes (2011, 131), "Morales straddles two traditions of popular organization: the *sindicalista* tradition and the *indigenista.*" His down-to-earth personal style reinforced his authenticity as a man of the people. Morales became a "nodal point for the unification of highly fragmented popular actors into a new common popular identity" (Phillips and Panizza 2012, 12).

Managing the fractious coalition upon which MAS depends proved to be one of Morales's most important tasks as party leader and president. Built on foundational support in rural unions and indigenous communities, MAS won in 2005 and thereafter because of its capacity to appeal to a diverse range of urban organizations (Anria 2013, 33). These included neighborhood associations along with sectorial groups representing formal and informal workers, white-collar professionals, pensioners, and small-business owners (Madrid 2012, 60).

### Ecuador's Pachakutik and PAIS

For a decade prior to Correa's election, Pachakutik was a political movement at the forefront of the struggle against neoliberalism. Like MAS, Pachakutik was founded as a political instrument for channeling the demands of popular social movements, especially the indigenous movement led by CONAIE. In the same vein, Pachakutik projected itself as an inclusive "third option" that would bring indigenous groups and other popular organizations around a progressive agenda (Becker 2008; Cordero 2008). That agenda included stopping negotiations with the U.S. on a free-trade agreement, ending Ecuador's leasing of a coastal air base to the U.S. military for counternarcotics operations, and convoking a constituent assembly to overhaul the country's constitution.

Pachakutik made electoral inroads from 1996 to 2002, winning municipal elections and legislative seats. Unlike MAS, however, Pachakutik ultimately failed in its effort to consolidate as a "big tent" for discontented voters and remained largely identified with the indigenous movement. The high-profile role played by some indigenous leaders in the 2000 coup that toppled President Mahuad raised questions about CONAIE's commitment to democracy. By 2002, Pachakutik's alliance with the urban mestizo-led confederation of social movements, Coordinadora de Movimentos Sociales, was over. Pachakutik's organizational apparatus and leaders were practically synonymous with CONAIE. Like many other parties, Pachakutik's support was circumscribed geographically. Its voters resided in highland provinces and the less-populated Amazon. Pachakutik's limited appeal was compounded further by the relatively low level of indigenous ethnic identification in the electorate.

"Losing by winning" is how Mijeski and Beck (2011) described Pachakutik's fateful decision in 2002 to support the populist presidential bid of Lucio

Gutiérrez. As Roberts (in this volume) observes, many politicians in Latin America engaged in the "bait and switch" on neoliberalism: they campaigned as populists but governed as neoliberals. Gutiérrez was in this genre. He campaigned vigorously on an anti-neoliberal platform, only to abandon it a few months into his presidency. Pachakutik's participation in Gutiérrez's cabinet abruptly ended, but its association with the unpopular government was a long-term liability. In April 2005, Gutiérrez became the third president in less than a decade to be forced out before completing his term in office. Awash in corruption charges and accusations that he had violated the constitution by purging the judiciary, Gutiérrez was forced out by massive antigovernment demonstrations in the streets of Quito. This time, however, CONAIE stayed on the sidelines while Quito's middle class led the charge (Ramírez Gallegos 2005).

As national elections loomed on the horizon for 2006, the void in Ecuador's party system was palpable. With traditional parties on the decline, Pachakutik debilitated, and Gutiérrez's populism discredited, the stage was set for yet another "outsider" candidate. The likelihood that the vote would be dispersed among many parties in the first round of the presidential election enhanced the potential for such a candidate. Thirteen candidates secured slots on the first-round ballot, making it the largest field since the democratic transition of 1979.

By late 2005, efforts to construct a new vehicle to unite forces on the left and discontented voters from across the spectrum were underway. Rafael Correa, a young economist and university professor, burst onto the national scene during the interim government of President Alfredo Palacio (2005–2006). A relative unknown with little experience apart from media punditry, Correa was named as Palacio's minister of finance. His stint was short-lived, but long enough to establish his credentials as a left-leaning technocrat and a virulent critic of neoliberalism. Audacious and outspoken, Correa naturally attracted media attention.

A small group of leftist advisers played a critical role in the formation of PAIS. The group included Guayaquil economist and former Socialist Party activist Ricardo Patiño. Another economist, Alberto Acosta, was a leftist intellectual previously allied with Pachakutik. Gustavo Larrea, a human rights activist and former minister in the Bucaram government, was also on board along with Fander Falconí, a young economist and academic. A public relations guru with experience in presidential campaigns, Vincio Alvarado, was another key member of the team.

These figures and others in PAIS's inner circle had a history of working with leftist causes, but none were bona fide leaders of movements, unions, or civic organizations. Neither Correa nor any other PAIS leader was like Morales. In the absence of organic links with social movements, PAIS strategists opted for a territorially structured campaign that revolved around organizing familial and social networks at the local level (Ramírez Gallegos 2010b).

In the lead-up to the October 2006 election, forces on the left remained dispersed. Many of the young and largely middle-class dissidents in Quito who had mobilized to topple the Gutiérrez government lined up with Correa. Yet other leftists did not. Internally divided over its ill-fated alliance with Gutiérrez, Pachakutik declined Correa's overtures and decided instead to run Luis Macas as its first indigenous candidate for president. The leftist Movimiento Popular Democrático (MPD), based in the national teachers' union, also fielded its own candidate. Center-left forces and the remnants of the social-democratic ID rallied around León Roldós, the candidate of the newly formed Red Ética y Democracia (RED). Roldós, the former socialist and presumptive front-runner, was the brother of the beloved deceased president Jaime Roldós.

Running on an aggressive anti-establishment, anti-neoliberal platform and promising to transform the country with a new constitution, Correa surged past Roldós just weeks before the first round. His media campaign was fresh and attention grabbing, featuring television spots with catchy jingles that mocked the political class (De la Torre and Conaghan 2009). Youthful and kinetic on the campaign trail, Correa embodied the message of change.

Held in October 2006, the first round of the presidential election confirmed the ongoing decline of all the established parties from left to right. Álvaro Noboa, the billionaire running with his own vehicle, PRIAN, finished first with 27 percent, drawing support mostly from the coastal provinces. Correa followed with 23 percent. The PSP, running Lucio Gutiérrez's brother as its nominee, trailed with 17 percent of the vote, along with RED's Roldós with 15 percent of the vote. The rest of the field, including the candidates from PSC, PRE, MPD, and Pachakutik, registered percentages in the single digits.

Not surprisingly, the second-round matchup between Correa and the right-wing populist Noboa brought centrists and leftists together in support of Correa. Both contenders promised voters heavy doses of public spending for social assistance, small-business credit, and housing loans. The second-round election in November 2006 concluded with a sweeping victory for Correa. Winning 57 percent of the vote, Correa expanded his electoral base in the interior highlands and Amazonian provinces, while Noboa's votes were confined largely to the coast.

Unlike Morales and the MAS, Correa's victory was not the product of years of grassroots organizing. Instead, Correa sprinted to the presidency in a partisan void, inventing PAIS along the way and expecting that leftists and other reformers would jump on a winning bandwagon. Correa's assumption proved to be correct. As Pachakutik, CONAIE, and other forces on the left discovered, however, lining up with PAIS did not mean that they would be welcome partners in Correa's inner circle.

## PARTISAN POWER AND INCORPORATING POLICIES

Serial elections and referendums served as the gateway for Morales and Correa to consolidate their own power while entrenching MAS and PAIS as dominant organizations in the reconfigured party systems. Convincing, consecutive victories by MAS and PAIS made for a bipolar dynamic in party competition: MAS and PAIS on one side facing a fractured set of opponents on the other (Alpert, Centellas, and Singer 2010; Eichorst and Polga-Hecimovich 2013).

After winning in the first round of 2005, Morales handily fought off a 2008 presidential recall election, taking 67 percent of the vote. Voters also endorsed MAS's new 2008 constitution with 61 percent approval. Morales went onto his 2009 reelection, winning in the first round with 64 percent of the vote. On the legislative side, MAS expanded its control in the national legislature. Securing a majority of 72 of out 130 lower-chamber seats in 2005, MAS won a supermajority of 96 seats in the 2009 election.

Correa and PAIS enjoyed a similar string of election victories. Eighty-two percent of the electorate endorsed Correa's 2007 proposal for a constituent assembly. Months later, voters opted for a PAIS majority of 73 seats in the 130-member body. In 2008, 64 percent of voters approved the new constitution. In 2009, Correa sailed to a first round reelection victory with 52 percent of the vote; in 2013, he secured reelection once again on the first round with 57 percent of the vote. As in Bolivia, PAIS was transformed from a majority into a supermajority party in the national legislature. PAIS's 59-seat caucus in the 124-member body of 2009 turned into a 100-seat caucus in the 137-seat body of 2013.

By securing convincing serial election victories that legitimated their visions of change, Morales and Correa were equipped to accomplish what they had set out to do. Executive power, enhanced by new constitutions and legislative majorities, would be harnessed to dismantle neoliberalism and launch policies incorporating the social, economic, and cultural demands of lower-class groups.

### MAS's Incorporation

After a highly contentious constituent assembly process forced some concessions to opponents, Morales and MAS finally delivered a constitution in 2009

(Schavelzon 2012). The document laid out a bold agenda to transform the role of the state and expand the rights of citizenship. The "essential functions" assigned to the state in Article 9 of the constitution outline an ambitious set of priorities. Among the state's duties are ensuring "decolonialization;" consolidating "plurinational identity;" guaranteeing access to education, health, and work; advancing industrialization; and conserving the environment. As Artaraz argues (2012, 170), the Bolivian constitution constituted a significant redefinition of the social contract. Instead of leaving individuals and communities at the mercy of unpredictable market forces and homogenizing globalization, the state was charged with assuming a proactive role in leading economic development, deepening social welfare, and safeguarding the myriad indigenous cultures of the country.

The redefinition of the social contract under Morales involved creating new policies and expanding on those already in place. Social protection programs targeting infant and maternal health, childhood nutrition, and other problems in poor communities existed prior to the Morales government (World Bank 2005a). Morales significantly expanded the welfare assistance by creating new direct cash transfers to targeted groups. Low-income schoolchildren became recipients of monthly-assistance payments through the Bono Juancito Pinto program (Artaraz 2012, 45). Expectant and recent mothers also received significant monthly-assistance payments in the Bono Juana Azurduy program. Another breakthrough came with a major restructuring of Bonosol, the universal pension program created as part of Sánchez de Lozada's second-generation reforms. In its place, Morales created the Renta Dignidad plan, which greatly expanded eligibility for noncontributory participants along with payments (Müller 2009). Taken together, three out of every four households received some form of assistance. Low-income consumers benefited greatly from subsides that included the Tarifa Dignidad, the reduced electricity rate applied to low-use households. Public health care missions were directed to fight hunger, improve eye care, and assist the disabled. Through these programs, the Morales administration succeeded in edging down the overall poverty rate, especially in the countryside.

The collective demands for respect and inclusion long made by indigenous peoples and other marginalized groups were incorporated into the constitution as well as public policy. The new constitution established Bolivia as a "plurinational" state with a foundational commitment to protecting the autonomy and rights to self-government of "indigenous first-peoples peasants" (*indígena originario campesinos*). Along with according thirty-six indigenous languages official status, the document contained provisions that gave indigenous communities the right to administer traditional justice practices, established that government exercise "prior consultation" with communities in advance of projects affecting the environment, and created indigenous districts for the allotment of seats to the National Assembly. Gender equality was entrenched in articles stipulating nondiscriminatory practices for workplaces, schools, and with regard to property owning. The rights of other categories of people (children, the disabled, the elderly, adolescents, prisoners, and consumers) were also explicitly delineated along with universal access to water, energy, and medicines (República de Bolivia 2009).

To make this new social citizenship a reality, the Morales administration depended on revenues from the country's natural resource industries. To this end, Morales enacted policies aimed at capturing more rent from the country's major natural resource industries through royalties and taxation. Thus, the government significantly increased its revenues, making increases on social spending and infrastructure possible (Gray Molina 2010, 65–68). The pursuit of this ambitious incorporation project became linked, at least in the short and medium term, to an extractive model of economic development.

## PAIS's Incorporation

Ecuador's constitution, written by a PAIS majority in the 2007–2008 Constituent Assembly, also laid out an expansive set of collective and substantive rights. Designating the state as "plurinational" and "intercultural," the document extended special ethnic recognition and collective rights to indigenous and African-descendent communities along with culturally distinctive coastal peasants known as *montubios*. The state was assigned responsibilities to look after the needs of specific categories of persons (the elderly, youth, the disabled, pregnant women, people with catastrophic illnesses, Ecuadorians living abroad, consumers). In addition to traditional civil liberties and commitments to universal education and health, the constitution stipulated universal rights that included access to water, food, a clean environment, and even recreation (República del Ecuador 2008).

As in Bolivia, increased social spending went hand in hand with the constitutional commitment to social citizenship. Cash-transfer programs figured largely in this equation. Cash payments to the poor started under the Mahuad administration as the Bono Solidario. Under Correa, the number of beneficiaries and benefits increased in the Bono de Desarrollo program (Ray and Kozameh 2012). Other *bono* programs provided support for schoolchildren, medical treatments, small-business projects, assistance to the disabled, home construction credit, and subsidized utility rates. Improving the living standards of low-income citizens was not the only focus of government efforts. Modernizing and improving the efficiency and quality of state services for all citizens was also a goal; turning the government into a "friendly and nearby" partner for citizens was an important component of the national development plan (Secretaría Nacional de Planificación y Desarollo 2009).

Like Bolivia, Ecuador's ability to implement social policies depended enormously on financing from natural resource exports. Revenues from petroleum, generating around 35 percent of all government income, underwrote social programming, and helped fuel the overall growth of public spending in the period 2007–2011. While this strategy facilitated the initial implementation of incorporating policies and proved extremely popular at the ballot boxes in both countries, sustaining this formula is another matter. Social resistance to extractivist development (Silva in this volume), especially among indigenous groups, and unstable or declining profits proved problematic for the model over time.

## GOVERNANCE AND PARTISAN POLITICS

In constitutions and public policies, the governments of MAS and PAIS confirmed their commitment to collective and substantive incorporation; they extended a broad array of new rights and benefits to low-income and previously marginalized groups. The policies that provided for substantive incorporation, however, did not entail a parallel procedural incorporation of targeted beneficiaries into the actual decision-making processes, either in the party proper or in strategic locations inside the government bureaucracy (León Trujillo and Spronk in this volume; Silva in this volume).

Of the two cases, Bolivia's MAS juggled the most complex set of relationships between society and government. MAS, formed as the "political instrument" of contentious social movements, retained its foundational base. At the same time, it transformed into a ruling party with goals that included winning more elections and governing competently. That required reaching an ever-growing number of urban voters and carving out some capacity to resist the sectorial demands of organized groups, including MAS's own constituents. Amid these often competing and contradictory tasks stood Evo Morales, the tireless mediator and "nodal point" that held MAS together. MAS functioned as a hybrid. It was neither fully controlled from "below" nor entirely dictated to "above." In Ecuador, the lack of foundational ties between social movements and PAIS made for a more "top-down" model of how the movement would function in relation to society and the state. Correa, in conjunction with insiders at the apex of PAIS, determined which individuals and groups would be accorded entry to places of power.

## In Power: Morales and MAS

Do Alto and Stefanoni (2010) maintain that MAS is best understood as a system of "satellites" that revolve around Morales. The satellites include social movement organizations, the legislative caucus, public sector appointees, and the technocratic corps within the state apparatus. Representatives of popular class organizations often move across these realms, but their pervasive presence did not translate into a steady exercise of power across all areas of policy making. They vie for power with middle-class professionals and activists, known as "*invitados*" (guests). Recruited directly for administrative posts or as candidates by Morales, the *invitados* serve multiple purposes. They demonstrate MAS's willingness to make alliances beyond its peasant base and acquire skilled professional personnel. The most notable *invitado* is Vice President Alvaro García Linera, the prolific leftist theoretician and former guerrilla. The leftist La Paz-based party, Movimiento Sin Miedo (MSM), was also among those invited to collaborate as part of MAS's legislative slate in 2005 (Brockman and Aparicio 2012). *Invitados* have been a crucial component in expanding MAS's electoral appeal.

MAS's growing diversity, however, did not eclipse its ties with rural social movements. MAS's dual membership structure, combining territorially based units and "corporate" entities, demonstrates how deeply entrenched these ties are (Anria 2010). The highest portfolios in its national board remained reserved for leaders from MAS's three foundational peasant organizations: CSUTCB, Confederación Sindical de Comunidades Interculturales Originarias de Bolivia (CSCIOB), and Confederación Nacional de Mujeres Campesinas Indígenas de Bolivia-Bartolina Sisa (CNMCIOB-BS). In a powerful symbolic act that underscored this continuing relationship, Morales retained his titular position as head of the *cocaleros* union after he was inaugurated as president. Even more importantly, Morales continued to lead in a manner attuned to the traditions and practices of social movements: face-to-face consensus building (Zegada, Arce, and Canedo 2011, 255; Silva in this volume).

On the ground level, popular organizations intervene actively in the recruitment and selection of MAS candidates. The rivalries among organizations are often intense, making for messy and weakly institutionalized candidate selection procedures (do Alto and Stefanoni 2010). Nonetheless, the competition allows for popular class participation in the internal operations of MAS and provides these organizations with a way to ensure some access to the collateral patronage jobs that come attached to elective office (do Alto and Stefanoni 2010; Zuazo 2010). Access to public sector serves as visible proof of the power of movements in MAS and in the state.

MAS's electoral success translated into political power and upward mobility for popular class leaders. Morales drew his first 2006 cabinet entirely from the ranks of MAS militants, with social movement leaders figuring prominently among the appointees along with leftist intellectuals (Muñoz-Pogossian 2008, 201). While technocrats edged out social movement leaders over time, the elevation of popular class leaders was a breakthrough of significant political and symbolic importance. It was a visible demonstration of MAS's "decolonizing" of the state, reversing the country's history of exclusion. Ministries headed by indigenous leaders have included foreign relations, justice, education, and rural development.

MAS's takeover of the state effectively transformed the social composition of the country's political elite (Mayorga 2011). For the first time, indigenous and peasant leaders constituted a "critical mass" inside the state. Since 2006, approximately half of members of MAS's caucuses in the legislature and the Constituent Assembly have been indigenous (Madrid 2012, 167–68). The new constitution reinforced this opening up of the state by designating indigenous seats to the national and local electoral tribunals along with requiring special consideration for indigenous peoples in recruitment for public sector posts. Nonetheless, as several Bolivian scholars point out, cabinet appointments are regarded as personal invitations extended by Morales. Individual leaders, not their organizations, are invited to partake in power.

While unrivaled in its electoral strength since Morales's 2005 election, MAS remained institutionally underdeveloped. MAS opened party politics and public administration to its social movement allies, but the primary loyalties of members resided with their organization rather than MAS. The party itself did not emerge as the key institutional side for policy design or conflict resolution. Instead, as Fernando Mayorga shows (2011, 97), organizations allied with MAS worked together in special entities created to deal with "high aggregation" issues—that is, policy challenges central to MAS's project and the defense of the Morales government. The Pacto de Unidad made up of CSUTCB, CSCIOB, CNMCIOB-BS, and other organizations developed the blueprint for the government's constitutional project; the Coordinadora Nacional por el Cambio (CONALCAM) defended against intensified opposition over the new constitution. In contrast to high aggregation issues that unify MAS's coalition, "low aggregation" issues involve specific sectorial demands that weaken organizational support for MAS (Silva in this volume).

Launched by peasants as a "political instrument," MAS made the leap to become a multiclass party with support from urban popular and middle-class voters across the country (Oviedo 2010; Anria 2013). Yet the blurry lines between MAS and social movements made it difficult to institutionalize clear rules for its internal operations. At the helm of an institutionally weak but electorally potent organization, Morales acts as a centralizing force that keeps MAS together. Drawing on his skills as a grassroots organizer, his charisma, and the powers of the presidency, Morales juggled MAS's unstable coalition in a way that provided some measure of access and influence to its constituents. Social movements are heeded, in part because they are important political actors inside MAS and because they remain willing to use contentious tactics when they disagree with Morales. The notion that Bolivia is ruled by a "government of social movements," however, is an oversimplification. As Silva (in this volume) shows, certain realms of policy making (like agriculture) are more open to social movement lobbying while others (like finance) are controlled by technocrats. The idea that Morales leads a "government of social movements" should be understood as aspirational, not operational: an evocative phrase that encapsulates MAS's message of inclusion (Zegada, Arce, and Canedo 2011, 274–75).

### In Power: Correa and PAIS

Correa won in 2006 with the support of groups, parties, and activists rallying around PAIS in the second-round runoff election. Leftists from Pachakutik, MPD, and CONAIE believed that the Correa presidency could become a launching pad for social reform and constitutional change. Closing ranks around Correa were reform-minded groups interested in constitutional change such as the young professionals of Movimiento Ruptura 25 (MR-25), who had mobilized to bring down the Gutiérrez government in 2005.

Correa's first cabinet established his leftist credentials, but it did not signify a dramatic social breakthrough for marginalized groups like that of Morales. Nor did it reflect any pact-making sympathetic groups or parties. The only indigenous appointee was Mónica Chuji as secretary of communication; the only African-descendent appointee was the poet Antonio Preciado as minister of culture. Excluding the one cabinet slot given to the Socialist Party, no other parties were invited to join the cabinet. Correa's preference for working with loyal PAIS professionals and technocrats was reflected in every subsequent cabinet.

Despite the absence of a formal pact with other parties, informal cooperation between PAIS and other forces on the left proved critical to the advancing of a new constitution. Underscoring his disdain for traditional party politics, Correa ran solo for the presidency in 2006 without a slate of PAIS congressional candidates. In the Machiavellian maneuvering that preceded the installation of the Constituent Assembly in the first half of 2007, Correa relied on congressional votes from leftist and populist parties to endorse his plan for suspending Congress and turning power over to a constituent assembly likely to be controlled by PAIS.

PAIS's slate of candidates for the assembly election was a product of top-down decision making in the organization. Correa and the top echelon of PAIS controlled the candidate selection process. Provincial leaders and other allied groups offered up potential nominees for the poll testing that preceded final approval (El Universo 2007). The candidate selection process yielded an eclectic list that combined veteran politicians fleeing traditional parties with novices who had never before run for office.

Riding on Correa's enormous popularity, PAIS won a smashing victory by taking 80 of the 130 assembly seats. Pachakutik and MPD added another nine on the left. The ongoing collapse in the party system was evident in the very poor electoral performance of standard contenders such as PSC, PRE, and PRIAN. Correa had cleared a path for PAIS to dominate the deliberations on the new constitution. Alberto Acosta, a PAIS founder, was elected president of the assembly. The ten thematic working groups in the assembly, charged with consulting the public and drafting articles, were also under PAIS control; eight of the thirteen seats in each working group were allotted to PAIS (Carter Center 2008).

The constitutional assembly previewed the problems that later led to a complete breakdown in the relation between PAIS and the organized left. Disagreements on policy substance and decision-making style were plain to see. Dedicated to the notion that the constitution required extended consultations with groups in civil society, Acosta sent working groups out across the country to collect proposals. Frustrated with the slow pace of the proceedings, Correa pressured Acosta to speed up the process. Acosta balked and resigned. Pachakutik and CONAIE also found themselves on the losing side of fights with Correa, who rejected their demands to give official status to all indigenous languages and to give indigenous communities veto power over mining projects.

Yet, despite the disappointments with the process and the limits in the text, the expansive rights laid out in the constitution were sufficient to keep most movements and left parties on board for its ratification in the 2008 referendum (Hernández and Buendía 2011, 135). The broad coalition for "yes" yielded an important victory when 64 percent of the electorate approved the new constitution. The approval set the stage for a new set of national elections in April 2009, keeping Correa in power with 52 percent of the vote in a single round.

The divide between dissenters on the left and PAIS intensified thereafter. Correa saw PAIS's project as one of building an efficient, strong, autonomous state. That meant stripping away what he viewed as "corporatist practices" in the form of interest group influence over policy making. This applied to interest groups as well as to CONAIE and environmental groups that challenged the government's extractive development model (Collins 2012). After fractious conflicts over education reform, MPD also joined the opposition (Silva in this volume).

A 2011 referendum engendered further conflicts between disillusioned leftists and the president. Unhappy with the slow pace of judicial reforms, Correa asked voters to authorize a process to replace judicial personnel in a manner contrary to procedures laid out in the new constitution. Excluded from PAIS's political bureau after his conflict with Correa over management of the Constituent Assembly, Alberto Acosta criticized Correa's authoritarian style and called on voters to reject the change. Gustavo Larrea, another PAIS founder frozen out of the inner circle, joined in the call for a no vote. Also breaking with the government was MR-25, whose young leaders, María Paula Romo and Norman Wray, played a prominent role in the Constituent Assembly. While the government won all nine questions on the May 2011 ballot, the referendum rendered the narrowest victory for PAIS since taking power in 2007.

The collapse in the cooperation between the left and Correa in 2011 complicated his legislative agenda, as did the desertion of several high-profile PAIS caucus members. Without an absolute majority, PAIS was forced into constant negotiations with "independent" legislators. Major pieces of legislation needed to enable constitutional provisions such as water rights and mining regulations languished with no resolution.

The 2013 national elections gave PAIS the opportunity to resolve the impasse caused by the lack of a legislative supermajority. The results of the National Assembly election confirmed the power of Correa's coattails and PAIS's ascent as the hegemon in the party system. PAIS trounced its rivals, taking 48 percent of the overall legislative vote, adding thirty-eight additional legislators to its caucus for a total of one hundred members. PAIS's two-thirds majority, entrenched for the period 2013–2017, now enjoyed untrammeled power to legislate without the need for negotiations or pacts.

With solid approval ratings and a buoyant economy, Correa's own presidential reelection was never in doubt. He secured the victory by taking 57 percent of the votes in the first round. His strongest competitor was Guayaquil banker Guillermo Lasso, who rallied conservative and centrist voters around his newly created vehicle Movimiento Creando Oportunidades (CREO). Lasso won 23 percent of the vote, but Correa's remaining rivals drew percentages in the single digits. The losing candidates included Correa's leftist rivals who had broken with PAIS, Alberto Acosta, and Norman Wray. Acosta led a united leftist front supported by Pachakutik, MPD, and CONAIE, while Wray ran as the MR-25 candidate.

Born as a vehicle for Rafael Correa, PAIS became an electoral powerhouse. Unlike Ecuador's other parties, PAIS successfully reached across the country's regional divides and become a "truly national party" in 2013 (Eichorst and Polga-Hecimovich 2013). The "nationalization" of PAIS was reflected in its capacity to mount candidate slates in every province and electoral district. Expanding PAIS's membership base and solidifying its organizational structure was one of the keys to its success. After the 2009 reelection, which left Correa short of a supermajority, PAIS focused on strengthening its territorial reach through a proliferation of Comités de la Revolución Ciudadana (CRC): groups of anywhere from five to twenty supporters, typically based in neighborhood networks. For the 2013 elections, PAIS mobilized an estimated four to five thousand CRC units for its door-to-door campaign. A youth wing, Juventud PAIS, became part of the organizational grid mobilized for electioneering (Alianza País 2013).

Organizational expansion, however, did not change the ethos inside PAIS. Control over the critical decisions in the organization remained in the hands of Correa and nonelected members of the Dirección Nacional (DN). In Correa's second administration, the DN included several government ministers, the president of the National Assembly, the mayor of Quito, the prefect of Pichincha Province, and PAIS's executive secretary, who served formerly as Correa's presidential secretary. The DN's composition collapsed any distinction between PAIS and the government; officials became interchangeable and served at the pleasure of the president (Pachano 2012b). Correa candidly acknowledged that enjoying his "confidence" was the key criteria for appointment to the DN (Harnecker 2010).

PAIS's rank and file never played a significant role in shaping the government's policy agenda. At most, membership served as a gateway for participating in the politicking surrounding the nominations of candidates for local and regional offices along with the provincial assembly lists. In 2009, PAIS's first attempt at staging internal primaries generated chaotic infighting. In 2013, provincial assemblies took place in lieu of primaries, but the candidate lists remained subject to vetting by the DN, which deployed public opinion polls to identify the most electable. The DN selected the candidates for the assembly's "national" seats.

PAIS owed much of its electoral success to a masterfully designed media operation orchestrated by Vinicio Alvarado, the architect of the 2006 victory. He brought his skills to the presidential palace, serving as the Secretary General of Public Administration (2009–2013) and Secretary General of Communication (2009–2013). Alvarado oversaw the development of a large media operation inside the government designed to drive home the administration's accomplishments, stoke Correa's personal appeal, and attack critics of the Citizens' Revolution. In advertising campaigns, imagery and slogans blurred the lines between PAIS and the government.

In addition to the heavy use of paid advertising and the free broadcast time that media outlets were obliged to provide, Correa directly connected with the public on his Saturday morning radio and television broadcast, *Enlace Ciudadano*. Running for several hours, the show was staged each week at different locations around the country. With cabinet members in tow, Correa used the show to rally and reward local PAIS supporters and keep in touch with municipal and regional officials. For the broader audience, the show functioned as a venue for the president to educate the public on his policies (with the obligatory PowerPoint slides) while naming and shaming his opponents.

From its inception in 2006, PAIS proved to be an effective vehicle for winning elections but not for representing or even interacting with organized interests of any sort. PAIS reached out to voters as individuals, not as group members, with the brilliantly marketed promise of a "Citizens' Revolution." Absent was any intimation that the revolution was intended as a real exercise in deliberative democracy or a way toward a "government of social movements."

## MAS, PAIS, AND PARTY SYSTEMS TRANSFORMED

In Bolivia and Ecuador, voters turned their backs on the parties associated with neoliberalism and the accompanying policies of disincorporation (Rossi and Silva in this volume). Now more than twenty-five years after the implementation of neoliberal policies, the purveyors of the model are either entirely gone from political life or have been reduced to mere shadows of their former selves.

In the 2009 Bolivian national elections, none of the original parties associated with neoliberalism (MNR, ADN, MIR) even appeared on the ballot. In Ecuador, the two parties most identified with neoliberal policies (DP, PSC) floundered. After sitting out presidential elections in the 2000s and seating just a handful of legislators, what had been DP (renamed as Unión Democrata Cristiana) finally lost its legal status as a party in 2013. After polling poorly against Correa in 2006, the PSC sat out the 2009 and 2013 presidential elections. Once commanding legislative caucuses of more than twenty members in the 1990s, the PSC delegation stood at just six legislators by 2013.

Populist vehicles that veered in and out of relationships with traditional parties during the neoliberal era also fared poorly. In Bolivia, CONDEPA and UCS proved incapable of overcoming the deaths of their charismatic founders. In Ecuador, Bucaram's failed presidency and his subsequent exile in Panama sealed PRE's decline. Gutiérrez's PSP suffered a similar fate with a botched presidency in 2005. The PSP struggled to recoup in subsequent elections, but to no avail. Alvaro Noboa's successive defeats in presidential elections (1998, 2002, 2006, 2009, 2013) eviscerated PRIAN's legislative caucus.

The fall of the traditional parties and populist contenders created a void that MAS and PAIS filled. Yet MAS and PAIS were not the only forces vying for the power to overturn neoliberalism. In these multiparty systems, they faced other parties that articulated many of the same claims. In its early stage of development, MAS was competing with other indigenous and leftist parties such as Felipe Quispe's MIP and Movimiento Bolivia Libre (MBL). In Ecuador, PAIS emerged only after Pachakutik miscalculated miserably in its alliance with the Gutiérrez government and failed to expand beyond its strongholds in indigenous highland communities. What catapulted MAS and PAIS to power over the competitors was a potent combination: compelling, broad programmatic appeals delivered by a captivating leader committed to the cause. The formula turned these organizations into catchall parties with support across ethnic, class, and regional divides.

After winning their first presidential elections, Morales and Correa labored to ensure that they and their political organizations would dominate the party system. Delivering on the promise of a new era of incorporation in the form of new constitutions and enhanced welfare programs was vital to maintaining and expanding support for the new governments. They also deployed state power to effect partisan advantage. In both countries, the constitutional change allowing for immediate reelection transformed each president from a lame duck to a powerful incumbent with an array of resources available to wield in every election cycle. Poorly enforced campaign regulations and the government's ability to outspend opponents worked in favor of MAS and PAIS.

With each election, Morales and Correa reduced the space for political opponents and consolidated more power in their respective organizations. Encumbered by conservative control over the senate and opposition from regional governors during his first term, Morales led MAS through serial elections in 2009 and 2010 that addressed the problem. MAS took control of the senate, taking twenty-six out of thirty-six seats in 2009. In the following year, MAS increased its departmental governorships from two to six out of ten and won two-thirds of the municipal government races nationwide.

Correa similarly secured untrammeled legislative power for PAIS by turning its wobbly 2009 majority into a commanding supermajority of one hundred legislators in 2013. Analysts pointed to the advantages that accrued to PAIS in the wake of the government's change in election rules and election districts. A mixed Hare/D'Hondt formula, used for calculating the proportion of seats assigned to parties in 2009, was switched entirely to the D'Hondt formula, known to overrepresent the winning slate. The creation of new electoral districts in the three most densely populated provinces, and the fragmentation of the votes therein, further advantaged PAIS (Zeas 2013).

By dominating elections, MAS and PAIS effectively polarized their fragmented party systems: the political arena divided between the governing party and the forces opposed, with little room for compromise between the two sides. One notable exception to the polarized political combat occurred in late 2008 when MAS agreed to end the spiraling conflict over the constitution by accepting some of the modifications demanded by Quiroga's PODEMOS. The subsequent collapse of PODEMOS made for an even more scattered field of opposition. Some regionally based opponents rallied around Manfred Reyes, the populist leader from Cochabamba; others looked to the businessman and two-time presidential candidate Samuel Doria Medina and his centrist Unidad Nacional (UN). In 2010, the leftist La Paz–based reformist party Movimiento sin Miedo (MSM) officially ended its alliance with MAS.

Similarly, PAIS faced a mixed bag of opponents. No unifying leader or organization emerged. With traditional parties and populist vehicles of the past obliterated or greatly debilitated, new efforts to mount antigovernment movements on the left and on the right yielded varied returns. The best performance by the opposition in the 2013 national elections came from Guayaquil Guillermo Lasso and his organization, CREO. While Lasso failed to force Correa into a second-round runoff, he garnered 23 percent of the vote in his debut appearance as a presidential candidate, and CREO became the single largest opposition caucus in the assembly with eleven deputies. In contrast to Lasso's credible performance on the center-right, leftists at odds with Correa from the ranks of Pachakutik and MPD failed miserably in their attempt to mount an alternative in the Coordinadora Plurinacional de las Izquierdas. As its presidential candidate, Alberto Acosta took just 3 percent of the vote, and its legislative list rendered only five seats in the assembly.

MAS and PAIS shifted the parameters of the national political debate. Unvarnished neoliberalism was off the table for vote-seeking candidates of every partisan persuasion. In Ecuador's 2013 elections, every presidential candidate promised increases in the antipoverty *bono* assistance and to continue proactive government policies in health, education, and employment. Recognizing the public's strong approval of economic and welfare policies, partisan opponents have differentiated themselves from the governing party most explicitly on matters related to democratic governance, especially what they view as the excessive concentration of powers in the presidency. Arguments about the lack of checks and balances, however, never resonated significantly with the public at large in the period under discussion. Morales and Correa readily brush off such procedural criticisms, citing their substantial election victories as the source of their governments' democratic legitimacy.

Overtaking all competitors, MAS and PAIS went from being political movements to constituting governments. Missing in this transition, however, was any clear consensus or blueprint for their long-term development as political parties. Under the control of charismatic presidents intent on consolidating power and pursuing their transformative projects, MAS and PAIS were first and foremost instruments in the service of those ends. Overshadowed by and dependent on their one-of-a-kind leaders, the organizations remained underinstitutionalized.

Leading MAS and PAIS, Morales and Correa turned initial victories into unprecedented electoral hegemony. Their transformation of the party system laid the basis for other equally momentous transformations in constitutions, laws, and public policy. Enjoying the continuity provided by reelection, Morales and Correa spearheaded a new era of incorporation for popular sectors. Nationalism, social welfare, and a "rights revolution" were part of the potent mix that brought voters from across the social spectrum into the folds of MAS and PAIS. Whether and how MAS and PAIS can sustain their winning formula in the long haul is a complex matter. It will demand keeping their "catchall" coalitional capabilities intact and withstanding the inevitable conflicts about who will take the reins from their exceptional founders.

Chapter 12

# THE SECOND WAVE OF INCORPORATION AND POLITICAL PARTIES IN THE VENEZUELAN PETROSTATE

## DANIEL HELLINGER

Venezuela is just one of several Latin American countries where mass protest movements drove elected presidents from office, motivated at least in part by a sense of betrayal or frustration as elected leaders attempted to implement neoliberal policies (see Roberts and Rossi in this volume). As Roberts puts it, what occurred in some countries was a "basic rupture of the constitutional order" and "a sharp turn away from neoliberal orthodoxy." Certainly that applies to the course of events following the forced resignation of President Carlos Andrés Pérez in early 1993. The backlash against the government also undermined the hegemony of his party, the social democratic Acción Democrática (AD). The succeeding period saw rise of the cashiered lieutenant colonel Hugo Chávez Frías, leader of a failed coup against Pérez in 1992. Chávez and his Bolivarian movement "outflanked" the traditional leftist parties, including the Movimiento al Socialismo (MAS), which for twenty-five years had posed as the authentic left option to the "pacted democracy" known as Punto Fijo.

As the country limped to the end of 2014, a rare year in which no national elections took place, neither Chavismo nor the opposition had consolidated itself fully into an institutionalized party or coalition of parties. The PSUV certainly has developed some organizational stability, but its procedures, the nomination process, and ideological goals remain diffuse, and it faces the possible exit or expulsion of its most committed, grassroots cadre. The Mesa de la Unidad Democrática (MUD) emerged from the ashes of the opposition's extra-constitutional efforts to depose Chávez in 2001 and 2002 and its failure to acknowledge and learn from Chávez's overwhelming victory in the recall election of August 2004. The MUD attempted to forge its own ties to social

movements, notably among students. However, from the start its heterogeneous members have shown little consensus programmatically, and its most
outspoken and extreme leaders embraced sectors in the streets committed to
the violent, disruptive tactics of the earlier period.

It has become increasingly apparent in the period since the death of
Chávez in 2014 that like so many other processes and organizations, the political party system is weakly institutionalized. In part, this can be attributed to the failure of Chávez to transfer his charisma to institutions. However,
the polarization between the parties and the growing divisions within them
have roots in struggles to define how they will relate to the Venezuelans who
were reincorporated politically, economically, and socially under Chávez's
leadership.

The period after 1998 saw Chávez attempt to consolidate a new regime
marked by two features common to regime change: (1) new "rules of the
game" embodied in the 1999 constitution and (2) a redefinition of the relationship between the state and civil society. In the first few years, Chávez concentrated on the first task. The second began to take shape after 2001 with a
reform of the oil laws and the successful struggle by Chávez to assert control
over the state oil company, PDVSA, in effect giving Chavismo control over oil
rents (superprofits), the main source of accumulation of capital in the country. In 2006, Chávez, with much less success, moved to redefine relations between the state and civil society through institutionalization of a communal
state, first through accelerated efforts to channel oil rents through grassroots,
communal councils and then an attempt to institutionalize a "new geography
of power" by drawing the communal councils together into networks constituting "communes." The communes, which would not correspond to existing
state and municipal boundaries, clearly pose a challenge, if not a threat to the
authority of elected officials, regardless of their party.

It was Hugo Chávez's intention, then, not only to reincorporate the popular sector politically but to restructure state relations with civil society, and it
was not until 2006 that he acknowledged the need for a revolutionary political
party to accomplish that goal. Yet at the same time, that party, the PSUV, was
tasked with mobilizing votes, with every election turned into a referendum
on the entire Bolivarian project. With the exception of defeat in a referendum for constitutional reform (in December 2007), the Bolivarian movement
swept to electoral victories in every national, state, and local election held
right through to Chávez's last campaign in 2013. From the start, the PSUV
struggled to reconcile electoral mobilization and social mobilization. Within
its ranks, tensions always existed between professional politicians and grassroots activists. In November 2014, less than two years after Chávez's death,

this tension fully revealed itself as, in anticipation of internal elections, the PSUV moved to the brink of expelling leaders of the left wing of the PSUV, Marea Roja ("Red Tide," a deliberate play on "Pink Tide").

The lone defeat in the referendum, in retrospect, was telling. It represented the failure of Chávez and his most enthusiastic, grassroots supporters to gain the type of majoritarian mandate needed to embark on the second aspect of the project, the communal state. The worst fears of Bolivarian activists were nearly realized when in April 2014, Chávez's chosen successor, Nicolás Maduro, only very narrowly held the presidency for the PSUV, defeating the MUD's Enrique Capriles by less than 2 percent of votes cast.

Both the PSUV and the MUD were held together by a common political lodestone: the paramount political power of Hugo Chávez. In the post-Chávez era, the political success of either one depends upon its ability, whether in office or opposition, to win or maintain the confidence of a population that found in Chávez a vehicle to reclaim its right to inclusion in sharing access to the oil rents that flow from their common ownership of the hydrocarbons under their soil.

## ANTECEDENT CONDITIONS: THE FIRST INCORPORATION

The masses of Venezuelans were first incorporated into economic, social, and political circuits during an extended era of populism that began in the 1940s and reached its apogee, politically and economically, during the 1970's OPEC oil bonanza. Rómulo Betancourt and Acción Democrática (AD) were the main catalysts for this project, which was first spelled out in Betancourt's seminal Plan de Barranquilla, written while he was in exile in Colombia in 1931. The Plan linked political incorporation in the form of democracy and universal adult suffrage with (1) economic development and (2) the anti-imperialist demand for a "just share" of profits generated by the oil exports (Betancourt 1995 [1931], 241–42). Then, as now, the accumulation and distribution of oil rents lay at the heart of the Venezuelan politics.

Betancourt and his main rival, the Communist Party, found allies between 1935 and 1948 in a variety of movements (labor, women, peasants) and organizations (unions, *gremios*, interest groups). Early on, there was a degree of spontaneity and autonomy in this process, but gradually the movements and organizations of the incipient civil society subordinated themselves to discipline imposed by parties, including AD. This latter feature reemerged in the contemporary era as grassroots Chavista leaders and intellectuals bemoan the lack of internal debate and tolerance for dissent within the Bolivarian movement (see Garcia-Guadilla and also Ellner in this volume).

Betancourt and AD governed during a three-year democratic interlude between 1945 and 1948 (the *trienio*). They benefited from the success of the previous government (a modernizing military regime) in enacting in 1943 an oil reform law that wrested a larger share of the superprofits from the foreign oil companies. AD used those resources to pursue an inclusionary program of human development (health, education, housing, labor organizing) and development of national infrastructure (favoring construction over industrialization). In 1948, the fledgling democracy was overthrown by a military coup that established a ten-year dictatorship under Marcos Pérez Jiménez. Pérez Jiménez may have been a brutal authoritarian, but he was a populist who freely dispensed patronage and embarked on megaprojects, especially in housing. A civil-military movement overthrew his government in 1958 and returned Venezuela to democracy that same year.

The Punto Fijo system refers to a power-sharing pact signed at a Caracas villa of the same name among three parties, the most important by far being AD and COPEI, the Comité de Organización Política Electoral Independiente, a Christian democratic party founded in opposition to AD during the *trienio*. (The third party faded quickly in the ensuing decade.) "Puntofijismo" also came to signify a series of other pacts that secured the support of the military, the Church, the AD-dominated union movement, and business leaders for the new regime in an effort to prevent a repetition of the 1948 coup. Just as important, however, the political pact excluded the Communist Party, despite the important role it played in the resistance to the dictatorship, a factor that arguably weakened the link of the party system to the interests of the popular sector. The 1961 Constitution reinforced the pact by creating a system of representation that reinforced the discipline of party leaders over their followers, especially by providing for a closed-list system of proportional representation. This list system extended to civil society, which was colonized by the parties, the main mediators between the petrostate and interest groups. The party leadership exercised strict control as well over nominations for a broad range of elected officials in unions, student organizations, professional associations, and myriad other organizations of civil society, most of which were heavily subsidized by the state.

In contrast to other cases examined in this volume, political incorporation was more closely linked to the distribution of oil rents through social welfare, construction, services, and commerce than to a program of import substitution industrialization. Even during the bonanza period of the 1970s, the new subsidized heavy industries (especially the metallurgical enterprises in Ciudad Guayana) were created with the aim of serving export markets, not import substitution in the domestic market. Together, the Pact of Punto

Fijo and the Constitution of 1961 defined a regime by which the state related to civil society as the allocator of oil rents that it appropriated from the oil industry, at that time dominated by three foreign companies (Standard, Shell, Gulf) operating under forty-year concessions granted in 1943.

Interest aggregation under Puntofijismo took the form of institutionalizing competition for rents among the competing factions of the bourgeoisie, while at the same time channeling a portion of oil rents toward the popular sectors through organizations (unions, professional associations, student groups, neighborhood associations, peasant leagues) directly linked to the state through party structures. This aggregation process involved not only periodic electoral competition for control of state institutions but internal party posts and—it cannot be emphasized enough—intense partisan competition among the parties for control of civic organizations (Rey 1991). Until the devaluation of 1983, this was not a zero-sum game. That changed with devaluation and became even more zero-sum in 1989 with a structural adjustment agreement. The resulting social exclusion undermined the myth that electoral democracy would guarantee progress for all as promised in the Plan de Barranquilla.

After nationalization in early 1976, the Pérez government proudly proclaimed, "the oil is ours." Actually, the subsoil had always belonged to the nation; it was the industry that had changed hands. However, once the economy collapsed in the 1980s, leading to the proletarianization of much of the middle class and the pauperization of most of the informal sectors, the motto seemed little more than a bitter irony. After all, if the nation owned the "wealth" and most of the population was poor, could this condition be blamed on "*imperialismo petrolero*"? Venezuelans had to turn inwardly for answers, and their gaze would fall harshly on representative democracy, which no longer seemed capable, as the Plan de Barranquilla had promised of ensuring progress for all.

We see, then, that Venezuela shares with most of Latin America the central characteristic of the first populist era, an attempt to modernize and develop by channeling profits from the key export sectors into a program of economic modernization. But in the Venezuelan case, the populist coalition that pursued this developmental project placed considerably less emphasis on import substitution industrialization. It preferred to develop commerce and services that circulated oil rents. The question of appropriation and distribution of rents by the petrostate were, and remain, at the center of political struggle, much more so than any of Latin America's economically dependent countries.

## THE NEOLIBERAL JUNCTURE: DISINCORPORATION

The currency devaluation of February 18, 1983, during the presidency of Herrera Campíns (COPEI), to this day called "Black Friday," can be considered the beginning of "first-generation reforms" because it radically lowered the quality of life, but it was not part of a broader neoliberal reform. The more drastic fiscal belt tightening came after 1988. This was followed by the *apertura petrolera*, a policy of increasing production by permitting foreign capital to reenter the basic industry on extraordinarily favorable terms (Mommer 2002), which weakened the capacity of the state to capture rents and also lowered them in absolute terms by contributing to lower global market prices (Hellinger 1996).

Jaime Lusinchi, the *adeco* (member of AD) president (1984–1988) who followed Herrera Campíns, borrowed liberally and spent profligately in an attempt, somewhat successful, to slow the economic decline, a tactic that ultimately deepened the economic morass and vulnerability to pressure from international lenders. The Lusinchi administration generated terrible corruption scandals that seemed to have no end or limit, reaching into the presidential palace in tawdry cases of enrichment by the president's mistress. Pérez kept up the populist illusion in his presidential campaign of 1988. When he began his second presidency in 1989, the rapidly deteriorating economy forced an about-face. His announcement of a structural adjustment agreement touched off the *Caracazo*.

Outside of the oil sector, the Venezuelan bourgeoisie was hardly enthusiastic about austerity, given its dependence on the consumer culture fostered by the circulation of oil rents. Outside of several state metallurgical companies in Ciudad Guayana, which were joint ventures, there was little of great interest to privatize outside of the oil sector. Not surprisingly, then, the key target of neoliberal reform was Petróleos de Venezuela (PDV). Superficially, the company was off-limits for privatization by terms of the 1976 nationalization law, but PDV was and is a holding company for subsidiaries that produce, refine, and market hydrocarbons. It never produced a drop of oil. PDV executives, Venezuelans who had already ascended in the pre-nationalization era to top management positions, maneuvered to undermine the state's control over the hydrocarbons in the subsoil under the control of capital and its cooperation with OPEC. The latter sought to defend prices by limiting production; the oil men wanted to expand production, at the expense of maintaining rents.

As the state lost governing capacity and legitimacy, the influence of PDV increased. The state and the parties, not the company, were held responsible for the collapse of oil prices, the devaluation of February 1983, and the deteriorating standard of living. This generated a crisis of representation that was magnified by the corruption scandals, eroding the legitimacy of the pact that defined the country's key institutions. COPEI and AD, and even the smaller political parties, were unwilling to enact reforms that might threaten Punto-fijismo. Nationalization of oil in 1976 had eliminated one of the three legs on which the populist regime had been constructed since 1935. No longer could *imperialismo petrolero* be regarded as an obstacle to fulfillment of the developmental project associated with AD and Punto Fijo.

## SECOND-GENERATION NEOLIBERALISM: POLITICAL REFORMS AND DE-ALIGNMENT

The political environment after the *Caracazo*, mainly the collapse of state institutions (including the oil ministry) and the desperation of the Punto Fijo ruling elite to restore economic growth, prepared the way for the second generation of neoliberal reforms, which consisted of fiscal belt tightening, the *apertura petrolera*, and partial political reforms that only partly loosened the grip of party elites. The parties may have been at the heart of the system, but that vital organ was deprived of its lifeblood—oil rents—and the causes were not entirely exogenous.

PDV executives justified the *apertura petrolera* as a strategy to stimulate economic productivity in both the oil sector and the economy as a whole by attacking rent seeking, portrayed as the underlying source of corruption in Venezuela. One way to do that was to eliminate "rents" themselves, and this was effectively what the *apertura petrolera* achieved by allowing foreign capital to return to the fields under fiscal policies that drastically reduced royalty and made majority ownership by the state little more than a legal subterfuge (see Mommer 2002). Production recovered in the 1990s, but not oil earnings, and things got worse when prices collapsed again in 1998, an election year.

In response to concerns that Venezuelans were becoming increasingly disenchanted with the political system, President Lusinchi in 1984 created a Commission for Political Reform (COPRE). While COPRE largely avoided specific recommendations on economic policy, it saw its work of reforming the state as a contribution to a break with rentier capitalism—the need to make reforms to smooth the passage from a subsidized economy to an economy of the market. COPRE's reports had little impact, however, until the *Caracazo* explosion revealed the depths of popular discontent. It took the crisis of the 1992 coup attempts to induce modest reform of the system of representation, dividing seats in Congress between those elected proportionately and those by "first past the post" for the 1993 elections. The *cogollos* (cliques of party leaders) still maintained a tight fist on nominations, allocation of oil income to state and local levels, appointments to the judiciary, and legislative voting. And they absolutely refused reforms to the civil service, which would have deprived them of an estimated forty thousand patronage positions (Conde 2004).

The election of governors and mayors was approved by Congress after Pérez and his main opponent in the 1988 campaign both promised to bring it about. A case of "too limited and too late," partial implementation of COPRE's agenda widened cracks in the Punto Fijo regime. While leaving most of the rest of the architecture of Punto Fijo in place, the reform created a political opportunity structure that became evident in the state and local elections of 1989 and 1992, when regional electoral movements took advantage of direct elections for mayors and governors. The regional character and idiosyncratic programs of these campaigns were more indicative of de-alignment than re-alignment. Mainly they served to further reveal the deterioration of two-party hegemony than to stimulate reform or realignment.

As is well known, the depth of the political crisis became evident in 1992 with two failed coups, in February and November. The first and more conse-quential of the two was led by Hugo Chávez. His televised speech for the rebels to surrender, with his admission that the objective had not been achieved but only "for now," brought in play the element of charismatic populist leadership from an unexpected sector, the military. That did not necessarily manifest itself in opinion polls, even after Chávez and other officers were released from jail by President Caldera in 1994. However, the February coup made clear the gap between almost the entire population and the political class. The politi-cians railed in Congress against the coup makers but dared not call their bases out into the streets (López Maya 2005, 110).

The presidential election of the following year (1993) was the definitive moment of de-alignment (see Roberts in this volume). Whereas Pérez and his main rival, COPEI's Eduardo Fernández, together took 93 percent of the vote in the 1988 election, in 1993 official results gave the nominees of AD and COPEI together only 46 percent of the vote. The proclaimed winner of the election was Caldera, who had broken from COPEI and formed a coalition of small regional, personalist, and leftist parties that came to be called the "chiripas," after the small chirping crickets heard in the evenings in Caracas. Caldera won on the basis of (1) his speech to Congress after the February 1992 coup in which he, almost alone among the political class, insisted that public sympathy for the coup makers was an expression of loss of confidence in the political system; (2) his criticism of neoliberalism and promise to offer an al-ternative economic program; and (3) his standing as a patriarch that offered one last chance for the reform of the system from within. His percentage of the official national vote was a mere 30.5 percent, and the 60.5 percent turnout was the lowest ever in a presidential election.

Two other clear signs of de-alignment were the emergence of a strong challenge of a movement-based political party, La Causa R (LCR), and the emergence for the first time of serious questions about the transparency of an election at the presidential level. Andrés Velásquez, the LCR candidate, originally rose to prominence as a leader of the worker democracy movement in the heavy industrialized zone of Ciudad Guayana, itself a blow to the political hegemony of AD and COPEI because it was a serious breech in AD's hold over the union movement (see Ellner in this volume).

In the presidential election of 1993, Velásquez officially finished fourth with over 22 percent of the vote in an election marked by fraud. Whether the fraud actually cost Velásquez the election is not clear, but minimally the electoral chicanery should be taken as more evidence of the desperation of political elites to maintain their grip on power. Among the most damaging evidence of fraud was the discovery of systematic electoral fraud, including boxes with thousands of pro-Velásquez ballots found in a Caracas garbage dump. Julia Buxton (2001, 93 and 95) points out that by failing to challenge voter theft, the national leadership of smaller alternative parties lost respect from their grassroots members and supporters, thus jeopardizing their own place in the party system.

The LCR's electoral success had some impact on Chávez and his civilian-military coalition, the Movimiento Bolivariano Revolucionario (MBR), which was behind the failed coup of February 1992. Francisco Arías Cardenas, a coup leader, caused reassessment of the MBR's abstentionist strategy when he won the governor's mansion in Maracaibo, Zulia, center of the oil industry, as a candidate of LCR in 1995. The LCR subsequently suffered a deep split, mainly between Velásquez and Pablo Medina, the secretary general and one of those who tried to organize civilian support for the coup. The party's inability to resolve its differences can be attributed in part to a common malady of movement-based parties—their lack of institutionalized mechanisms for decision making (Hellinger 1996). Medina and others of his group would form the Patria Para Todos (PPT). Some leaders (but not Medina) of the PPT became close trusted members of the cabinet and Chávez's inner circle. From its ranks came Alí Rodríguez, who would serve as president of PDV and then oil minister during the period of struggle between Chávez and PDV executives over oil policy.

Caldera's administration only contributed to the frustration of social movements. Promising to provide an alternative to neoliberal economic policies, the patriarch was confronted almost immediately by a near collapse of the banking system. He was forced to bail out the banks and turn to the IMF for a new structural adjustment agreement, which he had vowed he would never do. His attempt to reform labor laws further alienated the working class. Most of the Venezuelan business community was unenthusiastic about fiscal discipline of privatization, but FEDECAMARAS (the Federación de Cámaras de Comercio) welcomed policies to deregulate and weaken labor rights. As the economic crisis deepened, it sought to reduce the influence of the Confederación de Trabajadores Venezolanos (CTV) and roll back social security and unemployment benefits won in the time of prosperity (see Ellner in this volume).

In 1997, the MBR registered as the Movimiento Quinta República (MVR).[1] The MVR presented itself as an "electoral movement" seeking the votes of those fed up with parties. A sign of the rapid de-alignment that characterized the party system in the late Punto Fijo era, the MVR was one of several electoral movements formed to support national and regional political ambitions. Like LCR, all avoided the label of "party" because of popular antipathy toward Puntofijismo. In 1998, the top-three presidential contenders were all leaders of organizations that presented themselves as "antiparty" electoral movements. Irene Saez, a former mayor of Chacao, created the ephemeral IRENE (Integración y Renovación para la Nueva Esperanza), and Enrique Salas Romer, a former *copyano* and a governor, created his Proyecto Venezuela.

Romer was nominated by his own personalist party, Proyecto Venezuela. Proyecto (2006) offered a vague program but one close enough to attract the backing of Marcel Granier, a maverick entrepreneur and TV personality with political aspirations. Granier used his show on RCTV, a network he controlled, to espouse shrinking the state and to blast corruption, especially in the Venezuelan banking system. However, much of the business community, especially other media and the financial sector, hedged its bets by discreetly supporting financially both Romer and Chávez (Granier 1984, esp. 127; Ortiz 2004, 86; Gates 2010). AD's nominee was running so poorly in the polls that the party withdrew its support at the last moment and threw it to Romer. The winner, however, was Hugo Chávez Frías.

## REINCORPORATION AND RESHAPING THE PARTY SYSTEM

The MVR was more than a "personalist party." Its predecessor, the MBR, held widespread consultations with sympathizers throughout the country before holding a congress in 1997 to decide whether to launch Chávez's candidacy or to continue advocating abstention. It formed an alliance, the Polo Patriótico (PP), with smaller parties, the PPT, the Communist Party, and other parts of the MAS. Still, from the start Chávez dominated the MVR and the PP. He rapidly rose in the opinion polls from a mere 8 percent to nearly equal status with the leading contenders, using his formidable social-communication skills to present himself as the best option to resist neoliberalism and exclusion. As with Brazil's Lula before him and Bolivia's Evo Morales's afterwards, we should not underestimate the symbolic importance of his multiracial appearance, humble social origins, and popular-folk rhetoric. This was particularly evident in Chávez's invocation of mythology surrounding Enrique Zamora, a populist general and martyr of the nineteenth-century Federal War (1859–1863), a symbol of popular resistance to exploitation by a rapacious oligarchy (Pereira Almao 2001; Ellner 2008).

The Chávez campaign succeeded, however, not just because its leader was so charismatic but because unlike Romer, the leader of the MVR clearly promised to reject neoliberal economic policy and because he promised to convene a constituent assembly to write a new constitution. He also benefited politically from the drop in oil prices that discredited the PDVSA executives and promised to restore the oil company to the people. Much more than Romer, Chávez was able to tap into the hopes of social movements seeking to construct a more authentic democracy (see García-Guadilla in this volume). In this first election, even much of the middle class welcomed challenge to the corruption and antidemocratic character of Puntofijismo.

Chávez led Venezuela through thirteen years of political experimentation as he attempted to build a new regime for appropriating and distributing the wealth generated by the country's enormous hydrocarbon deposits. Ultimately, Chávez failed to translate his charismatic authority into stable institutions. Here we concentrate on the void, never filled, left by the collapse of the party system. In the next few pages we trace the evolution of party politics through five phases: (1) the period (1999–2001) of final collapse of the Punto Fijo system and the design of a new constitutional system; (2) political polarization and emergence of disloyal opposition (2001–2004); (3) the Chavista high tide and attempted radicalization, including the founding of the PSUV (2004–2007); (4) opposition resurgence (December 2007–2013); and (5) Chavismo without Chávez, a return to polarization and an uncertain future (post-March 2013).

### Phase 1: Punto Fijo's Final Collapse, 1999–2001

The first phase of the Chávez era began with the convening of the Constituent Assembly, followed by the writing and approval of the new Bolivarian Constitution in 1999 and the "mega-elections" of July 2000. As part of the referendum to a constituent assembly to write a new constitution, voters approved choosing delegates via a first-past-the post system. This system clearly advantaged the MVR; however, "uninominal" representation (single-member district) was not simply an electoral maneuver by the president and his followers. It had been put forth by social movements, especially Queremos Elegir, an organization that arose from the neighborhood association movement and was based mostly in the middle class, which did not regard Chávez with the same visceral opposition as it would later in his term.

After the constitution was ratified by another referendum, Chávez insisted that all elected officials subject themselves to the voters in the nationwide "mega-elections" of July 2000. Delegates to the new unicameral National Assembly were elected through a mixed system, half by uninominal, half by proportional representation, with seats allocated by a formula intended to help smaller parties compensate on a state-by-state basis for underrepresentation generated by the first-past-the-post system. In the "megas," the MVR took 44.3 percent of the vote and 91 out of 165 seats in the National Assembly. COPEI shrunk to a mere 5.1 percent of the vote and six seats. AD suffered great attrition, but emerged as the largest opposition party with 16.1 percent of the vote and thirty-three seats. However, focusing on its relative success among opposition parties obscures the true dimensions of its fall. The taint of too-close association with AD or COPEI caused other opposition forces to maintain a distance from the old-guard parties (Neuman 2012).

Despite the dual system of representation, the Chavistas (first as the MVR, and after 2007 as the PSUV) enjoyed a substantial advantage by dominating the uninominal ballot and by running allied but technically independent parties. (The tactic was actually first employed by the opposition.) That advantage was substantially reduced after the opposition managed to coordinate candidacies in the 2010 elections, but in these first three phases of the Chavista era, the system favored the Bolivarian forces more. The culture of Puntofijismo had not died, nor has it evaporated today.

A key player in Chávez's electoral success was Luis Miquelena, a former communist with ties to the financial community and long experience as a political infighter. Although Miquilena was reviled by radical sectors of Chavismo, his political experience was vital to maintaining a majority for the president in the Assembly, especially after defections from the Chavista delegation left it with a thin majority. The antiparty MVR had virtually no institutional infrastructure. A party congress had been held in 1997, mainly to debate the question of whether to enter the 1998 electoral contest or to maintain a position of abstention, but the MVR depended heavily on the personality of Chávez for direction and on diffuse social-protest movements for support.

In this phase, Chávez did not pursue a radical economic agenda, and some critics wondered if he indeed would break from neoliberalism (e.g., Blanco 2002). Chávez did, however, reaffirm Venezuela's commitment to OPEC by convening the second summit of OPEC heads of state in Caracas in September 2000, contributing to the recovery of oil prices from a nadir of $10 in 1999 to $35 by that time. He put his own trusted allies in the presidency of PDVSA, but these were not oilmen, and he had not moved to change any key policies associated with the *apertura petrolera*. However, the latter part of this period saw Chávez begin to take on the most powerful sector of Venezuelan capitalism, the PDVSA executives.

### Phase 2: Polarization and Disloyal Opposition, 2001–August 2004

In November 2001, using authority granted to him almost a year earlier by the National Assembly, Chávez issued forty-nine decree laws, including one that dictated a new fiscal regime for oil—raising royalty from rates as low as 1 percent during the *apertura* era to 30 percent (allowing some discounts in the heavy oil sector) while maintaining the tax rate at a slightly lower 50 percent.[2] The new law also required real majority ownership of joint ventures. Separately, Chávez insisted that PDV repatriate profits transferred to subsidiaries abroad to its books in Venezuela. By these actions, he directly took on the PDV executives, effectively rolling back the *apertura petrolera*. If that was not enough, other decree laws initiated a land reform and protected the rights of small fishermen against larger industrial fishing interests.

Certainly patronage politics and charisma remained sources of power for Chavismo. Venezuela was and remains today a country where the main basis of capitalist accumulation is capturing international oil rents; the state must distribute those rents through some political mechanism. The question of democracy revolves necessarily therefore around the rules for responding to this central fact of political life. The November decrees were decisive in establishing that Chávez intended a thorough overhaul of the neoliberal *apertura*, and the decree laws suggested that the president intended to use rents to modify property relations, not just to ameliorate the injustices of a market society. The decrees alienated Miquilena, who was already in an awkward position with his patrons because Chávez had proved unwilling to meet the expectations of the finance community of quid pro quo for the funding they provided through Miquilena in the 1998 campaign (Gates 2010). The old pol left the MVR to protest the decree laws and ultimately supported the short-lived coup of April 2002.

The decree laws of November 2001 galvanized the opposition behind an extra-constitutional strategy. The five months leading up to the coup of April 14, 2002, were marked by mounting opposition protests, often illegal and increasingly violent. The coup itself was carried out by sectors of the military following a violent and bloody massive march that was to end at PDV headquarters peacefully but was at the last moment diverted by march organizers toward the presidential palace with a demand that Chávez resign. The coup lasted only forty-eight hours. Chávez's restoration was brought about by the enormous grassroots mobilization of barrio dwellers in Caracas and other major cities and by divisions within the opposition over the suspension of the constitution, closing of Congress, and other draconian decrees proclaimed by Pedro Carmona, the FEDECAMARAS president named to head the military junta. The grassroots mobilization was activated by the Bolivarian Circles that had begun to appear in 2001. These were formed partly in response to a call by Chávez but also as an extension of social movements, such as the barrio assemblies (see García-Guadilla in this volume) and radical "patriotic assemblies" (Ciccariello-Maher 2012, 200). The mass resistance to the coup solidified the relationship between the social base and Chávez, but the relationship was direct, not mediated by the MVR.

After the coup, Chávez significantly expanded the social programs, a move made possible by the new fiscal framework and rising global oil prices. The surge in oil rents enabled the government to address poverty and exclusion— an effort that accelerated after the attempted coup of April 2002 and especially after Chávez's victory in the *revocatoria*—the recall election of August 2004. The earliest programs were the *misiones* in health care and literacy launched in 2003, followed by others that addressed the needs of popular sectors that had been neglected, especially during the neoliberal period. As García-Guadilla shows in this volume, these and other programs also would become vehicles for popular sector organization and electoral mobilization.

The mixing of these two functions became salient during the campaign around the recall election of August 2004. Chávez was disconcerted that the MVR had first failed to prevent the opposition from securing enough signatures on the petition to call the recall election, and then that the party might not perform adequately in the election itself. The Bolivarian leader reorganized the campaign to rely more directly on local "electoral battle units" made up of local activists and leaders involved in the *misiones*. Chávez won the election resoundingly, but the question of how to reconcile electoral campaigning with mobilization for revolutionary change remained unanswered. Bolivarian activists were mistrustful of MVR politicians, and the politicians were not as eager as the activists to transfer authority from representatives and the bureaucracy to grassroots organizers.

The opposition faced a somewhat different problem. In this period, the main opposition organization was the Democratic Coordinator, founded as an umbrella group of opposition parties and organizations, but it too collapsed in the wake of (1) the failed oil work stoppage, part of a larger strike begun in December 2002 and lasting to March 2003; (2) the refusal of some of the opposition to accept the validity of the Chávez victory in the 2004 recall referendum; and then (3) the decision to abstain from contesting the 2005 elections for the National Assembly, which produced a supermajority for the president in the legislature.

**Phase 3: The Chavista High Tide, August 2004–December 2007**

Chávez may have been disappointed by the MVR, but he faced contesting two elections within eighteen months after the *revocatorio*. The first of the two was for election of municipal authorities in October. Arguing that it would be difficult to organize primaries or some other grassroots process, and needing to allocate nominations to some of the MVR's alliance partners in the PP, Chávez and his inner circle selected the nominees. Grassroots Chavistas tolerated the centralized system, though it smacked of Puntofijismo to many.

In the second election, for National Assembly elections, which took place in December 2005, the MVR picked its candidates for municipal posts via a primary, a first in the country's history. A U.S. embassy cable released by WikiLeaks summarized the ambiguous response of activists to the primary. "While not trouble-free, the MVR primaries are a 'first' which Chavez supporters will tout as credentials of their commitment to democracy in contrast to whatever process the opposition parties have used to pick their candidates. For some Chavez supporters, these primaries were indeed an end to Chavez's hand-picked candidates, although rumblings of fraud, obvious favoritism, personal gain and division marred the process" (U.S. embassy, Caracas, 2011). Chávez, aware that his political survival was due mainly to popular support organized by local activists, would grow increasingly restive about the MVR. Tensions between the MVR politicians and grassroots activists would increase over time. Chávez would seek to resolve these through establishment of the PSUV, but only after the presidential election of 2006.

After his high-water victory (63 percent of the vote) in the December 2006 presidential election, Chávez issued a call for a "single party of the left," going so far as to brand left parties, such as the PPT and the Communist Party, as "opposition" if they failed to join. Ultimately, Chávez backed away from this demand, which provoked considerable criticism within the left for reducing space for debate and pluralism—although it should be noted that Chávez was not proposing a single-party regime for Venezuela. The PSUV held its founding congress in January 2008 and thus became the main party of government.

**Phase 4: Opposition Resurgence, December 2007–March 2013**

The fruitlessness of opposition tactics between 2001 and 2005—in particular, a decision to boycott the December 2005 Assembly elections, which permitted the MVR to achieve a supermajority in the unicameral legislature—led to a shift in opposition strategy. Most of the opposition galvanized behind the Zulia governor Manuel Rosales in the 2006 elections. Rosales was a former *adeco* who founded a regional party, Nuevo Tiempo (NT), to support both his state and national aspirations. Rosales acknowledged Chávez's landslide victory, and the opposition signaled that it would concentrate its efforts on constitutional and electoral opposition. This shift produced benefits when the opposition narrowly defeated a package of constitutional amendments advanced by Chávez in a referendum in December 2007. The opposition coalition became formal with the creation of the MUD in January 2008.

The MUD was, and remains today, an archipelago of smaller parties that includes leftist dissidents (e.g., Causa R, parts of MAS); the remnants of AD and COPEI (somewhat sizable in the case of AD); personalist and regional parties, such as Proyecto Venezuela and NT; and the center-right Primero Justicia. Opposition to Chávez was the main motive for this heterogenous collection of coalition partners to suppress divisions among themselves. Perhaps the party that has offered the most coherent programmatic and ideological content to the MUD is Primero Justicia, which began in 1992 as a middle-class movement promoting "clean government" and moderate neoliberalism. From its ranks would come Henrique Capriles and other younger leaders less associated with Puntofijismo.

By the mid-2000s, Primero Justicia candidates had begun to have some success in the Caracas metropolitan area, mainly in the more affluent suburbs of the east. Moreover, the party's middle-class leaders also began to make some headway by campaigning to improve the quality of governance, with notable success in attracting votes in the massive barrio of Petare on the eastern edge of the Caracas area, in Miranda state. In 2008, its candidate, Henrique Capriles, scion of one of the country's most important business families, won the governorship of Miranda. Another of its younger candidates, Leopoldo López, served as mayor of Chacao from 2000 to 2008, though he moved to NT in 2007.

In anticipation of the 2010 National Assembly elections, it became clear that the MUD would need to devise mechanisms to choose candidates to oppose the PSUV. The result was a mixture of negotiation among party leaders and primaries in some districts. The success of the opposition in capturing almost half of the national vote proved the value of unity, but as already noted, the unifying factor was opposition to Chávez. The primaries helped MUD both to project a democratic image and to repair some of the self-inflicted damage done in the past. The MUD leaders said that slightly over three million voters went to the polls in their primaries held in February 2012, which would constitute approximately 17 percent of the electorate and about half of the vote that Capriles obtained in the December election.

The PSUV has displayed an inconsistent commitment to internal democracy. The party has had to confront the issue of how to reconcile the competing demands of grassroots Chavistas for more horizontal decision making about candidacies with the practical need for (1) alliances with other parties, such as the PPT, the Communist Party, and supportive factions of the old MAS that expect some share of posts; and (2) accommodation of sinecures for important national leaders—for example, loyal MBR military officers who enjoy a close relationship to the president. The conflicting priorities are especially acute when elections closely follow presidential campaigns in which militants subordinate all other tasks and goals of social movements and missions to the singular objective of defending the presidency itself.

The electoral agenda for 2012 included not only a presidential contest in October but also elections for state governor, state legislatures, and municipal councils in December. Mayoral elections were originally to take place in early 2013 but were postponed until December that year. The MUD chose its presidential candidate (Capriles) for December 2012 and most of its candidates for other elections via a primary in February 2012. The PSUV reverted to centralized nominations after consultation, but the grassroots leadership was unhappy with the system. Gustavo Borges, a well-known Bolivarian activist in the 23 de Enero housing projects, commented, "The big question is what the hell do we do with these candidates for provincial government? . . . Do we block them, do we vote for them, do we get made, so we keep the [electoral] map 'red, very red,' do we fold our arms or keep fighting?" (quoted in Boothroyd 2012).

Chávez defeated Capriles in the October 2012 election by a margin of 55 to 44 percent of votes in an election that saw an astounding 81 percent of the electorate turnout. The high turnout was likely due to a combination of opposition optimism that the election would be tight, along with the decision of many wavering voters in poor areas to defend Chávez because his defeat would put in jeopardy the programs that have substantially improved their lives. Chávez's overall percentage of the vote was down from the 63 percent he won in 2006, but he won almost every state. Capriles carried two western Andean states—Merida, which has a reputation as the most traditionally conservative and religious, and Táchira, where insecurity along the border with Colombia may have been a factor. Chávez narrowly carried Miranda, Capriles's home state, which he served as governor. He also carried Zulia (the Maracaibo region), the most populous state and one where the PSUV struggled in prior

TABLE 12.1. Intention to vote, Capriles v. Chávez, by social class, May 2012

| | Percentage intending to vote in upper (A, B), middle (C), lower (D), very poor (E) | | | |
| | A, B | C | D | E |
|---|---|---|---|---|
| Chávez | 19.8% | 30.3% | 58.6% | 68.3% |
| Capriles | 55.4% | 42.3% | 20.7% | 12.5% |

Source: Jesse Chacón, Candidatos y Encuestas, realidad y espedculaciones, GIS XXI, previously available at http://www.gisxxi.org/articulos/candidatos-y-encuestas-realidad-y-espe culaciones-jesse-chacon-gisxxi/#.UIImqK50iYc, accessed October 22, 2012. Percentages do not add up to 100 because of undecided voters.

elections. Two months later, the PSUV captured twenty of twenty-three state governorships, but turnout fell to 53 percent.[3]

For a while it appeared as though a party system like the Chilean one, organized around two blocks of parties, might emerge around competition between the PSUV (in an alliance with some smaller left parties) and the MUD. In June 2012, the Varianzas poll (2012), generally associated with the opposition, found that 44.4 percent of Venezuelans identified as "Chavista," 39.1 percent as "opposition," and 16.5 percent as "neither one". In August, Consultores 33.11, generally favorable to the government, found that 44.1 percent of the electorate identified as "Chavista" and 24.7 percent as "anti-Chavista." While the two polls differed on the size of the opposition base, both of them seemed to agree that the emerging electoral alignment was somewhat favorable to Chavismo but that an important bloc of voters could swing an election to the opposition.

Although the Chávez vote showed some decline in the barrios, polling data during the 2012 campaign continued to show a highly polarized electorate, not only in partisan terms but also around the axis of class. GIS XXI, a polling firm closely allied with the government but also the one that most closely predicted the outcome, found a stark degree of social-class polarization in May 2012, three months before the election (see table 12.1). This class polarization stands in notable contrast to the Punto Fijo era, when both AD and COPEI functioned as catchall parties with appeal across class lines. Baloyra and Martz (1979), drawing on their survey work conducted during the electoral campaign of 1973—which solidified the two-party condominium of AD and COPEI—concluded simply and directly, "There are no strong linkages between class and party in Venezuela" (74).

The strong lower-class preference for Chávez support was elicited as a result of the inclusionary programs launched under his unmediated, charismatic leadership. Worth special mention is Misión Identidad, which distributed eight million new national-identity cards in 2003 and 2004—seven hundred thousand to immigrants and indigenous peoples. This program legally reincorporated masses of poor who never received or never replaced cards, making them eligible for social benefits and to cast ballots. However, soon after the death of Chávez it became clear that lower-class support for Chávez would not automatically transfer to the PSUV or the Bolivarian leader's designated successor. The close election of April 2013 was won by the PSUV's Nicolás Maduro by less than two percentage points.

**Phase 5: Chavismo without Chávez, March 2013 to Present**

The close election between Capriles and Maduro was a surprise to almost all observers, but there were already signs of problems for the PSUV in Chávez's last victory. The MUD had already made some key inroads in traditional Chavista support. For example, in Petare, a huge barrio in the eastern Caracas metropolitan area, Capriles won 53 percent of the vote, a reversal of 2006, when Chávez won 53.6 percent in 2006. At 23 de Enero, the epicenter of Chávez support in Caracas, the president's vote declined from 75 percent to 66.4 percent; in the western barrio of Sucre it fell from 74.3 percent to 64.3 percent, and in Antímano, from 81.8 percent to 75.1 percent. Capriles rolled up the customary 80+ percent figures for the opposition in most of the more affluent, middle-class areas.

The shift toward Capriles in the April 2013 presidential election seems not to have been due significantly to abstention, as some past opposition success was (e.g., the 2007 referendum defeat). The national rate of abstention was only one percentage point higher in April than it was in October (20.3 vs. 19.5 percent).[4] Table 12.2 shows that there was erosion of the Chavista vote almost across the board in all types of municipalities. The bigger shifts tended to be in rural areas and in more working-class areas near oil fields and industrial zones. For example, Zulia has been a hard-fought region, but Chávez and the PSUV ran well in the state in the October and December elections. Maduro, however, failed to hold even 90 percent of the vote for Chávez in some key industrial areas. The shift toward the MUD candidate in the four rural states (Portuguesa, Cojedes, Barinas, Táchira) is also notable. While they remained in the majority column for the Chavistas, Capriles gained more than 12 percent over his October performance.

This partial ecological analysis of the votes suggests that the MUD and PSUV (with its allies) were on relatively balanced terms as they entered the post-Chávez era. However, there are two caveats to consider. First, while the MUD's performance is consistent with the 2010 legislative elections, the coalition was thoroughly trounced in the December 2012 elections for governors

TABLE 12.2. Sustaining electoral mobilization from Chávez to Maduro

| Municipality | Chávez, October 2012, total votes and percentage | Abstention rate as percent (%) | Maduro, April 2012, total votes and percentage | Abstention rate as percent (%) | Maduro vote as percentage of Chávez vote; Capriles, April as percentage of Oct. vote Maduro— Capriles |
|---|---|---|---|---|---|
| State of Zulia—Western oil producing | | | | | |
| Cabimas* | 85,901—56.8% | 15.2% | 78,340—51.2% | 16.0% | 91.2%—114.8% |
| Colón* | 30,107—55.9 | 19.4 | 27,327—49.7 | 20.3 | 92.4—115.2 |
| Lagunillas* | 46,976—47.2 | 17.4 | 40,645—39.8 | 17.0 | 86.5—116.5 |
| Mara† | 65,991—70.4 | 21.4 | 61,776—66.5 | 23.5 | 93.6—112.8 |
| Maracaibo‡ | 332,313—45.8 | 20.6 | 296,111—40.3 | 20.4 | 89.1—111.9 |
| San Francisco*** | 124,004—56.8 | 18.5 | 108,677—48.8 | 18.2 | 87.6—121.3 |
| Santa Rita* | 18,422—58.1 | 17.6 | 16,805—53.0 | 17.3 | 91.2—114.9 |
| Simón Bolívar* | 14,231—54.6 | 17.4 | 12,569—47.5 | 17.6 | 88.3—105.9 |
| Valmore Rodrig.* | 16,043—54.8 | 18.6 | 14,416—48.6 | 19.1 | 89.9—116.2 |
| State of Bolívar—Eastern industrial state | | | | | |
| Caroní† | 202,054—55.1 | 18.1 | 187,660—49.7 | 17.6 | 92.9—117.0 |
| Heres‡ (capital) | 86,573—49.8 | 20.5 | 73.726—41.9 | 20.6 | 85.2—118.9 |
| State of Anzoategui—Eastern oil producing | | | | | |
| Anaco* | 34,617—49.8 | 17.4 | 31,836—44.7 | 17.5 | 92.0—114.4 |
| Freites* | 24,258—57.0 | 18.2 | 23,059—54.3 | 19.6 | 95.1—107.2 |
| State of Monagas—Eastern oil producing | | | | | |
| Maturín‡* (capital) | 150,338—55.7 | 17.9 | 143,236—52.2 | 18.2 | 95.3—110.8 |
| Piar* | 15,501—63.8 | 21.5 | 14,570—60.4 | 23.3 | 94.0—110.2 |
| Santa Barbara* | 3,720—62.1 | 18.8 | 3,641—60.7 | 20.4 | 97.9—105.2 |
| State of Miranda (three municipalities, plus Petare, a parish in Sucre) | | | | | |
| Chacao†† | 10,910—18.4 | 26.4 | 10,079—17.0 | 27.8 | 92.4—101.3 |
| Petare (in Sucre)** | 116,235—46.2 | 20.4 | 109,880—43.4 | 21.0 | 94.5—106.0 |
| Guaicaipuro** | 77,121—51.1 | 17.8 | 72,214—47.2 | 18.0 | 93.6—110.0 |
| Cristobal Rojas** | 41.403—64.6 | 16.4 | 39,866—61.0 | 16.8 | 96.3—113.5 |
| Baruta†† | 36,461  20.7 | 22.0 | 34,128—19.7 | 23.7 | 93.6—100.0 |

| Municipality | Chávez, October 2012, total votes and percentage | Abstention rate as percent (%) | Maduro, April 2012, total votes and percentage | Abstention rate as percent (%) | Maduro vote as percentage of Chávez vote; Capriles, April as percentage of Oct. vote Maduro—Capriles |
|---|---|---|---|---|---|
| Capital District (Libertador), selected parishes | | | | | |
| 23 de Enero** | 38.663—66.4 | 17.7 | 36,586—62.5 | 18.6 | 94.6—112.3 |
| La Vega** | 44,943—58.0 | 18.4 | 42,117—54.3 | 19.4 | 93.7—109.3 |
| San Bernardino† | 6,273—32.4 | 25.9 | 5,904—30.7 | 17.3 | 94.1—101.7 |
| El Paraiso*** | 26,591—37.1 | 19.3 | 24,627—34.5 | 20.6 | 92.6—103.6 |
| La Pastora*** | 29.109—52.3 | 19.21 | 26,863—48.3 | 20.2 | 92.3—108.7 |
| Three rural states | | | | | |
| Portuguesa††† | 327,960—70.9 | 17.8 | 303,982—65.5 | 19.8 | 92.7—121.3 |
| Cojedes††† | 116,578—65.3 | 17.5 | 108,018—61.2 | 20.3 | 92.7—116.9 |
| Barinas††† | 243,618—59.2 | 19.3 | 214,671—52.2 | 21.2 | 88.1—118.8 |
| Tachira††† | 274,573—43.3 | 18.8 | 235,303—37.0 | 20.0 | 85.7—112.1 |

Key: * Municipalities located near or in significant oil fields.
† Industrial—petrochemical for Mara, metallurgical for Caroní.
‡ Capital with industrial areas.
†† Middle-class areas in the Caracas metro area.
** Predominantly poor and working-class barrios.
*** Mixed-, middle-, working-class, commercial area.
††† Rural ranching and agrarian states.

Note: The results for 2013 are those posted by the CNE before it began its audit of voting machines in May 2013.

Source: Dirección de Estadísticas Electorales, CNE.

and state legislatures, when Chávez was still alive but not able to campaign. The relatively strong performance of the PSUV and its allies was repeated in the December 2013 municipal elections, when the Chavistas won a clear majority of mayoralties and a national majority of the vote.

There was no major test of electoral prowess between the PSUV and the MUD in 2014, but by the end of the year both were threatened by schism and a leadership crisis. For Maduro to be tasked with succeeding Chávez was difficult in any case, but few would argue that he has shown himself adept at governance. To add to his troubles, Maduro saw oil prices tumble from $115 in June to $70 in December 2014. By one estimate, in 2012 the "break-even price" per barrel for Venezuela —that is, the price need to prevent fiscal cuts, borrowing, or use of monetary reserves to cover expenditures—was over $100 (Stevens and Hulbert 2012, 8). This figure may be somewhat exaggerated, as production levels for Venezuela are seriously underestimated in international reports,[5] but falling prices, coupled with PDV's failure to hit targets for increased production, means that the unfortunate Maduro may find himself administering adjustments to falling rents.[6] How that adjustment is made will play out in the uncertain context of parties and coalitions of parties battling for power in the context of partisan polarization, economic stress, and shaky institutions.

In regard to the latter, of greatest significance for the party system is the inability of the PSUV and MUD to agree on renewal of appointments to the five-member Consejo Nacional Electoral (CNE). The CNE generally garners high marks for maintaining the integrity of the ballot count. After the April 2013 elections, violent protests by Capriles supporters responding to their candidate's allegations of fraud seem to have hurt the MUD's prospects in the December municipal elections (COHA 2014). The CNE's record of adjudicating complaints about campaign abuses, especially by incumbents (*ventajismo*), is quite another matter. The PSUV lost its qualified majority to act unilaterally on appointments in the 2010 National Assembly elections. Failure of the parties to agree on renewing the CNE makes it more likely that losing candidates in the 2015 election will refuse to recognize the legitimacy of the count, a development that could redound negatively on both the PSUV and the MUD in the public eye.

## CONCLUSION: POLITICAL PARTIES IN THE SECOND WAVE OF INCORPORATION IN VENEZUELA

From Rómulo Betancourt's Plan de Barranquilla to Hugo Chávez's concept of a "protagonistic democracy," Venezuelans have wrestled with how to "sow the oil" rents into an inclusive, economically developed, democratic political order. Political parties may have ultimately failed to carry that project forward in the Punto Fijo era, and they have never recovered the confidence of Venezuelans since. Nonetheless, they remain the key institutions that resolve who gets what, when, and how (Lasswell 1936) in Venezuelan politics. Chávez understood that, but he failed to institutionalize his charismatic authority over distribution of rents, particularly with regard to resolving the tension between a party charged simultaneously with guiding social mobilization and with winning elections.

Roland Denis, a former government official and a well-known leftist organizer and commentator, supported Chávez again in the 2012 election but expressed his pessimism about the direction of the Bolivarian Revolution:

> The PSUV is a disaster. . . . We have a two-fold, contradictory process. The process has allowed for a process of radicalization, so radical that it is a surprise to many people. It started with democracy, and moved to re-founding the nation, Constituent Assembly, anti-imperialism, socialism, and self-management. At the same time, the process is becoming more and more bureaucratic. On the one hand, the process advances in discursive terms, and on the other hand, the organic process suffers a setback. These are two processes that are in complete conflict with each other. One form of organization is vertical and authoritarian—the PSUV, for example, is a machine that says that "you are the candidate," and that's it, Chávez arrives and nominates whomever he feels like. The development of this political culture is an obvious retrogression from the point of view of the popular movements, and from a socialist or communist perspective. (Denis 2012)

Nonetheless, Venezuela is not simply regressing to the late Punto Fijo era. The MUD in particular faces the question of what alternative it can offer to Venezuelans to take advantage of dissatisfaction with Maduro and the PSUV. Oscar Schemel, director of the Hinterlaces polling firm, says that Venezuela has undergone a "process of profound empowerment of the popular sectors that began because presidential discourse called attention to the popular condition, validated the protagonism of the popular sectors that felt excluded, humiliated. Nonetheless, the opposition has not managed to grasp this new reality, but rejects it. It is lost" (quoted in Leon 2012). For the MUD, there is no question of moving toward a communal state, of course, but its members are divided over the issue whether the future Venezuelan state should be social democratic or neoliberal. Certainly Capriles has presented himself as favoring the social democratic alternatives, but some of his supporters, including Primero Justicia, the party he helped found, envision implementation of a neoliberal project advocated in a controversial document leaked by dissident sectors of the MUD.[7]

In the post-Chávez era, the political success of any party depends upon its ability, whether in office or opposition, to win or maintain the confidence of a population that found in Chávez a vehicle to reclaim its right to inclusion in sharing access to the oil rents that flow from its common ownership of the hydrocarbons under its soil. The Chávez years have seen the reincorporation of the masses, and this will continue to shape politics in the post-Chávez era, but Chávez clearly failed to transfer his authority to institutions of state or to the PSUV. That leaves the future of party politics and democracy in Venezuela very fluid.

Chapter 13

# THE POLITICS OF INCORPORATION

Party Systems, Political Leaders, and the State
in Argentina and Brazil

## PIERRE OSTIGUY AND AARON SCHNEIDER

Parties and party systems in Argentina and Brazil have displayed divergent paths in the process of popular sectors' reincorporation, both institutionally and in terms of party system dynamics. They have in common that neither political landscape was entirely recreated anew after neoliberalism, in sharp contrast to the Andean cases; and in both cases, political actors came to power with an agenda of incorporating popular sectors excluded by neoliberalism. In Brazil, a party that opposed neoliberalism, the Partido dos Trabalhadores (PT), came to power in 2002 with a mandate to incorporate popular sectors and middle classes. In Argentina, Kirchnerismo consolidated itself in power from shaky beginnings by reaching out to popular sectors that had been disincorporated during neoliberalism.

Party system dynamics since 2002, however, look quite different in the two countries. Brazilian parties have increasingly formalized state bureaucratic links to popular movements, leading to a more institutionalized and stable party system and a coalitional mode of governance across a broad ideological spectrum. Argentina has moved closer to a personalistic, "transformative" form of political leadership and linkage to popular sectors, a de-institutionalized party system, and more radical strategies of governance.

### PARTY SYSTEMS PRIOR TO THE REINCORPORATION PERIOD

#### Brazil: Dictatorship, Democracy, and the Legitimation of New Political Actors

The military leaders who governed Brazil from 1964 to 1985 brutalized opponents and carefully manipulated political institutions to reinforce military control. The limited space available for partisan and civic organizing allowed social actors to constitute themselves as legitimate political actors, helped them learn strategies of organization and collaboration, and established political party vehicles and patterns of party-system cleavage defined by the struggle for democratic transition. The period established the antecedent conditions for subsequent struggles of exclusion and incorporation: the old regime broke down, new social actors established themselves, and intermediary associations such as political parties began to structure political conflict.

Middle-class sectors, including public sector workers and private urban professionals, had been among the original supporters of the military regime, responding to the inflationary spirals, perceptions of corruption among the political elite, and the increasing political polarization of the period (Skidmore 1988). Their support for the military began to fade as persecution intensified through the Institutional Act 5 (AI5) of 1968, which particularly targeted opponents among the political elite, activist students, intellectuals, peasant and worker leaders, and others defined as threats (Stepan 1988). The first signs of declining support appeared in the 1973 elections, which were interpreted as a resounding defeat for the military. Urban professionals and public sector workers increasingly joined active movements for democratization.

The movement against the regime brought middle classes together with wide-ranging social movements, including many organized around neighborhood services, gender, Afro-Brazilian identity, and other demands to deepen democracy (Escobar and Alvarez 1992; Alvarez 1990; Rossi in this volume). In addition, working classes mobilized, as they bore the brunt of both military repression and regressive growth strategies. As the military regime required larger concentrations of capital for industrial deepening, Depression-era corporatist institutions came to be used primarily as mechanisms to repress worker organizing, depress wages, and concentrate profits (Leff 1982; Evans 1979). As discussed in Gindin and Cardoso, a new more autonomous union movement developed in response, and strike waves were especially vigorous in the manufacturing belt around São Paulo, where an alternative national federation of unions, CUT, formed in 1983.

With the gradual opening of electoral competition after 1973, at least part of the democratization struggle shifted into the party system, opening a primary cleavage according to support or opposition to the military regime. The main aggregator of opposition was the Movimento Democrático Brasileiro (MDB, later Partido do Movimento Democrático Brasileiro, PMDB), with the Aliança Renovadora Nacional party (ARENA) serving as the pro-military party. Beginning in 1973, there was a controlled and gradual opening, with elections first for the House of Representatives and senate, next for local executives, next for state executives, and only finally with indirect elections for president in 1985 (Kinzo 1993). Frequent changes to electoral laws largely had the effects intended by the military—fragmenting and underrepresenting opposition parties (Lavarreda 1991).

After electoral rules allowed the emergence of additional parties, the PT formed in 1980, offering an organizational and ideological vehicle of coordination for urban and rural working classes and their social movement and middle-sector allies, including the political left of various Marxist hues and ex-guerrillas.[1]

As a party that emerged "from the bottom up" (Nylen 1997, 429) with "extra-parliamentary" origins (Meneguello 1998, 33), the PT was committed to the autonomy of its movement and union allies. There was a "formal separation" between the party and civil society organizations, avoiding the subordination that characterized the traditional Brazilian left and the relationship between populist parties and labor movements (Keck 1992, 68–69 and 184–85). The party maintained a vibrant internal debate that encouraged the emergence and competition of more than thirty factions, chief among them the Articulação, led by autoworker and future president Luis Inácio Lula da Silva (Keck 1992, 114).

After direct elections for governors were allowed in 1982, the PT and other opposition parties pressed for direct presidential elections supported by unprecedented mass mobilizations. Though they failed to achieve direct elections, they forced the military to accept the candidate of the PMDB and leave the presidency in 1985 (Stepan 1988). This was followed by a constituent assembly in 1988 in which many of the demands of social movements and democratic parties were included.

### Argentina and Peronism: Top-Down and Bottom-Up Logic in a Double Political Spectrum

Peronism as a whole gives Argentina significant sociopolitical continuity far beyond the military period. As a political movement, it originated in the 1940s from the merging of top-down and bottom-up dynamics. Perón, a high-ranking military officer, deployed from the state top-down material, cultural, and symbolic appeals to seduce workers. Peronism also arose initially from a spontaneous, ebullient, bottom-up, working-class base—even bypassing its own union leadership on October 17, 1945. This duality, structurally constitutive of Peronism, has persisted over time (cf. McGuire 1997). Also, while organizations are omnipresent in Peronism, institutions are not (Levitsky 1998, 2001). "Institutionally," links between Peronism's leaders or *conductores* and its militants, while marked by a clear Peronist "mystique," are much more decisive than the actual PJ itself. Unsurprisingly, work on populism and Peronism is tightly intertwined.

"Peronism's" policy and political orientation is also always a product of "naked" relations of power, displayed and measured through means as varied as numbers of people in the plaza, polls, violence and intimidation, and electoral outcomes—though usually not through primaries or party congresses. This "forcing of a situation" between different leaderships often leads to abrupt swings within Peronism.

These various features allow actors remarkable autonomy within what is rightly called a movement more than a political party. What is permissible is limited not by ideology (as with the PT) or party statutes but by actors' explicit refusals to follow leaders' orders. Peronism may well often operate as a political party (the PJ) and have a "parasitic" relationship with the state, but Peronism can also survive electorally and socially without either of them. Because of these features, including that of politically "forcing situations," the links between the Peronist state/ "party" and society are much more intense and two-directional than those of a typical electoral, bureaucratized, liberal-democratic political party and its voters.

In contrast to Brazil, the severe repression of Argentina's 1976–1983 dictatorship did not significantly modify the post-1945 party system. After the transition, the two main political forces remained the Peronists and the Radicals (i.e., UCR), alongside smaller socialist, conservative, and provincial forces. Uniquely enough, what differentiates Peronists and Radicals is not so much left-right differentiation but markedly different social bases.

Fundamental to the evolution of the Argentine party system and its logic is the fact that its political space is structured by not one but two orthogonal dimensions. One is the classic left-right dimension (more as spectrum than cleavage); the other, specific to Argentina and politically more important and socially deeper, is the Peronist/anti-Peronist cleavage. This second divide is a true cleavage much more than an ordinal dimension. Because of the cleavage's intensity and prominence (and of Peronism's and anti-Peronism's genesis), one finds key Peronist figures on the right, in the center, and on the left. Symmetrically, one finds very staunch anti-Peronist socialists, centrist Radicals, and conservative neoliberals. Historically, Argentina's 1946–2001 party system thereby constituted a double political spectrum: a Peronist and an anti-Peronist political spectrum, each widely ranging from left to right (Ostiguy 1998, 2009).

## NEOLIBERALISM AND ITS CONSEQUENCES FOR THE PARTY SYSTEMS

### Reorienting Politics around Neoliberal Adjustment in Brazil

As discussed in Rossi, and Gindin and Cardoso's chapters, in 1990 Fernando Collor de Mello began the liberalization of trade and deregulation of the

Brazilian economy that was accelerated under Fernando Henrique Cardoso's Partido da Social Democracia Brasileira (PSDB)-led government from 1994 to 2002. While Brazil experienced more gradual and less complete liberalization during this period than some other countries in Latin America, the 1990s represented a historical juncture for the country, especially in terms of the political cleavages among important social groups and the institutional response they provoked in the party system and state institutions. During the decade, the party system reoriented around a primary cleavage of support or opposition to liberalization (Roman 2012; Hagopian, Gervasoni, and Andrés Moraes 2009), governance settled into an elite-level pattern of "presidential coalitionism" (Abranches 1988; Figueiredo 2011), and social policies aimed at mitigating some of the dislocations caused by adjustment. The PT preserved its core bases of support by remaining in opposition to neoliberalism at the national level, experimenting with participatory institutions in localities where it won office, and learning the accommodation tactics of presidential coalitionism.

The priority of the Cardoso period was stabilizing the currency. As finance minister in 1994, Cardoso introduced the Real Plan, including a new currency and policies of fiscal discipline, as well as deregulation and removing subsidies and price controls. In addition to economic stabilization, the government sought to "improve competitiveness" through liberalized trade, privatizing public enterprises, and pursuit of foreign investment (Amaral, Kingstone, and Krieckhaus 2008, 141–42).

The policies associated with this version of stabilization shifted the nature of political alignments in society and engagement with the state (Stokes 2001b). Continued liberalization of trade and prices allowed portions of poor and middle classes to consume again after facing runaway prices and limited supply during 1980s cycles of hyperinflation and low growth (Baker 2009, 229–54). The Cardoso government also followed through on welfare state commitments from the 1988 constitution, which mandated universal provisions in health and education, expanded funding for housing and sanitation, and targeted income transfer programs (Draibe 2003, 69; Melo 2008). At least temporarily, new consumers and those benefiting from elements of social protection lined up behind the PSDB and its allies, providing convincing electoral victories to Cardoso. They joined the PSDB's original base of mostly middle- and upper-class supporters attracted by the technocratic and social democratic credentials of party founders who had exited the PMDB during the 1980s (Power 2008). Still, the party failed to build an organizational base outside of its core constituency in São Paulo and a few other states, and it came to depend on the clientelist networks of its conservative allies to deliver elections in the rest of the country (Roma 2002).

TABLE 13.1. Fragmentation and coalitional presidentialism in the 1990s

|      | PCdoB | PT | PSB | PDT | PSDB | PMDB | PTB | PL | PFL | PSD | PRN | Other |
|------|-------|----|-----|-----|------|------|-----|----|-----|-----|-----|-------|
| 1990 | 5 | 35 | 11 | 46 | 37 | 109 | 34 | 15 | 83 | 42 | 41 | 55 |
|      | PCdoB | PT | PSB | PDT | PMDB | PSDB | PTB | PL | PFL | PP | PPR | Other |
| 1994 | 10 | 49 | 16 | 34 | 107 | 63 | 31 | 13 | 89 | 35 | 51 | 15 |
|      | PCdoB | PT | PSB | PDT | PMDB | PSDB | PTB | PL | PFL | | PPB | Other |
| 1998 | 7 | 58 | 19 | 25 | 83 | 99 | 31 | 12 | 105 | | 60 | 14 |

Key: PCdoB: Partido Comunista do Brasil; PDT: Partido Democrático Trabalhista; PFL: Partido da Frente Liberal; PL: Partido Liberal; PMDB: Partido do Movimiento Democrático Brasileiro; PP: Partido Progressista; PPB: Partido Progressista Brasileiro; PPR: Partido Progressista Reformador; PRN: Partido da Reconstrução Nacional; PSB: Partido Socialista Brasileiro; PSD: Partido Social Democrático; PSDB: Partido da Social Democracia Brasileira; PT: Partido dos Trabalhadores; PTB: Partido Trabalhista Brasileiro.

Source: Adapted from Power and Zucco (2009, 228), Hunter (2010), Amorim (2002, 64), and electoral data from the Supreme Electoral Tribunal.

The more neoliberal elements of stabilization generated strong opposition from key social groups mobilized during the democratization struggle (Rossi in this volume). As Gindin and Cardoso's chapter pointed out, neoliberal stabilization also disincorporated formal sector workers, especially as de-industrialization and privatization eliminated the workplaces and associated benefits of workers in public enterprises and large-scale manufacturing. In this context, the CUT and other labor federations fought to slow the pace of neoliberal reforms (Hunter 2010, 61–71), which they framed as eroding rights won in previous decades of struggle.

These social cleavages articulated through the party system into support or opposition to the stabilization program of the Cardoso government. Table 13.1 is organized according to parties' relative ideological position, as derived from surveys of legislator self-placement and placement of other parties (Power and Zucco 2009; Hunter 2010, 48–49). Parties to the left are more intensely opposed to neoliberal adjustment; the numbers in each cell indicate the number of seats won by each party.

The table suggests characteristics of the party system, with important implications for party and government strategy. During the 1990s, the party of the president had consistently low representation, never above the 99 out of 513 seats won in 1998, and as low as 41 seats under Collor's 1990 Partido da Reconstrução Nacional (PRN) government (Kinzo 2004, 27). Coalitions were therefore needed to secure majorities, and the shaded boxes indicate the parties that were at one point or another in governing coalitions.

Some observers labeled this fragmented and volatile party system "inchoate" (Mainwaring and Scully 1995b). It was characterized by instability and weak party institutionalization (Mainwaring 1993; Power 2000) "over-determined by both electoral and executive-legislative institutional incentives" (Ames and Power 2007). These incentives include a proportional representation electoral system with large, multimember federal districts that enables small parties to secure representation. Multiround elections for executive office give politicians additional incentive to create small parties offering potential allies for second-round elections, producing a proliferation of small parties varying across jurisdictions (Jones 1994).

Incentives within executive-legislative relations further complicate governing majorities. There are few limits on switching parties after elections, and politicians migrate into and out of parties to secure executive patronage or place themselves strategically for the next election (Ames 2002; Melo 2004; Desposato 2006). In addition, the open-list ballot drives politicians to compete for votes within their own party to secure a high position on the party list. These institutional problems maintained relatively high levels of volatility and fragmentation in a party system characterized by personalist politicians and weak party organizations (Mainwaring 1999).

To deal with these issues, Cardoso managed governance through "presidential coalitionism" (Abranches 1988), building legislative supermajorities that could withstand occasional defections. A host of interlocutors manage such coalitions, including single-issue caucuses, governors with leverage over state delegations, party leaders, and individual politicians with large vote-banks. To secure their support, Cardoso deployed a bevy of resources, such as ministerial appointments, tens of thousands of federal jobs, and release of investments in the bailiwicks of individual legislators (Pereira, Power, and Rennó 2005). The executive enjoyed agenda-setting privileges, dictating the order of congressional activity. In the event of legislative obstructionism, the president could also use provisional decrees to temporarily impose measures and renew them repeatedly (Figueiredo and Limongi 1999).

As the government built supermajorities and passed much of its agenda, the party system reoriented around support or opposition to the PSDB stabilization strategy (Power and Zucco 2009; Lyne 2008; Hagopian, Gervasoni, and Andrés Moraes 2009). Along with a few other left-of-center parties, as Roberts argues in the introduction to part 3, the PT maintained principled opposition.

At the same time, the PT competed for and won executive office at the local level, experimenting there with strategies that would eventually be scaled upwards. One such strategy was institutional innovation to give popular sectors and social movements greater direct access to government decision making. Such institutions tended to be structured so that preferential access for working class and popular sector actors and redistribution were built into institutional design and practice. One example was participatory budgeting, which gave citizens the opportunity to vote directly for investment priorities in the use of public resources and which includes allocation mechanisms that target working-class neighborhoods in the redistribution of resources.[2] As a result, participatory budgeting tended to "invert priorities" in budgeting processes that had long favored elites (Avritzer Marquetti and Navarro 2003).

Participatory institutions also responded to the demands of social movements, many of which had been the most vocal advocates of participation in the drafting of the constitution. Participatory councils operated in areas such as social policy, providing privileged access to social movement representatives with specific sectorial orientations, allowing them to tilt outcomes in more progressive directions. For example, education councils included reserved seats for civil society organizations active in education policy, and similar arrangements operated in health and housing (Cornwall 2008). Social movements seized on such institutions as autonomous spaces for the articulation of novel social and political identities and the elaboration of a democratic civil society (Avritzer 2002).

## The Consequences of Neoliberalism by Surprise in Argentina

Menem's turn to neoliberalism came as an abrupt surprise. Many thought it a betrayal of Perón's legacy. Nonetheless, Peronist popular sector voters, in particular, repeatedly and persistently renewed Menemista Peronism in government and in the legislature. Menem's PJ won each of the first four national elections in which Menemistas ran.

The second major paradox is that this repeated outcome occurred despite the declining popularity of neoliberalism as individuals descended the socioeconomic scale (Ostiguy 1998, 464–79) and despite the presence of more leftist Peronist electoral alternatives. Inversely, the historically anti-Peronist middle classes, despite benefiting from the credit surge and supporting neoliberalism to a greater extent, remained fiercely anti-Peronist and anti-Menemistas. Meanwhile, the demographically small upper classes in Buenos Aires voted "Menem" only briefly, in the early 1990s, in that they voted for the small neoliberal Unión de Centro Democrático (UCeDe) party, allied with Menem's PJ. Once Domingo Cavallo, architect of Argentina's neoliberalism, was forced out from government in 1995, the socioeconomic elite followed him electorally against Menem (Ostiguy 1998).

There was, however, discontent within militant left-of-center Peronism. Saúl Ubaldini, leader of the CGT throughout the 1980s, was highly critical. Many left-of-center Peronist cadres left the PJ block in the legislature, most notably the "Group of 8" led by Carlos "Chacho" Álvarez. Both the Group of 8 and Ubaldini separately hoped to capitalize electorally in Menem's new-found neoliberalism in the 1991 legislative elections. They were severely disappointed.

As a consequence, Carlos "Chacho" Álvarez and the Group of 8 decided to take some distance from traditional Peronism. They eventually forged the oppositional Frente Grande (FG) coalition, together with leftist non-Peronist parties. In 1994, the FG "merged" with the historically anti-Peronist Socialist Party and the more Peronist centrist PAIS, creating the Frepaso (Frente País Solidario).

Argentina's political space was polarizing between the Peronist right, of Carlos Menem, and the non-Peronist moderate left (Frepaso). For the 1995 elections,[3] the Frepaso had to choose a presidential candidate; unexpectedly, the very centrist candidate of PAIS, not particularly anti-neoliberal, defeated Álvarez, thus moving the Frepaso to the center. The Frepaso's orientation became less and less a leftist opposition to the economic model and focused instead more and more on Peronist (Menemista) corruption, advocating transparency, "decency," and making Argentina "a serious country."

Moving this way toward the anti-Peronist center, the Frepaso could only collide with the Unión Cívica Radical (UCR), which had always occupied that space. Indeed, in the 1995 presidential election, the two parties ended up "stealing" each other's voters, while Menem freely continued cultivating his populist, Peronist linkage to the Argentine popular sectors (Ostiguy 1998, 209–28 and 2009, 48–55).

Shortly after, the Frepaso and UCR formed an alliance to defeat Peronism in the following presidential race: the Alianza por el Trabajo, Justicia y Educación, or simply "Alianza." The Alianza did pay off, as it won the legislative elections of 1997. For the 1999 presidential elections, a presidential candidate had to be nominated at a much higher level of aggregation now, thus requiring a primary between the UCR, which spread from the right of center to the left of center, and the formally clearly left-of-center Frepaso. The UCR nominated a clearly right-of-center and anti-Peronist candidate: Fernando De la Rúa. The Frepaso this time nominated a clearly left-of-center candidate. Ironically for the Frepaso and for opponents of neoliberalism, De la Rúa won the primary, thus leaving no major presidential candidate in Argentina who would be critical of neoliberalism in the race against Menem's PJ, partly in line with Roberts's (2014) thesis.

Meanwhile, Eduardo Duhalde (the "natural heir"), thwarting with difficulty Menem's unconstitutional attempt to stand again for reelection, finally achieved becoming the PJ's candidate. Though Menem's historical partner,

Duhalde was nonetheless a very traditional Peronist—that is, not a neoliberal—concerned moreover with the material well-being of the popular sectors, in part through clientelistic measures. The 1999 presidential contest, therefore, came to be waged just like in 1989 a decade before, along anti-Peronist/ Peronist lines, with Duhalde perhaps arguably to the left of De la Rúa—or at least much more linked culturally and socially to the popular sectors.

Fatigue with Peronism, particularly Menemismo, contributed to the Alianza's 1999 victory. Going full circle, in early 2001 De la Rúa then appointed as his minister of economy none other than Cavallo: the same top technocrat who had crafted and implemented Menem's neoliberal project (Ostiguy 2009). Many Frepaso people, meanwhile, were deserting the governmental coalition. From 1991 to 2001, Argentina had gone 180 degrees politically, back again to Cavallo on the right but now in an anti-Menemista, anti-Peronist coalition, and with Peronism in the opposition.

It is highly consequential in the transformation of the Argentine party system and its partial implosion to understand that it was under the watch of the anti-Peronist, Radical president De la Rúa, and under neoliberal, right-wing Cavallo as minister of economy, that the country collapsed economically in December 2001. As a consequence, De la Rúa and the century-old UCR were basically wiped off the political map, with enormous negative consequences for the anti-Peronist half of the political space.

The causes of the collapse of the Argentine economy and neoliberal model had been simmering for years. Technically, the direct cause was the pegging of the local currency to the dollar in early 1991 at a significantly overvalued rate.[4] One solution to that problem would have been to devaluate during the late 1990s, but a comeback to the familiar vicious cycle of devaluation, high inflation, and a run on the dollar, as in 1989–1991, was correctly feared. Cavallo tried to address the logically resulting growing trade deficit as a neoliberal: by lowering the cost of Argentine labor through "labor flexibilization" to make exports more competitive. With the ever-declining support of the IMF, Argentina also resorted to foreign loans to cover its balance of payments. Cavallo cut state spending to address the fiscal deficit, thus further slowing down the economy. By 2001, Argentina's balance of payments was so deficitary and its reserves so low that it became unlikely it could meet its debt obligations in dollars. Cavallo first obtained a delay from creditors in exchange for higher interest rates. The operation triggered alarm and confidence in deposits dwindled, provoking a run on the dollar and an emptying of bank deposits. To prevent a banking collapse and financial breakdown, Cavallo enacted on December 1 the so-called *corralito*, freezing people's bank accounts and prohibiting the movement of dollars out of the country. The resulting massive cut in liquidity acted as a stupendous brake on economic activity. Huge protests resulted, from both radical, unemployed *piqueteros* organizations, and middle sectors whose bank accounts had been frozen (see Rossi in this volume). By December 19, there was major looting, violence, and anarchy throughout the country. De la Rúa declared a state of siege; significant repression thus followed, leaving twenty-seven dead and over two thousand injured. Violence, protests, and looting did not abate, however. Instead, they were crowned by a national strike of the CGT and mass demonstrators banging pots and pans asking for the president's resignation. On the evening of December 20, a stunned De la Rúa resigned and fled the Casa Rosada by helicopter.

This collapse of the Argentine neoliberal model led directly and abruptly to the collapse of the Argentine party system and to the famous slogan "¡Qué se vayan todos!" ("They should all go"). Indeed, at this point, all major political forces had been in government, each appointing Cavallo and each following the same economic model, which had imploded. Since Vice President "Chacho" Álvarez (Frepaso) had resigned in disgust in late 2000, there was no more vice president; the presidency thus went to the head of the senate. Congress appointed the longtime Peronist governor of San Luis, Adolfo Rodríguez Saá, as president. During his one week in power, Rodríguez Saá "patriotically" repudiated all of Argentina's (by then unpayable) foreign debt, thus shutting the country off from all international financial circuits.[5] Lacking the support of Peronist governors, Rodríguez Saá then resigned; the chamber of deputies then asked Duhalde to take over.

The year 2002 was a watershed in Argentine history. That year, as a result of the collapse, Argentina's real GDP contracted by nearly 15 percent; per capita income in dollar terms dropped by an astonishing 62 percent,[6] and factories closed. Even the use of money decreased, at times replaced by barter. Many workers started taking over their closed factories. In June 2002, Duhalde finally unpegged the peso from the dollar (parity), bringing its managed floating value to 26 cents USD.

As the economy collapsed, institutional representative democracy (or party democracy) gave way to direct democracy, with neighborhood assemblies, public meetings in parks, and regular demonstrations (see Rossi in this volume). The economic dystopia gave rise to the anarchist utopia of the end of the political class and of bourgeois democracy. In contrast to Brazil's PT or the MAS in Bolivia, there were thus no new political parties in Argentina offering a drastically alternative model or acting as the political umbrella for radical social movements at the time. The situation was in fact far too dramatic for such institutionalized political channeling. Instead, 2002 looked like the radical ending of institutional representative democracy.

## CRITICAL CHANGES ON THE ROAD TO TRANSFORMATIVE ELECTIONS

### PT Accommodations as Limits to Future Incorporation

The party also spent its years in power at the local level learning how to govern within the Brazilian system. This included a simultaneous strategy of articulating anti-neoliberal positions while mimicking "coalitional presidentialism" in dealing with rival political elites. Office-oriented factions within the party, especially Lula's Articulação, urged accommodation as they sought to manage governance challenges in the jurisdictions where their members governed and as they eyed national power (Gómez Bruera 2013, 47–48). Over time, they pushed the PT rightward, taking over important positions within the party and shifting the party platform set in biannual party conventions away from a commitment to socialism (Freire de Lacerda 2002, 58; Mendes 2004). The legislative bloc pushed to the center as moderate candidates demonstrated greater capacity to win elections (Power 2008 as cited in Hunter 2010, 77), and party leaders allowed for the possibility of forming alliances for elections, even with more conservative parties (Hunter 2010).

In substantive terms, the party considered compromise on certain components of adjustment such as privatization and fiscal restraint (Manzetti 1999, 39). When Lula finally won presidential power in 2002, "coalitional presidentialism" and the accommodations made to conservative forces as the price of governing placed an upper limit on the degree the PT would break from neoliberalism or attempt to reorganize political and partisan institutions.

As Gindin and Cardoso argue in this volume, Lula's government had to demonstrate that it could maintain macroeconomic stability and governability. To signal a commitment to macroeconomic stability, Lula committed during the 2002 presidential campaign to respect agreements with the IMF, picked a businessman from the conservative Partido Liberal (PL) as his running mate, and appointed Antonio Palocci, from the most conservative wing of the party, as minister of finance, along with a Central Bank president from the banking sector, Henrique Meirelles of Bank of Boston. The government maintained Cardoso's inflation targeting regime, setting primary surplus targets even higher than required, at 4.25 percent of GDP.[7]

The PT would lead the second incorporation of popular sectors, but it would be constrained as it did so.

### Contingency and the Unexpected Emergence of Kirchner in Argentina

The transition to reincorporation in Argentina was the product of highly contingent decisions by state leaders, most particularly Duhalde. Second, the unexpected withdrawal of Menem in the second round of the presidential election, the initial dependence of Néstor Kirchner on Duhalde's endorsement, apparatus, and machine politics, and the particularly explosive social situation of the time all led to a situation of remarkable political fragility for Kirchner. It is precisely that fragility that incentivized him in a daring strategy of reincorporation. This section describes the political set up that made possible and led to the incorporation described in the following section.

During the infamous year of 2002, though neoliberalism had de facto been repudiated by the government of Duhalde and his minister Lavagna, there was nonetheless little by way of an alternative socioeconomic project. But with the 2003 presidential elections coming and the gradual fading of the "¡Qué se vayan todos!" outcry, the interim president and power holder, Duhalde (who had committed not to run), had to appoint an heir apparent, not only against non-Peronist candidates as to be expected but much more importantly against Menem, turned into archrival and once again presidential candidate. If the Menem-Cavallo duo had been the public face of neoliberalism in Argentina, Duhalde's brand has always been social spending in clientelistic way and machine politics—with the Menem-Duhalde duo the public face of Peronism (on the "low") during the 1990s.

The virulent rift between Menem and Duhalde that began in the late 1990s ended up defining the evolution, post-economic collapse, of Argentina's party system. The 1994 constitution's prohibition against a third reelection had indeed required Menem to step down in 1999. Duhalde by 1998 therefore considered himself Menem's "natural heir," but Menem instead announced that he was going to run for re-reelection. Menem only renounced it after Duhalde threatened a popular plebiscite on the topic—and not after the court injunction.

In 2002, even if Duhalde was now president, with all corresponding powers, Menem made clear again he was going to run for president in 2003—and win. His level of rejection in the population, however, was even higher than in 1998, because of the economic collapse. Menem's calculation was that he was still president of the national council of the PJ and from there could "twist" (through unorthodox means) a Peronist primary to his advantage. Then, as the official Peronist candidate, he would then be invincible against the now defunct anti-Peronist opposition forces.

The odd way this key Menem-Duhalde rift was resolved explains how the transition to reincorporation was made possible in the political field: only months before the presidential election, three Peronist presidential candidates were prodded to run on their own, against both the anti-Peronists and against one another, each with his own political party.[8] Duhalde's calculation was that even if Menem achieved going to the second round (something quite possible), that strange arrangement would provoke an unwinnable second-round national runoff of Menem against another Peronist. What he may not have predicted was the subsequent closeting of the PJ as political party.

When Duhalde's first two choices as heir failed to mobilize support,[9] he threw all of his weight behind Néstor Kirchner, a not very well-known governor of the very small and remote province of Santa Cruz who had been critical of the neoliberal project of Carlos Menem. Kirchner chose for his own party the name "Frente para la Victoria" (FpV), named after his PJ-led coalition in Santa Cruz. For his running mate, Kirchner chose Daniel Scioli, a centrist Peronist politician who had been brought into Peronist politics by Menem himself in the 1990s.

For the race, Kirchner relied on Duhalde's powerful political machine in the province of Buenos Aires and his own anti-neoliberal and "progressive" discourse. Menem had a strong social basis of support in the impoverished federalist provinces of the northwest and among the "popular conservative" electorate. The organization of Rodríguez Saá's party was much smaller and appealed to a traditionally Peronist electorate.

This foundational election of 2003 produced an unheard-of five-way contest, with three Peronist personalistic political parties (Menem, Rodríguez Saá, and Kirchner, from right to left) and two anti-Peronists parties, one led by Ricardo López Murphy on the right and one by Elisa Carrió, then left of center. The candidates and their parties were thus perfectly distributed, politically, in a two-dimensional political space (Ostiguy 2009). Carrió, then on the (always anti-Peronist) center-left, created–together with ex-Frepasistas—the new political party Afirmación para una República Igualitaria (ARI).[10] López Murphy ran on the anti-Peronist right, having created the party Recrear para Crecer. He combined free-market economic appeals with a defense of ethics and of transparency.[11] Both anti-Peronist candidates strongly opposed what O'Donnell (1994) calls "delegative democracy."

Menem did win the first round, with 24.4 percent of the vote. In line with Duhalde's calculations, Kirchner came in second, with 22.2 percent. Certainly, there was no discernable shift to the left at the time in the electorate: López Murphy's Recrear, also on the right, came in third. The very dissimilar Rodríguez Saá and Carrió came last, each with around 14 percent of the vote. In all, right-wing candidates obtained 41 percent of the vote; left-wing candidates, 36 percent. From the more politically salient Peronist versus anti-Peronist divide, the Peronists largely won the election with 61 percent of the vote, while the anti-Peronists together garnered only 31 percent.

Duhalde's political gamble proved correct: Menem's high rate of rejection throughout society ensured Kirchner's "catchall" victory for the second round. But, wanting to go down as "never defeated" and deprive Kirchner of the legitimacy of a landslide victory, Menem simply declared he was no longer running. Kirchner was therefore forced to start his presidency with a meager 22.2 percent mandate in a society in turmoil. His response was to attempt to reincorporate the popular sectors (and many progressives) and, in the process, also restructure the Argentine party system.

In contrast to Brazil, the social reincorporation that followed Kirchner's 2003 victory was not the product of a leftist shift in the electorate, polls, or the party system. Nor was Kirchner's victory associated with the forceful sociopolitical struggles from below. In Brazil, there had been a long, deliberate political and social struggle on the part of the PT and then an intentional moderating move of the party toward the center-left in 2002 in order to win the election. In contrast, it was "the Kirchners' *lack* of prior organizational links with the popular sectors . . . [,] highly mobilized" (Etchemendy and Garay 2011, 300) that, in the context of a very weak electoral starting point, led to the daring incorporation of most of the social movements, popular organizations, and militant trade unions that had previously destabilized all neoliberal (Peronist and especially anti-Peronist) governments.

## POPULAR SECTOR REINCORPORATION AND THE POST-NEOLIBERAL POLITICAL ECONOMY

In both Brazil and Argentina, left-oriented parties that had opposed neoliberal adjustment (the PT and to a much lesser extent the FpV) reached national power and pursued strategies of reincorporation. As described by Rossi and Silva in this volume, the process of reincorporation involves "the expansion of substantive rights in ways that the expressed interests of major, politically significant new and old popular sector organizations find, at minimum, programmatic expression in left governments. Reincorporation also involves the concrete institutional mechanisms that link popular sector organizations to the political arena and policy making."

In Argentina and Brazil, this process of reincorporation included policy change and the institutional incorporations of group actors in a reincorporation process that was segmented (see Silva's concluding chapter in this volume) according to who was being targeted and what mechanisms were available. Policy changes responded to the demands of groups and citizens excluded by neoliberalism (and at times before) and were the object of significant sociopolitical contention; a new social pact was articulated that included benefits for newly incorporated recipients as well as greater universality in several social rights. In addition, reincorporation included politico-institutional innovations that linked newly incorporated actors and the state, offering opportunities such as absorbing movement leaders into state offices (yet another original form of interest intermediation), allowing previously excluded militant groups and popular sector cooperatives direct involvement in public spending in Argentina, and direct participation and some degree of influence over public power in Brazil.

These policy and institutional innovations promised significant changes in patterns of partisan competition, which did not fully materialize (more so in Brazil, less so in Argentina). However, those innovations focused conflict around the efforts of popular-left parties to preserve and deepen social pacts and the establishment of privileged relationships between previously excluded militant groups and the state, while opponents sought to roll those back and "normalize" the country.

### Reincorporating Popular Sectors (and Middle Classes) in Brazil

In Brazil, the 2002 presidential election marked a shift in the party system, one that allowed Lula's government to incorporate core social actors. In part, the PT in power shifted incorporation to the state, as the party could use state institutions and policy to incorporate core constituencies. This reoriented politics, with partisan competition focused on preserving or eliminating the routinized relationships embodied in state institutions and the terms of the social pact expressed in targeted policies.

The fiscal room to pursue this dual strategy came from a period of global expansion, an opportunity the PT did not miss as it pursued neo-developmentalist strategies to insert Brazilian economic actors in the global economy. Neo-developmentalism was not a complete break with 1990s neoliberalism, as it continued the inflation-targeting regime of the Cardoso period. Still, developmentalist policies use fiscal and credit policy to promote growth, expand consumption, and distribute wealth.

Policy space to pursue neo-developmentalism came from growth in the rest of the international economy, benefiting in particular from high prices for commodities. These were sustained by demand in emerging markets, as China came to absorb 40 percent of Brazilian soy exports, a third of iron exports, and 10 percent of meat, pulp, oil, and paper. By 2011, commodities exports were $162.2 billion, versus only $60.3 billion in manufactures (WDI 2012). Finance, which had already benefited from high interest rates associated with the stabilization strategy begun under Cardoso, also continued to enjoy high returns, boosting the services sector.

These sectors mostly benefited economic elites, lessening their political opposition, but the government would have to find mechanisms to distribute some of the growth to its core supporters, such as public employees and middle-sector professionals hard-hit by neoliberal state retrenchment in the 1990s. Increased fiscal space allowed more aggressive macroeconomic stances beginning in 2006, including expanded public employment and investment, especially when the 2008 crisis gave the government room to embark on aggressive countercyclical investment, dubbed the Growth Acceleration Program (Ministry of Finance 2012, 26–28).

Public sector expansion included increased salaries and pensions for middle-sector professionals, who were further privileged by an expansion in consumer and housing credit, stimulated by public banking institutions (Barbosa 2010). Lower-middle-class families received subsidized home-buying credit that aimed to distribute R$200 billion by the end of 2014 and were further benefited by labor market policies that increased rates of formal employment from 45 percent to 55 percent and kept unemployment at historic lows. The combination of growth and efforts to distribute benefits grew the middle class to 55 percent of the population, with 105.5 million people.

Efforts to expand popular sector incomes and consumption were even more significant. Successive increases in the monthly minimum wage, from R$350 in 2002 to R$560 in 2012, improved conditions across the board, as many low-income jobs and pensions are indexed to minimum wages. Extending pensions to informal sector workers extended the impact, providing twenty-eight million Brazilians with old-age protection. In the rural sector, small farmer credits and agricultural extension reached almost two million small producers.

Spending on social policies of housing, health, and education also rapidly expanded after 2003, moving closer to the 1988 constitution promise of universal access to health and education, as well as subsequent legislation that promised a right to housing. The flagship social policy, an income transfer program called Bolsa Familia, absorbed and expanded various social programs to extend income support, education, and health to low-income families. Bolsa Familia currently reaches more than forty million Brazilians and has been credited with cutting poverty, improving health outcomes, and improving educational attainment (Castiñera, Rivera, Currais Nunes, and Rungo 2009; Hall 2006).[12] The percentage of the population in poverty fell from 26.7 percent in 2002 to 10.9 percent in 2012; the incomes of the poorest three deciles have seen annual average rates of growth of 7.2, 6.3, and 5.9 percent as compared to 1.4, 2.5, and 3.3 percent for the highest deciles, and this has produced a fall in Gini coefficients from 0.596 in 2001 to 0.519 by 2012 (Ministry of Finance 2012).

In the context of neo-developmentalist growth strategies, this collection of policies articulated a new social pact. By extending credit, boosting wages, increasing formal sector employment, transferring income, and expanding social protections, the PT in government enabled lower- and middle-class consumption and participation in the labor market. In the context of flagging external demand for Brazilian commodities after the 2008 financial crisis, expanded domestic consumption came to be a core driver of neo-developmentalist growth, in which expanded material benefits for lower and middle classes coincided with high rates of growth for upper-class-dominated financial and commodity sectors. Andre Singer, Brazilian academic and spokesperson for Lula, described the phenomenon as "Lulismo"—"gradual reform within a conservative pact" (Singer 2012).

An additional set of state innovations institutionalized channels of communication and incorporation for social movements. With the arrival of the PT at the national level, public policy participatory councils experienced a significant expansion in funding and importance. Operating in thirty-one different policy areas, they included 1,350 members, with slightly more civil society (55 percent) than government (45 percent) representation, and undertook both deliberative and advisory tasks (Lopez, Souza Leão, and Grangeia 2011; Lopez and Pires 2010). As of 2005, there were over three hundred thousand registered civil society organizations, and by 2009, they were receiving over R$14 billion in government transfers. Participatory institutions had been mandated in the 1988 constitution, but they were advanced only in narrow policy areas and partially across the country, usually where the PT governed at the local level (Gurza Lavalle, Acharya, and Houtzager 2005). With PT arrival on the national scene, these institutions could be scaled up and funneled more significant funding.

These national institutions absorbed many of the same actors who had honed their participation skills at the local level. At the state and national levels, middle-sector professionals operating through recognized sectoral organizations were especially adept at securing access, and this was especially the case in policy-specific councils that placed a priority on deliberative skills and professional expertise. For example, health professionals and health NGOs occupied important positions in state and national health councils (Houtzager and Gurza Lavalle 2010).

Other institutional innovations offered additional opportunities to absorb social movement and union allies. Upon one's entering office, among the first executive orders was the creation of secretariats for women, human rights, and promotion of racial equality. The leadership and staff for these secretariats were drawn directly from among feminists, Afro-Brazilians, and civil rights activists, and they were eventually gathered and upgraded into a single ministry in Dilma's second government, the Ministry for Women, Racial Equality, Youth, and Human Rights.

In sum, the institutional innovations enacted by the PT were important for its capacity to routinize patterns of interaction with popular sectors and middle classes, absorbing key leaders into newly created entities where they could symbolically represent their members at the same time they influenced policy. Such institutional mechanisms of incorporation coincided with policies targeted to the core constituencies of the PT, which articulated a social pact that paired expanded material benefits for lower and middle classes with high rates of stability and growth for elites.

## Incorporation through Absorption, Mobilization, and Financing in Argentina

By the time Kirchnerismo emerged in 2003, neoliberalism in Argentina had already ended, following Argentina's inability to pay foreign debtors and the *corralito*, followed by default, liquidity crisis, and collapse. Neoliberalism, first, and then the collapse of the economy in late 2001–2002 had unleashed an array of new, radical, highly mobilized social forces, including popular assemblies and *piqueteros* (see Rossi in this volume). Starting in 2003, Kirchnerismo positioned itself as a political force against the already deceased neoliberal project and as a new sociopolitical project to solve Argentina's very real socioeconomic problems and include previously excluded social groups.

A new macroeconomic setting that combined consumption-fostering radical anti-austerity measures and a novel commodity boom (driven in Argentina by soya prices) made possible the second incorporation, in terms of overall project, extension of social rights, contentious public policies, and "absorbing" institutional innovations. From 2003 forward, the Argentine economy grew at historically high rates despite debt, default, and lacking foreign direct investment and access to international financial markets. During the Néstor Kirchner years, poverty fell, income inequality declined, formal employment rose, and social spending expanded, especially on education, health, income transfers, and pension programs. Public spending increased to 40.6 percent of GDP. Social spending rose from 13 percent of GDP in 2002 to 20.6 percent of a much larger GDP in 2009 (Lustig and Pessino 2013, 4). These policies favoring particularly the urban popular sectors were supported by increasingly targeting the booming agricultural export sector. Duhalde had increased export taxes to 10 percent; in 2007 Kirchner raised them to 20 percent (35 percent on soy); shortly after, Cristina Kirchner raised them to 44 percent. Eventually, massive social and political opposition during all of 2008 forced the government to back down in a social polarization about the core of the sociopolitical project. After the 2009 downturn, the government instead increased direct taxes, raising corporate tax rates from 20 percent to

35 percent, the highest in Latin America.[13] Throughout, a different social pact was sought.

To distribute some of the growth, organized labor increased strike activity (see Gindin and Cardoso's chapter). Moreover, Kirchner brought unions back to the table by reestablishing tripartite negotiations over wages and employment in key sectors (Etchemendy and Collier 2007). CGT negotiators pushed adjustments of minimum taxable income and other deductions upward, and strikes by oil workers in 2007 led the government ultimately to eliminate minimum deductions altogether (Fairfield 2015, 271).

The widely distributed cash transfers and pensions, targeting groups traditionally excluded from corporatist mechanisms of incorporation (particularly people who had worked without accruing retirement contributions), led to a significant reduction in poverty and inequality. In 2004 and 2005, legislation established noncontributory pensions, and by 2009 there were 2.2 million beneficiaries, with over 80 percent of the poor covered, 30 percent more than in 2003 (Lustig and Pessino 2013, 19).[14] Two cash-transfer programs also stood out: the Programa Jefes y Jefas de Hogar Desempleados, initially accounting for 1 percent of GDP (Higgins and Pereira 2013, 5) and, as unemployment decreased, the 2009 Asignación Universal por Hijo program, which targeted household heads who were either unemployed, working in the informal sector, or earning subminimum wages—that is, 20 percent of all households in 2009. Social rights were thus extended to categories of people previously excluded and who had been making such claims.

In the political arena, the political force[15] that carried out the reincorporation of the popular sectors was "Kirchnerismo." Its political party is, formally, the FpV. Kirchnerismo is neither synonymous with, nor a fraction of, the PJ. It includes both a part of Peronism and significant non-Peronist (politically left-of-center and socially popular) forces, including in active leadership roles. Conversely, several PJ/Peronist leaders are clearly and forcefully in the opposition, while others had to explicitly "endure" Kirchnerismo. The relation between the PJ and Kirchnerismo/FpV changed significantly over time and has certainly not been free of tensions. At its peak under Cristina Kirchner in the early 2010s, the FpV and Kirchnerismo should also be understood as an ambitious political project (especially by its left wing) to replace Peronism and the PJ with Kirchnerismo and the FpV, establishing Kirchnerismo as the relevant—post-2001—signifier and collective sociopolitical actor in Argentine politics.

Politically, Kirchnerismo is on the left. But in the Argentine party system and (two-dimensional) political space, there is also a significant anti-Kirchnerista left, rooted in the socialist, anti-Peronist tradition. In contrast to this (anti-Peronist) left and to the PJ, the FpV is politically not much more than the personal political will of the Kirchners' and others' willingness to follow it. Sociopolitically, "pure Kirchnerismo" is a set of movement organizations in line with, and militantly supporting, the Kirchners' "national and popular project,"[16] together with relatively minor political parties unambiguously doing the same with public resources. With regard to social movements and labor unions specifically, the Kirchnerista coalition had a Peronist leg (the semicorporatist CGT under Hugo Moyano) and a non-Peronist, "social," leftist one that included the CTA and other movements.[17]

Argentina's second incorporation process was carried out through "absorption"—a novel mechanism of state intermediation—and the related financing of previously autonomous (as well as new militant) leftist, popular social organizations.[18] The first unique characteristic of the Argentine case is that it was carried out, from above and in a relation of weakness, to bring "inside the project" highly mobilized and militant groups with whom Kirchner had no substantial previous connections and that were hostile to the PJ (from which Kirchner distanced himself). The second unique characteristic was the heavy, discretionary funding of those same organizations on the part of the Kirchnerista state so that the former could carry out local public policy and public work functions. That is, in sharp contrast to state managerialism, the Kirchnerista state "subcontracted" to these previously highly oppositional leftist groups (most of them not Peronist) the construction of public housing, the formation of cooperatives, the provision of land, and so forth. Social assistance was thus in part subcontracted to organizations of the unemployed such as the Tupac Amaru, the FTV, Barrios de Pie (up to 2008), the Fundación of the Madres Plaza de Mayo ("Shared Dreams"), and the more Peronist—2003 and beyond—Movimiento Evita.[19] It appears incorrect to claim that they were "co-opted" by the state; rather, they received heavy funding, kept all of their autonomy, and moderated none of their previous sociopolitical orientation (but became politically "Kirchneristas").

Right at the beginning of his "mandate," Néstor Kirchner daringly asked organizations of the militant *piquetero* movement—which was born and had grown outside of, and mostly against, the PJ and Peronism (also see Garay 2007, 317)—to take command of high echelons of the state's decision-making apparatus. Most of them became "ultra-Kirchneristas," while remaining hostile to many PJ mayors. This politicized institutional arrangement of incorporation, which included looking at formal state institutions to delegate the provision of many social services and public housing construction, also led to a certain de-bureaucratization of state administration intertwined in the process with grassroots militant organizations and mobilization of supporters.

For example, as discussed in Rossi's chapter, in 2003 Kirchner put Luis D'Elía, the leader of the largest *piquetero* federation (FTV), in charge of providing popular housing for the poor and unemployed as head of the government's Subsecretariat for Social Habitat. He also founded in 2004 the party Frente para Todos, and later in 2011 the party Miles, supporting Kirchner with electoral lists external to the PJ.

A similar arrangement occurred with the popular sector organization Tupac Amaru in the impoverished north of the country, personalistically headed by Milagro Sala, a militant Bolivarian of lower-class origins. She and her grassroots organization came to manage million-dollar contracts conferred directly by Cristina's central government, even rivaling the provincial government of her state of Jujuy. These, along with the CTA, fostered the "left-wing" component of Kirchnerismo, to the detriment of traditional Peronism and its political structure.

In the Peronist leg of the governing coalition, an important ally was the CGT union movement (see Gindin and Cardoso's chapter). The specifics are as follows: Hugo Moyano was the central actor in the three-way interface between the union movement, Kirchnerismo, and the PJ. Head of the MTA in frontal opposition to the De la Rúa government, he became close to Peronist Duhalde in 2002 and as such fully supported Kirchner's bid in 2003. Under Kirchner, Moyano came to control the pan-Peronist CGT, having it fully allied with the government. When Kirchner took control of the PJ in 2008, Moyano was named interim president of the PJ in the province of Buenos Aires, becoming the PJ's national executive. At the peak of her power after 2011, Cristina decided to rely instead more on her ultraloyalist "K" organizations, and Moyano thus broke off, taking a significant part of the CGT with him and becoming Peronist opposition to the government.

Indeed, throughout its years in power, Kirchnerism in addition inspired the creation of many powerful, new popular sociopolitical organizations, particularly under Cristina.[20] Like the Chavista base organizations, these are not technically part of the state but nor are they "participatory bottom-up" social organizations. Some are defined functionally (e.g., youth, slum dwellers, inmates); others are geographically concentrated (e.g., Sala in the north of the country, D'Elía in Greater Buenos Aires). Above all, they are personalist organizations with particular social or functional vocations, each responding to a particular leader, him or her personally loyal to Cristina. Their personalism should not, however, mask their unambiguous leftism.

These post-2003 Kirchnerista social-political movements, together with small political parties (e.g., Nuevo Encuentro and the Communist Party) and other "national and popular leftist" forces, were all subsumed in 2012 under

TABLE 13.2. PT support by income in minimum salaries (MS), education, and region

| | 1998 | 2002 (first round) | 2002 (second round) | 2006 (first round) | 2006 (second round) | 2010 (first round) | 2010 (second round) |
|---|---|---|---|---|---|---|---|
| **Income** | | | | | | | |
| < 2 MS | | | | 46 | 61 | 53 | 56 |
| < 5 MS | 25 | 45 | 59 | | | | |
| 2–5 MS | | | | 41 | 53 | 43 | 49 |
| 5–10 MS | 23 | 48 | 63 | 29 | 44 | 37 | 45 |
| > 10 MS | 25 | 50 | 60 | 27 | 41 | 31 | 39 |
| **Education** | | | | | | | |
| Primary | 24 | 42 | 56 | 46 | 69 | 52 | 57 |
| Secondary | 25 | 47 | 63 | 38 | 53 | 45 | 48 |
| Tertiary | 31 | 52 | 58 | 27 | 43 | 31 | 40 |
| **Region** | | | | | | | |
| South | 18.4 | 37 | 55 | 26 | 42 | 40 | 42 |
| Southeast | 44.5 | 37 | 58 | 35 | 50 | 41 | 48 |
| North/ Central West | 10.6 | 36 | 60 | 39 | 55 | 44 | 50 |
| Northeast | 26.5 | 36 | 55 | 58 | 71 | 61 | 63 |

*Source*: Datafolha public opinion surveys of various years from the last date before the elections (http://datafolha.folha.uol.com.br/, accessed August 15, 2013); second-round data for 1998 and 2002 from IBOPE public-opinion survey (http://www.ibope.com.br/, accessed August 15, 2013).

Cristina Kirchner's vast umbrella organization Unidos y Organizados, challenging the PJ. In the political arena, in sharp contrast to the PJ, Unidos y Organizados is purely Kirchnerista ("ultra-Kirchnerista").

## PARTY SYSTEMS IN THE REINCORPORATION PERIOD

### Workers' Party Institutionalization, Left-Right Competition, and Elite Accommodation in Brazil

Workers' Party policies targeted working-class and poor beneficiaries and institutionalized PT electoral support around a class cleavage apparent in both individual levels of support and regional patterns of voting. During the 1990s, Cardoso's mix of inflation beating, social spending expansion, and alliances with clientelist rural politicians had earned enough support from lower classes to muddy class-based voting patterns, and the PT continued to draw support from educated and middle-class voters as a result of its successful local governments in a number of urban centers. Between 2002 and 2006, however, a class cleavage consolidated in voting patterns, as the PT polled better among poorer voters and in poorer regions (Roman 2012). Table 13.2 shows voter intention for the PT in the last poll before the election in 2002, 2006, and 2010, with voters categorized by income, education, and region, with the northeast being the poorest region of Brazil, and the south and southeast being more developed. Bolsa Familia and other state programs had institutionalized the association between the PT, growth, and redistributive programs associated with neo-developmentalism (Hunter 2007; Bohn 2011).

Like the PSDB under Cardoso, the PT failed to secure legislative majorities for its party in elections, taking 91 of 513 seats in 2002, 83 in 2006, and 88 in 2010. To govern, the PT at first resisted coalitional presidentialism, building only a minority coalition of 218 seats. Legislative paralysis and the crisis of a scandal related to purchasing legislative votes, the "*mensalão*," forced the party to revise its strategy. It then built coalitions stretching across the ideological spectrum.[21]

The most important indicator of the PT embrace of coalitional presidentialism was signaled by the inclusion of the PMDB, always among the top-three parties in terms of its seats in the legislature and an anchor of coalitional presidential strategies since the 1980s (Abranches 1988). From its origins as a partisan umbrella to a wide range of opponents to the military, the PMDB evolved into a catchall vehicle. This gave a central role to "PMDBismo," understood as free entry to all interests, obscuring the substantive content of partisan polarization and veto power for internally organized factions, limiting what legislative majorities can do, and playing into the hands of regional economic elites. While state-level elites had lost much of their fiscal influence as a result of 1990s adjustment, they could use influence through the PMDB to veto redistributive efforts or challenges to the extractive development model (Figueiredo 2011). In 2011, for example, they secured a long-debated new forestry law, decentralizing control over forest management and reducing federal protections for indigenous and environmentally sensitive lands, playing into the hands of regional economic elites and their political allies organized into a "ruralist" caucus (Ferraz da Fonseca and Moreira da Silva 2011).

Coalitional presidentialism allowed the PT to govern and coincided with steadily increasing support for Lula as president and ensuring Dilma Rousseff's 2010 victory as his successor. The PT and its allies filled the center-left to the center-right of the party space, facing a main bloc of rightist opposition led by the PSDB and provoking crisis for the extreme-right party, the Democratas party (DEM).[22]

Some of the most active maneuvering has occurred on the left of the party system, stimulated by the PT strategy of coalitional presidency and fealty to neoliberal macroeconomic stability. A left challenge was signaled first by the upstart candidacy of Heloisa Heloina in 2006, which garnered 7 percent of the vote after she left the Lula government and formed her own party. In 2010, Marina Silvà, another defector from the Lula cabinet, was the candidate of the Partido Verde (PV) and secured 19.3 percent of the 2010 first-round popular vote. While Dilma ultimately prevailed, the space on the left of the political system was highlighted once again in 2013, when protests indicated that reincorporation under PT-led neo-developmentalism had failed to reach important social movements (McCormick 2010; Rossi in this volume).

Over time, criticism of PT neo-developmentalism coincided with criticisms of the horse-trading and outright corruption of coalitional presidentialism. After Rousseff's slim second-round 2014 reelection over the PSDB candidate, the opposition coalesced around a right-wing program, eventually pulling the PMDB to the right and uniting to depose Rousseff in an impeachment that culminated in August 2016.

The party system since reincorporation would appear to have settled into a pattern of left-right competition. The PT and its allies occupy most of the space on the center-left, and its main competitors have emerged on the right, with the PMDB operating as the pivot that can stabilize or destabilize coalitional strategies. The most significant electoral challenge comes from the PSDB and its allies on the right, while the left flank collects support from disaffected members of the PT's social and political coalition. With the 2016 impeachment, the PT is faced with right-wing attempts to undo the social pact expressed in neo-developmentalist growth and social policies and efforts to dismantle the institutional mechanisms of communication to key PT constituencies, and its removal from power has weakened its primacy among the partisan organizations operating on the left.

### The Kirchnerismo-PJ Treacherous Relationship and the Two-Dimensional Party System

The Kirchnerista project and coalition is made up of a Peronist (and not particularly leftist) leg and a purely Kirchnerista (and not particularly or even Peronist) leg (Rocca Rivarola 2013). Significant tensions have existed between them throughout the thirteen years of the Kirchner presidencies. We cover here this key tension, in line with Roberts's (2014) thesis and the overall party system's evolution.

As we previously stated, the Argentine political arena or political space is markedly two-dimensional: left and right; Peronism and anti-Peronism (or "low" and "high"). This feature is the hard political reality of Argentina and has persisted even after the collapse of the party system's anti-Peronist half (in power when the economy collapsed). Despite the implosion of the traditional two- (or "two-and-a-half") party system[23] in 2002, the Argentine political space is in fact even more two-dimensional than before (Ostiguy 1998, 2005, 2009). There are four very clearly demarcated and explicitly acknowledged political quadrants. Kirchnerismo occupies the lower-left, or populist left quadrant. It faces opposition from all three other quadrants, albeit from different angles. The anti-Peronist left reproaches Kirchnerismo (and certainly Peronism generally) for its authoritarianism, thuggishness, corruption, lack of ethics, low respect for division of powers and the rule of law, its Caesarism and bid for unending personal rule. The Peronist right reproaches Kirchnerismo for lacking "true Peronism," disregarding the regions, being confrontational, obliterating Perón's teachings, not focusing on security, prioritizing defendants' rights over victims,' supporting gay marriage, and lacking concern for the country's "productive forces." The anti-Peronist right levels both kinds of criticisms. Importantly, class and educational differences in Argentina correlate to an immensely greater extent than do left and right with the Peronist/anti-Peronist cleavage. Indeed, there are many middle-sector urban progressives left of center and many popular "hard-working" rural Peronist conservatives or security-concerned popular sector urban dwellers right of center.

Our key thesis is that the Kirchners repeatedly attempted to transform Argentina's party system and consolidate a left-right cleavage that would obliterate the traditional one between Peronism and anti-Peronism while sidelining the PJ organizationally and politically. Indeed, the two key facts in party politics of the first two years of the Kirchner presidency were "transversalism" and the shutting down of the PJ.

The possibility of reconfiguring the party system appeared with Duhalde's 2003 maneuver to splinter the PJ into three separate parties. To "normalize" the Argentine political space along a more typical left-right, unidimensional axis, Néstor Kirchner initially promoted a leftist "transversalism." He called it such because it was meant to be a left-wing force transversal to the Peronist/anti-Peronist cleavage.[24] In the 2003 electoral campaign, Néstor had also attracted many progressive anti-neoliberal urban voters.

Transversalism antagonized the right (both anti-Peronist and Peronist) and was also much resented by traditional Peronist actors, especially the Greater Buenos Aires municipalities' powerful mayors, who embodied the local Peronist political machines. As part of this effort, Kirchner even sided with the Madres de Plaza de Mayo against the PJ. Following a 2004 congress to re-unify the party, he ordered all elected PJ party authorities to resign, including the many ones favorable to him. A year later, a federal judge ordered the clos-ing or "intervention" of the PJ pending election of new authorities, something then not about to happen. Kirchner even stated that he "did not need either the [Peronist] governors or the [Justicialist] party to govern."[25] Institutionally, the reincorporation of the popular sectors in the 2000s was therefore clearly not conducted under the PJ.

The year 2005 was a turning point. In these first post-2003 legislative elections, Cristina Kirchner and the FpV ran in the all-powerful province of Buenos Aires against the PJ and the wife of Duhalde. In that fight between two major parties and figures, Cristina prevailed, 43 percent to 15 percent. The balance of power within the broad Peronist movement shifted thereafter toward the Kirchners. Local Peronist politicians opportunistically deserted the Duhalde machine for Kirchnerismo. These events emancipated Kirchner from his "godfather" Duhalde and granted him an electoral mandate denied by Menem's withdrawal.

For the 2007 presidential election, Néstor got Cristina to run for the pres-idency, which she did so explicitly as a self-styled "progressive." Attempting to create a generic, plural "left," opposed to a right, she created a "plural con-certation." Kirchnerismo did very well, and Cristina was elected president. However, electoral results showed that the Kirchners' "transversalist" attempt to restructure the party system had entirely failed. The non-Peronist left voted in massive numbers against the Kirchners (Ostiguy 1998, 2009). In fact, elec-toral sociology remained as always—in line with the cleavage between Per-onism and anti-Peronism, as since the mid-1940s, the predictors of the vote were class and education, not left-right political position or ideology. Equally telling, conservative right-wing elements of the popular sectors, especially in the more remote poorer provinces (Menem's traditional bastion), ended up voting for the FpV at rates above 70 percent. Conversely, Cristina's leftist appeals failed to sway middle-sector progressives she had appealed to, who largely voted for the anti-Peronist and still left-of-center Coalición Cívica of Elisa Carrió and the Socialists. To crown this coherent picture, the anti-Peronist right voted for the left-of-center anti-Peronist Socialist option that had greater chances. It thus became clear that it made no sense for the Kirch-ners to ignore Peronism as a political force and identity: it was precisely the Peronist electorate that was voting for them.

Therefore, with Cristina Kirchner assuming the presidency in early 2008, Néstor Kirchner did the only logical thing (Ostiguy 2007): he reactivated the PJ and hegemonized it. Thanks to Cristina's overwhelming electoral victory—

crushing the parties of the Peronist right in the process—Kirchnerismo and the FpV could claim the PJ for itself. At the national level, the FpV and the PJ officially merged, with their respective symbols used in parallel. Important dissident Peronist figures more on the right then excluded themselves from the PJ. They remained very active within Peronist politics, including holding onto various governorships and/or creating alternative Peronist parties. The PJ leadership and apparatus and the national government were meanwhile largely reunited under Néstor and Cristina. Néstor, particularly as head of the PJ, restored direct and fluid contacts with the old guard of the PJ in the municipalities of Greater Buenos Aires (see Rossi in this volume). Peronism, now led by the FpV-PJ, appeared once again fully invincible in Argentina. But this fusion between Peronism/PJ and Kirchnerismo lasted only two years, from 2008 to 2010.

To fund their "national and popular" project, the Kirchners launched in early 2008 a frontal attack on rural agro-exporters (labeled the "old oligarchy," though many were small producers as well) benefiting from the commodity boom with massive tax increases on soya. The country polarized in a major way, splitting also the Peronist base. In the subsequent 2009 legislative elections, the FpV-PJ, headed by none other than Néstor Kirchner himself, lost against the Peronist right (allied with the non-Peronist right) in the all-powerful province of Buenos Aires as well as in several agricultural provinces. Once again, the Kirchners were forcing a left-right polarization against the traditional Peronist/anti-Peronist cleavage.

After Néstor Kirchner's death in 2010 and Cristina's overwhelming 2011 presidential election victory, she dropped the PJ again. She also radicalized. But the party system in the 2011 presidential election had not aligned along left and right. In second place after the FpV was the main party of the anti-Peronist left, that of the Socialist Hermes Binner. In 2011, Binner had founded the Frente Amplio Progresista, imitating its Uruguayan Frente Amplio counterpart. The two parties of the Peronist right combined came in third. Meanwhile, Carrió, who had by then moved quite to the anti-Peronist right, was wiped out, while the "high right" per se did not present a presidential candidate.

Confident after her sizable victory, Cristina reverted fully to her FpV, putting the national PJ in total oblivion. She even fostered a quite modified version of "transversalism," this time more verticalist and without the futile appeals to the anti-Peronist left, creating as we saw the umbrella organization (on the left) Unidos y Organizados. The "pure Kirchnerista" La Cámpora youth organization also moved to the national forefront—to the major frustration of Peronist Greater Buenos Aires mayors and the governors.

TABLE 13.3. Argentine party spectrum and alignments

| | Left of center | Right of center | Left of center, left, center | Right of center | |
|---|---|---|---|---|---|
| | Peronism | | Anti-Peronism | | |
| | Kirchnerism | Dissident/ "Orthodox" Peronism | Anti-Peronist center-left, left, and center | "Neoliberal" right | |
| Elections | Name of the political party | | | | |
| 2005 | FpV | PJ | ARI | UCR | PRO (Macri; Lopez Murphy) |
| 2007 | FpV | Frente Justicia, Unión y Libertad (FREJULI) | Coalición Cívica (incl. PS) | Recrear (Lopez Murphy) (with PRO, in provinces) | |
| 2009 | FpV-PJ | Unión-PRO (De Narváez); Frente Santa Fe Federal PJ; Unión por Córdoba (incl. PJ) | Acuerdo Cívico y Social (PS, GEN, UCR, CC) | PRO (Macri) | |
| 2011 | FpV | Compromiso Federal; Frente Popular | Frente Amplio Progresista (FAP) (PS, GEN, Luis Juez) | PRO | |
| 2013 | FpV | Frente Renovador Compromiso Federal Unión por Córdoba (PJ Córdoba) Unidos por la Libertad y el Trabajo | UNEN and Frentes Progresistas Cívicos y Sociales (incl. UCR in various provinces) | UCR (going alone in some provinces) | PRO |

*Key*: CC: Coalición Cívica; GEN: Generación para un Encuentro Nacional; PS: Partido Socialista; UNEN: Frente Amplio Unión de Encuentros Nacionales.

*Note*: For the years corresponding only to national legislative elections (i.e., not to presidential elections), by definition the abbreviations correspond to parties at the provincial level (because of the particular form of Argentine federalism).

In the 2013 legislative elections, having sharply mistreated her Peronist organizational bases (especially the Peronist mayors of Greater Buenos Aires), Kirchner once again lost in the powerful province of Buenos Aires, thus also foreclosing—what was perceived by some—as her dream of reelection through a constitutional reform. Still more lethal yet, several of those PJ barons defected to a new challenger, Cristina's former chief of cabinet Sergio Massa. Massa deserted at the last minute to found the Frente Renovador, a right-of-center political party in tune with important segments of the Peronist electorate, instantly winning the province of Buenos Aires.[26]

As a product of that outcome, the governor of the province of Buenos Aires, Daniel Scioli—a "centrist" Peronist who is officially Kirchnerista but was despised and attacked by much of the Kirchnerista leadership—stepped forward (without her blessing) to succeed Cristina as the next presidential candidate, reviving the PJ. Thus, Peronism in 2014 once again oddly ranged from left to right: from the Kirchnerista Peronists on the left to Scioli in the center, with support of much of the traditional PJ; to Massa of the Frente Renovador, more right of center, with the support of other PJ mayors; to conservative Peronists. While Scioli and the Kirchneristas are allied, Kirchneristas campaign as Cristinistas, and Scioli does so as a Peronist, mostly separately.

Since 2003, thus, the national political situation in Argentina has been one in which Kirchnerismo has dominated the "low-left" quadrant, with vociferous opposition from actors in each of the other three quadrants. Kirchnerismo has therefore been helped electorally by the fact that the opposition was divided, with little uniting the other three quadrants. A danger for Kirchnerismo comes from the "slippery slope" on the left-right Peronist political spectrum.

Table 13.3 represents, chronologically and in terms of political parties, the governing political force (which is not party coalitional) and the three-way opposition to it.

Oddly, the main party victim of neoliberalism and its failure was not the political force that implemented it (the PJ) but the two political parties of the Alianza government: the Frepaso disappeared, and the centenary UCR shrank electorally to tiny proportions. The UCR was in fact destroyed by its association with not one but two devastating economic crises erupting under its watch: the hyperinflation of 1989 at the very end of Raúl Alfonsín's presidency, and the December 2001 collapse. Beyond the failure of the Alianza, the political label that went with neoliberalism was not "Peronism" but "Menemismo." The demonized "other" for the FpV is always Menemismo, put in the same normative category as the IMF and the military dictatorship.

While this could politically and discursively explain the permanence of "Peronism," the situation as we saw is not that simple and may not require such a recourse to discourse. On the one hand, it is true that neoliberalism in Argentina ended on its own (through "internal contradictions") and not through the victory of an entirely absent powerful new political party on the left pre-2002—that is, no outflanking occurred (Roberts 2014). But on the other hand, as we just saw, a powerful new political force and political party— Kirchnerismo and the FpV—did emerge in reaction to, and (most of the time) in a negative relation to, the PJ after 2002 and the drastic collapse of neoliberalism, thus confirming after the fact Roberts's (2014) thesis. And in 2016, since the victory of Macri, Kirchnerismo and Peronism have increasingly gone their own separate ways.

With regard to the governing coalition that led the reincorporation, there is however a major political difference depending on whether one looks at the national level or the provincial and municipal level. The top governing officials under Cristina nationally were increasingly made up of non-Peronist (though not anti-Peronist) leftists, including many previously attached to the Frepaso, the Communist Party, or other Marxist (and never Peronist) groups. At the provincial and municipal level, however, those governing remain overwhelmingly Peronist. To summarize, the governmental orientation is leftist; the government's organizational medium of contact with voters is Peronist. Key national decision makers closest to Cristina (e.g., Axel Kicillof, Carlos Zannini, Martín Sabbatella, Juan Manual Abal Medina) are all educated leftists. Their profile could not conceivably be more different from that of the coarse and unquestionably Peronist Hugo Curto or from thuggish Raúl Othacehe[27] or, at the national level, of Néstor's era all-powerful Secretary of Commerce Guillermo Moreno or from Julio De Vido, Néstor's equally powerful Santa Cruz "buddy." And certainly, despite their very rocky relationship, the Kirchners would have been unable to govern without the PJ-identified Peronist mayors and governors they often frustrated.

The FpV remains a primarily personalist and programmatic but weakly institutionalized political party.[28] In that sense, it is unclear how much party structure the FpV retains between elections, beyond being a tight legislative bloc in Congress and a closed name list in a proportional representation electoral system.

Vis-à-vis Peronism, Kirchnerismo's intentions seem to have been to become a political force "outdating" (*instancia superadora*) Peronism, highly valued but as something in past history. Kirchnerismo sought to embody a socalled "national and popular" form of left, having its ideological and symbolic origins in the militant (and mostly middle-sector) youth of the early 1970s. Understood in terms of that immense ambition, Kirchnerismo arguably failed, despite becoming the main political force in Argentina for over a decade.

## CONCLUSION

This chapter relates the incorporation of popular sectors after neoliberalism to divergent forms of organized state-party-society relations and the trajectory of the Brazilian and Argentine party systems. In both countries, groups mobilized by the exclusionary impacts of neoliberalism gained access to the political system, and their incorporation, together with the particular kind of political leadership shown institutionally by the incorporating side, has had significant effects on the party system. Brazil has stabilized and institutionalized left-right partisan competition, with the PT and its coalitional allies pursuing a presidential strategy of elite alliances. Argentina, after the collapse of late 2001 and the emergence of Kirchnerismo, moved toward a less institutionalized system where partisan actors remain greatly weakened. A new hybrid kind of organization arose between sectors of Peronism (both at the political and the trade-union level), non-Peronist left-wing actors, and social movements (both predating and postdating the arrival of Néstor Kirchner to power) hostile to neoliberalism, in a whole dominated by the increasingly highly personalist (historically "Peronist-style") leadership of the Kirchners. The years of reincorporation have seen repeated attempts, mainly from the Kirchnerista left but also some from the right, to forge new alliances and coalitions across the Peronist/anti-Peronist line, thereby potentially even "normalizing" Argentina's politics and party system along more standard left-right lines. Such efforts have repeatedly failed to take hold, and even when political leaders made such moves, voters proved loath to follow. While large political parties have decayed in Argentina, its political space has thus remained very much two-dimensional.

In Brazil, the democratic struggle constituted and legitimated new political actors in the working classes, social movements, and the middle classes. Their link to the PT consolidated as a result of neoliberalism implemented by conservative parties; post-neoliberal neo-developmentalism implemented by the PT in government introduced partisan and state mechanisms of incorporation that stabilized the party system around a left-right cleavage in which the PT and its allies occupy the center-left. The limits to this social pact and incorporating institutions—neoliberal stabilization and coalitional presidentialism—placed an upper limit on the degree to which the PT could break with neoliberalism and reorganize political institutions.

In Argentina, by contrast, the traditional political force that incorporated working class and popular sectors, Peronism, was also the one that implemented neoliberalism, though it lost power to its traditional rival prior to neoliberalism's spectacular collapse in 2001–2002. Because the PJ and its rivals were both associated with neoliberalism, the social actors who mobilized in opposition were initially distant from all established political parties, and it was a series of circumstantial events that brought Néstor Kirchner to power in 2003 atop what was initially a faction of Peronism, his electoral FpV. Unencumbered with economic and political elite allies of the sort that moderated the PT in Brazil, Kirchner pursued a daring political, social, and organizational strategy of incorporation to consolidate his initially meek power, as well as more aggressive neo-developmentalist policies. The mechanisms of incorporation for militant, excluded groups were channeled through "Kirchnerismo," a combination of a politicized state, social movements politically administering state funds on the ground, and the partisan electoral engine of the FpV—with the PJ taking a back seat and the figures of Néstor and then Cristina embodying the project's "transformative" orientation. Since Néstor's death, Cristina has continued to occupy the left-Peronist quadrant of the partisan space, and no combination of right-wing and centrist Peronists and/or anti-Peronists (whether conservative or left-progressive) have been able to dislodge them, until late 2015.

In both Brazil and Argentina, there are important limits to current combinations of party system, mechanisms of incorporation, and social base. In Brazil, the 2013 protests revealed simmering discontent over the unaccountability of the neo-developmentalist growth model, especially in its only partial responsiveness to key concerns of groups that ought to have been incorporated as members of working classes, social movements, and middle sectors. Still, the PT has been the partisan vehicle for incorporating those who have felt excluded for the last three decades, and there is little to suggest that actors on either the left or the right are capable of taking over that function. Similarly, in Argentina the dominant position of the Kirchners has been challenged by sectors that feel victimized by the current model of neo-developmentalism, as in the case of the agricultural producers' strike, or that feel intense dislike for the praxis of Kirchnerismo, as in the large and various anti-Kirchnerista "citizen protests" that occurred in the 2010s. Still, until early 2015, no challenge at the political-electoral level was able in twelve years to hold together a lasting winning combination of the actors of very disparate sociopolitical orientations— left, center, right, Peronist, anti-Peronist—that could replace Kirchnerismo. To be sure, "institutional" does not mean permanency. While there can be a routinized and habituated interaction between the state, social groups, and society, this reorganization is a political (or sociopolitical) project—a social "pact," not a bureaucratic one.

These two cases suggest a few areas of further investigation regarding responses to the neoliberal juncture that have established mechanisms of incorporation integrated to varying extent into the party system. First, there are structural, economic limits to the post-neoliberal moment, which in both countries depends on the continued surplus (generating fiscal resources) produced by an extractive export model. Both countries weathered the 2009 international financial crisis, but a long-term decline in the demand for their primary exports could undercut their neo-developmentalist model. Argentina in 2014 was furthermore experiencing economic challenges related to energy, currency reserves, and inflation—all familiar problems in Argentina's history. Second, in contrast to their Andean neighbors, neither Argentina nor Brazil carried out a refoundation of the republic, including a new social constitution "freezing in" the new model and arrangements. Therefore, political fatigue, after more than a decade of the PT and of Kirchnerismo in power, could simply bring the pendulum to swing back electorally to a more center-right orientation in government and, more damaging yet, a pro-private enterprise model or perhaps even free market. The mechanisms for such a reversal would likely be different in each country: a normal alternation in power in Brazil or to the PRO and allies in Argentina, or a slippage of Peronism toward the center. In Brazil, a winning coalition of left or (much more likely) right actors could conceivably displace the PT. So far, politics in both countries have been stabilized in large measure by the incapacity of partisan and political elite competitors to advance an alternative winning coalition. Whether such mechanisms of incorporation can outlive the current partisan coalition or personalistic hybrid organization in power is doubtful and remains to be seen.

Chapter 14

# CONCLUSION

Reflections on the Second Wave of Popular
Incorporation for a Post-Neoliberal Era

## EDUARDO SILVA

This book has shown that the neoliberal period had profound effects on the principal actors and mechanisms of the first incorporation analyzed by Ruth Berins Collier and David Collier in their seminal work *Shaping the Political Arena* (1991). It weakened labor unions, political parties, and state corporatism. As was argued in the introduction to this book, neoliberal policies disincorporated the popular sectors from politics, although they did so incompletely and unevenly across the cases.

Neoliberal economic, social, and political reforms also generated significant backlash. The reactive phase to neoliberalism, to borrow a phrase from Ken Roberts, involved protest and electoral mobilization by both popular sector and middle-class groups. As Rossi argued in the introduction to part 1, new organized popular sector and subaltern groups led reincorporation struggles, such as the indigenous, indigenous-peasants, the unemployed, landless peasants, and the denizens of poor urban neighborhoods, to mention a few. Although their impact was less, human rights', women's, environmental, and *alter-mundialista* movements also joined the fray.

These social forces, instead of the traditional labor movement, which of course also participated, were at the forefront of anti-neoliberal resistance alongside new political movements and parties that capitalized electorally on mounting social discontent. They crafted political projects from below for a post-neoliberal period. Which popular sector social groups and political parties, in what combinations, and the specific forms of reincorporation depended a great deal on the degree of institutional disruption (Bolivia, Ecuador, and Venezuela) or continuity (Argentina and Brazil) during the reactive phase to neoliberalism (Levitsky and Roberts 2011; Roberts 2014).

Bolivia, Ecuador, and Venezuela experienced major institutional disruption. Established political parties practically disappeared as voters switched allegiances to new ones. Significantly, voters have reelected presidents from the left parties and coalitions that emerged from the neoliberal period again and again. New constitutions gave teeth to the ideals of substantive democracy and expanded rights.

Compared to the Andean cases, Brazil and Argentina experienced more institutional continuity, although the former more so than the latter. In Brazil, mild constitutional reform expanded rights and introduced some political reforms. The party system did not suffer a radical overhaul. It absorbed a new left political party, the Workers' Party. It seems the party system has become more institutionalized and stable, Dilma Rousseff's impeachment in 2016 notwithstanding. Argentina experienced more volatility, but less so than the Andean cases, and eschewed constitutional reform. The party system suffered major changes with the virtual disappearance of the Unión Cívica Radical However, despite upheavals and changes, the Partido Justicialista lives on.

After left and center-left governments came to power, inaugurating a post-neoliberal era, conflicts during the second incorporation period involved two types. As occurred during the first incorporation (Collier and Collier 1991), one centered on clashes over the project from below vs. the project from above. Here, newly installed left governments implemented policies that clashed with the proposals of the wider coalitions that had crafted broad-based projects from below during the resistance to neoliberalism. Many but not all of those tensions involved popular struggles against the intensification of extractive models of accumulation. Frequently these intertwined with indigenous claims for territorial autonomy and control and with ecologists who envisioned the promotion of more ecologically friendly policies.

Building on the introductory chapter, Rossi's introduction to part 1, and the case studies, this chapter reflects on the meaning of incorporation in a post-neoliberal era and the processes of incorporation. It then fleshes out those reflections in a brief comparative exercise. The chapter closes with some thoughts on the potential legacies of the second incorporation and subjects for further research.

## REFLECTIONS ON THE MEANING OF INCORPORATION

In *Shaping the Political Arena*, Collier and Collier argued that incorporation involved the regularization and institutionalization of labor union linkages to the state and/or political parties with the principal objective of controlling or mobilizing them (Collier and Collier 1991). Regularization and institutionalization were *the* central dimensions of the first incorporation because of the central position of the principal social actor—urban labor—in the process of capitalist production. Labor unions were strengthening during a period of social, economic, and political turmoil and it was imperative that they be controlled or mobilized or both. Moreover, labor unions also expressed broader demands for inclusion from other segments of the popular sectors that were either more weakly organized or not organized at all.

By contrast, regularization and institutionalization, while not absent, were not always the principal focus during the second incorporation. The context was more complex. As Rossi stressed in this volume and I (2012) have argued elsewhere, social forces other than labor more often than not led the struggle for popular sector inclusion. These social groups were not always crucial links in economic production (hence the territorial nature of organization), nor, at times, were their demands even principally economic; however, their anti-neoliberal protests and mobilization had been extraordinarily disruptive. Thus, in our cases formal regulation and institutional incorporation for some popular sector actors were either not a priority or were rejected outright.

Given these circumstances, following Rossi (2015a, 2017, and in this volume), it is useful to think of incorporation as a process of recognition and inclusion of popular sector and subaltern social groups' interests, as well as frequently but not necessarily their organizations in the political arena, which comprises political parties, elections, executive and legislative institutions, and policy making. This formulation accounts for greater variation in state popular sector relations in the second incorporation, acknowledging that inclusion (or "regularization") may even be informal. Moreover, the state may recognize explicitly expressed popular sector interests and demands articulated during the reactive phase of neoliberalism without bringing in their formal organizations or, as on occasion occurs, while actively disarticulating them. A government may address popular sector interests directly via public policy. Ecuador may be the paradigmatic case, but it also occurs in Venezuela and Bolivia as well as Brazil and, to a lesser extent, Argentina.

## REFLECTIONS ON THE PROCESS OF INCORPORATION

Collier and Collier (1991) adopted a critical juncture framework that shaped how they approached historical sequencing. They carefully isolated an incorporation period, which then shaped an aftermath and a legacy. Insufficient time has passed in the period covered in this volume to make a critical juncture argument. Only the future can tell if the contemporary reincorporation of popular sectors might constitute a critical juncture. This volume, then, necessarily focused more on specifying the modes of reincorporation, the contemporary reconfiguration of the relationship of popular sectors to the political arena after the installation of resilient left governments in reaction to the neoliberal period.

Given these considerations, this volume has focused more on specifying the process of reincorporation. In temporal terms, the process spans the neoliberal period, including popular reaction to it, initial incorporation, and the beginnings of a consolidation phase (Rossi 2015a and 2017). What of the content of each period? To systematize analysis it may be useful to think of processes of incorporation as involving three key dimensions in a temporal sequencing that correspond to the aforementioned periods.

Building on Collier and Collier (1991), the first dimension refers to the emergence of an incorporation project, which in our cases is in reaction to neoliberalism. This involves the emergence of a post-neoliberal agenda for change during the period of cycles of anti-neoliberal contention. As the introduction and Rossi (2015a) have argued, this dimension includes the rights being demanded (largely socioeconomic ones for the second incorporation), the characteristics of the popular sectors involved, and the political agents doing the incorporating. It also includes the incorporation projects, which our collection has specified in each case.

The second dimension covers what one might call the substance of incorporation as left governments struggle to establish themselves. An overlooked characteristic is that it involves the degree to which they reorganize popular sector representation to support a long-term left project. This includes established popular sector organizations, such as unions and new ones such as Rossi's reincorporation movements. As this volume has emphasized, it also considers the relationship of popular sectors to political institutions in the policy process, primarily political parties and the institutions of the executive and legislative branches of government. Are they direct, as in having formal or informal roles in decision making and policy? Are they at arm's length? Absent formal and informal roles in the policy process, do popular sectors benefit from government policies and, therefore, support such governments electorally?

The third dimension concerns the type of interest intermediation between state and society that emerges in a consolidation phase. Is it primarily pluralist (Oxhorn 1998, 2012), corporatist (Doctor 2007), clientelist (Hilger 2012), or something else? One could argue that a new type emerges: *segmented popular interest intermediation regimes*. In segmented regimes, no single form of interest intermediation dominates (as had been the case in the first incorporation with state corporatism as the modal form). Given the proliferation and heterogeneity of popular sector groups that matter politically for left governments, they establish different forms of intermediation with different groups.

In the segmented interest regimes of the second incorporation we see the emergence of two new forms of interest intermediation that mix with reorganized corporatist regimes and clientelism: state managerial and informal contestatory. State managerialism refers to recognition of popular sector demands and public policy to address them, but the state does not involve the popular sector organizations that raised them in the policy process. In this type, the state manages popular sector demands directly. Informal contestatory types involve the following routinized interactions: The government proposes a policy, affected popular sector organizations protest, and negotiation ensues. The pattern repeats regularly; thus, it constitutes an informal institutional form of interest intermediation. The importance of interest intermediation regimes rests on their capacity to keep tensions over interests and policy preferences among organized social groups in the policy process manageable.

## Processes of Incorporation in Cases with Significant Institutional Discontinuity: Bolivia, Ecuador, and Venezuela

As was argued in the introduction to this volume, Bolivia, Ecuador, and Venezuela were the cases with the most institutional discontinuity from the neoliberal period and, hence, less institutional constraints in reorganizing state-popular sector relationships. To summarize for our purposes here, I first compare them in terms of the relationship of the popular sectors to the policy-making process. Secondly, I compare them on the degree to which left governments have reorganized popular sector representation to support a long-term left project, a theme not explicitly addressed in the volume. Thirdly, I expand the comparison with respect to their emerging interest intermediation regimes.

### Relationship of Popular Sectors to the Policy Process

Compared to the first incorporation, the relationship of popular sectors to the policy process is less direct and more at arm's length. Much of this has to do with the weakening of political parties. In the first incorporation, labor parties often directly incorporated unions into the policy process via labor bureaus. This was especially the case in Venezuela, but also more informally in Bolivia where the COB had influence on MNR policy (see Ellner and León Trujillo and Spronk in this volume). By the same token, state corporatist interest intermediation, despite their co-optative characteristics, offered direct conduits to policy making in the executive.

In the second incorporation, new parties in these three cases were generally less institutionalized and played a more marginal role in forming policy platforms (see the chapters by Hellinger and Conaghan in this volume). Moreover, popular organizations, by and large, no longer have strong, direct policy influence in them as labor had in the past.[1] The heterogeneous nature of the popular sector organizations that forged the post-neoliberal project contributes to this situation. Many more popular groups with varying degrees of organization and strength clamor for access. The often conflicting relationships among them make it difficult to formally incorporate them in a political party. Corporatist-like arrangements, in the rare cases we see them, are not institutionalized.

Despite these developments, we can nevertheless still make meaningful distinctions between more direct or more arm's-length relationships to the policy process. Of the three cases, it was most direct in Bolivia, where *cocaleros* and indigenous peasants (CSUTCB) and *interculturales* (frontier colonists) and, until 2011, indigenous organizations (CIDOB and CONAMAQ) were straightforwardly incorporated in the MAS. Indeed, they had created the party. Nevertheless, policy emanates from the presidency, where the CSUTCB has a more institutionally based role in its design, although not in its formulation. More important is the informal regularization of relations that involve consultation between Evo Morales's government and organizations of the core coalition that sustains it. At strategic moments, this applies to organized labor—the COB—as well (see Silva and León Trujillo and Spronk in this volume).

Ecuadorian popular sectors, by far, have the most arm's-length relationship to the policy process (see Conaghan, León Trujillo and Spronk, and Silva in this volume). All of the major popular organizations are deliberately excluded. Social policy designed by technocrats in the executive is the main instrument for the incorporation of many popular interests without organization input. Some smaller, more peripheral organizations are sometimes included on an ad hoc basis, as was the case with FENOCIN to gain legitimacy for agrarian policy and to compete with conservative party clientelist networks for electoral purposes. Corporatist mechanisms have been practically eliminated.

Venezuela may be considered an intermediate case because some popular sector organizations have more direct connections to the policy process both through the principal left political party—the PSUV—and via linkages to the executive (see Ellner, García-Guadilla, and Hellinger in this volume). Labor, as Steve Ellner showed, has more recently developed an institutionalized connection to the PSUV in the form of a new "labor bureau." It was involved in the design of the 2012 labor law. However, this covers only the newly created "official" labor confederation. Traditional labor organizations, both in the diminished CTV and the former Causa R–connected unions of Guayana, are excluded. There is also a social movements coordinator in the PSUV, but the movement organizations are not involved in policy design, as García-Guadilla (in this volume) showed. The myriad social organizations of popular power are directly and institutionally linked to the executive by law; however, at best only as implementers of policies created by the presidency. Overall, the main function of party incorporation or direct linkage to the state seems to be to secure support of these organizations for the government. Still, this is qualitatively different from the arm's-length Ecuadorian formula. Material benefits flow accordingly.

*State-led Reorganization of Popular Representation*

The degree of state-led reorganization of popular representation can also be placed on a continuum. It was least pronounced in Bolivia, largely due to the fact that Bolivia's major social movement organizations were founding members of the MAS and Evo Morales's government. Labor was in strategic alliance with it. Thus, despite tensions, Morales's government generally chose to negotiate with them rather than intervene in them. The major exception was the break with lowland indigenous and more traditional highland indigenous over territorial autonomy rights (see León Trujillo and Spronk; also Silva in this volume).

Due to its anticorporate stance (and the weakness of the opposition to his government), Correa's administration intervened in popular sector organizations to a larger extent than did Morales in Bolivia. He removed social movement organizations from policy-making boards. He also weakened major movement organizations themselves. With CONAIE, the government undermined links between its base organizations in local communities and the national organization by keeping national leaders excluded from policy making and going directly to local community leaders offering to solve their pressing problems with infrastructure, schools, housing, and social policy. Local leadership realized national leaders were no longer necessary intermediaries between them and the state (Silva in this volume).

The situation was more severe with labor unions. Because of labor's role in economic production, it was more regulated than indigenous peoples' organizations. Labor, and especially public sector employees, enjoyed formal rights and protections beyond other social movements. In response to labor's "privileged" position, Correa's administration set about to decollectivize it. In a series of amendments to labor laws during the Constituent Assembly, it reclassified work categories to render hiring and firing more flexible and to weaken strike capabilities. It also weakened collective bargaining rights. Throughout, Correa's government tried to disarticulate unions and it was not until 2016 that they finally began to fight back (León Trujillo and Spronk in this volume).

State-led reorganization of popular sectors to create support for a left agenda was most pronounced in Venezuela. García-Guadilla's chapter details how the Bolivarian government radically expanded its efforts to create new popular social organizations after the turbulent events of 2002–2004. These were supported by generous expenditures directly from the presidency to combat poverty, especially through the missions. Unlike in Bolivia and Ecuador, this largely involved organizing the unorganized. By 2006, the communal council emerged as a paradigmatic organization. Moreover, as the government and PSUV create popular power to defend the Bolivarian revolution, they are penetrating the communal councils, aggregating them into larger units, and directing them in as much as possible.

In addition to organizing the unorganized, as Ellner's chapter showed, the Venezuelan government is also reorganizing union federations, creating, recognizing, and bargaining with a new one that is committed to defending the process of change politically, even if it has to put workers' issues second. Meanwhile, as mentioned previously, it excludes union federations that do not join the officially sanctioned one. Moreover, the government ignores or tries to break popular organizations that insist on autonomy or side with the opposition.

### Segmented Interest Intermediation Regimes

Distinctive segmented interest intermediation regimes that differed substantially from the state corporatism of the first incorporation crystalized in Bolivia, Ecuador, and Venezuela. By 2013, Bolivia had predominantly mixed two forms of interest intermediation. Silva's chapter showed that the main social movements in the MAS—the CSUTCB, its feminist branch, and colonists (mestizo peasants in frontier zones)—have been incorporated more or less directly in a corporatist-like form. They are state recognized—but not state chartered—representative organizations. After 2010 they developed a privileged relationship with the state, which included appointments to key ministries, participation in policy making, and selection of MAS candidates for elected offices. However, this is not corporatism in the traditional sense because MAS's relationship to the state and policy process is not codified and institutionalized. It depends on the government in office. Meanwhile, Silva's and León Trujillo and Spronk's chapters demonstrate that contestatory interest intermediation characterized the relationship to the state for many other movement organizations, such as the COB, cooperative miners, and indigenous organizations such as CIDOB (after 2012), and environmentalists.

The chapters on parties, unions, and social movements in this volume illustrate that Ecuador developed its own distinctive segmented popular intermediation regime, one that mixed three forms of popular interest intermedi-ation. First, it established a type of state managerialism that delivered public policies to reduce poverty and increased access to services while keeping organized popular sector interests from participating in the policy process. Second, Correa's administrations also relied on clientelism, a traditional form of popular interest intermediation. This system worked best in the barrios of Guayaquil, a city with well-established clientelist networks controlled by po-litical parties that were rivals of PAIS.

Third, Correa's government made occasional halfhearted efforts to devel-op mechanisms that involved popular sectors and civil society in the policy process so long as they did not and could not challenge administration goals. First, as we saw in Silva's chapter, at times the government selectively invited weaker popular sector organizations to participate in policy making. This was especially the case of FENOCIN in the reform of agrarian policy. Second, the government also developed a system of nonbinding citizen consultation for policy in the national planning process (Nicholls 2014). Citizens generally did not represent important organizations. Usually they participated as individu-als or were members of small local civic organizations. State agencies mainly administered surveys during citizen planning workshops.

What of Venezuela's segmented popular interest intermediation regime? The chapters in this volume reveal, first, that given the emphasis on popu-lar power, Hugo Chávez's government developed a very different style of state managerial popular interest intermediation than Ecuador. Although state mangers developed policy and pushed popular sector organization, most communal councils cultivated ties to the government agencies in charge of ap-proving and funding projects, and increasingly to the PSUV. The currency of exchange was political loyalty to the Bolivarian socialist revolution, although, in fairness, this was not always instrumental logic. Many community councils believed in the legitimacy of Venezuela's process of change and the necessity of defending it.

A second feature of Venezuela's segmented popular interest intermediation system was clientelism. According to García-Guadilla, the direct dispensation by the central government of resources to urban popular organization such as the communal councils has encouraged the practice by government operators from the PSUV and various ministries. It is unknown how pervasive the prac-tice might be, but conservative estimates place it at about 50 percent.

A third element of Venezuela's segmented popular interest intermediation system was the corporatist-like incorporation of the reorganized labor move-ment. Ellner's chapter showed that the new labor confederation is officially recognized by the government and is incorporated in the PSUV. It is the sole interlocutor for organized labor in the policy process as evidenced by its participation in crafting the 2012 labor law. However, its relationship to the state is not formally institutionalized. It depends on the government in office. All other labor confederations are kept at arm's length from the policy process and are in more or less conflictive relationships with the government.

## Processes of Incorporation in Cases with Significant Institutional Continuity: Brazil and Argentina

Given the relative institutional continuity of Brazil and Argentina's transition to post-neoliberalism, one expects reincorporation processes to exhibit less profound changes due to greater institutional constraints. This is not to say that changes in popular representation, the popular sector's relationship to the policy process, or in the structure of interest intermediation did not occur. However, regularization of their interactions with the state and institutionalization were greater.

### Relationship of Popular Sectors to the Policy Process

One fundamental difference with the Andean cases lies in the relationship between labor unions and left governments. In the Andean cases they were strained. Indeed, it appeared that in many respects those governments were decidedly antilabor union. In large measure this was due to the close association of unions with the *ancien* political regime in a context where the traditional party system had collapsed and new left governing parties saw their mission as one of recasting (or refounding) politics (see Collier in this volume). This was not so much the case in Argentina and Brazil. There were certainly changes in political parties but, given greater institutional continuity, the left parties that took power in the early 2000s had a closer association with the labor movement.

A second fundamental difference with the Andean cases refers to the nature of the reincorporation struggles for social movements. As Rossi emphasized in this volume, in Brazil and Argentina the MST and the unemployed workers' movement had not yet been recognized as social or political actors in their own right. Therefore, the incorporation process involved obtaining both recognition and achievement of political and substantive socioeconomic rights. In the Andean cases, recognition and political rights (especially of indigenous peoples) had been won during the neoliberal period.

Unlike in the Andean cases, in Argentina and Brazil unions had a closer relationship to governing left parties and to the state. In both cases, party incorporation ensured that key policy issues such as wages, commitment to formal employment, and—importantly—the strengthening of labor unions themselves were attended to. In both cases, the Ministry of Labor was the key institution they related to. This was a traditional arrangement. The difference with the neoliberal period is that this institution was no longer being used to disincorporate unions.

That said, the nature of the relationship of unions to parties differed. In Brazil, the PT was born a new labor party, thus it was an organic relationship with a major labor confederation, the CUT (see Gindin and Cardoso, Ostiguy and Schneider in this volume). The government saw the CUT as a source of state managers. Being in the state had a moderating effect on the CUT, not the least due to cadres leaving because of its increasingly mild reformist stance. In Argentina, as Gindin and Cardoso show, by the 2010s the union movement had lost influence with the PJ, although substantial segments supported Kirchnerismo politically.

In sharp contrast to Bolivia and Venezuela, social movements in Argentina and Brazil were subordinate to the labor movement in the policy process.[2] In Argentina, Kirchnerismo established linkages with *piquetero* organizations and the state in the policy process, as detailed in Rossi's chapter. At first, new and reoriented state institutions incorporated them in the process, especially in the administration of welfare programs. Eventually the Ministry of Social Development became the major point of contact. However, *piquetero* leaders in the government had little or no influence in policy formulation (Rossi 2015a, 2017). The movement's impact eventually declined as targeted welfare programs and state or party political employment demobilized them. The Brazilian MST went through a similar trajectory. However, the principal distancing agent was MST disenchantment with the government's commitment to mild reformism instead of structural changes. In both of these cases the relationship of the social movements to the state were not institutionalized and, therefore, depended on the government in office.

On balance, compared to the Andean cases, popular sector organizations in Argentina and Brazil experienced greater regularization and institutionalization of their relationship to the state and the policy process. Labor unions were the primary target of reinstitutionalization, resulting in the reorganization of their relationship to the state on more favorable terms than under neoliberalism. However, social movements also saw their relationship to the state improved with predictable demobilizing results. Although attenuated, their policy impact was, on average, greater than in the Andean cases, with the possible exception of Bolivia.

### Reorganization of Popular Representation

The evidence from the chapters on unions, social movements, and political parties suggests that state-led reorganization of popular representation in Argentina and Brazil was less pronounced than in the Andean cases. In these two cases left governments worked with—or courted—existing popular sector representative organizations that supported them politically. With few exceptions, they did not create them. In Brazil, coming out of the struggles for democratization and anti-neoliberalism, the CUT unions were founding members of the ruling party, and the MST initially was a close strategic supporter. Policy strengthened union centrals, both urban and rural. Any reshaping was done through promotion of leadership to political posts, which involved embracing mild reformism. The effect was a voluntary exit of cadres due to the conservative turn of the PT in government. This process, more than overt purges, shaped leadership and popular organizations over fourteen years of PT rule.

A similar process occurred in Argentina, although union and social movements were more fractured, as shown in Rossi's and in Ostiguy and Schneider's chapters. There, shifting constellations of union centrals and *piquetero* organizations strategically aligned with Kirchnerismo from the early 2000s to this writing. The choice of whether to support the government politically depended on autonomous strategic decisions from the movement organizations themselves. Popular organizations not aligned with Kirchnerismo were not directly intervened with.

### Segmented Interest Intermediation Regimes

What of Argentina and Brazil's popular interest intermediation regimes? They too may be characterized as segmented, although, unlike the Andean cases, the continuation of neocorporatist arrangements is strong. If we follow Molina and Rhodes (2002), neocorporatism is best thought of as an institutionalized exchange between recognized representative social actors and the state in the policy process. Thus, we can focus on patterns of cooperation between state and societal actors even with the loosening, weakening—or in the absence—of traditional structural conditions. By extension, "corporatist-like" arrangements refer to the absence of institutionalization or legally binding consultation and/or negotiation in what otherwise look like corporatist exchanges.

Gindin and Cardoso argued that in Brazil unions had never been outside of corporatist structures. This continued under PT governments. Decentralized collective bargaining rules, however, weakened direct central government control over the labor movement compared to the past. Rossi's chapter showed that social movements in general and the landless workers' movement in particular were incorporated in new neocorporatist-like structures specially created by PT governments (Goldfrank 2011; Doctor 2007).[3]

Whether they decided to participate or not varied over time with their tolerance for government control mechanisms, especially as they related to policy moderation.

In Argentina, labor unions also remained in a corporatist system of labor relations that, although modified, was never dismantled (Etchemendy and Collier 2007). Kirchnerismo fortified those structures, which, along with centralized collective bargaining, strengthened the central government in relation to unions. Nevertheless, as Gindin and Cardoso illustrate, union autonomy from direct state control also contributed to heightened, politicized confrontation.

Social movements, however, were not channeled into corporatist structures as in Brazil. Instead, as Rossi documents, the Kirchner administrations created new agencies or adapted existing ones to incorporate them on a more informal basis: leaders occupied posts in government agencies. The government targeted their social bases with a multiplicity of policies to meet their varied needs. This accounts for the fluidity and variability in the state institutions charged with interfacing with *piquetero* organizations. Moreover, their incorporation was along territorial lines in relation to multiple state agencies rather than on a functional logic of official representation with one specialized government department (Rossi 2015a, 2017). Later, the restructuring of the General Secretariat attempted "to build a routinized—albeit not legally institutionalized—relationship equivalent to the corporatist one, but for actors and conflicts of a territorial nature" (Rossi 2015a, 15). However it is characterized, this was clearly a more regularized arrangement than that found in the Andean cases, with the exception of Bolivia.

Neocorporatism and corporatist-like arrangements were not the only game in town. Just as in the Andean cases, in Brazil and Argentina a strong dose of state managerialism was also in evidence with similar social assistance policies: Bolsa Familia in Brazil and the Asignación Universal por Hijo program in Argentina. They address the material interests of the popular sectors, especially for income and consumer subsidies. As occurs everywhere, they create individual linkages between individuals and the state.

What of contestatory and clientelistic forms of interest intermediation? At one time, contestatory forms may have characterized the relationship of *piquetero* protests and governments at the local and state level. The same can be said of MST protests and land invasions. However, the widespread development of social assistance policies has significantly demobilized people who used to participate in them. Their immediate demands for income and income supplements have been attended to. As a result, compared to Bolivia, protests of this nature are not significant at a nationally relevant political level. By the same token, clientelistic practices remain ubiquitous in the delivery of social assistance, but do not constitute a novelty (Weitz-Shapiro 2014; Montero 2014).

## POTENTIAL LEGACIES OF SECOND INCORPORATION PROCESSES

What might the longer-term consequences of these reincorporation processes be for major policy issues and political stability? Of course, we cannot know what the outcomes of the reincorporation processes will be. However, we can hypothesize about possible legacies.

The significance of popular incorporation for political stability is a key subject. Collier and Collier (1991) focused on the consequences of the incorporation of unions for political dynamics during the 1950s to 1970s. A key argument was that state incorporation of labor under authoritarian regimes with the aim of demobilization and control led to the alignment of unions with Marxist or radical populist left parties in a subsequent democratic period. This fueled political polarization and repressive coups d'état of the bureaucratic authoritarian variety in Chile, Brazil, and Argentina.

In sharp contrast, second incorporation processes are taking place in the context of democratic political systems where reasonably competitive elections decide who governs.[4] In the second incorporation we know that parties and party systems have changed. New or substantially altered left parties have been incorporating a much broader swath of popular sectors and poor subaltern social groups (Levitsky and Roberts 2011). As Collier and Rossi point out in their chapters, the second incorporation focuses more on those left out of the first incorporation, although unions retain a prominent place in Brazil and Argentina—the two cases with greater institutional continuity.

Because most of the popular sectors broadly writ are, at minimum, electorally incorporated, a move to a competing radicalized left movement or party is unlikely. The governing left parties take up most of the ideological space on the left. Thus, left parties and movements critical of the current governments have difficulty gaining traction either electorally or in terms of attracting popular sector organizations.

This is clearest in the cases of Brazil, Bolivia, and Ecuador but also plausible for Argentina. Party systems as a whole have permanently changed and, for now, become more stable. Since the left has governed programmatically, with widely supported and relatively prudent state involvement in social policy and the economy, it is unlikely that conservative parties, when they gain power in the future, would return to the stark free-market models that reigned from the 1970s through the 1990s. Policy debates will likely be over adjustments at the margins, even during economic downturns, rather than wholesale dismantling.

Subaltern social groups, such as indigenous peoples and other racial or ethnic minorities, have built on legal recognition gained during the neoliberal period to obtain more substantive rights and equality. Thus, in Bolivia and Ecuador it is unlikely that indigenous peoples will be as uniformly subjugated and discriminated against as in the past. As Rossi argues in this volume, in these and in the other cases, largely invisible subaltern social groups have gained greater space to mobilize, protest, and apply institutional pressure to gain recognition and advance their cause.

With respect to longer-term political stability, much depends on whether unions and social movements align with currently governing left parties, with minority left opposition, or with conservative opposition. Protest and street mobilization are to be expected as a normal function of democratic politics as Latin American democracies come to resemble the "movement societies" of economically advanced countries (Tarrow 2011). In at least four of our cases, more serious events such as coups d'état or powerful revolutionary or reactionary destabilizing political movements are unlikely. Left parties, whether in or out of office, still command strong electoral support from popular sectors and, thus, offer strong competition for center-right party coalitions. Unions and social movements not aligned with the government align with electorally less significant left parties rather than with conservative opposition.

Under these circumstances, one would expect alternation in power with center-right political parties along with moderate swings in social policy, labor relations, and other policy issues that affect popular sectors when that occurs (Garay 2017). This appears to be the trend in Argentina after the defeat of Kichnerismo's Frente para la Victoria in November 2015 to Mauricio Macri's center-right Cambiemos alliance. It also seems to hold true for former vice president Michel Temer's embattled administration after Dilma Rouseff's impeachment in August 2016.

Venezuela is an outlier. Similar to the other cases, it too has witnessed a permanent change in its party system. It is also unlikely that an eventual conservative government would try to roll back social policy in a radical neoliberal style, although privatization of public companies would feature more prominently on the agenda. However, strong political polarization has existed since 2002. Coups d'état have already been attempted, and a bout of middle- and upper-class mass mobilization aimed at destabilizing the government (reminiscent of 2002) occurred in 2013–2014. The exclusionary form of incorporation described by García-Guadilla and the alignment of old-line union sectors with the political opposition analyzed by Ellner mean that potential popular sector support for such destabilizing adventures exist. However, for now, these sectors remain fragmented and divided among conservative opposition and more radical left critique. Hence, the Chavista regime muddles through somehow. A self-coup by elements of Maduro's government may not be out of the question either.

What lines of future research on contemporary incorporation processes does this volume suggest? Tracking the durability of the relationships established during the incorporation process is certainly one fruitful course. Do the effects previously hypothesized materialize, or do we see larger swings in social policy and state involvement in the economy? Does the expectation of relative political stability hold?

Another line of research could focus on the emerging environmental-indigenous-territorial axis of contention against the deepening of the traditional extractive development model. Will it, and the critical left, expand or whither? What are the consequences for policy and politics?

Finally, one could expand comparison. A potentially fruitful comparison might be between the cases in this volume and cases of more conservative governments, such as Colombia and Mexico. The "social question" Rossi discussed in the introduction to part 1 also affected them. Have they had their own reincorporation processes in reaction to orthodox neoliberalism? Are dynamics there radically different or similar and with what consequences for policy and politics? In this vein, other cases such as Chile, Peru, Paraguay, and Uruguay could also be studied. What of dynamics in Central America?

This volume, in any case, has established that for Argentina, Brazil, Bolivia, Ecuador, and Venezuela, the neoliberal period and the reaction to it had profound and permanent consequences for policy and politics. The different modes and processes of incorporation are deeply intertwined, with increased complexity of social organization in general and popular and poor subaltern group organization in particular. Transformations in state capacities and policy instruments permit more sophisticated mechanisms of incorporation and have changed the face of popular interest intermediation. The commodity boom of the 2000s made much of this possible. Left governments could govern on the left. It remains to be seen how the inevitable slowdown in the commodity boom will affect the relationship between the popular sectors, the state, and left political parties in the future.

# NOTES

## CHAPTER 1. INTRODUCTION: RESHAPING THE POLITICAL ARENA IN LATIN AMERICA

1. Traditionally, popular sectors referred to urban, lower-class, predominantly mestizo peoples and social groups with distinctive cultural traits and folklore. Politically, they were generally the electoral base of leftist, frequently populist, parties; but they could also support conservative populist parties. Popular sectors are also associated with urban self-help movements for housing, land titling, and services such as water, electricity, and transportation. In this volume, we extend the term to include all social groups that are not from the upper and middle classes. We do so largely for the sake of narrative shorthand to cover the heterogeneity of social groups involved in anti-neoliberal struggles that became the subjects of the second incorporation in the cases in this collection. However, when analysis involves specific social groups, we identify them specifically.

2. We thank Ken Roberts for this insight.

3. We are indebted to one of our anonymous reviewers for this insight.

4. As previously mentioned, during the neoliberal period governments also promoted the recognition and organization of nonunion popular actors in identity politics, environmentalism, and urban self-help—often in collaboration with NGOs. However, the spaces for their participation excluded socioeconomic policy.

5. Of course, despite the fact of institutional continuity in the two cases, there were considerable differences in the degree of political and economic crisis and levels of mass mobilization.

6. On a continuum, Brazil probably is the least "statist" and Venezuela is unquestionably the most "statist" (Flores-Macías 2012).

## CHAPTER 2. INTRODUCTION TO PART I: SOCIAL MOVEMENTS AND THE SECOND WAVE OF (TERRITORIAL) INCORPORATION IN LATIN AMERICA

1. This chapter reproduces paragraphs of my book *The Poor's Struggle for Political Incorporation* (New York: Cambridge University Press, 2017) and my article "The Sec-

ond Wave of Incorporation in Latin America: A Conceptualization of the Quest for Inclusion Applied to Argentina" (*Latin American Politics and Society* 57, no. 1 [Spring 2015]: 1–28).

2. For a discussion of the relative role of collective feelings versus materialistic struggles, see Honneth (1995) and Hobson (2003).

3. For this conceptual proposal, I have followed the approach of Collier and Mahon (1993) for the formation of radial categories.

4. Manin (1992) defines the "crisis of party communities" as the metamorphosis of political representation. Representation changed from a form based on programmatic parties reflecting the concerns of social classes or communities to a more personality-based form of politics, in which a multidimensional society is represented through governing elites that attempt to interpret public opinion. See also Roberts (in this volume).

5. This means that reincorporation movements can follow multiple goals simultaneously, but incorporation must be the main medium-term focus. The use of "revolutionary" (or other) rhetoric by movements struggling for the second incorporation of the popular sectors does not mean that movement leaders are confused or uncertain about movement goals. Instead, it means that a movement can be defined as a "reincorporation movement" by its relation to a macrohistorical process of (dis/re) incorporation, even though the main long-term goal for some organizations might be something else. Thus, following this definition, all movements that have struggled for the popular sectors' incorporation since neoliberal state reforms were applied can be defined as reincorporation movements, be this a short-, medium-, or long-term goal within "revolutionary," "reformist," or "conservative" rhetorical forms.

### CHAPTER 3. SOCIAL MOVEMENTS AND THE SECOND INCORPORATION IN BOLIVIA AND ECUADOR

1. Emily Achtenberg, NACLA Report on the America, Rebel Currents, June 15, 2015.   http://nacla.org/blog/2015/06/15/morales-greenlights-tipnis-road-oil-and-gas -extraction-bolivia%E2%80%99s-national-parks.

2. These policy choices have prompted heated, vituperative accusations that the government has lost its way, is insufficiently revolutionary, and too neoliberal (Manifiesto 2011).

3. Source: database of government officials compiled by the author.

4. See "Indigenous People Converge on Capital to Protest Government Mining Projects." http://dgrnewsservice.org/2012/03/24/indigenous-people-converge-on-ec uadors-capital-to-protest-government-mining-projects/.

5. "Barrio Politics and Government Politics in Guayaquil and Quito." August 2012. Interviews with barrio political leaders and residents. Centro de Documentación e Información de los Movimientos Sociales del Ecuador (CEDIME).

## CHAPTER 4. THE INCORPORATION OF POPULAR SECTORS AND SOCIAL MOVEMENTS IN VENEZUELAN TWENTY-FIRST-CENTURY SOCIALISM

1. Popular organizations are permanent and relatively institutionalized, with authority limited to the local level. Although nominally inscribed in the Bolivarian Revolutionary project, their goals do not transcend concrete local issues, such as the physical improvement and quality of life of their neighborhoods. They may or may not share the Revolution's ideology. Among those who question the Bolivarian project, we find some nongovernmental organizations that identify with the middle class and the political opposition. Social movements, by contrast, are defined through their identity, mobilization strategies and, above all, by their autonomy, understood as the capacity to make their own decisions. In addition to self-organization from below, they tend to exhibit a low degree of institutionalization and mobilize in function of a shared project of social transformation.

2. For details on the Punto Fijo system, see Hellinger in this volume. Data for this chapter came from García-Guadilla (2010), FONACIT/GAUS-USB research project "Construction of New Citizenships and Post-Constitutional Sociopolitical Conflicts in Venezuela," as well as periodical sources, primary documents, databases and interviews with urban land committees, communal councils, and communes between 2000–2017 as part of the research project "Participatory Democracy and the Bolivarian Social Organizations in the Socialism of the 21st Century" conducted by the "Grupo de Investigación en Gestión Ambiental, Urbana y Sociopolítica" (GAUS-USB), Caracas, Venezuela.

3. The MVR succeeded the Movimiento Bolivariano Revolucionario 200 (MBR-200), which was the first political expression of the Chavista movement (see Hellinger in this volume for details).

4. According to the National Technical Office for Land Regularization, there were almost six thousand CTUs in 2006, distributed in the majority of Venezuela's poor barrios and covering nearly a million families.

5. The webpage of the Ministerio del Poder Popular para las Comunas y los Movimientos Sociales states that there were more than 46,000 communal councils by the year 2017. Nonetheless, according to our database, many of them were inactive due to a lack of resources, and the majority have not renewed their leadership since 2016 as required, which raises questions about the legitimacy of those leaders (GAUS-USB 2000–2017).

6. After President Chávez died in 2013 and Nicolás Maduro was elected president, the economic crisis caused by the dramatic drop in oil prices reached its peak. This aggravated the political, social, and territorial exclusionary processes under way. The lack of public funding for government initiatives precipitated substantial cuts to the Social Missions and related initiatives. It also prompted authorities to redesign the

criteria for resource distribution according to political-partisan lines to favor groups aligned with the Bolivarian regime. The scarcity of resources also affected the protagonism of popular organizations and drastically reduced their role in policy decision making. Under the pretext that it faced an economic war, the administration issued a Decree of State of Emergency and Economic Emergency in 2016. The decree gave extraordinary powers to the Comités Locales de Abastecimiento y Producción (CLAPs, Local Committees for Provisions and Production), which in practice replaced not only the social missions and related programs but the existing network of social organizations as well. The CLAPs were formed from ideologically pro-Chávez organizations such as the Bolívar-Chávez Battle Units (Unidades de Batalla Bolívar-Chávez), the Francisco Miranda Ideological Front (Frente Ideológico Francisco de Miranda), the National Union of Women (Unión Nacional de Mujeres), and representatives of communal councils, among others. Thus, the comunal councils changed from being a space for participating in local policy decision-making to vehicles of political-partisan control of programs to alleviate poverty, to manage deficits of food and medicines, and to distribute them according to a political-partisan logic.

7. The socio-environmental movement articulates the human rights, indigenous, and ecological social movements.

8. See www.amigransa.blogia.com.

9. According to the Gaceta Oficial 40.855, Decree No. 2.248, the "Zona de Desarrollo Estratégico Nacional Arco Minero del Orinoco (AMO)" was created on February 24th, 2016, by the Venezuelan government. It has an extension of almost twelve hundred thousand square kilometers, and the objective is the extraction of gold, diamonds, cooper, bauxite, coltan, and other important minerals. More than 150 companies from 35 countries are involved, and the main investors at this moment are Canada, United States, China, and Democratic Republic of the Congo. The socio-environmental movement has criticized the project, claiming it will cause great ecological damage on the river basins of the Orinoco and Caroni. In addition to destroying the tropical forest and its diversity, it will have a severe negative impact on cultural diversity, affecting indigenous communities such as the Baniva, Piaroa, Yekuana, and Jivi and their territories.

### CHAPTER 5. SOCIAL MOVEMENTS, THE NEW "SOCIAL QUESTION," AND THE SECOND INCORPORATION OF THE POPULAR SECTORS IN ARGENTINA AND BRAZIL

1. This chapter reproduces paragraphs of my book *The Poor's Struggle for Political Incorporation* (New York: Cambridge University Press, 2017).

2. In 1994, traditional landowners decided to close the UDR because they were feeling that agrarian reform was abandoned as a national policy.

3. CONTAG was also critical of the agrarian policies of the Lula governments.

4. Other organizations, such as the LCP, were always in opposition to Lula, but they still had a regular dialogue with INCRA officials.

5. Ministry of Social Development and Fight against Hunger, www.mds.gov.br/saladeimprensa/noticias/2012/outubro/imagens/19102012-evolucaoanualbf-9anos .jpg (viewed October 20, 2012).

6. The return to power of conservative neoliberals reinforced this situation. The first decision taken by President Mauricio Macri was to—almost completely—eliminate any kind of export taxes to commodities in December 2015. This has severely unfinanced the national state, self-justifying the need for austerity policies.

7. As part of the aftermath of second incorporation, the Macri government continued with the same social policies inherited from the Fernández de Kirchner government. As a result of a proposal of the CCC and the Movimiento "Evita," Macri even further institutionalized the relationship with the reincorporation movement in the Ministry of Social Development with the creation of a social security system for informal and cooperative-based workers.

8. The second PAC started in January 2010 and ended in December 2014.

9. Ministry of Social Development and Fight against Hunger, www.mds.gov.br/saladeimprensa/noticias/2012/outubro/imagens/19102012-evolucaoanualbf-9anos. jpg, viewed October 20, 2012).

### CHAPTER 6. INTRODUCTION TO PART II: LABOR UNIONS IN LATIN AMERICA: INCORPORATION AND REINCORPORATION UNDER THE NEW LEFT

1. Note the difference in polarity of the two indices: greater deregulation is higher on the flexibility index and lower on the labor standards index, which aggregates provisions regarding freedom of association, collective bargaining, and the right to strike. For a description of the indices, see Stallings (2010, 145–48).

### CHAPTER 7. SOCIALISM WITHOUT WORKERS? TRADE UNIONS AND THE NEW LEFT IN BOLIVIA AND ECUADOR

1. *Dancing with Dynamite* is the title of Ben Dangl's (2010) excellent book on the relationships between the MAS and social movements.

2. Executive Order 1701 limited collective bargaining and possibilities to unionize. The constitutional mandate 04 reduces compensation for "unattended layoffs," favoring the layoffs of skilled workers and bypassing the Public Service Organic Law. Decree 813 (July 2011) creates the purchase of "mandatory waivers." The new constitution (2008) prohibits strikes by all public sector workers in defiance of the ILO standard to differentiate between essential and nonessential services. The Criminal Code makes organizing or participating in strikes an act of terrorism punishable by eight to

twelve years of imprisonment. Executive Orders 1701 (May 2009) and 225 (February 2010), plus ministerial agreements 080 (August 2008) and 0155-A (October 2008) limit the legal right to strike before the revision of the collective bargaining agreement.

3. Co-author Jorge León Trujillo interviews with Mesias Tatamuez, president of CEDOCUT and former FUT president; José Chávez, former president of CEOSL; Fernando Ibarra, president of CEDOC-CLAT and also of the newly established Parlamento Laboral Ecuatoriano; and Jaime Arciniega, former president of CEOSL, from which he breaks off to form the CSE (Confederación Sindical del Ecuador). CEDOC-CLAT and CSE form the Parlamento Laboral Ecuatoriano.

4. The website of *El Universo*, http://www.eluniverso.com/noticias/2014/11/11/nota/4213486/nace-nueva-central-unitaria-trabajadores-que-dice-es-resultado.

5. Critics consider these measures demagogic because they lack designated funding.

### CHAPTER 8. CONFLICTING CURRENTS WITHIN THE PRO-CHAVEZ LABOR MOVEMENT AND THE DYNAMICS OF DECISION MAKING

1. One manifestation of this divergence was the last-minute decision of the ex-guerrilla group "Bandera Roja" to drop out of the February 4, 1992, coup attempt on grounds that the MBR-200 allegedly planned to maintain complete control over the operation rather than promote an armed insurrection through the immediate distribution of arms to the general population.

2. Under Ramos's plan, unlike Vera's, workers who contributed more to the system would receive greater benefits.

3. Oswaldo Vera, personal interview, July 25, 2012, Caracas.

4. Eduardo Sánchez [leader of the CTR current and president of the Sindicato de Trabajadores de la UCV], personal interview, July 26, 2012, Caracas.

5. Alejandro Alvarez [secretary general of Sindicato Único de Trabajadores Socialistas Sidetur], telephone interview, September 16, 2012, Puerto Ordaz.

6. Franklin Rondón [president of the Federación Nacional de Trabajadores Públicos and CBST vice president], personal interview, August 30, 2011, Puerto La Cruz, Venezuela.

### CHAPTER 9. THE LABOR MOVEMENT AND THE EROSION OF NEOLIBERAL HEGEMONY: BRAZIL AND ARGENTINA

1. The Obras Sociales are supported by mandatory contributions. The Obras Sociales and national collective bargaining played a major role in centralizing even those unions that adopted federative structures. Initially, each union managed the Obra Social correspondent to its category, and it wasn't until the 1990s that the system suffered its first (and partial) defeat. See Perelman (2006).

2. This social group had not been the subject of policies in the Vargas period (1930–1945), although it constituted the majority of the Brazilian population, due to Vargas's compromise with large rural landowners. See Stein (2008).

3. According to a census of unions (IBGE, 2002), 24 percent of manufacturing workers' unions were affiliated to the CUT, 21 percent to the FS; 15 percent of the commerce workers' unions were affiliated to the CUT and 13 percent to the FS; 12 percent of land transports unions were affiliated to the FS and 8 percent to the CUT.

4. Assuming as a reference 1980 = 100, in 1990, the real minimum wage value had dropped to 40.2 in Argentina (Panorama Laboral of the Latin American Office, International Labor Organization 2001).

5. Of the fifteen main unions presented in figure 9.1, class-based mobilization is influential in four: Unión Ferroviaria, UF (railway workers), Federación de Trabajadores de la Industria de la Alimentación, FTIA (food workers), Unión Tranviarios Automotor, UTA (bus and subway drivers), and CTERA (public teachers).

6. In 2010, for example, the food-service federation resigned from the CGT, claiming that the truck drivers' federation was disputing the affiliation of workers from a catering company.

7. In 2012, the government repealed the policies implemented in 2003 that benefited Moyano's union.

8. The labor legislation guarantees the possibility of "assistance contribution" at the occasion of the signing of collective agreements or conventions, and the 1988 Constitution also guarantees the deduction of fees for the confederative system of representation, which must be approved in an assembly. These two deductions, unlike the union tax, are not mandatory; however, all three are applied to all unionized workers.

9. Source: PNAD 2006 and 2011.

10. The number of seats taken by the PT in the chamber of deputies increased from fifty-eight to ninety-one in the 2002 elections. Out of these ninety-one representatives, forty-four had roots in the labor movement. Other sectors of the FS and the Social Democracia Sindical, SDS (created in 1997 by dissenting FS unions) rallied around the PSDB candidate (Lucca 2011).

11. Unionists, either former CUT cadres or due to histories within the PT, took over positions of command in several ministries, banks, state companies, and pension funds. The Ministry of Labor was occupied successively by Jaques Wagner, Ricardo Berzoini, and Luiz Marinho, all of them PT militants who started in unionism.

12. The CUT, for example, promoted a union for the aerospace industry at the rank-and-file level of the São José dos Campos metalworkers' unions (headed by the CONLUTAS) and also the organization of federal university professors (whose traditional union is also affiliated to the CONLUTAS).

13. There are other more radical left-wing parties in Brazil, such as the PSTU and the PSOL, which are close to the CONLUTAS or other left-wing central federations, but their electoral relevance is small.

### CHAPTER 10. INTRODUCTION TO PART III: POLITICAL PARTIES IN LATIN AMERICA'S
### SECOND WAVE OF INCORPORATION

1. Chile and Uruguay were other prominent cases of programmatic alignment; see Roberts (2014).

2. Brazil and Chile did experience major protest cycles at later stages, in 2013 and 2011, but these did not culminate in the overthrow of incumbent rulers.

### CHAPTER 12. THE SECOND WAVE OF INCORPORATION AND POLITICAL PARTIES
### IN THE VENEZUELAN PETROSTATE

1. The Punto Fijo era is often wrongly equated with the "Fourth Republic." In reality, Chávez and his followers dated the "Fourth Republic" from 1826, when the larger Andean "Gran Colombia" founded by Bolívar collapsed.

2. Royalty is levied directly on production at the market price; taxes are only on profits, and they are more difficult to audit. Hence, the raising of royalty more than compensated for lowering the tax rate.

3. Official results are available from the National Electoral Council at: http://www .cne.gov.ve.

4. All electoral results are taken from the National Electoral Council at: http:// www.cne.gov.ve/web/index.php.

5. Production reported by PDV has been fairly steady at three million barrels per day, whereas international estimates are typically 400,000 to 500,000 barrels lower. In part, the difference is explained by how international estimates often excluded extra-heavy oil production.

6. Despite the aforementioned decline in these rents, we should remember that even at the relatively high cost of production of $15 for extra-heavy oil, at the end of 2014 each barrel exported to major consumer markets was generating a superprofit of $50 above normal rates of profit.

7. The Capriles campaign denied the authenticity of the document.

### CHAPTER 13. THE POLITICS OF INCORPORATION: PARTY SYSTEMS, POLITICAL LEADERS,
### AND THE STATE IN ARGENTINA AND BRAZIL

1. The PT was considered an "anomaly" as it emerged from a "solid base in labor and social movements," with much of "its leadership drawn from the labor movement" (Keck 1992, 3).

2. The poor tend to participate more than the wealthy because of institutional incentives and intermediary organizations such as unions and neighborhood associations (Goldfrank 2011).

3. The 1993 Pact of Olivos between Alfonsín and Menem opened the way to a 1994 constitutional reform that allowed, amongst other things, presidential reelection.

4. This overvaluation was the product of unavoidable inertia in the inflation rate even after its structural causes had been addressed.

5. In the second half of 2001, the IMF resolved to let Argentina sink (in contrast to Brazil) by not providing any bridging loans.

6. Only since 2010 has Argentina surpassed its 1998 GDP per capita in dollar terms.

7. To sustain this fiscal effort, among the first reforms the government pursued in 2003 was a cutback in benefits to public pensioners, a move that even the Cardoso government had been unable to impose (Bresser-Pereira 2010). This provoked the first and to date most significant exodus of PT politicians, as Heloísa Helena was expelled/left the party to form the Partido Socialismo e Liberdade (PSOL).

8. All three presidential candidates were permitted to use Peronist symbols but could not use the PJ stamp or claim to represent the PJ.

9. Duhalde's first two choices were Governor Carlos Reutemann of Santa Fe, who declined, and then Governor Juan Manuel de la Sota of Córdoba, who accepted but lacked much appeal.

10. Originally a Radical, Carrió left the Alianza in 2000 to form a more personalist party, and she split from the Socialists in 2002, moving left together with anti-Peronist Socialist deputies from the Frepaso. They created the movement "Argentina para una República de Iguales," or ARI. Before the economic collapse, ARI won several legislative seats. In late 2002, Carrió split from the Socialists to form "Afirmación para una República Igualitaria".

11. López Murphy was also an ex-Radical and had been minister of economy briefly in 2001in De la Rua's government. In contrast to Carrió, he exited the UCR on to the right, with support in 2003 from most advocates of neoliberalism, including the well-to-do.

12. Bolsa Familia distributes R$20 billion per year to 13.4 million households, though it costs only 0.4 percent of GDP.

13. In the absence of external borrowing, taxes, monetary expansion, and nationalizations (e.g., of the private pension funds) financed most of the fiscal expansion.

14. Poverty (defined as earning less than $4 per day) had increased from 15.9 percent of the population in 1992 to 23.7 percent in 1999 to 45.5 percent with the crisis of 2001–2002. By 2010 it was down to 14.3 percent, and infant mortality and inequality both also fell.

15. We prefer to refer to "political forces" than to "political parties," since in post-2002 Argentina political parties (per se) have become largely irrelevant organizationally.

16. Some organizations have come from within Peronism, others have come from outside of it, and some seem to blend Peronism and the anti-imperialist Latin American left in unorthodox ways. All support the Kirchners.

17. The CGT has been Peronist since the late 1940s. Under Menem it split, and the leftist CTA has been highly critical of both the PJ and of traditional Peronism since its foundation. The larger *piquetero* movements became fierce leftist defenders of Kirchnerism and distrustful of the PJ apparatus throughout the Kirchner era (see Gindin and Cardoso, and Rossi in this volume, Rocca Rivarola 2013).

18. See, for example, the excellent and acclaimed narrative of Boyanovsky Bazán (2012).

19. Not surprisingly, such an arrangement led eventually to not a few major financial scandals, particularly in the case of the particularly left-wing Tupac Amaru and the "Shared Dreams" of the Madres de Plaza de Mayo.

20. The most important such organization is La Cámpora. This Cristinista youth organization was founded by the Kirchners' son Maximo, and it ranges socially from bright, young, radical administrators of top state and public enterprises to militants proselytizing in public schools or impoverished neighborhoods. There are several other such important organizations. The large Movimiento Evita works in poor neighborhoods and responds to Emilio Pérsico. The Kolina movement, led by Néstor's sister Alicia, is responsible for the country's social programs. Other such organizations abound, including the Frente Transversal Nacional y Popular, the Corriente Peronista Descamisados, and the Corriente Nacional Martín Fierro.

21. The *mensalão*, or "big monthly payment," scandal was named for the monthly payments to deputies in exchange for votes.

22. The DEM party was the new name for the Partido Frente Liberal (PFL), evolved from the pro-military ARENA and the biggest legislative party and main ally to Cardoso during the 1990s.

23. Ever since return to democracy in 1983, Argentina has had important third parties, usually centered in the Buenos Aires metropolitan area: the Partido Intransigente, the UceDé, the Movimiento por la Dignidad y la Independencia (MODIN), Frepaso and, since the 2000s, the center-right Propuesta Republicana (PRO).

24. Kirchnerismo was against neoliberalism, Menem, and the 1990s, and favored militant human rights organizations and of jailing officials from the former dictatorship, praised the militants of the 1970s, and favored a "nationalist" stance.

25. *La Nación*, March 28, 2004.

26. Massa initially positioned himself at the center of each of Argentina's two divides, but was later pulled into the low right.

27. Hugo Curto is a union man turned into Greater Buenos Aires mayor, continuously since 1991. Othacehe is also a Greater Buenos Aires mayor fearsomely in power for twenty-three continuous years and now moved to Massa's Frente Renovador.

28. Despite its extremely high level of personalism, Kirchnerismo is more programmatically cohesive than the PJ (or the UCR historically) and Peronism.

## CHAPTER 14. CONCLUSION: REFLECTIONS ON THE SECOND WAVE OF POPULAR INCORPORATION FOR A POST-NEOLIBERAL ERA

1. The CSUTCB and the *cocaleros* in the MAS in Bolivia are exceptions.

2. In Ecuador, none of the major popular sector organizations counted.

3. The "corporatist-like" categorization refers to the absence of institutionalization or binding consultation and/or negotiation in what otherwise look like corporatist exchanges in Molina and Rhodes's (2002) approach.

4. The outlier here is Venezuela, where some (or many) may argue that it is no longer any type of democracy. It may be an illiberal democracy or a competitive authoritarian regime (Levitsky and Way 2010), but elections still decide who rules, and the opposition has a fighting chance. That it hasn't won more is, in great measure, due to its own internal factionalism, including widely differing ideological standpoints.

# REFERENCES

Abers, Rebecca Neaera, and Luciana Tatagiba. 2015. "Mobilizing for Women's Health from Inside the Brazilian Bureaucracy." In *Social Movement Dynamics: New Perspectives on Theory and Research from Latin America*, 73–101. Edited by Federico M. Rossi and Marisa von Bülow. London: Routledge.

Abers, Rebecca Neaera, Lizandra Serafim, and Luciana Tatagiba. 2014. "Changing Repertoires of State-Society Interaction under Lula." In *Brazil Under the Workers' Party: Continuity and Change from Lula to Dilma*, 36–61. Edited by Fabio de Castro, Kees Koonings, and Marianne Wiesebron. New York: Palgrave-Macmillan.

Abranches, Sérgio. 1988. "Presidencialismo de coalizão: o dilema institucional brasileiro." *Dados* 31, no. 1: 5–33.

Abrucio, Fernando Luiz. 1998. *Os Barões da Federação: os governadores e a redemocratização brasileira*. São Paulo: Editora Hucitec.

Acosta, Alberto (Memo). 2015. *Extractivismo del siglo XXI. Una "revolución ciudadana" sin revolución social, ni productiva*. Quito.

Acosta, Alberto. 1991. "Ecuador. La realidad de una fantasia." *Nueva Sociedad* 112 (April): 16–23.

Albó, Xavier. 2009. "Muchas naciones en una." In *¿Nación o naciones boliviana(s)? Una institucionalidad para nosotros mismos*. Edited by Gonzalo Rojas Ortuste. La Paz: CIDES-UMSA.

Albó, Xavier. 2007. "Movimientos indígenas desde 1900 hasta la actualidad." In *Bolivia en movimiento: acción colectiva y poder político*, 67–100. Edited by Jesús Espasandín López and Pablo Iglesias Turrión. Madrid: El Viejo Topo.

Albró, Robert. 2006. "Bolivia's 'Evo Phenomenon': From Identity to What?" *Journal of Latin American Anthropology* 11, no. 2: 408–28.

Alexander, Robert Jackson. 2005. *A History of Organized Labor in Bolivia*. Santa Barbara, CA: Praeger Press.

Alexander, Robert Jackson. 1973. *Aprismo: The Ideas and Doctrines of Victor Raúl Haya de la Torre*. Kent, OH: Kent State University Press.

Alianza País. 2013. *Movimientoalianzapais* (blog). http://www.movimientoalianzapais.com.ec/.

Almeida, Paul D. 2007. "Defensive Mobilization: Popular Movements against Economic Adjustment Policies in Latin America." *Latin American Perspectives* 34, no. 3: 123–39.

Alpert, Alexandra, Miguel Centellas, and Matthew Singer. 2010. "The 2009 Presidential and Legislative Elections in Bolivia." *Electoral Studies* 29: 757–61.

Altmann, Phillip. 2013. "El movimiento indígena ecuatoriano como movimiento social." *Revista Andina de Estudios Políticos* 3, no. 2: 6–31.

Alto, Hervé do. 2007. "El MAS-IPSP boliviano, entre la protesta callejera y la política institucional." In *Reinventando la nación en Bolivia,* 71–110. Edited by Karín Monaterios, Pablo Stefanoni, and Hervé Do Alto. La Paz: Editorial Plural.

Alto, Hervé do, and Pablo Stefanoni. 2010. "El MAS y las ambivalencias de la democracia corporativa." In *Mutaciones del campo político en Bolivia,* 353–63. Edited by Luís Alberto García Orellana and Fernando Luís García Yapur. La Paz: UNDP.

Alvarez, Sonia. 1990. *Engendering Democracy in Brazil: Women's Movements in Transition Politics.* Princeton: Princeton University Press.

Álvarez, Rosangel, and María Pilar García-Guadilla. 2011. "Contraloría social y clientelismo: la praxis de los consejos comunales en Venezuela." *Revista Politeia* (Instituto de Estudios Políticos, UCV), 34, no. 46: 175–207

Amaral, Aline Diniz, Peter R. Kingstone, and Jonathan Krieckhaus. 2008. "The Limits of Economic Reform in Brazil." In *Democratic Brazil Revisited,* 137–160. Edited by Peter R. Kingstone and Timothy J. Power. Pittsburgh: University of Pittsburgh Press.

Ames, Barry. 2002. *The Deadlock of Democracy in Brazil.* Ann Arbor: University of Michigan Press.

Ames, Barry, and Timothy Power. 2007. "Parties and Governability in Brazil." In *Political Parties in Transitional Democracies,* 179–212. Edited by Paul Webb and Stephen White. New York: Oxford University Press.

Amorim Neto, Octavio. 2002. "Presidential Cabinets, Electoral Cycles, and Coalition Discipline in Brazil." In *Legislative Politics in Latin America,* 48–78. Edited by Scott Morgenstern and Benito Nacif. New York: Cambridge University Press.

Amorim Neto, Octavio, Gary W. Cox, and Matthew D. McCubbins. 2003. "Agenda Power in Brazil's Camara dos Deputados, 1989–98." *World Politics* 55, no. 4: 550–78.

Andolina, Robert. 2003. "The Sovereign and Its Shadow: Constituent Assembly and Indigenous Movement in Ecuador." *Journal of Latin American Studies* 35: 721–50.

Andrade, Pablo. 2010. *Democracia y cambio politico en el Ecuador.* Quito: Universidad Andina Simón Bolívar.

Andrade, Pablo. 2008. *Democracia y cambio político en el ecuador: liberalismo, política de la cultura y reforma institucional.* Quito: UASB-Corporación Editora Nacional.

Anria, Santiago. 2013. "Social Movements, Party Organization, and Populism: Insights from the Bolivian MAS." *Latin American Politics and Society* 55, no. 3 (Fall): 19–46.

Anria, Santiago. 2010. "Bolivia's MAS: Between Party and Movement." In *Latin America's Left Turns: Politics, Policies and Trajectories of Change*, 101–26. Edited by Maxwell A. Cameron and Eric Hershberg. Boulder, CO: Lynne Rienner.

Antillano, Andrés. 2005. "La lucha por el reconocimiento y la inclusión en los barrios populares: La experiencia de los comités de tierras urbanas." *Revista Venezolana de Economía y Ciencias Sociales* 11, no. 3: 205–18.

Arconada, Santiago. 2005. "Seis años después: mesas técnicas y consejos comunitarios de aguas." *Revista Venezolana de Economía y Ciencias Sociales* 11, no. 3: 187–203.

Ardaya, Gloria. 2009. "La autonomía y la descentralización como posibilidad de la recomposición del estado y de la política en Bolivia." In *¿Nación o naciones boliviana(s)? Una institucionalidad para nosotros mismos*, 151–73. Edited by Gonzalo Rojas Ortuste. La Paz: CIDES-UMSA.

Arenas, Nelly, and Luis Gómez Calcaño. 2006. *Populismo autoritario: Venezuela 1999–2005*. Caracas: CENDES-CDCH, UCV.

Arrieta, José Ignacio. 1997. "La reforma de la Ley del Trabajo llegó a puerto." *SIC*, no. 596: 261.

Arrioja, José Enrique. 1998. *Clientes Negros: Petróleos de Venezuela bajo la generación de Shell*. Caracas: Los Libros de El Nacional.

Arruda, Lilian Rose. 2010. "Do local ao global. O processo de reestruturação na Volkswagen/Anchieta entre 2001 e 2006." PhD diss., São Paulo: Pontifícia Universidade Católica.

Artaraz, Kepa. 2012. *Bolivia: Refounding the Nation*. London: Pluto Press.

Arze, Carlos, and Tom Kruse. 2004. "The Consequences of Neoliberal Reform." *NACLA Report on the Americas* 38, no. 3: 23–28.

Asamblea Metropolitana de Comités de Tierra Urbana de Caracas. 2004. *Democratización de la ciudad y transformación urbana: Propuesta de los CTU a la Misión Vivienda*. Caracas: Vicepresidencia de la República, Oficina Técnica Nacional para la Regularización de la Tenencia de la Tierra.

Asamblea Nacional. 2010. "Ley Orgánica de las Comunas." Caracas, Venezuela.

Aspiazu, Eliana, and Sebastián Waisgrais. 2007. "La encuesta a trabajadores en empresas." *Trabajo, Ocupación y Empleo* 6. Buenos Aires: MTESS.

Assies, Willem. 2004. "Bolivia: A Gassified Economy." *European Review of Latin American and Caribbean Studies* 76 (April): 25–43.

Auyero, Javier. 2003. *Contentious Lives: Two Argentine Women, Two Protests, and the Quest for Recognition*. Durham, NC: Duke University Press.

Auyero, Javier. 2002. "Los cambios en el repertorio de la protesta social en la Argentina." *Desarrollo Económico* 42, no. 166: 187–210.

Auyero, Javier, and Timothy Patrick Moran. 2007. "The Dynamics of Collective Violence: Dissecting Food Riots in Contemporary Argentina." *Social Forces* 85, no. 3: 1341–67.

Avritzer, Leonardo. 2002. *Democracy and the Public Space in Latin America*. Princeton: Princeton University Press.

Avritzer, Leonardo, Adalmir Marquetti, and Zander Navarro. 2003. *A Inovação Democrática no Brasil: Orçamento Participativo*. Curitiba: Cortez Editora.

Ayala, Rodrigo, Gustavo Fernández, Fernando Mayorga, Jorge Lazarte, Fernando Prado, Gonzao Rojas, José Mirtenbaum. 2009. *Conflictos: Una mirada hacia el futuro*. La Paz: Fundación Friedrich Ebert.

Baker, Andy. 2009. *The Market and the Masses in Latin America*. New York: Cambridge University Press.

Baloyra, Enrique, and John D. Martz. 1979. *Political Attitudes in Venezuela: Political Cleavages and Political Opinion*. Austin: University of Texas Press.

Barbosa, Nelson. 2010. "Counter-Cyclical Policy in Brazil 2008–2009" *Journal of Globalization and Development* 1, no. 1: 1–14.

Barrera, Augusto. 2001. *Acción colectiva y crisis política. El movimiento indígena ecuatoriano en la década de los noventa*. Quito: OSAL / CLACSO, Centro de Investigaciones Ciudad y Abya-Yala.

Basabe-Serrano, Santiago, and Julián Martínez. 2014. "Ecuador: cada vez menos democracia, cada vez más autoritarismo . . . con elecciones." *Revista de Ciencia Política* 34, no. 1: 145–70.

Baud, Michiel. 2007. "Indigenous Politics and the State. The Andean Highlands in the Nineteenth and Twentieth Centuries." *Social Analysis* 51, no. 2.

Becker, Marc. 2014. "Rafael Correa and Social Movements in Ecuador." In *Latin America's Radical Left: Challenges and Complexities of Political Power in the Twenty-First Century*, 127–48. Edited by Steve Ellner. Lanham, MD: Rowman & Littlefield.

Becker, Marc. 2011. *¡Pachakutik! Indigenous Movements and Electoral Politics in Ecuador*. Lanham, MD: Rowman & Littlefield.

Becker, Marc. 2008. *Indians and Leftists in the Making of Ecuador's Modern Indigenous Movements*. Durham, NC: Duke University Press.

Berg, Janine, Christoph Ernst, and Peter Auer. 2006. *Meeting the Employment Change. Argentina, Brazil and Mexico in the Global Economy*. Geneva: ILO.

Betancourt, Rómulo. 1995. "Plan de Barranquilla (1931)." In *Romulo Betancourt Antología Política*. Caracas: Volumen Primero *1928–1935*. Caracas: Editorial Fundación Rómulo Betancourt.

Birdsall, Nancy, Augusto de la Torre, and Felipe Valencia Caicedo. 2011. "The Washington Consensus: Assessing a 'Damaged Brand.'" In *The Oxford Handbook of Latin American Economics*, 79–101. Edited by José Antonio Ocampo and Jaime Ros. New York: Oxford University Press.

Blanco, Carlos. 2002. *Revolución y desilusión: La Venezuela de Hugo Chávez*. Madrid: Calarata.

Blanco Muñoz, Agustín. 1998. *Habla el comandante*. Caracas: UCV.

Bohn, Simone. 2011. "Social Policy and Vote in Brazil: Bolsa Familia and the Shifts in Lula's Electoral Base." *Latin American Research Review* 46, no. 1 54–79.

Boito Jr., Armando, and Paula Marcelino. 2011. "Decline in Unionism? An Analysis of the New Wave of Strikes in Brazil." *Latin American Perspectives* 38, no. 5: 38–62.

Boothroyd, Rachael. October 12, 2012. "PSUV Announces Candidates for Regional Elections, Some Criticism." *Venezuelanalysis.com*. http://venezuelanalysis.com/news/7349.

Boyanovsky Bazán, Christian. 2012. *El aluvión. Del Piquete al Gobierno: Los movimientos sociales y el Kirchnerismo*. Buenos Aires: Sudamericana.

Branford, Sue, and Jan Rocha. 2002. *Cutting the Wire: The Story of the Landless Movement in Brazil*. London: Latin American Bureau.

Bresser-Pereira, Luiz Carlos. 2011. "From Old to New Developmentalism in Latin America." In *The Oxford Handbook of Latin American Economics*, 108–29. Edited by José Antonio Ocampo and Jaime Ros. New York: Oxford University Press.

Bresser-Pereira, Luis Carlos. 2010. "Novo Desenvolvimentismo: Uma Proposta para a Economia do Brasil." *Nueva Sociedad* 230: 59–72.

Bringel, Breno. 2013. "MST's Agenda of Emancipation: Interfaces of National Politics and Global Contestation." In *Brazil Emerging: Inequality and Emancipation*, 97–120. Edited by Jan N. Pieterse and Adalberto Cardoso. New York: Routledge.

Brockman, Erika, and Fabiola Aparicio. 2012. *Partidos politicos y democracia: El MSM y el MIR bajo la lupa*. La Paz: Friedrich Ebert Stiftung.

Buainain, Antônio Márcio. 2008. "Reforma agrária por conflitos." In *Luta pela Terra, Reforma Agrária e Gestão de Conflitos no Brasil*. Edited by Antônio Márcio Buainain. Campinas: UNICAMP.

Buitrago, Deisy. 2009. "Rámirez dice esperar elección de la Futpv para discutir el contrato." *El Universal*, July 18.

Burdick, John, Philip Oxhorn, and Kenneth M. Roberts, eds. 2009. *Beyond Neoliberalism in Latin America? Societies and Politics at the Crossroads*. New York: Palgrave-Macmillan.

Burgess, Katrina. 2010. "Remittances as Non-State Transnational Transfers: Lessons from Mexico and El Salvador." *Studies in Comparative International Development* 45, no. 2: 198–224.

Burkart, Mara, Lorena Cobe, Bruno Fornillo, and Patricia Zipcioglu. 2008. "Las estrategias políticas de las organizaciones de desocupados a partir de la crisis de 2001." In *La huella piquetera. Avatares de las organizaciones de desocupados después de 2001*, 35–64. Edited by Sebastián Pereyra, Germán Pérez, and Federico Schuster. La Plata: Ediciones Al Margen.

Buxton, Julia. 2001. *The Failure of Political Reform in Venezuela*. Aldershot, UK: Ashgate.

CAAP. 2010. "Conflictividad socio-política Noviembre 2009–Febrero 2010." *Ecuador Debate*: 31–46.

Calderón, Fernando, and Eduardo Gamarra. 2003. "Crisis, inflexión y reformas de sistema de partidos en Bolivia." *Revista Colombia Internacional* 58 (July–December): 90–121.

Calla Ortega, Ricardo. 2012. "TIPNIS y Amazonía: Contradicciones en la agenda ecológica de Bolivia." *European Review of Latin American and Caribbean Studies* 92 (April): 77–83.

Calvo, Dolores. 2006. *Exclusión y política. Estudio sociológico sobre la experiencia de la Federación de trabajadores por la Tierra, la Vivienda, y el Hábitat (1998–2002)*. Buenos Aires: Miño y Dávila.

Calvo, Ernesto, and Marcelo Escolar. 2005. *La nueva política de los partidos en la Argentina: Crisis política, realineamientos partidarios y reforma electoral*. Buenos Aires: PENT-Prometeo.

Cameron, Maxwell A., and Eric Hershberg, eds. 2010. *Latin America's Left Turns: Politics, Policies and Trajectories of Change*. Boulder, CO: Lynne Rienner.

Canessa, Andrew. 2006. "Todos somos indígenas: Towards a New Language of National Political Identity." *Bulletin of Latin American Research* 25, no. 2: 241–61.

Cardoso, Adalberto. 2013. "Para onde foram os sindicatos?" Paper presented at the XXXVII ANPOCS Meeting, Águas de Lindoia, Brazil.

Cardoso, Adalberto. 2010. "Uma Utopia Brasileira: Vargas e a Construção do Estado do Bem-Estar numa Sociedade Estruturalmente Desigual." *Dados* 53, no. 4: 775–819.

Cardoso, Adalberto. 2004. *Industrial Relations, Social Dialogue and Employment in Argentina, Brazil and Mexico*. Employment Strategy Papers, no. 2004/7. Geneva: ILO.

Cardoso, Adalberto. 2003. *A década neoliberal e a crise dos sindicatos no Brasil*. São Paulo: Boitempo.

Cardoso, Adalberto. 1999. *A trama da modernidade. Pragmatismo sindical e democratização no Brasil*. Rio de Janeiro: Revan.

Cardoso, Adalberto, and Alvaro Comin. 1995. "Câmaras setoriais, modernização produtiva e democratização nas relações entre capital e trabalho no Brasil." In *A maquina e o equilibrista: inovações na industria automobilística brasileira*, 387–427. Edited by Nadya Araujo Castro. São Paulo: Paz e Terra.

Cardoso, Adalberto, and Julián Gindin. 2009. "Industrial Relations and Collective Bargaining: Argentina, Brazil and Mexico Compared." Working Paper 5, Industrial and Employment Relations Department, Geneva: ILO.

Cariola, Cecilia, and Miguel Lacabana. 2005. *Pobreza, nueva pobreza y exclusión social: los múltiples rostros de Caracas*. Caracas: BCV.

Cariola, Cecilia, Beate Jungeman, Alejandro Maldonado, and Miguel Lacabana. 2010. "Las Mesas Tecnicas de Telecomunicaciones e Informática." *Cuadernos del Cendes* 27, no. 74.

Carter, Miguel. 2009. *Combatendo a Desigualdade Social. O MST e a Reforma Agrária no Brasil.* São Paulo: Editora da UNESP.

Carter Center. 2008. *Informe sobre la Asamblea Constituyente de la República del Ecuador,* no. 1 (January). Quito, Ecuador.

Carvalho Rosa, Marcelo. 2010. "Para além do MST: O impacto nos movimentos sociais brasileiros." In *Combatendo a desigualdade social: O MST e a reforma agrária no Brasil,* 461–78. Edited by Miguel Carter. São Paulo: UNESP.

Castañeda, Jorge G. 2006. "Latin America's Left Turn." *Foreign Affairs* 85, no. 3: 28–43.

Castillo, Gerardo, and Álvaro Orsatti. 2005. *Trabajo informal y sindicalismo en América Latina y el Caribe: Buenas prácticas formativas y organizativas.* Montevideo, Uruguay: CINTERFOR/OIT.

Castiñera, Berta Rivera, Luis Currais Nunes, and Paolo Rungo. 2009. "The Impact of Conditional Cash Transfers on Health Status: The Brazilian Bolsa Familia Programme." *Revista Española de Salud Pública* 83, no. 1: 85–97.

Chalmers, Douglas A., Carlos M. Vilas, Katherine Hite, Scott B. Martin, Kerianne Piester, and Monique Segarra, eds. 1997. *The New Politics of Inequality in Latin America: Rethinking Participation and Representation.* Oxford: Oxford University Press.

Chávez, Carlos Alberto. 2000. "El sindicalismo boliviano: crisis y perspectivas." *Opiniones y Analisis,* no. 51: 45–71.

Chávez, Hugo. 2009. *Chávez y el control obrero. Intervención del Presidente Chávez en el taller de transformación socialista: Ciudad Guayana, 21–05–09.* Los Teques: Fundación Federico Engels de Venezuela.

Chiriboga Zambrano, Galo, and Vjekoslav Darlic´ Mardesic´. 1995. *Conflictos colectivos, huelgas y paros patronales 1973–1994.* Quito: MTRH-ILDIS.

Chirino, Orlando. 2006. "We Have the Right to Move toward Socialism." *International Socialist Review* 47.

Ciccariello-Maher, George. 2012. *We Created Chávez: A People's History of the Venezuelan Revolution.* Durham, NC: Duke University Press.

Ciudadanía Informada. 2009. "ERCO: persisten conflictos laborales." http://www.ciudadaniainformada.com/noticias-politica-ecuador0/noticias-politica-ecuador/browse/31/ir_a/politica/article//erco-persisten-conflictos-laborales.html, 14/10/2009.

COHA. 2014. *The Municipal Elections in Venezuela as a Plebiscite on Chavismo.* Washington, DC: Council on Hemispheric Affairs.

Collier, Ruth Berins. 1999. *Paths Toward Democracy: The Working Class and Elites in Western Europe and South America.* New York: Cambridge University Press.

Collier, Ruth Berins, and David Collier. 1991. *Shaping the Political Arena: Critical Junctures, the Labor Movement, and Regime Dynamics in Latin America*. Princeton: Princeton University Press.

Collier, David, and James Mahon. 1993. "Conceptual 'Stretching' Revisited: Adapting Categories in Comparative Analysis" *American Political Science Review* 87, no. 4: 845–55.

Collier, Ruth Berins, and Sebastián Etchemendy. 2007. "Down but Not Out: Union Resurgence and Segmented Neocorporatism in Argentina (2003–2007)." *Politics & Society* 35, no. 3: 363–401.

Collier, Ruth Berins, and Samuel Handlin. 2009. *Reorganizing Popular Politics: Participation and the New Interest Regime in Latin America*. University Park: University of Pennsylvania Press.

Collins, Jennifer. 2012. "The Rainbow Fades to Green: The Marginalization of Ecuador's Indigenous Movement in Correa's Citizen Revolution," May 23–26. Paper delivered at XXX International Congress of the Latin American Studies Association, San Francisco, CA.

Collins, Jennifer. 2004. "Linking Movement and Electoral Politics: Ecuador's Indigenous Movements and the Rise of Pachakutik." In *Politics in the Andes: Identity, Conflict, Reform*, 38–57. Edited by Jo-Marie Burt and Philip Mauceri. Pittsburgh, PA: University of Pittsburgh Press.

Colque, Gonzalo. 2011. "Revolución Productiva." *Página Siete*, July 12.

Combellas, Ricardo. 1993. "La reforma constitucional en Venezuela: retrospectiva de una experiencia frustrada." In *Venezuela: Crisis política y reforma constitucional*, 9–31. Edited by Ricardo Combellas. Caracas: Universidad Central de Venezuela.

Conaghan, Catherine M. 1988. *Restructuring Domination: Industrialists and the State in Ecuador*. Pittsburgh, PA: University of Pittsburgh Press.

Conaghan, Catherine M., and James M. Malloy. 1994. *Unsettling Statecraft: Democracy and Neoliberalism in the Central Andes*. Pittsburgh, PA: University of Pittsburgh Press.

Conaghan, Catherine M., James M. Malloy, and Luis A. Abugattas. 1990. "Business and the 'Boys': The Politics of Neoliberalism in the Central Andes." *Latin American Research Review* 25, no. 2: 3–30.

CONAIE. June 7–8, 1994. "Mandato de la movilización por la vida." Asamblea Extraordinaria de la CONAIE, Riobamba. http://abyayala.nativeweb.org/ecuador.

Conde, Edith Mabel Cuñarro. 2004. "Venezuela 1984–1999: 15 años de historia (La Comisión Presidencial para la Reforma del Estado [COPRE] como mecanismo de innovación política)." *Cuestiones Políticas* 33. http://revistas.luz.edu.ve/index.php/cp/article/viewFile/626/587.

Congreso Nacional de Bolivia. 2006. "Discurso de Posesión del Presidente Juan Evo Morales Ayma en el Congreso," January 22.

Cook, Maria Lorena. 2006. *The Politics of Labor Reform in Latin America: Between Flexibility and Rights.* University Park, PA: Pennsylvania University Press.

Cordero, Sofía. 2008. "MAS y Pachakutik: La lucha por la inclusión política en Bolivia y Ecuador." Master's thesis, FLACSO Ecuador.

Cornwall, Andrea. 2008. "Deliberating Democracy: Scenes from a Brazilian Municipal Health Council." *Politics & Society* 36, no. 4: 508–31.

Corrales, Javier. 2011. "Conflicting Goals in Venezuela's Foreign Policy." In *Venezuela's Petro-Diplomacy: Hugo Chávez's Foreign Policy*, 32–48. Edited by Ralph S. Clem and Anthony P. Maingot. Gainesville: University Press of Florida.

Corrales, Javier. 2003. "Market Reforms." In *Constructing Democratic Governance in Latin America*, 2nd ed., 74–99. Edited by Jorge I. Domínguez and Michael Shifter. Baltimore, MD: Johns Hopkins University Press.

Correa, Rafael. August 10, 2010. "Lo que nos falta por hacer, es mucho más de lo que ya hemos hecho." *Informe del Presidente a la Nación, Salón Plenario de la Asamblea Nacional.* Quito.

Crabtree, John. 2011. "Electoral Validation for Morales and the MAS." In *Evo Morales and the Movimiento al Socialismo in Bolivia: The First Term in Context, 2006-2010*, 117–42. Edited by Adrian J. Pearce. London: Institute for the Study of the Americas, University of London.

Crabtree, John. 2005. *Patterns of Protest: Politics and Social Movements in Bolivia.* London: Latin America Bureau.

CSUTCB. 2011. "Propuesta de Ley de Tierras." Borrador, La Paz.

CTA. 2005. *Informe sobre cláusulas obligaciones: contribuciones patronales y aportes de los trabajadores pactados en los convenios colectivos de trabajo. Periodo 2002 a 2004.* Buenos Aires: Observatorio del Derecho Social—CTA.

Cunha, Clayton, and Rodrigo Santella. 2010. "The National Development Plan as a Political Economic Strategy in Evo Morales' Bolivia." *Latin American Perspectives* 37, no. 4 (July): 177–96.

Dandler, Jorge. 1976. "Peasant Sindicatos in Bolivian Politics." In *Popular Participation in Social Change: Cooperatives, Collectives, and Nationalized Industry*, 341–52. Edited by June C. Nash, Jorge Dandler, and Nicholas S. Hopkins. The Hague and Chicago: Mouton.

Dangl, Ben. 2010. *Dancing with Dynamite: Social Movements and States in Latin America.* Oakland, CA: AK Press.

Darlic, Vjekoslav. 1997. *Organizaciones sindicales 1934–1996.* Quito: ILDIS-MRTH.

Da Silva, Sidney Jard. 2000. *Companheiros servidores: Poder político e interesses econômicos do sindicalismo do setor público na CUT.* Master's thesis, São Paulo: Universidade de São Paulo.

Dávila Loor, Jorge. 1995. *El FUT, trayectoria y perspectivas.* Colección Popular 15 de Noviembre. Quito: CDS- Corporación Editora Nacional.

Delamata, Gabriela. 2002. "De los 'estallidos' provinciales a la generalización de la protesta en Argentina. Perspectiva y contexto en la significación de las nuevas protestas." *Nueva Sociedad* 182 (November–December): 121–37.

De la Torre, Carlos. 2013. "El populismo latinoamericano, entre la democratización y el autoritarismo." *Nueva Sociedad* 247 (September–October): 120–37.

De la Torre, Carlos. 2012. "Rafael Correa's Government, Social Movements, and Civil Society in Ecuador." In *Civil Society and the State in Left-Led Latin America: Challenges and Limitations to Democratization*, 48–62. Edited by Barry Cannon and Peadar Kirby. London: Zed Books.

De la Torre, Carlos. 2010. *The Populist Seduction in Latin America*, 2nd ed. Athens, OH: Ohio University Press.

De la Torre, Carlos, and Catherine Conaghan. 2009. "The Hybrid Campaign: Tradition and Modernity in Ecuador's 2006 Presidential Campaign." *International Journal of Press/Politics* 14, no. 3 (July): 335–52.

Delgado, Nelson Giordano, and Sergio Pereira Leite. 2011. "Políticas de Desenvolvimento Territorial no Meio Rural Brasileiro: Novas Institucionalidades e Protagonismo dos Atores." *Dados* 54, no. 2: 431–73.

D'Elia, Yolanda. 2006. *Las Misiones Sociales en Venezuela: Una aproximación a su comprensión y análisis*. Caracas: ILDIS.

D'Elia, Yolanda, and Luis F. Cabezas. 2008. *Las Misiones Sociales en Venezuela*. Caracas: ILDIS.

D'Elia, Yolanda, and Cristyn Quiroz. 2010. *Las Misiones Sociales: ¿Una alternativa para superar la pobreza?* Caracas: ILDIS.

Denis, Roland. 2012. "Open Horizons." *The Bullet* (Socialist Project E-Bulletin) 687 (August 24). http://www.socialistproject.ca/bullet.

Denis, Roland. 2006. "El nuevo Estado en Venezuela y los movimientos populares," April 14. Interview with Roland Denis by Raúl Zelik. http://www.rebelion.org/mostrar .php?id=El+nuevo+estado+en+Venezuela&submit=Buscar&inicio=0&tipo=3.

Desposato, Scott W. 2006. "The Impact of Electoral Rules on Legislative Parties: Lessons from the Brazilian Senate and Chamber of Deputies." *Journal of Politics* 68, no. 4: 1018–30.

Diario Hoy. April 22, 2011. "Empresarios salen al frente de los reclamos laborales." http://www.semanariolaverdad.com/noticias/empresarios_salen_al_frente_de_ los_reclamos_laborales.asp.

Diario Hoy. September 15, 2010. "Plantean mediación para solucionar conflicto de ERCO." http://www.hoy.com.ec/noticias-ecuador/plantean-mediacion-para-solu cionar-conflicto-de-erco-430276.html.

DIEESE. 2011. "Balanço das negociações dos reajustes salariais em 2010." *Estudos e Pesquisas* 55 (March). São Paulo: DIEESE.

Doctor, Mahrukh. 2007. "Lula's Development Council: Neo-Corporatism and Policy Reform in Brazil." *Latin American Perspectives* 34, no. 6: 131–48.

Draibe, Sônia. 2003. "A Política Social no Período FHC e o Sistema de Proteção Social." *Tempo Social* 2: 63–101.

Dunkerley, James. 2007. "Evo Morales, the 'Two Bolivias' and the Third Bolivian Revolution." *Journal of Latin American Studies* 39, no. 1: 133–66.

Dunkerley, James. 1993. "The Crisis of Bolivian Radicalism." In *The Latin American Left: From the Fall of Allende to Perestroika*, 121–38. Edited by Barry Carr and Steve Ellner. London: Westview Press and Latin American Bureau.

Dunkerley, James. 1990. *Political Transition and Economic Stabilisation: Bolivia, 1982–1989*. London: Institute of Latin American Studies.

Dunkerley, James. 1984. *Rebellion in the Veins: Political Struggle in Bolivia, 1952–82*. London: Verso.

Eaton, Kent. 2007. "Backlash in Bolivia: Regional Autonomy as a Reaction to Indigenous Mobilization." *Politics & Society* 35, no. 1: 71–102.

Edwards, Sebastian. 1995. *Crisis and Reform in Latin America: From Despair to Hope*. Washington, DC: World Bank Publication.

Egaña, Pablo, and Alejandro Micco. 2012. "Labor Markets in Latin America and the Caribbean: The Missing Reform." In *The Oxford Handbook of Latin American Political Economy*, 585–608. Edited by Javier Sentiso and Jeff Dayton-Johnson. New York: Oxford University Press.

Eichorst, Jason, and John Polga-Hecimovich. March 14, 2013. "Party Nationalization after the 2013 Ecuadorian Presidential and Legislative Elections." *The Monkey Cage*. http://themonkeycage.org/2013/03/14/party-nationalization-after-the-2013-ecuadorian-legislative-and-presidential-election.

El Comercio. February 6, 2010. "El sindicato de Erco aceptó los despidos." http://www.elcomercio.com/actualidad/sindicato-erco-acepto-despidos.html.

El Tiempo. 2010. "Conflicto laboral." Cuenca, 7–14.

El Universo. October 8, 2007. "Una selección basada en los sondeos."

Ellner, Steve. 2012a. "Au Venezuela: Un chavisme sans Chavez?" *Le Monde Diplomatique* (September): 18–19.

Ellner, Steve. 2012b. "The Heyday of Radical Populism in Venezuela and Its Reappearance." In *Populism in Latin American*, 2nd ed., 132–58. Edited by Michael L. Conniff. Tuscaloosa: University of Alabama Press.

Ellner, Steve. 2008. *Rethinking Venezuelan Politics: Class, Conflict and the Chávez Phenomenon*. Boulder, CO: Lynne Rienner.

Ellner, Steve. 1999a. "Assault on Benefits in Venezuela." *NACLA: Report on the Americas* 32, no. 4: 18–19.

Ellner, Steve. 1999b. "The Impact of Privatization on Labor in Venezuela: Radical Reorganization or Moderate Adjustment?" *Political Power and Social Theory* 13: 109–45.

Ellner, Steve. 1993. *Organized Labor in Venezuela, 1958–1991: Behavior and Concerns in a Democratic Setting*. Wilmington, DE: Scholarly Resources.

Escobar, Arturo, and Sonia E. Alvarez. 1992. *The Making of Social Movements in Latin America: Identity, Strategy, and Democracy.* Boulder, CO: Westview Press.

Esping-Andersen, Gøsta 1990. *Three Worlds of Welfare Capitalism.* Princeton: Princeton University Press.

Etchemendy, Sebastián. 2011. *El diálogo social y las relaciones laborales en Argentina 2003–2010: Estado, sindicatos y empresarios en perspectiva comparada.* Buenos Aires: Oficina de País de la OIT para la Argentina.

Etchemendy, Sebastián. 2004. "Repression, Exclusion, and Inclusion: Government-Union Relations and Patterns of Labor Reform in Liberalizing Economies." *Comparative Politics,* 36, no. 3: 273–90.

Etchemendy, Sebastián. 2001. "Reform Coalitions: The Politics of Compensations in the Argentine Path to Economic Liberalization." *Latin American Politics and Society* 43: 1–35.

Etchemendy, Sebastián, and Ruth Berins Collier. 2007. "Down but Not Out: Union Resurgence and Segmented Neocorporatism in Argentina (2003–2007)." *Politics & Society* 35, no. 3: 363–401.

Etchemendy, Sebastián, and Candelaria Garay. 2011. "Argentina: Left Populism in Comparative Perspectives, 2003–2009." In *The Resurgence of the Latin American Left,* 283–305. Edited by Steven Levitsky and Kenneth M. Roberts. Baltimore, MD: Johns Hopkins University Press.

Evans, Peter. 1979. *Dependent Development.* Princeton: Princeton University Press.

Fagen, Stuart I. 1977. "Unions and Democracy" In *Venezuela: The Democratic Experience,* 174–94. Edited by John D. Martz and David J. Myers. New York: Praeger.

Fairfield, Tasha. 2015. *Private Wealth and Public Revenue in Latin America: Business Power and Tax Politics.* New York: Cambridge University Press.

Falleti, Tulia. 2010. *Decentralization and Subnational Politics in Latin America.* New York: Cambridge University Press.

Farinetti, Marina. 1999. "¿Qué queda del movimiento obrero? Las formas del reclamo laboral en la nueva democracia argentina." *Trabajo y Sociedad,* 1, no. 1: 1–34.

Farrel, Gilda. 1985. "El movimiento sindical frente a la segmentación tecnológica y salarial del mercado de trabajo." In *El sindicalismo latinoamericano en los ochenta,* 73–86. Santiago: CLACSO (Comisión de Movimientos Laborales).

Farrel, Gilda. 1982. *Mercado de trabajo urbano y movimiento sindical.* Quito, IIE-PUCE-ILDIS.

Farthing, Linda. 1991. "The New Underground." *NACLA Report on the Americas* 25, no. 1: 18–23.

Farthing, Linda, and Benjamin Kohl. 2014. *Evo's Bolivia: Continuity and Change.* Austin: University of Texas Press.

Fausto, Boris, and Fernando Devoto. 2004. *Brasil e Argentina. Um ensaio de história comparada (1850–2002).* São Paulo: Paralelo 34.

Feliciano, Carlos Alberto, ed. 2011. *Banco de Dados da Luta pela Terra: Relatório 2010.* Presidente Prudente: NERA.

Fenwick, Tracy Beck. 2009. "Avoiding Governors: The Success of Bolsa Família." *Latin American Research Review* 44, no. 1: 102–31.

Fernandes, Bernardo Mançano. 2000. *A formação do MST no Brasil.* Petrópolis: Vozes.

Fernandes, Bernardo Mançano. 1998. *Gênese e desenvolvimento do MST.* São Paulo: MST.

Fernandes, Bernardo Mançano, and João Pedro Stédile. 1999. *Brava gente: A trajetória do MST e a luta pela terra no Brasil.* São Paulo: Fundação Perseu Abramo.

Fernández, Arturo. 1998. *Crisis y decadencia del sindicalismo argentino.* Buenos Aires: Centro Editor de América Latina.

Ferraz da Fonseca, Igor, and Ana Paula Moreira da Silva. 2011. "Mudança Institucional: O Novo Código Florestal e a Descentralização da Política Ambiental." In *Boletim de Análise Político-Institucional No. 1*, 43–53. Brasília: IPEA.

Figueiredo, Argelina Cheibub. 2011. "Government Coalitions in Brazilian Democracy." *Brazilian Political Science Review* 1, no. 2: 182–216.

Figueiredo, Argelina, and Fernando Limongi. 1999. *Executivo e Legislativo na Nova Ordem Constitucional.* São Paulo: FGV.

Flores, Héctor. 2005. "De la culpa a la autogestión." In *De la culpa a la autogestión*, 13–45. Edited by Héctor Flores. Buenos Aires: Peña Lillo-Continente.

Flores-Macías, Gustavo. 2012. *After Neoliberalism: The Left and Economic Reform in Latin America.* New York: Oxford University Press.

Fontana, Lorenza Belinda. 2013. "On the Perils and Potentialities of Revolution: Conflict and Collective Action in Contemporary Bolivia." *Latin American Perspectives*, 40, no. 3: 26–42.

Frank, Jason. 2010. *Constituent Moments: Enacting the People in Postrevolutionary America.* Durham, NC: Duke University Press.

Freidenberg, Flavia. 2012. "Ecuador 2011: Revolución ciudadana, estabilidad presidencial y personalismo político." *Revista de Ciencia Política* 32, no. 1: 129–50.

Freidenberg, Flavia. 2003. *Jama, Caleta y Camello: Las estrategias de Abdalá Bucaram y el PRE para ganar las elecciones.* Quito: Universidad Andina Simón Bolívar, Sede Ecuador.

Freire de Lacerda, Alan Daniel. 2002. "O PT e a Unidade Partidária como Problema." *Dados* 45, no. 1: 39–76.

French, John D. 1992. *The Brazilian Workers' ABC: Class Conflict and Alliances in Modern São Paulo.* Chapel Hill: University of North Carolina Press.

Fuentes, Miguel Lora. December 29, 2010. "Gasolinazo para aumentar las ganancias de las petroleras e "incentivar" la extracción de crudo." *Bolpress.* http://www.bolpress.com/art.php?Cod=2010122901.

Fundación Tierra. 2012. *Marcha indígena por el TIPNIS: La lucha en defensa de los territorios*. La Paz: Fundación Tierra.

FUT. January 26, 2015. "Denuncia a la OIT." Quito: Frente Unitario de los Trabajadores (CTE—CEDOCUT—CEOSL).

Gallagher, Kevin. 2008. "Understanding Developing Country Resistance to the Doha Round." *Review of International Political Economy* 15, no. 1: 62–85.

Gamarra, Eduardo, and James M. Malloy. 1995. "The Patrimonial Dynamics of Party Politics in Bolivia," In *Building Democratic Institutions in Latin America*. Edited by Scott Mainwaring and Timothy R. Scully. Stanford, CA: Stanford University Press.

Garay, Candelaria. 2016. *Social Policy Expansion in Latin America*. New York: Cambridge University Press.

Garay, Candelaria. 2007. "Social Policy and Collective Action: Unemployed Workers, Community Associations, and Protest in Argentina." *Politics & Society* 35, no. 2: 301–28.

Garcés, Fernando. 2010. *El Pacto de Unidad y el proceso de construcción de una propuesta de constitución política de Estado: Sistematización de una experiencia*. La Paz: Centro Cooperativo Sueco.

García-Guadilla, María Pilar. 2013. "Neo-Extractivism, Neo-Rentierism, and Social Movements in Venezuela's 21st–Century Ecosocialism." In *Environmental Movements around the World: Shades of Green in Politics and Culture, Volume 1*, 77–130. Edited by Timothy Doyle and Sherilyn McGregor. Santa Barbara: Praeger.

García-Guadilla, María Pilar. 2011. "Urban Land Committees: Cooptation, Autonomy, and Protagonism." In *Venezuela's Bolivarian Democracy*, 80–103. Edited by David Smilde and Daniel Hellinger. Durham, NC: Duke University Press.

García-Guadilla, María Pilar. 2010. *Emergencia de nuevas ciudadanías y conflictos sociopoliticos Post-Constitucionales en Venezuela*. Vols. 1–9. FONACIT/GAUS-USB.

García-Guadilla, María Pilar. 2008. "La praxis de los consejos comunales: ¿Poder popular o instancia neoclientelar?" *Revista Venezolana de Economía y Ciencias Sociales* 14, no. 1: 125–51.

García-Guadilla, María Pilar. 2005. "La sociedad civil venezolana 1961-2004: Institucionalización de nuevas ciudadanías y luchas por la democracia." In *Lectura sociológica de la Venezuela actual II*, 83–120. Caracas: Ediciones Universidad Católica Andrés Bello.

García-Guadilla, María Pilar. 2003. "Civil Society: Institutionalization, Fragmentation, Autonomy." In *Venezuelan Politics in the Chavez Era: Class, Polarization and Conflict*, 179–96. Edited by Steve Ellner and Daniel Hellinger. Boulder: Lynne Rienner.

García-Guadilla, María Pilar, and Rosangel Álvarez. 2013. "Mitos y realidades de poder comunal: Las comunas del Socialismo del Siglo XXI," November 4–6. Paper presented at XII Simposio Venezolano de Ciencia Política, UCV, Venezuela.

García-Guadilla, María Pilar, and Mónica Hurtado. 2000. "Participation and Consti-
tution Making in Colombia and Venezuela: Enlarging the Scope of Democracy?,"
March 16–18. Paper presented at the XXII International Congress of the Latin
American Studies Association, Miami, FL.

García-Guadilla, María Pilar, and Ana Mallen. 2013. "A Rude Awakening: The Under-
side of Venezuelas Civil Society in the Time of Hugo Chávez." *Politeia (Venezuelan
Studies)* 24: 141–62.

García-Guadilla, María Pilar, and Ernesto Roa. 1996. "Gobernabilidad, Cambio Político y Sociedad Civil: el Proceso Constituyente en Venezuela." *Revista Venezolana
de Ciencias Económicas y Sociales* 2–3: 85–112.

García Linera, Álvaro. 2012. *Las tensiones creativas de la revolución. La quinta fase del
proceso de cambio en Bolivia.* Buenos Aires: Ediciones Rosa Luxemburgo.

García Linera, Álvaro. 2011. *El "Onegismo," enfermedad infantil del derechismo (o
como la reconducción del proceso de cambio es la restauración neoliberal).* La Paz:
Vicepresidencia del Estado.

García Linera, Álvaro. 1999. *Reproletarización: nueva clase obrera y desarrollo del capital industrial en Bolivia (1952–1998): El caso de La Paz y El Alto.* La Paz: Muela del
Diablo Editores.

Gasparini, Leonardo, and Nora Lustig. 2011. "The Rise and Fall of Income Inequality
in Latin America." In *The Oxford Handbook of Latin American Economics,* 691–
714. Edited by José Antonio Ocampo and Jaime Ros. New York: Oxford University
Press.

Gates, Leslie. 2010. *Electing Chávez: The Business of Anti-Neoliberal Politics in Venezuela.* Pittsburgh, PA: University of Pittsburgh Press.

GAUS-USB. 2002-2017. "Base de datos de las organizaciones sociales bolivarianas:
Comités de Tierra, Consejos Comunales, Comunas y Comités de Abastecimien-
to y Producción CLAPS". Laboratorio de Investigación en Gestión de Conflictos
Ambientales Urbanos y Sociopolíticos (GAUS). Manuscrito. Caracas: Universidad
Simón Bolívar.

Gerlach, Alan. 2003. *Indians, Oil, and Politics: A Recent History of Ecuador.* Wilmington: Scholarly Resources.

Gibson, Edward, and Ernesto Calvo. 2000. "Federalism and Low-Maintenance Constituencies: Territorial Dimensions of Economic Reform in Argentina." *Studies in
Comparative International Development.* 35, no. 3: 32–55.

Gindin, Julián. 2011. "Por nós mesmos. As práticas sindicais dos professores públicos
na Argentina, no Brasil e no México." PhD diss., Rio De Janeiro: Universidade do
Estado do Rio de Janeiro.

Gindin, Julián. 2008. "Argentina: Growth, Height and Crisis of the Teacher's Opposition to Neoliberal Reforms (1991–2001)." In *Globalisation, Neoliberalism, Education and Resistance, Volume 3: Low and Middle Income Countries.* Edited by Dave
Hill and Ellen Rosskam. London: Routledge.

Godio, Julio. 2003. "Los movimientos piqueteros ante una seria disyuntiva." *Rabana-das de Realidad.* 6, no. 1.

Godio, Julio. 2000. *Historia del movimiento obrero argentino.* Buenos Aires: Corregidor.

Goldfrank, Benjamin. 2011. "The Left and Participatory Democracy: Brazil, Uruguay, and Venezuela." In *The Resurgence of the Latin American Left*, 162–83. Edited by Steven Levitsky and Kenneth M. Roberts. Baltimore, MD: The Johns Hopkins University Press.

Goldfrank, Benjamin, and Brian Wampler. 2008. "From Petista Way to Brazilian Way: How the PT Changes in the Road." *Revista Debates* 2, no. 2: 245–71.

Gomes, Ângela do Castro. 1988. *A invenção do trabalhismo.* Rio de Janeiro: Vértice/ IUPRJ.

Gómez, Luis. 1987. *Crisis y movimientos sociales en Venezuela*, Caracas: Ed. Tropykos.

Gómez Bruera, Hernán F. 2013. *Lula, the Workers' Party, and the Governability Dilemma in Brazil.* New York: Routledge Press.

Gómez Calcaño, Luis, and Margarita López Maya. 1990. *El Tejido de Penélope. La Reforma del Estado en Venezuela 1984–1988*, CENDES APUCV. Caracas: Colegio de Sociólogos y Antropólogos de Venezuela.

Gonçalves Couto, Cláudio, and Paulo Fernandes Baia. 2004. "O governo Lula: Uma avaliação política e econômica." In *Brasil e Argentina hoje: Política e economia*, 215–54. Edited by Brasilio Sallum Jr. Bauru: Edusuc.

Gotkowitz, Laura. 2007. *A Revolution for Our Rights: Indigenous Struggles for Land and Justice in Bolivia, 1880–1952.* Durham, NC: Duke University Press.

Granier, Marcel. 1984. *La generación de relevo vs. el Estado omnipotente.* Caracas: Talleres Cromotip.

Gray Molina, George. 2010. "The Challenge of Progressive Change under Evo Morales." In *Left Governments in Latin America: Successes and Shortcomings*, 57–76. Edited by Kurt Weyland, Raúl Madrid, and Wendy Hunter. New York: Cambridge University Press.

Gray Molina, George. 2007. "Ethnic Politics in Bolivia: 'Harmony of Inequalities' 1900–2000." CRISE Working Paper No. 15 (February). Oxford: Centre for Research on Inequality, Human Security and Ethnicity, Oxford University.

Griffin, Keith, and Víctor Tokman. 1977. *Situación y perspectivas del empleo en Ecuador.* Santiago: PREALC.

Grindle, Merilee. 2003. "Shadowing in the Past: Policy Reform in Bolivia, 1985–2002." In *Proclaiming Revolution: Bolivia in Comparative Perspective*, 318–39. Edited by Merilee S. Grindle and Pilar Domingo. Boston, MA: Harvard University Press.

Gudynas, Eduardo. 2012. "Estado compensador y nuevos extractivismos. Las ambivalencias del progresismo sudamericano." *Nueva Sociedad* 237 (January–February): 128–46.

Gurza Lavalle, Adrián Arnab Acharya, and Peter P. Houtzager. 2005. "Beyond Comparative Anecdotalism: Lessons on Civil Society and Participation from São Paulo, Brazil." *World Development* 33, no. 6: 951–64.

Guzman, Ismael. 2012. *VIII marcha indígena en Bolivia: Por la defensa del territorio, la vida, y los derechos de los pueblos indígenas.* La Paz: Editorial CIPCA.

Hagopian, Frances, Carlos Gervasoni, and Juan Andrés Moraes. 2009. "From Patronage to Program: The Emergence of Party-Oriented Legislators in Brazil." *Comparative Political Studies* 42, no. 3: 360–91.

Hall, Anthony. 2006. "From Fome Zero to *Bolsa Família*: Social Policies and Poverty Alleviation under Lula" *Journal of Latin American Studies* 38, no. 4: 689–709.

Hall, Anthony. 2005. "Globalized Livelihoods: International Migration and Challenges for Social Policy, The Case of Ecuador," December 12–15. Paper delivered at Arusha Conference, New Frontiers of Social Policy.

Hammond, John L., and Federico M. Rossi. 2013. "Landless Workers Movement (MST) Brazil." In *The Wiley-Blackwell Encyclopedia of Social and Political Movements,* 680–83. Edited by David A. Snow, Donatella della Porta, Bert Klandermans, and Doug McAdam. Oxford: Wiley-Blackwell.

Handlin, Samuel, and Ruth Berins Collier. 2011. "The Diversity of Left Party Linkages." In *The Resurgence of the Latin American Left,* 139–61. Edited by Steven Levitsky and Kenneth M. Roberts. Baltimore, MD: Johns Hopkins University Press.

Harnecker, Marta. 2010. "Tiempos Políticos, Procesos Democráticos: Entrevista de Marta Harnecker a Alberto Acosta." Interview manuscript. http://www.rebelion .org/docs/113474.pdf.

Harnecker, Marta. 2009. "De los consejos comunales a las comunas. Construyendo el socialismo del siglo xxi." http://es.scribd.com/doc/27443484/Harnecker-Marta -De-los-consejos-comunales-a-las-comunas-2009.

Harnecker, Marta. 2002. *Sin Tierra: Construyendo movimiento social.* Madrid: Siglo XXI.

Harten, Sven. 2011. *The Rise of Evo Morales and the MAS.* London: Zed Books.

Hawkins, Kirk A. 2010a. "Who Mobilizes? Participatory Democracy in Chávez's Bolivarian Revolution." *Latin American Politics & Society* 52, no. 3: 31–66.

Hawkins, Kirk A. 2010b. *Venezuela's Chavismo and Populism in Comparative Perspective.* Cambridge: Cambridge University Press.

Hawkins, Kirk A. 2003. "Populism in Venezuela: The Rise of *Chavismo*." *Third World Quarterly* 24, no. 6: 113–80.

Hawkins, Kirk, and David R. Hansen. 2006. "Dependent Civil Society: The Círculos Bolivarianos in Venezuela." *Latin American Research Review* 41, no. 1: 101–32.

Healy, Kevin. 1991. "Political Ascent of Bolivia's Coca Leaf Producers." *Journal of Inter-American Studies and World Affairs* 33, no. 1: 87–121.

Healy, Kevin, and Susan Paulson. 2000. "Political Economies of Identity in Bolivia, 1952–1998." *Journal of Latin American Anthropology* 5, no. 2: 2–29.

Hellinger, Daniel. 2006. "Venezuelan Oil: Free Gift of Nature or Wealth of a Nation?" *International Journal* 62 (Winter): 55–67.

Hellinger, Daniel. 2005. "When 'No' Means 'Yes' to Revolution: Electoral Politics in Bolivarian Venezuela." *Latin American Perspectives* 32, no. 3: 8–32.

Hellinger, Daniel. 1996. "The Causa R and the Nuevo Sindicalismo in Venezuela." *Latin American Perspectives* 23, no. 3: 110–31.

Hernández, Virgilio, and Fernando Buendía. 2011. "Ecuador: Avances y desafíos de Alianza País." *Nueva Sociedad* 234 (July–August): 129–42.

Herrera, Stalin Gonzalo. 2013. "El Movimiento indígena campesino y vías de democratización en el Ecuador: Los Ríos y Chimborazo." Master's thesis, Global Studies Unit, Universidad Andina Simón Bolívar, Quito.

Hertzler, Douglas. 2005. "Campesinos and Originarios! Class and Ethnicity in Rural Movements in the Bolivian Lowlands." *Journal of Latin American Anthropology* 10, no. 1: 45–71.

Hey, Jeanne A. K., and Thomas Klak. 1999. "From Protectionism towards Neoliberalism: Ecuador across Four Administrations (1981–1996). *Studies in Comparative International Development* 34, no. 3: 66–97.

Higgins, Sean, and Claudiney Pereira. 2013. "The Effects of Brazil's High Taxation and Social Spending on the Distribution of Household Income." Working Paper 7, Commitment to Equity. New Orleans: CEQ.

Hilger, Tina, ed. 2012. *Clientelism in Everyday Latin American Politics*. New York: Palgrave.

Hobson, Barbara. 2003. "Introduction." In *Recognition Struggles and Social Movements: Contested Identities, Agency and Power*, 1–17. Edited by Barbara Hobson. Cambridge: Cambridge University Press.

Honneth, Axel. 1995. *The Struggle for Recognition: The Moral Grammar of Social Conflicts*. Cambridge: Polity Press.

Hopenhayn, Martín. 2000. *El gran eslabón: Educación y desarrollo en el umbral del siglo XXI* México: Fondo de Cultura Económica.

Houtzager, Peter, and Adrian Gurza Lavalle. 2010. "Civil Society's Claims to Political Representation in Brazil." *Studies in Comparative International Development* 45, no. 1: 1–29.

Huber, Evelyn, and John D. Stephens. 2012. *Democracy and the Left: Social Policy and Inequality in Latin America*. Chicago: University of Chicago Press.

Hunter, Wendy. 2010. *The Transformation of the Workers' Party in Brazil, 1989–2009*. New York: Cambridge University Press.

Hunter, Wendy. 2007. "Rewarding Lula: Executive Power, Social Policy, and the Brazilian Elections of 2006." *Latin American Politics and Society* 49, no. 1: 1–30.

Hylton, Forrest, and Sinclair Thomson. 2007. *Revolutionary Horizons: Past and Present in Bolivian Politics.* London: Verso.

Ibáñez Rojo, Enrique. 2000. "The UDP Government and the Crisis of the Bolivian Left, 1982–1985." *Journal of Latin American Studies* 32, no. 1: 175–205.

INEC. 2016 *Reporte de economia laboral.* Quito: INEC.

INEC. 2015. *Indicadores laborales.* Quito: INEC.

INEC-UNFPA. (2015–2016). *Análisis y proyección de la población económicamente activa (PEA) del Ecuador.* Quito: INEC.

Inter-American Development Bank. 1997. *Latin American after a Decade of Reforms.* Washington, DC: Inter-American Development Bank.

International Monetary Fund (IMF). 2011. "Bolivia: 2011 Article IV Consultation Cover," 11–124. Washington, DC: IMF Country Report.

Isaacs, Anita. 1993. *Military Rule and Transition in Ecuador, 1972–92.* Pittsburgh, PA: University of Pittsburgh Press.

Isuani, Ernesto. 1985. *Los orígenes conflictivos de la seguridad social argentina.* Buenos Aires: Centro Editor de América Latina.

James, Daniel. 1988. *Resistance and Integration: Peronism and the Argentine Working Class, 1946–1976.* Cambridge: Cambridge University Press.

Jenness, Valerie, David Meyer, and Helen Ingram. 2005. "Conclusion. Social Movements, Public Policy, and Democracy: Rethinking the Nexus." In *Routing the Opposition: Social Movements, Public Policy, and Democracy,* 288–306. Edited by David Meyer, Valerie Jenness, and Helen Ingram. Minneapolis: The University of Minnesota Press.

John, S. Sándor. 2009. *Bolivia's Radical Tradition: Permanent Revolution in the Andes.* Tuscon: University of Arizona Press.

Johnston, Jake, and Stephan Lefebvre. 2014. "Bolivia's Economy under Evo in 10 Graphs." Washington, DC: Centre for Economic Policy Research. http://www.cepr.net/index.php/blogs/the-americas-blog/bolivias-economy-under-evo-in-10-graphs.

Jokisch, Brad, and Jason Pribilsky. 2002. "The Panic to Leave: Economic Crisis and the 'New Emigration' from Ecuador." *International Migration* 40, no. 4: 75–102.

Jones, Mark P. 1994. "Presidential Election Laws and Multipartism in Latin America." *Political Research Quarterly* 47, no. 1 (March): pp. 41–57.

Kaup, Brent Z. 2010. "Neoliberal Nationalization? The Constraints on Natural Gas-Led Development in Bolivia." *Latin American Perspectives* 37, no. 3: 123–38.

Keck, Margaret. 1992. *Workers' Party and Democratization in Brazil.* New Haven, CT: Yale University Press.

Kinzo, Maria D'Alva. 2004. "Partidos, Eleições, e Democracia no Brasil Pós-1985." *Revista Brasileira de Ciências Sociais* 19, no. 54: 23–40.

Kinzo, Maria D'Alva. 1993. *Radiografia do quadro partidário brasileiro.* São Paulo: Fundação Konrad-Adenauer.

Klein, Herbert S. 2003. *A Concise History of Bolivia.* New York: Cambridge University Press.

Kohl, Benjamin. 2010. "Bolivia under Morales: A Work in Progress." *Latin American Perspectives* 37, no. 3: 107–22.

Kohl, Benjamin. 2004. "Privatization Bolivian Style: A Cautionary Tale." *International Journal of Urban and Regional Research* 28, no. 4: 893–908.

Kohl, Benjamin. 2002. "Stabilizing Neoliberalism in Bolivia: Popular Participation and Privatization in Bolivia." *Political Geography* 21, no. 4: 449–72.

Kohl, Benjamin, and Linda Farthing. 2006. *Impasse in Bolivia. Neoliberal Hegemony and Popular Resistance.* London: Zed Press.

Kruse, Tom. 2001. "Transición política y recomposición sindical: Reflexiones desde Bolivia." In *Los sindicatos frente a los procesos de transición política,* 219–51. Edited by Enrique de la Garza Toledo. Buenos Aires: CLACSO.

Kurtz, Marcus. 2004. "The Dilemmas of Democracy in the Open Economy: Lessons from Latin America." *World Politics* 56, no. 2: 262–302.

Lalander, Rickart. 2009. "Los indígenas y la revolución ciudadana: Rupturas y alianzas en Cotacachi y Otavalo." *Ecuador Debate* 77: 185–220.

Lalander, Rickard, and Pablo Ospina Peralta. 2012. "Movimiento indígena y revolución ciudadana en Ecuador." *Cuestiones Políticas* 28, no. 48: 13–50.

Lander, Edgardo. December 12, 2011. "El movimiento popular venezolano." *CETRI.* http://www.cetri.be/spip.php?article2423&lang=es.

Lanzara, Gregorio, and Boris Arias. 2010. *Represa Cachuela Esperanza: Posibles consequencias socioeconómicas y ambientales de su construcción.* La Paz: Editorial CIPCA.

Larrea, Carlos. 2006. "Neoliberal Policies and Social Development in Latin America: The Case of Ecuador," June 2. Paper presented at Congress of the Social Sciences and Humanities, CERLAC, University of York, York.

Larrea, Gustavo. 2009. *Revolución Ciudadana.* Quito: Editorial Planeta.

Lasswell, Harold. 1936. *Politics: Who Gets What, When and How.* New York: Whittleshouse.

Lavarreda, Antonio. 1991. *A Democracia nas Urnas.* Rio de Janeiro: Rio Fundo Ed.

Lazar, Sian. 2008. *El Alto, Rebel City: Self and Citizenship in Andean Bolivia.* Durham, NC: Duke University Press.

Lazarte, Jorge. 1988. *Movimiento obrero y procesos políticos en Bolivia: Historia de la C.O.B. 1952–1987.* La Paz: EDOBOL.

Lazarte, Jorge. 1989. *Movimiento obrero y procesos políticos en Bolivia.* La Paz: Editorial Offse Boliviana.

Leal, Murilo. 2011. *A Reinvenção da Classe Trabalhadora (1953–1964).* Campinas: Editora da UNICAMP.

Lebowitz, Michael A. 2010. *The Socialist Alternative: Real Human Development*. New York: Monthly Review Press.

Leff, Nathaniel. 1982. *Underdevelopment and Development in Brazil: Economic Structure and Change*. New York: Harper Collins.

León, Oscar. August 27, 2012. "Venezuela: oposición perdida." http://alainet.org/active/57489.

León Trujillo, Jorge. 2011. "Política y movimientos sociales en el Ecuador de entre dos siglos." In *Estado del País. Informe Cero, Ecuador 1950–2010*, 207–30. Quito: FLAC-SO-ESPOL-PUCE-Universidad de Cuenca-Consorcio Social para la Educación -ODNA.

León Trujillo, Jorge. 2003a. *Estado del Movimiento sindical en Ecuador*. (Marzo) Quito: OIT-CEDIME.

León Trujillo, Jorge. 2003b. "Un sistema político regionalizado y sus crisis." In *Estado, etnicidad y movimientos sociales en América Latina. Ecuador en Crisis*, 25–55. Edited by Víctor Bretón and Francisco García. Barcelona: Icaria Editorial.

León Trujillo, Jorge. 2000. *Estado del Movimiento sindical en Ecuador*. Quito: OIT-CEDIME.

León Trujillo, Jorge. 1998. *Evolución y tendencias de la contratación colectiva, 19887–1998. Del proteccionismo a la desregulación de las relaciones de trabajo en Ecuador*. Quito: OIT-CEDIME.

León Trujillo, Jorge. 1997. "Movimientos sociales sin causa y con intereses: Entre la protesta y el corporativismo." *Íconos* 2: 29–33.

León Trujillo, Jorge. 1988. *Composición social y escena política en el sindicalismo ecuatoriano*. Quito.

León Trujillo, Jorge, and Juan Pablo Pérez Sáinz. 1987. "Les syndicats et la scène politique dans l'histoire de l'Equateur." *Mondes en développement* 15, no. 60.

León Trujillo, Jorge, and Juan Pablo Pérez Sáinz. 1985. "Crisis y movimiento sindical en Ecuador: las huelgas nacionales del FUT (1981–83)." In *Movimientos sociales en el Ecuador*. Edited by Luís Verdesoto, Manuel Chiriboga Vega, Jorge León, Juan Pérez, Simón Pachano, Mercedes Prieto, and Mario Unda. Quito: CLACSO-ILDIS.

Levine, Daniel. 1973. *Conflict and Political Change in Venezuela*. Princeton: Princeton University Press.

Levitsky, Steven. 2003. "From Labor Politics to Machine Politics: The Transformation of Party-Union Linkages in Argentine Peronism, 1983–99." *Latin American Research Review* 38, no. 3: 3–36.

Levitsky, Steven. 2001. "A 'Disorganized Organization': Informal Organization and the Persistence of Local Party Structures in Argentine Peronism." *Journal of Latin American Studies* 33, no. 1: 29–66.

Levitsky, Steven. 1998. "Peronism and Institutionalization: The Case, the Concept, and the Case of Unpacking the Concept." *Party Politics* 4, no. 1: 77–92.

Levitsky, Steven, and María Victoria Murillo. 2005. "Building Castles in the Sand? The Politics of Institutional Weakness in Argentina." In *Argentine Democracy,* 21–44. Edited by Steven Levitsky and María Victoria Murillo. University Park: Pennsylvania State University Press.

Levitsky, Steven, and Kenneth M. Roberts, eds. 2011. *The Resurgence of the Latin American Left.* Baltimore, MD: Johns Hopkins University Press.

Levitsky, Steven, and Lucan Way. 2010. *Competitive Authoritarianism: Hybrid Regimes after the Cold War.* New York: Cambridge University Press.

Llanos, Mariana. 2002. *Privatization and Democracy in Latin America: An Analysis of President-Congress Relations.* New York: Palgrave.

Lobo, Valéria M. 2010. *Fronteiras da Cidadania: Sindicatos e (des)mercantilização do trabalho no Brasil.* Belo Horizonte: Argvmentvm.

Lodola, Germán. 2005. "Protesta popular y redes clientelares en la Argentina: El reparto federal del Plan Trabajar (1996–2001)." *Desarrollo Económico* 44, no. 176: 515–16.

Lope Bello, Nelson G. 1979. *La defensa de la ciudad.* Caracas: Universidad Simón Bolívar-IERU.

Lopez, Félix, and Roberto Pires. 2010. "Instituições participativas e políticas públicas no Brasil: Características e evolução nas últimas duas décadas." *Brasil em desenvolvimento 2010: Estado, planejamento e políticas públicas,* 565–85. Edited by Roberto Pires et al. Brasília: IPEA.

López, Felix García, Luciana de Souza Leão, and Mario Luis Grangeia. 2011. "State, Third Sector, and the Political Sphere in Brazil." *International Journal of Sociology* 42, no. 2: 50–73.

López-Calva, Luis Felipe, and Nora Lustig, eds. 2010. *Declining Inequality in Latin America: A Decade of Progress?* Washington, DC: The Brookings Institution Press.

López Maya, Margarita. 2005. *Del viernes negro al referendo revocatorio.* Caracas: Afadil.

López Maya, Margarita. 1999. "La protesta popular venezolana entre 1989 y 1993." In *Lucha popular, democracia, neoliberalismo: Protesta popular en América Latina en los años del ajuste,* 211–35. Edited by Margarita López Maya. Caracas: Nueva Sociedad.

Lora, Eduardo. 2001. "Structural Reforms in Latin America: What Has Been Reformed and How to Measure It." Working Paper No. 466 (December). Inter-American Development Bank Research Department, Washington, DC.

Lora, Eduardo, Ugo Panizza, and Miriam Quispe-Agnoli. 2004. "Reform Fatigue: Symptoms, Reasons, and Implications." *Federal Reserve of Atlanta Economic Review* (Second Quarter): 1–28.

Lora, Guillermo. 1977. *A History of the Bolivian Labour Movement, 1848–1971.* Cambridge: Cambridge University Press.

Lucca, Juan Bautista. 2011. "Estudio comparado de la identidad partidaria-sindical durante el gobierno de Lula da Silva (Brasil, 2003–2006) y de Néstor Kirchner (Argentina, 2003–2007)." PhD diss., Buenos Aires: Facultad Latinoamericana de Ciencias Sociales.

Lucero, José Antonio. 2008. *Struggles of Voice: The Politics of Indigenous Representation in the Andes.* Pittsburgh, PA: University of Pittsburgh Press.

Lucio-Paredes, Pablo. 2015. "El (inexistente) debate sobre las jubilaciones." *Koyuntura,* 53, no. 7. Quito: Instituto de Economía de la USFQ.

Lucio-Paredes, Pablo. 2009. "30 años de democracia en lo económico y social: ¿Medio vaso lleno . . . o vacío?" Seminario Cordes-USFQ, September. Quito: Instituto de Economía, USFQ.

Lugo, Eduardo. 2012. "Dicen que es ilegítima." *Tal Cual,* March 14.

Luna, Juan Pablo. 2014. *Segmented Representation: Political Party Strategies in Unequal Democracies.* Oxford: Oxford University Press.

Lupien, Pascal. 2011. 'The Incorporation of Indigenous Concepts of Plurinationality into the New Constitutions of Ecuador and Bolivia." *Democratization* 18, no. 3: 774–96.

Lustig, Nora, and Carola Pessino. 2013. "Social Spending and Income Redistribution in Argentina During the 2000s: The Rising Role of Noncontributory Pensions." CEQ Working Paper 5. http://www.commitmentoequity.org/publications_files/Argentina/CEQWPNo5%20SocSpendRedist2000sArgentina%20Jan%202013%20REVISED%20Aug%2031%202013.pdf.

Lyne, Mona M. 2008. "Proffering Pork: How Party Leaders Build Party Reputations in Brazil." *American Journal of Political Science* 52, no. 2: 290–303.

Madrid, Raúl. 2012. *The Rise of Ethnic Politics in Latin America.* New York: Cambridge University Press.

Madrid, Raúl. 2009. "The Origins of the Two Lefts in Latin America." *Political Science Quarterly* 125, no. 4: 1–23.

Mahoney, James. 2001. *The Legacies of Liberalism: Path Dependence and Political Regimes in Central America.* Baltimore, MD: Johns Hopkins University Press.

Mainwaring, Scott. 2006. "State Deficiencies, Party Competition and Confidence in Democratic Representation in the Andes." In *The Crisis of Democratic Representation in the Andes,* 295–345. Edited by Scott Mainwaring, Ana María Bejarano, and Eduardo Pizarro Leongómez. Stanford, CA: Stanford University Press.

Mainwaring, Scott. 1999. *Rethinking Party Systems in the Third Wave of Democratization: The Case of Brazil.* Stanford, CA: Stanford University Press.

Mainwaring, Scott. 1993. "Presidentialism, Multipartism, and Democracy: The Difficult Combination." *Comparative Political Studies* 26, no. 2: 198–228.

Mainwaring, Scott, and Timothy Scully. 1995a. "Introduction: Party Systems in Latin America." In *Building Institutions in Latin America Democratic,* 1–36. Edited by Scott Mainwaring and Timothy R. Scully. Stanford, CA: Stanford University Press.

Mainwaring, Scott, and Timothy Scully, eds. 1995b. *Building Democratic Institutions: Party Systems in Latin America.* Stanford: Stanford University Press.

Malloy, James M. 1970. *Bolivia: The Uncompleted Revolution.* Pittsburgh, PA: University of Pittsburgh Press.

Malloy, James M., and Eduardo Gamarra. 1988. *Revolution and Reaction: Bolivia 1964–1985.* New Brunswick, NJ: Transaction Books.

Maneiro, María. 2012. *De encuentros y desencuentros: Estado, gobiernos y movimientos de trabajadores desocupados.* Buenos Aires: Biblos.

Manifiesto. 2011. "Por la recuperación del proceso de cambio para el pueblo y por el pueblo." *Página Siete.* La Paz, Bolivia, June 19.

Manin, Bernard. 1992. "Metamorfosis de la representación." In *¿Qué queda de la representación política?,* 9–40. Edited by Mario Dos Santos,. Caracas: CLACSO-Nueva Sociedad.

Manzetti, Luigi. 1999. *Privatization Latin American Style.* New York: Oxford University Press.

Marcelino, Paula Regina Pereira, Andréia Galvão, and Patrícia Vieira Trópia. 2011. "As bases sociais da União Geral dos Trabalhadores (UGT), " July 26–29. XV Congresso Brasileiro de Sociologia, Curitiba.

Martínez, Gabriel X. 2006. "The Political Economy of the Ecuadorian Financial Crisis." *Cambridge Journal of Economics* 30, no. 4: 567–85.

Martínez Abarca, Mateo. 2011. *El cascbel del Gatopardo: La Revolución ciudadana y su relación con el movimiento indígena.* Quito: FLACSO-Abya Yala.

Martins, Jose de Souza. 1994. *O poder do atraso: Ensaios de sociologia da história lenta.* São Paulo: Hucitec.

Marx, Roberto, and Adriana Marotti de Mello. May 30–June 1, 2012. "Automotive Industry Transformations and Work Relations in Brazil. What Is the Next Step?" *Gerpisa Colloque.*

Mayorga, Fernando. 2011. *Dilemas: Ensayos sobre democracia intercultural y Estado Plurinacional.* La Paz: CESU/Plural Editores.

Mayorga, René Antonio. 2003. "Bolivia: Metamorfosis del sistema de partidos." *Íconos* 16 (May): 96–105.

Mayorga, René Antonio. 1997. "Bolivia's Silent Revolution." *Journal of Democracy* 8, no. 1: 142–56.

MBR-200. 2002. "Ideas programáticas, gobierno estadal." In *Documentos de la revolución.* Edited by Alberto Garrido. MBR: Caracas.

McCormick, Sabrina. 2010. "Damming the Amazon: Local Movements and Transnational Struggles over Water." *Society and Natural Resources* 24, no. 1: 34–48.

McGuire, James. 1997. *Peronism without Peron: Unions, Parties, and Democracy in Argentina.* Stanford, CA: Stanford University Press.

Mejía Acosta, Andrés. 2010. "Rente pétrolière et politique budgétaire en Équateur." *Revue internationale de politique comparée* 17, no. 3: 111–26.

Mejía Acosta, Andrés. 2009. *Informal Coalitions and Policymaking in Latin America: Ecuador in Comparative Perspective*. London: Routledge.

Melo, Marcus André. 2008. "Unexpected Successes, Unanticipated Failures: Social Policy from Cardoso to Lula." In *Democratic Brazil Revisited*, 161–84. Edited by Peter Kingstone and Timothy J. Power. Pittsburgh, PA: University of Pittsburgh Press.

Melo, Marcus André. 2004. "Institutional Choice and the Diffusion of Policy Paradigms: Brazil and the Second Wave of Pension Reforms." *International Political Science Review* 25, no. 3: 320–41.

Mendes, Gabriel. 2004. "Da Frente Brasil Popular a Aliança Capital/Trabalho: As Campanhas de Lula a Presidente de 1989 a 2002." Master's thesis, Rio de Janeiro: UERJ.

Mendoza, Ignacio. 2009. "L@s trabajador@s y sus derechos en la nueva constitución." *Umbrales*, September 19.

Meneguello, Raquel. 1998. *Partidos e Governos no Brasil Contemporâneo*. São Paulo: Paz e Terra.

Merklen, Denis. 2005. *Pobres Ciudadanos. Las clases populares en la era democrática (Argentina, 1983–2003)*. Buenos Aires: Gorla.

Mijeski, Kenneth J., and Scott H. Beck. 2011. *Pachacutik and the Rise and Decline of the Ecuadorian Indigenous Movement*. Athens, OH: Ohio University Press.

Ministry of Finance. 2012. *Brazilian Economic Outlook*. Brasilia: Ministry of Finance.

Mitchell, Christopher. 1977. *The Legacy of Populism in Bolivia: From the MNR to Military Rule*. New York: Praeger.

Molina, Fernando. 2013. "¿Por qué Evo Morales sigue siendo popular? Las fortelezas del MAS en la construcción de un nuevo orden." *Nueva Sociedad* 245 (May–June): 4–14.

Molina, Oscar, and Martin Rhodes. 2002. "Corporatism: The Past, Present, and Future of a Concept." *Annual Review of Political Science* 5: 305–31.

Mommer, Bernard. 2002. "Subversive Oil." In *Venezuelan Politics in the Chávez Era: Polarization and Social Conflict*. Edited by Steve Ellner and Daniel Hellinger. Boulder, CO: Lynne Rienner.

Montero, Alfred. 2014. *Brazil: Reversal of Fortune*. Cambridge: Polity Press.

Montes Cató, Juan, and Patricia Ventrici. 2011. "Labor Union Renewal in Argentina: Democratic Revitalization from the Base." *Latin American Perspectives* 38, no. 6: 38–51.

Montúfar, César. 2000. *La reconstrucción neoliberal. Febres Cordero o la estatización del neoliberalismo en el Ecuador 1984–1988*. Quito-Ecuador: Ediciones Abya-Yala Universidad Andina Simón Bolívar.

Morresi, Sergio, and Gabriel Vommaro. 2014. "The Difficulties of the Partisan Right in Argentina: The Case of the Propuesta Republicana." In *The Resilience of the*

*Latin American Right*, 319–46. Edited by Juan Pablo Luna and Cristóbal Rovira. Baltimore, MD: Johns Hopkins University Press.

Müller, Katharina. 2009. "Contested Universalism: From Bonosol to Renta Dignidad in Bolivia." *International Journal of Social Welfare* 18, no.2: 163–72.

Muñoz Eraso, Janeth Patricia. 2010. "Gabinetes itinerantes, enlaces ciudadanos y consejos comunales." *Ecuador Debate* 80 (August).

Muñoz-Pogossian, Betilde. 2008. *Electoral Rules and the Transformation of Bolivian Politics: The Rise of Evo Morales.* New York: Palgrave Macmillan.

Murillo, María Victoria. 2005. "Partisanship amidst Convergence: Labor Market Reforms in Latin America." *Comparative Politics* 37, no. 4: 441–58.

Murillo, María Victoria. 2001. *Labor market, partisan coalitions and market reforms in Latin America.* Cambridge: Cambridge University Press.

Murillo, María Victoria, and Andrew Schrank. 2005. "With a Little Help from My Friends: Partisan Politics, Transnational Alliances, and Labor Rights in Latin America." *Comparative Political Studies* 38, no. 8: 971–99.

Navarro, Zander. 2008. "Social Movements of the Past Confront the Present: The Brazilian Landless Movement (MST) and the Challenges of Mobilising the Rural Poor in Neoliberal Times." Social Movements and the Politics of Neoliberalism: International Perspectives on the MENA Region conference. Florence & Montecatini Terme: European University Institute.

Neffa, Julio. 2008. *Desempleo, pobreza y políticas públicas. Fortalezas y debilidades del Plan Jefes y Jefas de Hogar Desocupados.* Buenos Aires: Miño y Dávila.

Neuman, William. 2012. "Venezuela's Opposition Struggles for Unity." *New York Times*, October 16, sec. A4.

Nicholls, Esteban. 2014. "Rearticulating the State through Governmental Regimes: State Power and Popular Indigenous Participation in Ecuador, 2008–2012." PhD diss., Political Science Department, Carleton University.

Noronha, Eduardo. 2009. "Ciclo de greves, transição política e estabilização: Brasil, 1978–2007." *Lua Nova* 76: 119–68.

North, Liisa L. 2004. "State Building, State Dismantling and Financial Crises in Ecuador." In *Politics in the Andes: Identity, Conflict, and Reform*, 187–206. Edited by Jo-Marie Burt and Philip Mauceri. Pittsburgh, PA: University of Pittsburgh Press.

Novaro, Marcos. 2009. *Argentina en el fin de siglo. Democracia, mercado y nación (1983–2001).* Buenos Aires: Paidós.

Novik, Marta. 2003. *La Negociación Colectiva en el Período 1991–1999.* Informe Elaborado para el Ministerio de Trabajo y Seguridad Social.

Nylen, William. 1997. "Reconstructing the Workers' Party: Lessons from Northeastern Brazil." In *The New Politics of Inequality in Latin America: Rethinking Participation and Representation*, 421–46. Edited by Douglas A. Chalmers, Carlos M. Vilas, Katherine Hite, Scott B. Martin, Kerianne Piester, and Monique Segarra. New York: Oxford University Press.

O'Donnell, Guillermo. 1994. "Delegative Democracy." *Journal of Democracy* 5, no. 1: 55–69.

O'Donnell, Guillermo. 1973. *Modernization and Bureaucratic-Authoritarianism: Studies in South American Politics.* Berkeley: Institute of International Studies.

Ojeda Díaz, Juan José. March 13, 2012. "Dirigentes sindicales anuncian cruzada nacional para el rescate de la CTV." http://twittervenezuela.co/profiles/blogs/dirigentes-sindicales-anuncian-cruzada-nacional-para-el-rescate.

Olivera, Oscar, and Tom Lewis. 2004. *Cochabamba: Water War in Bolivia.* Cambridge: South End Press.

Ondetti, Gabriel. 2008. *Land, Protest, and Politics: The Landless Movement and the Struggle for Agrarian Reform in Brazil.* University Park: Pennsylvania State University Press.

Ortiz, Nelson. 2004. "Entrepreneurs: Profits without Power?" In *The Unraveling of Representative Democracy in Venezuela,* 71–92. Edited by Jennifer McCoy and David J. Meyers. Baltimore: University of Maryland Press.

Ostiguy, Pierre. 2009. "Argentina's Double Political Spectrum: Party System, Political Identities, and Strategies, 1944–2007." Kellogg Institute Working Paper No. 361 (October).

Ostiguy, Pierre. 2007. "Del proyecto peronista." *Página/12,* October 31.

Ostiguy, Pierre. 2005. "Gauches péroniste et non péroniste dans le système de partis argentin." *Revue Internationale de Politique Comparée* 12, no. 3: 299–330.

Ostiguy, Pierre. 1998. "Peronism and Anti-Peronism: Class-Cultural Cleavages and Political Identity in Argentina." PhD diss., Department of Political Science, University of California, Berkeley.

Oviedo Obarrio, Fernando. 2010. "Evo Morales and the Altiplano: Notes for an Electoral Geography of the Movimiento al Socialismo, 2002–2008." *Latin American Perspectives* 37, no. 3: 91–47.

Oxhorn, Philip. 2012. "Understanding the Vagaries of Civil Society and Participation in Latin America." In *Routledge Handbook of Latin American Politics,* 248–61. Edited by Peter Kingstone and Deborah J. Yashar. New York: Routledge.

Oxhorn, Philip. 1998. "Is the Century of Corporatism Over? Neoliberalism and the Rise of Neopluralism." In *What Kind of Democracy? What Kind of Market? Latin America in the Age of Neoliberalism,* 195–217. Edited by Philip Oxhorn and Graciela Ducatenzeiler. University Park: Pennsylvania State University Press.

Pachano, Simón. 2012a. "RC—R'C' = 0," March 14–15. Paper presented at International Seminar, Ecuador, Bolivia and Peru: New Democratic Scenario in Comparative Perspective, FLACSO-Ecuador.

Pachano, Simón. 2012b. "El buró." *El Universo,* September 24.

Pachano, Simón. 2010. "Gobernabilidad democrática y reformas institucionales y políticas en Ecuador." In *Desafíos de la gobernabilidad democrática. Reformas político-institucionales y movimientos sociales en la región andina*, 79–111. Edited by Martín Tanaka and Francine Jácome. Lima: IEP; IDRC-CRDI; INVESP.

Pachano, Simón. 2006. "Ecuador: The Provincialization of Representation." In *The Crisis of Democratic Representation in the Andes*, 100–131. Edited by Scott Mainwaring, Ana María Bejarano, and Eduardo Pizarro Leongómez. Stanford, CA: Stanford University Press.

Palermo, Vicente, and Marcos Novaro. 1996. *Política y poder en el gobierno de Menem.* Buenos Aires: Norma.

Palomino, Héctor. 2008. "La evolución reciente del sistema de relaciones laborales en Argentina," September 2–4. VI Congreso Regional de las Américas, International Industrial Relations Association. Buenos Aires.

Pearce, Adrian. 2011. *Evo Morales and the Movimiento al Socialismo in Bolivia: The First Term in Context, 2006–2010.* London: Institute for the Study of the Americas.

Pereira Almao, Valia. 2001. "El Movimiento V República: fuerzas y debilidades." http://svs.osu.edu/jornadas/Pereira.pdf.

Pereira, Anthony. 2003. "Brazil's Agrarian Reform: Democratic Innovation or Oligarchic Exclusion Redux?" *Latin American Politics and Society* 45, no. 2: 41–65.

Pereira, Anthony. 1997. *The End of the Peasantry: The Rural Labor Movement in Northeast Brazil, 1961–1988.* Pittsburgh, PA: University of Pittsburgh Press.

Pereira, Carlos, Timothy J. Power, and Lucio Rennó. 2005. "Under What Conditions Do Presidents Resort to Decree Power? Theory and Evidence from the Brazilian Case." *Journal of Politics* 67, no. 1: 178–200.

Perelman, Laura. 2006. "Sindicalización y Obras Sociales." *Cuadernos del IDES* N° 10. Buenos Aires: Instituto de Desarrollo Económico y Social.

Pérez Sáinz, Juan Pablo. 1985. *Clase Obrera y Democracia en Ecuador.* Quito: El Conejo.

Phillips, George, and Francisco Panizza. 2011. *The Triumph of Politics: The Return of the Left in Bolivia, Ecuador and Venezuela.* Cambridge: Polity Press.

Polanyi, Karl. 1944. *The Great Transformation.* New York: Farrar and Rinehart.

Pontoni, Gabriela. 2012. "Identidad colectiva camionera, un recurso de poder sindical en Argentina entre 2003 y 2011." *Revista Gaceta Laboral* 18, no. 2: 151–72. Universidad del Zulia.

Postero, Nancy. 2010. "Morales's MAS Government: Building Indigenous Popular Hegemony in Bolivia." *Latin American Perspectives* 37, no. 3: 18–34.

Power, Timothy J. 2008. "Centering Democracy? Ideological Cleavages and Convergence in the Brazilian Political Class." In *Democratic Brazil Revisited*, 57–80. Edited by Timothy J. Power and Peter R. Kingstone. Pittsburgh, PA: University of Pittsburgh Press.

Power, Timothy J. 2000. "Political Institutions in Democratic Brazil: Politics as a Permanent Constitutional Convention." In *Democratic Brazil: Actors, Institutions, and Processes*, 17–35. Edited by Timothy Powers and Peter Kingstone. Pittsburgh, PA: University of Pittsburgh Press.

Power, Timothy J. 1996. "Elite Institutions in Conservative Transitions to Democracy: Ex-Authoritarians in the Brazilian National Congress." *Studies in Comparative International Development* 31, no. 3: 56–84.

Power, Timothy J., and César Zucco. 2009. "Estimating Ideology of Brazilian Legislative Parties, 1990–2005." *Latin American Research Review* 44, no. 1: 218–46.

Presidencia de la República del Ecuador. 2007. "Discurso de posesión del Presidente Rafael Correa." http://www.presidencia.gob.ec/discursos.

Prévôt-Schapira, Marie-France. 1996. "Las políticas de lucha contra la pobreza en la periferia de Buenos Aires, 1984–1994." *Revista Mexicana de Sociología* 58, no. 2: 73–94.

PROVEA. 2010. *Informe anual de derechos humanos 2010*. Caracas: Provea.

Proyecto Venezuela. 2006. "Declaración de Principios." http://americo.usal.es/oir/opal/Documentos/Venezuela/PV/DeclaracionPpiosPV.pdf.

Quiroga, María Soledad Trigo, Cristian León Coronado, Óscar Meneses Barrancos, Héctor Pacheco, and Pablo Ríos Dávalos. 2012. *Perfiles de la conflictividad social (2009–2011)*. La Paz: Fundación UNIR.

Ramírez Gallegos, Franklin. 2010a. "Fragmentación, reflujo y desconcierto. Movimientos sociales y cambio político en el Ecuador (2000–2010)." OSAL, Año XI, no. 28: 17–47.

Ramírez Gallegos, Franklin. 2010b. "Desencuentros, convergencias, polarización y viceversa: El gobierno ecuatoriano y movimientos sociales." *Nueva Sociedad* 227 (May–June): 83–101.

Ramírez Gallegos, Franklin. 2005. *La insurrección de abril no fue solo una fiesta*. Quito: Taller El Colectivo.

Ramírez Gallegos, Franklin, and Juan Guijarro. 2011. "Équateur une 'révolution citoyenne; contestée." *Alternatives Sud* 18: 53–59.

Ramos, Marisa. 1995. *De las protestas a las propuestas: Identidad, acción y relevancia política del movimiento vecinal en Venezuela*. Caracas: Editorial Nueva Sociedad.

Ray, Rebecca, and Sara Kozameh. 2012 (May). "Ecuador's Economy Since 2007." Center for Economic and Policy Research, Washington, DC.

Renner, Cecília Ornellas. 2002. *Duas estratégias sindicais. O Sindicato Metalúrgico de São Paulo e o de São Bernardo do Campo—1978-1988*. São Paulo: Letras a Margem.

Repetto, Fabián. 2000. "Gestión pública, actores e institucionalidad: Las políticas frente a la pobreza en los '90." *Desarrollo Económico* 39, no. 156: 597–618.

República de Bolivia. 2009. *Constitución de Bolivia 2009*. Political Database of the Americas, Georgetown University. http://pdba.georgetown.edu/Constitutions/Bolivia/bolivia09.html.

República del Ecuador. 2008. *Constitución del Ecuador 2008*. Political Database of the

Americas, Georgetown University. http://pdba.georgetown.edu/Constitutions/Ecuador/ecuador08.html.

Rey, Juan Carlos. 1991. "La democracia venezolana y la crisis del sistema populista de conciliación." *Revista de Estudios Políticos* 74: 533–78.

Rivas M., and W. Vásquez. May 1, 2014. "Marcha de la COB ingresa con Evo a la plaza Murillo." *La Razón*, sec. Economía. http://la-razon.com/economia/Marcha-COB-ingresa-Evo-Murillo_0_2044595547.html.

Rivera Cusicanqui, S. 1987. "Oppressed but Not Defeated: Peasant Struggles among the Aymara and Qhechwa in Bolivia, 1900–1980." United Nations Research Institute for Social Development, Geneva.

Roberts, Kenneth M. 2016. "Democratic Divergence and Party Systems in Latin America's Third Wave." In *Parties, Movements, and Democracy in the Developing World*, 93–121. Edited by Nancy Bermeo and Deborah J. Yashar. New York: Cambridge University Press.

Roberts, Kenneth M. 2014. *Changing Course in Latin America: Party Systems in the Neoliberal Era*. New York: Cambridge University Press.

Roberts, Kenneth M. 2003. "Social Polarization and the Populist Resurgence in Venezuela." In *Venezuelan Politics in the Chavez Era: Class, Polarization and Conflict*. 55–72. Edited by Steve Ellner and Daniel Hellinger. Boulder: Lynne Rienner.

Roberts, Kenneth M. 1998. *Deepening Democracy? The Modern Left and Social Movements in Chile and Peru*. Stanford: Stanford University Press.

Robertson, Ewan. August 3, 2012. "Revolutionary Democracy in the Economy? Venezuela's Workers' Control Movement." *Links International Journal of Socialist Renewal*. http://links.org.au/node/2995.

Rocca Rivarola, Dolores. 2013. "Sustentando al Presidente: Algunos Argumentos en Torno a los Conjuntos Oficialistas Organizados Alrededor de Kirchner (2003–2007) y Lula (2002–2006)," May 29–June 1. Paper delivered at the XXXI International Congress of the Latin American Studies Association, Washington, DC.

Rodrigues, Iram Jácome. 2002. "Um laboratório das Relações de Trabalho: O ABC paulista nos anos 90." *Tempo Social. Revista de Sociologia da USP* 14, no. 1: 137–57.

Rodríguez, Reinaldo. 2012. "Las letras pequeñas de la nueva LOTTT." *Militante: Voz marxista de la clase obrera y el PSUV* 35, no. 5.

Rojas Ortuste, Gonzalo. 2011. "La política en las calles: La cultura política y sus circunstancias," June 15. Study prepared for the Friedrich Ebert Stiftung and the Fundación Boliviana para la Democracia Multipartidaria.

Roma, Celso. 2002. "A Institucionalização do PSDB: Entre 1988 e 1999." *Revista Brasileira de Ciências Sociais* 17, no. 49: 71–92.

Roman, Andrei. 2012. "A Brazilian New Deal? Accounting for the Emergence of the Class Cleavage in Brazilian Politics," May 23–26. Paper delivered at the XXX International Congress of the Latin American Studies Association. San Francisco, CA.

Rosa, Marcelo C. 2011. *O Engenho dos Movimentos Sociais: Reforma agrária e signifi-cação social na zona canavieira de Pernambuco.* Rio de Janeiro: Garamond.

Rossi, Federico M. 2017. *The Poor's Struggle for Political Incorporation.* New York: Cambridge University Press.

Rossi, Federico M. 2015a. "The Second Wave of Incorporation in Latin America: A Conceptualization of the Quest for Inclusion Applied to Argentina." *Latin American Politics and Society* 57, no. 1: 1–28.

Rossi, Federico M. 2015b. "Beyond Clientelism: The Piquetero Movement and the State in Argentina." In *Handbook of Social Movements across Latin America,* 117–28. Edited by Paul Almeida and Allen Cordero. New York: Springer.

Rossi, Federico M. 2015c. "Building Factories without Bosses: The Movement of Worker-Managed Factories in Argentina." *Social Movement Studies* 14, no. 1: 98–107.

Rossi, Federico M. 2013. "*Piqueteros* (Workers/Unemployment Movement in Argentina)." In *The Wiley-Blackwell Encyclopedia of Social and Political Movements,* 929–32. Edited by David A. Snow, Donatella della Porta, Bert Klandermans, and Doug McAdam. Oxford: Wiley-Blackwell.

Rossi, Federico M. 2005. "Aparición, auge y declinación de un movimiento social: Las asambleas vecinales y populares de Buenos Aires, 2001–2003." *European Review of Latin American and Caribbean Studies* 78 (April): 67–88.

Roxborough, Ian. 1994. "The Urban Working Class and Labour Movement in Latin America since 1930." In *The Cambridge History of Latin America, Volume 6: 1930 to the Present,* 305–78. Edited by L. Bethell. Cambridge: Cambridge University Press.

Saad-Filho, Alfredo, Francesca Iannini, and Elizabeth Jean Molinari. 2007. "Neoliberalism, Democracy and Economic Policy in Latin America." In *Political Economy of Latin America: Recent Economic Performance,* 1–35. Edited by Philip Arestis and Malcolm Sawyer. New York: Palgrave-Macmillan.

Sachs, Jeffrey 2005. *The End of Poverty: Economic Possibilities for Our Time.* New York: Penguin Press.

Sallum, Brasilio Jr. 2003. "The Changing Role of the State: New Patterns of State-Society Relations in Brazil at the End of the Twentieth Century." In *Brazil since 1985: Politics, Economy and Society,* 179–99. Edited by Maria D'Alva Kinzo and James Dunkerley. London: Institute of Latin American Studies.

Saltos, Napoleón. 2001. "Movimiento indígena y movimientos sociales: Encuentros y desencuentros." *Instituto Científico de Culturas Indígenas* 3, no. 27. http://icci.nativeweb.org/boletin/27/saltos.html.

Sánchez, Pilar. 2000. *Correntinazo itéva.* Buenos Aires: Ágora.

Sánchez, Pilar. 1997. *El Cutralcazo: La pueblada de Cutral Co y Plaza Huincul.* Buenos Aires: Ágora.

Sánchez Parga, José. 2009. "Democracia caudillista y desmovilizaciones sociales en Ecuador." *Polis* 8, no. 24: 147–73.

Sánchez Parga, José. 1993. "Ecuador en el engranaje neoliberal." *Nueva Sociedad* 123 (January–February): 12–17.

Santana, Elías. 1988. "La política de los vecinos: Experiencias del Movimiento Comunitario como fuerza democrática y de cambio frente a la crisis." In *El venezolano ante la crisis*, 99. Caracas: Ediciones Amón C.A. Instituto IDEA.

Santana, Elías. 1986. *El poder de los Vecinos*. Caracas: Ediciones Ecotopia.

Santana, Marco A. 2001. *Homens Partidos. Comunistas e Sindicatos no Brasil*. São Paulo: Boitempo.

Schavelzon, Salvador. 2012. *El nacimiento del Estado Plurinacional de Bolivia: Etnografía de una Asamblea Constituyente*. La Paz: CEJIS/Plural editores.

Schefner, Jon, George Pasdirtz, and Cory Blad. 2006. "Austerity Protests and Immiserating Growth in Mexico and Argentina." In *Latin American Social Movements: Globalization, Democratization and Transnational Networks,* 19–41. Edited by Hank Johnston and Paul Almeida. Lanham, MD: Rowman & Littlefield.

Schilling-Vacaflor, Almut. 2011. "Bolivia's New Constitution: Towards Participatory Democracy and Political Pluralism?" *European Review of Latin American and Caribbean Studies* 90 (April): 3–22.

Secretaría Nacional de Planificación y Desarollo. 2009. "Plan Nacional para el Buen Vivir 2009–2013." http://www.planificacion.gob.ec/plan-nacional-para-el-buen -vivir-2009–2013.

Seidman, Gay W. 1994. *Manufacturing Militance: Workers' Movements in Brazil and South Africa, 1970–1985*. Berkeley: University of California Press.

Selverston-Sher, Melina. 2001. *Ethnopolitics in Ecuador: Indigenous Rights and the Strengthening of Democracy*. Coral Gables: North-South Center Press.

SENPLADES. 2000. *Plan Nacional de Desarrollo 2007–2010*. Quito: SENPLADES.

Silva, Eduardo. 2012. "Exchange Rising? Karl Polanyi and Contentious Politics in Latin America." *Latin American Politics and Society* 54, no. 3: 1–32.

Silva, Eduardo. 2009. *Challenging Neoliberalism in Latin America*. New York: Cambridge University Press.

Singer, André. 2015. "Cutucando onças com varas curtas." *Novos Estudos* 102: 43–71.

Singer, André. 2012. *Os sentidos do Lulismo: Reforma Gradual e Pacto Conservador*. São Paulo: Cia. Das Letras.

Singer, Matthew M. 2007. "The Presidential and Parliamentary Elections in Bolivia: December 2005." *Electoral Studies* 26: 200–205.

Siqueira, Alexander Dias. 2008. "Negociações Coletivas entre o Sindicato dos Metalúrgicos de Catalão e a Mitsubishi Motors Corporation Automotores do Brasil LTDA." Master's thesis, Uberlândia: Universidade Federal de Uberlândia.

Skidmore, Thomas. 1988. *The Politics of Military Rule in Brazil, 1964–1985*. New York: Oxford University Press.

Sluyter-Beltrão, Jeff. 2010. *Rise and Decline of Brazil's New Unionism. The Politics of Central Única dos Trabladores.* Bern: Peter Lang.

Solimano, Andrés, and Raímundo Soto. 2004. "Economic Growth in Latin America in the Late 20th Century: Evidence and Interpretation." Paper prepared for the ECLAC seminar Latin American Growth: Why So Slow?, December 4–5, Santiago, Chile.

Sosa, Arturo Abascal. 2001. *Rómulo Betancourt y el Partido del Pueblo (1937–1941).* Caracas: Universidad Católica Andres Bello.

Soul, Julia, and Julián Gindin. 2013. "La negociación colectiva después de la reconversión industrial. Siderúrgicas y terminales automotrices en Argentina y Brasil," July 2–5. VII Congresso Latino-Americano de Estudos do Trabalho, São Paulo.

Spronk, Susan. 2012. "Neoliberal Class Formation(s): The Informal Proletariat and 'New' Workers' Organizations in Latin America." In *The New Latin American Left: Cracks in the Empire,* 75–94. Edited by Jeffrey R. Webber and Barry Carr. Lanham, MD: Rowman & Littlefield.

Stallings, Barbara. 2010. "Globalization and Labor in Four Developing Regions: An Institutional Approach." *Studies in Comparative International Development* 45, no. 2: 127–50.

Stein, Leila C. 2008. *Trabalhismo, círculos operários e política—a formação do sindicato dos trabalhadores agrícolas no Brasil (1954–1964).* São Paulo: FAPESP/ Annablume.

Stepan, Alfred. 1988. *Rethinking Military Politics: Brazil and the Southern Cone.* Princeton: Princeton University Press.

Stevens, Paul, and Matthew Hulbert. 2012. *Oil Prices: Energy Investment, Political Stability in the Exporting Countries and OPEC's Dilemma.* London: Chatham House. http://www.chathamhouse.org/sites/files/chathamhouse/public/Research/Energy,%20Environment%20and%20Development/1012pp_opec.pdf.

Stokes, Susan C. 2001a. *Mandates and Democracy: Neoliberalism by Surprise in Latin America.* New York: Cambridge University Press.

Stokes, Susan C. 2001b. *Political Support for Market Reforms in New Democracies.* New York: Cambridge University Press.

Suriano, Juan, ed. 2000. *La cuestión social en Argentina, 1870–1943.* Buenos Aires: La Colmena.

Suriano, Juan. 1988. *Trabajadores, anarquismo y Estado represor: De la Ley de Residencia a la Ley de Defensa Social (1902–1910).* Buenos Aires: Centro Editor de América Latina.

Svampa, Maristella, and Sebastián Pereyra. 2003. *Entre la ruta y el barrio: La experiencia de las organizaciones piqueteras.* Buenos Aires: Biblos.

Tapia, Luis. 2008. "Constitution and Constitutional Reform in Bolivia." In *Unresolved Tensions: Bolivia Past and Present,* 160–72. Edited by John Crabtree and Laurence Whitehead. Pittsburgh, PA: University of Pittsburgh Press.

Tarrow, Sidney. 2011. *Power in Movement*, 3rd ed. New York: Cambridge University Press.

Teichman, Judith A. 2001. *The Politics of Freeing Markets in Latin America: Chile, Argentina, and Mexico*. Chapel Hill: University of North Carolina Press.

Thede, Nancy. 2011. "Democratic Agency in the Local Political Sphere: Reflections on Inclusion in Bolivia." *Democratization* 18, no. 1: 211–35.

Torre, Juan Carlos, and Elisa Pastoriza. 2002. "La democratización del bienestar." In *Los años peronistas (1943–1955)*, 257–312. Edited by Juan Carlos Torre. Buenos Aires: Sudamericana.

Trajtemberg, David, Cecilia Senén González, and Bárbara Medwid. 2011. "Determinantes individuales de la afiliación sindical: Resultados de la encuesta de trabajadores en empresa" *Trabajo, Ocupación y Empleo* (10). Buenos Aires: MTESS.

Trajtemberg, David, Cecilia Senén González, and Bárbara Medwid. 2009. "La expansión de la afiliación sindical: Análisis del módulo de relaciones laborales de la EIL." *Trabajo, Ocupación y Empleo* (8). Buenos Aires: MTESS.

Trópia, Patrícia Vieira. 2004. "O Impacto da ideologia neoliberal no meio operário— Um estudo sobre os metalúrgicos da cidade de São Paulo e a Força Sindical." PhD diss., Campinas: Universidade Estadual de Campinas.

Tuaza, Luis. 2011. "La relación del gobierno de Correa y las bases indígenas: Políticas públicas en el medio rural. *Ecuador Debate*. 83 (August): 127–50.

Universidad Andina Simón Bolívar. 2012. "Resultados electorales en el Ecuador, 2002–2011." Joint research project with the Consejo Nacional Electoral.

Urioste, Miguel. 2011. "Luces y sombras de la Ley de Revolución Productiva y Agropecuaria (Ley 144)." *Página Siete*. July 27.

Useem, Bert. 1980. "The Workers' Movement and the Bolivian Revolution." *Politics & Society* 9, no. 4: 447–69.

U.S. Embassy, Caracas. April 28, 2011. "Chávez's MVR Party: Primaries for Local Elections."

Van Cott, Donna Lee. 2008. *Radical Democracy in the Andes*. Cambridge: Cambridge University Press.

Van Cott, Donna Lee. 2005. *From Movements to Parties in Latin America: The Evolution of Ethnic Parties*. Cambridge: Cambridge University Press.

Van Cott, Donna Lee. 2003. "From Exclusion to Inclusion: Bolivia's 2002 Elections." *Journal of Latin American Studies* 35, no. 4: 751–75.

Van Cott, Donna Lee. 2000. *The Friendly Liquidation of the Past: The Politics of Diversity in Latin America*. Pittsburgh, PA: University of Pittsburgh Press.

Varela, Marcelo. 2010. "Las actividades extractivas en Ecuador." *Ecuador Debate*.

Varianzas. 2012. *Resultados Estudio de Opinión*, June 30. http://www.scribd.com/doc/99538236/Encuesta-Firma-Varianza-Fecha-7-de-Juio-de-2012.

Verdesoto, Luis. 2014 (Memo). "La democratización en Ecuador, pese a quien le pese, cumplió 35 años."

Verdesoto, Luis, and Gloria Ardaya. 2010. "La estatalidad de la democracia y la democratización del Estado en el Ecuador." In *Transiciones y rupturas. El Ecuador en la segunda mitad del siglo XX*, 115–58. Edited by Felipe Burbano de Lara. Quito: FLACSO.

Vieira, Margerete, ed. 2004. *Grito dos Excluídos: 10 anos de luta*. São Paulo: Expressão Popular.

Vogel, Luiz Henrique. 2010. "Negociar Direitos? Legislação trabalhista e reforma neoliberal no governo FHC (1995–2002)." PhD diss., Rio de Janeiro: Universidade do Estado do Rio de Janeiro.

von Bülow, Marisa, and Antônio Lassance. 2012. "Brasil después de Lula: ¿Más de lo mismo?" *Revista de Ciencia Política* 32, no. 1: 49–64.

Wainwright, Hilary, and Sue Branford. 2006. *En el ojo del huracán: Visiones de militantes de izquierda sobre la crisis política de Brasil*. Amsterdam: TNI.

WDI. 2012. *World Development Indicators*. Washington: World Bank.

Webber, Jeffery R. 2011. *From Rebellion to Reform in Bolivia: Class Struggle, Indigenous Liberation, and the Politics of Evo Morales*. Chicago: Haymarket Books.

Weisbrot, Mark, Rebecca Ray, and Jake Johnston. December 2009. "Bolivia: The Economy during the Morales Administration." Center for Economic and Policy Research.

Weitz-Shapiro, Rebecca. 2014. *Curbing Clientelism in Argentina: Politics, Poverty, and Social Policy*. New York: Cambridge University Press.

Welch, Cliff. 1999. *The Seed Was Planted: The São Paulo Roots of Brazil's Rural Labor Movement, 1924–1964*. University Park: Pennsylvania State University Press.

Weyland, Kurt. 2002. *The Politics of Market Reform in Fragile Democracies: Argentina, Brazil, Peru, and Venezuela*. Princeton: Princeton University Press.

Weyland, Kurt, Raúl Madrid, and Wendy Hunter, eds. 2010. *Left Governments in Latin America: Successes and Shortcomings*. New York: Cambridge University Press.

Williamson, John. 1990. "What Washington Means by Policy Reform." In *Latin American Adjustment: How Much Has Happened?*, 7–20. Edited by John Williamson. Washington, DC: Institute for International Economics.

Willis, Eliza, Christopher da C. B. Garman, and Stephan Haggard. 1999. "The Politics of Decentralization in Latin America." *Latin American Research Review* 34, no. 1: 7–56.

Wolff, Jonas. 2007. "(De-)Mobilising the Marginalised: A Comparison of the Argentine *Piqueteros* and Ecuador's Indigenous Movement." *Journal of Latin American Studies* 39, 1 (February): 1–29.

Woods, Alan. 2008. *Reformismo o revolución: Marxismo y socialismo del siglo XXI—respuesta a Heinz Dieterich*. Madrid: Fundación Federico Engels.

World Bank, Poverty Reduction and Economic Management Section Unit, Latin America and the Caribbean Region. October 31, 2005a. "Bolivia Country Economic Memorandum: Policies to Improve Growth and Employment." Report No. 32233-BO.

World Bank, Poverty Reduction and Economic Management Section Unit, Latin America and the Caribbean Region. December 15, 2005b. "Bolivia Poverty Assessment: Establishing the Basis for Pro-Poor Growth." Report No. 28068-BO.

World Bank, Poverty Reduction and Economic Management Section Unit, Latin America and the Caribbean Region. April 2004. "Ecuador Poverty Assessment." Report No. 27061-EC.

Wright, Angus, and Wendy Wolford. 2003. *To Inherit the Earth: The Landless Movement and the Struggle for a New Brazil.* Oakland: Food First.

Yashar, Deborah. 2005. *Contesting Citizenship in Latin America: The Rise of Indigenous Movements and the Postliberal Challenge.* New York: Cambridge University Press.

Zamosc, León. 2007. "The Indian Movement and Political Democracy in Ecuador." *Latin American Politics and Society* 49, no. 3: 1–34.

Zamosc, León. 2004. "The Indian Movement in Ecuador: From Politics of Influence to Politics of Power." In *The Struggle for Indigenous Rights in Latin America*, 131–57. Edited by Nancy Grey Postero and León Zamosc. Brighton: Sussex Academic Press.

Zamosc, León. 1994. "Agrarian Protest and the Indian Movement in the Ecuadorian Highlands." *Latin American Research Review* 29, no. 3: 37–68.

Zeas, Santiago. 2013. "D'Hondt, los distritos y la dispersion ayudaron a que A. País sea mayoría." *El Comercio*, February 25.

Zegada, Maria Teresa. 2011. "Conflictividad social, fragmentación e (in)capacidad de la COB." *Página Siete*, March 24.

Zegada, María Teresa, Gabriela Claudia Arce, and Alber Quispe Canedo. 2011. *La democracia desde los márgenes: Transformaciones en el campo politico boliviano.* La Paz: Muela del Diablo Editores.

Zuazo, Moira. 2010. "¿Los movimientos sociales en poder? El gobierno de MAS en Bolivia." *Nueva Sociedad* 227 (May–June): 120–35.

Zuazo, Moira. 2009. *Como nació el MAS: La ruralización de la política en Bolivia.* La Paz: FES-ILDIS.

# ABOUT THE CONTRIBUTORS

## GENERAL EDITORS

**Eduardo Silva** holds the Friezo Family Foundation Chair in Political Science, is professor of political science, and is a senior research associate of the Center for Inter-American Policy and Research at Tulane University. His books include *Challenging Neoliberalism in Latin America* (Cambridge University Press, 2009) and *The State and Capital in Chile* (Westview, 1996). He is editor of *Transnational Activism and National Movements in Latin America: Bridging the Divide* (Routledge, 2013) and coeditor of *Organized Business, Economic Change, and Democracy in Latin America* (North-South Center, 1998) and *Elections and Democratization in Latin America, 1980–85* (CILAS, 1986). His articles on social movements and political change, political ecology, and business-state relations have appeared in *World Politics, Comparative Politics, Development and Change, Latin American Research Review, Latin American Politics and Society*, the *Journal of Latin American Studies, Latin American Perspectives*, and the *European Review of Latin American and Caribbean Studies*, among others.

**Federico M. Rossi** is a research professor of the Consejo Nacional de Investigaciones Científicas y Técnicas of Argentina (CONICET) at the Escuela de Política y Gobierno of the Universidad Nacional de San Martín (UNSAM). He is the author of *The Poor's Struggle for Political Incorporation* (Cambridge University Press, 2017) and *La participación de las juventudes hoy* (Prometeo, 2009), and coeditor with Marisa von Bülow of *Social Movement Dynamics* (Routledge, 2015). His research, focused on social movements, trade unions democratization and contentious dynamics in Latin America and Europe, and youth political participation, has been published in several volumes, *Latin American Politics and Society, Latin American Perspectives, Mobilization, Social Movement Studies, International Sociology, Desarrollo Económico, América Latina Hoy* and the *European Review of Latin American and Caribbean Studies*, among others. He received his PhD at the European University Institute in Florence and has been a visiting or postdoctoral scholar in Tulane University, New York University, the University of Brasília, the European University Institute, and Singapore Management University.

## CONTRIBUTORS

**Adalberto Cardoso** is professor of sociology at the Instituto de Estudos Sociais e Políticos da Universidade do Estado do Rio de Janeiro (IESP-UERJ). His main fields of research include sociology of work (labor market, labor movement, class formation, social mobility, work-based inequalities, labor relations, and labor law), urban sociology (sociology of youth, urban segregation), and social theory. He has published extensively in these fields; his most recent books are *A construção da sociedade do trabalho no Brasil: Uma investigação sobre a persistência secular das desigualdades* (*The Building of Work Society in Brazil: An Inquiry on the Secular Persistence of Inequalities,* Rio de Janeiro: FGV, 2010); *Ensaios de sociologia do mercado de trabalho* (*Essays of Sociology of the Labor Market,* Rio de Janeiro: FGV, 2013); and *Work in Brazil: Essays in Economic and Historical Sociology* (EDUERJ, 2016).

**Ruth Berins Collier** is Heller Professor of the Graduate School, Department of Political Science at the University of California, Berkeley. Her research has focused on the interplay of regime change and forms of popular participation and has included comparative analyses of Latin America, Africa, and Europe. Her books are *Regimes in Tropical Africa: Changing Forms of Supremacy, 1945–1975* (University of California Press, 1982); *Shaping the Political Arena: Critical Junctures, the Labor Movement, and Regime Dynamics* (Princeton University Press, 1991); *The Contradictory Alliance: State-Labor Relations and Regime Change in Mexico* (University of California Press, 1992); *Paths Toward Democracy: The Working Class and Elites in Western Europe and South America* (Cambridge University Press, 1999); and *Reorganizing Popular Politics: Participation and the New Interest Regime in Latin America* (Pennsylvania State University Press, 2009).

**Catherine Conaghan** is the Sir Edward Peacock Professor of Latin American Studies and professor of political studies at Queen's University in Kingston, Ontario. She received her PhD from Yale University. Specializing in Andean politics, she is the author of three books on democracy and policy making in the region: *Fujimori's Peru: Deception in the Public Sphere* (University of Pittsburgh Press, 2006), *Unsettling Statecraft: Democracy and Neoliberalism in the Central Andes* (University of Pittsburgh Press, 1995), and *Restructuring Domination: Industrialists and the State in Ecuador* (University of Pittsburgh Press, 1989). Her articles have appeared in the *Journal of Latin American Studies,* the *Latin American Research Review,* and the *Journal of Democracy.* She has been a visiting scholar at Washington's Woodrow Wilson Center, the Instituto de Estudios Peruanos, and FLACSO-Ecuador.

**Steve Ellner** since 1977 has taught at the Universidad de Oriente in Puerto La Cruz, Venezuela. His book publications include *Venezuela's Movimiento al Socialis-*

mo: *From Guerrilla Defeat to Electoral Politics* (Duke University Press, 1988); *Organized Labor in Venezuela, 1958–1991* (Scholarly Resources, 1993); *Rethinking Venezuelan Politics: Class, Polarization and the Chávez Phenomenon*. (Lynne Rienner, 2008); and his edited *Latin America's Radical Left: Challenges and Complexities of Political Power in the Twenty-First Century* (Rowman and Littlefield, 2014). He earned his PhD in Latin American history at the University of New Mexico in 1980 and has been a visiting professor at Georgetown University (2004), Duke University (2005), Universidad Central de Venezuela (1994–2006), Universidad de Buenos Aires (2010), the National University of Australia (2013), and Tulane University (2015). He has published on the op-ed page of the *New York Times* and *Los Angeles Times* and is a regular contributor to *NACLA: Report on the Americas*.

**María Pilar García-Guadilla** is a professor of sociology and political science at the Universidad Simón Bolívar, Caracas, Venezuela. She coauthored (with Ana Mallen) *Venezuela's Polarized Politics: The Paradox of Direct Democracy under Chávez* (Lynne Rienner, forthcoming) and coedited (with Jutta Blauert) *Environmental Social Movements in Latin America and Europe* (NCB University Press, 1992). She has published in *Latin American Perspectives, América Latina Hoy, Politeia*, and *Revista del CENDES*, among others. She earned a PhD in sociology from the University of Chicago and postdoctorate in social movements from the University of London. She has been a visiting professor and research scholar at La Sorbonne, University of London, Universidad de Salamanca, Universidad Complutense, Universidad de Los Andes, Kellogg Institute University of Notre Dame, College of Charleston, University of New Mexico, University of Connecticut, University of Virginia, and Tulane University, and is an activist in the environmental, women's, and human rights social movements.

**Julián Gindin** is a professor at the Universidade Federal Fluminense (UFF, Rio de Janeiro). He specializes in the teachers' labor movement in Latin America and has edited the volumes *Pensar las prácticas sindicales docentes* (*Assessing Teachers' Union Practices*, Herramienta, 2011) and *Associativismo e sindicalismo em educação: Teoria, história e movimentos* (*Associationism and Unionism in Education: Theory, History and Movements*) with Márcia Ferreira and Sadi dal Rosso (Paralelo 15, 2013). He has also published *Por nós mesmos. O sindicalismo docente de base na Argentina, no Brasil e no México* (*By Ourselves. Base Teacher Unionism in Argentina, Brazil and México*, (Azougue, 2015).

**Daniel Hellinger** is professor of international relations at Webster University (St. Louis, Missouri). His most recent books are *Global Security Watch: Venezuela* (Praeger 2012), *Comparative Politics of Latin America: Democracy at Last?* (Routledge, 2011), and *Bolivarian Democracy in Venezuela: Participation, Politics and Culture* (contributor and coeditor with David Smilde, Duke University Press, 2011). He is coeditor with Steve Ellner of *Venezuelan Politics in the Chávez Era* (Lynne Rienner, 2003) and has published numerous scholarly articles on Latin American politics. He is past president of the Venezuela Studies Section of the Latin American Studies Association and the Midwest Latin American Studies Association. He serves on the advisory board for the Center for Democracy in the Americas, a Washington-based NGO that promotes better understanding between the United States and Latin America. He writes a monthly news analysis on Venezuela, *Caracas Connect*, distributed by the center.

**Jorge León Trujillo,** our colleague and friend, sadly, passed away on December 3. 2017. He was the director of the Centre for Development and Research on Social Movements in Ecuador (CEDIME) and professor of political science in FLACSO, Quito. He has also been visiting professor at Columbia (New York), Université du Québec à Montréal, and the Universidad Católica (Quito). He is the author of numerous books, articles, and chapters on social movements in Ecuador, including *De campesinos a ciudadanos diferentes: El levantamiento indígena* (CEDIME, 1994).

**Pierre Ostiguy** is a professor at the Instituto de Ciencia Política of the Universidad Católica de Chile and has previously taught in the United States and Canada. He is a specialist of Argentine politics, particularly Peronism and anti-Peronism, and has published numerous articles and book chapters on Peronism in Spanish, English, and French. Ostiguy's broader main research agenda is on populism, theoretically and cross-regionally. Release of his latest book, *Party Systems and Political Appeals: Populism and Anti-Populism in Argentina,* is expected in 2018 (University of Notre Dame Press). He is also the author of *Los capitanes de la industria: grandes empresarios, política y economía en la Argentina de los años 80* (Legasa, 1990). He is coeditor of *The Oxford Handbook of Populism* (Oxford University Press, 2017), which features a chapter on his theory of populism. Ostiguy frequently writes and appears as well in the Chilean and Argentine media.

**Kenneth M. Roberts** is the Richard J. Schwartz Professor of Government at Cornell University. His research and teaching interests are focused on Latin American political economy and the politics of inequality. He is the author of *Changing Course in Latin America: Party Systems in the Neoliberal Era* (Cambridge University Press, 2014) and *Deepening Democracy? The Modern Left and Social Movements in Chile and Peru* (Stanford University Press, 1998). He is also the coeditor of *The Resurgence of the Latin American Left* (Johns Hopkins University Press, 2011), *The Diffusion of Social Movements* (Cambridge University Press, 2010), and *Beyond Neoliberalism? Patterns, Responses, and New Directions in Latin America and the Caribbean* (Palgrave-MacMillan, 2009). His research on political parties, populism, and social movements has been published in the *American Political Science Review, World Politics, Comparative Political Studies, Comparative Politics, Politics and Society, Studies in Comparative International Development,* and *Latin American Politics and Society,* among others.

**Aaron Schneider** is the Leo Block Chair of International Studies and director of the Latin America Center at the Josef Korbel School of International Studies at the University of Denver, having recently moved from the Judy and Avram Chair in Political Science at Tulane University in New Orleans. Prior to joining Tulane University, Dr. Schneider worked at the Institute of Development Studies at the University of Sussex, UK. His book *State-Building and Tax Regimes in Central America* was published by Cambridge University Press in 2012 and subsequently translated into Spanish, and he has published over forty articles and book chapters. He is currently developing a project comparing the social and political determinants of international emergence in Brazil and India.

**Susan Spronk** is associate professor at the School of International Studies and Global Development, University of Ottawa. She has been studying anti-privatization movements in Bolivia since 2004 and is the author of several articles and book chapters on class formation and the New Left in Latin America. She is coeditor with Jeffrey R. Webber of *Crisis and Contradiction: Marxist Perspectives on Latin America in the Global Political Economy* (Historical Materialism, 2014). She is also a research associate with the Municipal Services Project, which investigates alternatives to neoliberalism in Asia, Africa, and Latin America in the health, water, and electricity sectors. Her current research project assesses the impact of cash transfer programs on women's and health movements in Bolivia and South Africa.

# INDEX

Note: Page numbers in *italics* refer to figures and tables.

274; patronage, 263; Peronist, 302;
personality-based form of, 326n4;
petro-, 20; policy and, 324; popular, 116; popular sectors and, 309;
post-adjustment, 212; recasting, 318;
reorienting, 278–82; territorialization of, 80; unions and, 140, 194, 207
Polo Obrero (PO), 88, 89, 97, 101
popular interest, 128; incorporation and,
116, 120; intermediation, 58, 316–17,
324; reorganization of, 58; segmented, 10–11
popular representation, reorganization
of, 315–16, 319–20
popular sector movements, 18, 26, 36,
45, 141, 313; creation of, 19, 66;
dominance of, 128; emergence of, 31;
popular power, 70–72; social change
and, 23; social movements and, 77;
social organizations of, 315; state
presence and, 28
popular sector organizations, 12, 27, 58,
59, 60, 61, 63–64, 66–73, 106, 123,
124, 149, 152, 158, 161–62, 234, 241,
295, 313, 314–15, 317, 319; attracting,
322; Bolivarian, 73; breaking, 316;
citizenship and, 76; consulting with,
49; cooperation/conflict among/
between, 5; coordination of, 137;
creation of, 18–19, 75–76; emerging,
64; fragmentation of, 156; Kirchnerismo, 193; policy-making and, 54;
policy process and, 13; politicized,
67–68; PT and, 128; reformist,
61–63; rejection of, 75; resources
and, 328n6; rural, 94–95; social
movements and, 66; state-promoted,
66; social pacts, 151, 289, 290, 293,
294, 299; urban, 11, 35
popular sectors, 12, 26, 29, 47, 48, 56,

65, 216, 275, 300, 301, 306, 312,
320, 322; in Bolivia, 43; in Brazil,
290–93; center-left/left governments and, 4; civil society and,
317; community associations and,
62; corporatist system and, 15;
decision-making and, 281; decollectivizing, 5; demands from, 42,
313; disincorporated, 24, 79–82;
fragmentation of, 9–10; inclusion
of, 311; incorporation of, 6, 7–11,
13, 24, 52, 60, 66, 67, 75, 78, 286,
306; marginalization of, 3; needs
of, 11, 215; neoliberal reforms and,
79–82; organization of, 8, 10, 296,
309; policy process and, 313–15,
317, 318–19; politics and, 156, 309;
recognition of, 11, 311; redefinition
of, 3; reincorporation of, 8–9, 30, 43,
73, 78, 84–85, 275, 289–97, 311, 316;
rural, 30, 85, 93, 115; social subjects
of, 154; state and, 313, 324; struggles
of, 14, 116; urban, 30, 85, 93, 115,
293; well-being of, 284
populism, 3, 12, 68, 158, 217, 218, 220,
226, 230, 231, 235, 253, 255, 258, 300;
Ecuadoran, 33–35; extreme, 160;
labor movements and, 277; national,
32; new forms of, 70–72; Peronism
and, 277; radical, 176
post-adjustment period, 212, 213,
215–18, 221
post-neoliberalism, 4, 15, 18, 20, 35, 308,
312, 318
poverty, 15, 47, 89, 129, 148, 154, 222,
227, 249, 294; fighting, 264, 316;
growth of, 63, 83; reducing, 48, 52,
62, 73, 86, 291, 293, 317
power, 290; centralization of, 52; constituted, 177, 178; decision-making,